JOURNAL FOR THE STUDY OF THE OLD TESTAMENT
SUPPLEMENT SERIES
130

JSOT Press
Sheffield

Structure and the Book of Zechariah

Mike Butterworth

Journal for the Study of the Old Testament
Supplement Series 130

Copyright © 1992 Sheffield Academic Press

Published by JSOT Press
JSOT Press is an imprint of
Sheffield Academic Press Ltd
The University of Sheffield
343 Fulwood Road
Sheffield S10 3BP
England

Typeset by Sheffield Academic Press
and
Printed on acid-free paper in Great Britain
by Billing & Sons Ltd
Worcester

British Library Cataloguing in Publication Data

Butterworth, Mike
    Structure and the Book of Zechariah.—
    (JSOT Supplement Series, ISSN 0309-0787;
    No. 130)
    I. Title II. Series
    224.9806

ISBN 1-85075-293-1

CONTENTS

PREFACE

This book was conceived in Bangalore in about 1977, and over the past fourteen years there have been many people who have helped towards its completion in one way or another.

Among them I must mention my former colleague Jim Gibbs, whose enthusiasm for chiasmus was infectious.

Professor Peter Ackroyd was my first advisor and then supervisor, and made valuable suggestions in the important initial stages of reading and planning.

The tape for producing the tables of repeated words came from Professor Radday in Tel Aviv. Without that I should still be less than half way through. The program that actually produced the results was written by Mrs Christine Brown, of the King's College Computer Department, and her successors have also given valuable help.

I owe most to my wife Jean, who has continued to encourage me to work on this book, at considerable cost to herself, when I could cheerfully have abandoned it.

In 1984 I spent a sabbatical at Hope College, Holland, Michigan. I owe a huge debt of gratitude to many people: to students for their interest; to Barry Bandstra and the Religion Department for the loan of books, and for getting a computer tape of the text of Isaiah; to the Computer Department, and especially to Dan Griswold, for enormous help in producing an analysed tape and a program to give me the results I needed. In the event, it proved too much to deal with Isaiah in the present thesis, but I have articles on the structure of Isaiah planned for controlled release over the next ten years. The support I received from scores of people at Hope College and Western Theological Seminary (with its Tower of Babel) was overwhelming.

Richard Coggins has been my supervisor for the greater part of the writing of the thesis upon which this book is based. His encouragement, constructive criticism and advice have been of enormous help.

The students and staff of Oak Hill College have given support in a number of ways: prayer, encouragement, stimulus to explain why the world needs to know about the structure of Zechariah, commiserations when progress was slow and so on. I should also mention the students of King's College London, who for nine years completely refrained from recalling any books on Zechariah in German or French.

Finally, I am most thankful to God, for all of the above, for illumination (I believe), and for helping me to persevere to the end.

TABLE OF FIGURES

ABBREVIATIONS

AB	Anchor Bible
AJSL	*American Journal of Semitic Languages and Literatures*
AnBib	Analecta biblica
ASTI	*Annual of the Swedish Theological Institute*
ATD	Das Alte Testament Deutsch
ATR	*Anglican Theological Review*
AUSS	*Andrews University Seminary Studies*
BBB	Bonner biblische Beiträge
BDB	F. Brown, S.R. Driver and C.A. Briggs, *Hebrew and English Lexicon of the Old Testament*
BHS	*Biblia hebraica stuttgartensia*
Bib	*Biblica*
BibRes	*Biblical Research*
BT	*The Bible Translator*
BTB	*Biblical Theology Bulletin*
BZ	*Biblische Zeitschrift*
BZAW	Beihefte zur ZAW
CBQ	*Catholic Biblical Quarterly*
EstBíb	*Estudios Bíblicos*
ExpTim	*Expository Times*
GKC	*Gesenius' Hebrew Grammar*, ed. E. Kautzsch, trans. A.E. Cowley
GTJ	*Grace Theological Journal*
HAR	*Hebrew Annual Review*
HeyJ	*Heythrop Journal*
HTR	*Harvard Theological Review*
HUCA	*Hebrew Union College Annual*
IB	*Interpreter's Bible*
ICC	International Critical Commentary
IDBSup	*Interpreter's Dictionary of the Bible, Supplementary Volume*
IEJ	*Israel Exploration Journal*
IF	Introductory Formula
Int	*Interpretation*
ISBE	G.W. Bromiley (ed.), *International Standard Bible Encyclopedia*, rev. edn

JBL	*Journal of Biblical Literature*
JEOL	*Jaarbericht. . . ex oriente lux*
JETS	*Journal of the Evangelical Theological Society*
JNES	*Journal of Near Eastern Studies*
JR	*Journal of Religion*
JSOT	*Journal for the Study of the Old Testament*
JSS	*Journal of Semitic Studies*
JTS	*Journal of Theological Studies*
KAT	Kommentar zum Alten Testament
KB	L. Koethler and W. Baumgartner, *Lexicon in Veteris Testamenti libros*
LB	*Linguistica Biblica*
NEB	New English Bible
OTG	Old Testament Guides
OTS	*Oudtestamentische Studiën*
RB	*Revue biblique*
RevQ	*Revue de Qumran*
RSV	Revised Standard Version
SBL	Society of Biblical Literature
SJT	*Scottish Journal of Theology*
ST	*Studia Theologica*
TynBul	*Tyndale Bulletin*
TZ	*Theologische Zeitschrift*
V	Vision
VT	*Vetus Testamentum*
VTSup	*Vetus Testamentum*, Supplements
WBC	Word Biblical Commentary
WO	*Die Welt des Orients*
ZAW	*Zeitschrift für die alttestamentliche Wissenschaft*
ZDPV	*Zeitschrift des deutschen Palästina-Vereins*
ZNW	*Zeitschrift für die neutestamentliche Wissenschaft*

BIBLE REFERENCES

Chapter and verse are separated by a full stop (period); where necessary the word number is indicated by '.#'. Thus Zech. 3.4.#5 means Zechariah ch. 3, v. 4, word 5.

References to word numbers in different verses are separated by a comma plus a space. Thus 3.8.#5, 9.#7 means ch. 3, the fifth word of the eighth verse, and the seventh word of the ninth verse.

References to word numbers in the same verse are separated by a comma and no space. Thus 5.##7,11 signifies the seventh and eleventh words in v. 5.

INTRODUCTION

This book has two mutually dependent parts. The task I have undertaken is to elucidate the structure of the book of Zechariah, but in
order to do this, a satisfactory method must be found. It seems to me
that there is no ready-made, proven method in use in biblical scholarship. The first two chapters attempt to demonstrate this and to draw
up criteria that will help us to frame a reliable way of proceeding.
The method I then devise is tested on the book of Zechariah, and the
results obtained are compared with those of biblical scholarship. The
procedure may be set out thus:

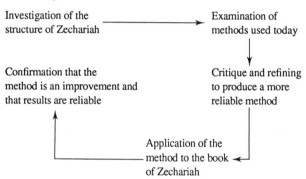

The circle could be closed by incorporating the results into 'methods
used today', and it is hoped that future studies will be able to build on
this one.

Although the present investigation arises out of an interest in literary structures and their function in the Bible, it is not a structuralist
work of the sort that traces its roots back to C. Lévi-Strauss and the
French Structuralists.[1] I believe that there may be some insights to be

---

1. As seen in works like: R. Barthes *et al.*, *Structural Analysis and Biblical
Exegesis: Interpretational Essays* (Pittsburgh: Pickwick Press, 1974); D. Patte, *What
is Structural Exegesis?* (Philadelphia: Fortress Press, 1976).

gained from this activity, but my own interest is much more in the authors' and redactors' intentions than in the meaning of the text as something with complete autonomy.

This, of course, raises the question whether this is a legitimate concern, and whether the 'intentionalist fallacy' is being allowed to put the study out of focus.[1] It is beyond my competence to enter into this literary discussion in any depth, but I remain interested almost wholly in the structures that have been produced by a human mind, rather than by accident. It will probably not be possible always to decide whether a writer consciously and deliberately created a particular structure, but I shall try and establish that the structures discerned are unlikely to be the result of a random positioning of particular words and phrases.[2]

This book makes use of the computer. It has little in common, however, with the computer studies produced by scholars such as Radday and Wickmann.[3] It makes no use at all of statistical theory. The computer is simply a means of doing a great deal of tedious work that would have taken much longer otherwise.

The starting point is main line biblical criticism. I assume that any serious biblical study must take account of textual criticism, literary and historical criticism, and form criticism. I believe, however, that biblical scholarship has rightly moved beyond form criticism,[4] and that the text as we have received it is a proper object of study.

This means that I have some sympathy for the views and programme of B.S. Childs.[5] However, I do not think that his canonical

1. Cf. J. Barton, *Reading the Old Testament* (London: Darton, Longman and Todd, 1984), pp. 147-51.

2. It is not possible to undertake a detailed statistical investigation, but some basic observations are made in Chapter 1.

3. E.g. Y.T. Radday and D. Wickmann, 'The Unity of Zechariah Examined in the Light of Statistical Linguistics', *ZAW* 87 (1975), pp. 30-55; cf. Y.T. Radday, *The Unity of Isaiah in the Light of Statistical Linguistics, with a Contribution by D. Wickmann* (Hildesheim: Gerstenberg, 1973); and S.L. Portnoy and D.L. Petersen, 'Biblical Texts and Statistical Analysis: Zechariah and Beyond', *JBL* 103 (1984), pp. 11-21.

4. As envisaged by J. Muilenburg, 'Form Criticism and Beyond', *JBL* 88 (1969), pp. 1-18.

5. As set out in several works, notably in his *Introduction to the Old Testament as Scripture* (London: SCM Press, 1979).

studies are entirely clear in their orientation and foundation. I do not know precisely what is intended by 'canonical shaping': it seems to imply the existence of a mind of some kind, which is distinct from the minds of the writers and editors who had a hand in the production of the Old Testament.[1] I do not think that Professor Childs means to investigate the mind of God. In any case, I confine my attention to the shaping undertaken by individual minds.

This study comes under the general title of 'rhetorical criticism', but even so it is restricted in scope. It does not deal, for example, with several of the concerns expressed by Muilenburg[2] or the authors of *Rhetorical Criticism*,[3] let alone the many studies that have been inspired by this initiative. For example, Johnny Lee Wilson investigates the use of different types of consonant to express a particular mood and meaning.[4]

---

1. Thus, for example, he says:

> A major literary and theological force was at work in shaping the present form of the Hebrew Bible. . . prophetic oracles directed to one generation were fashioned in sacred Scripture by a canonical process to be used by another generation.

('The Canonical Shape of the Prophetic Literature', in J.L. Mays and P.J. Achtemeier [eds.], *Interpreting the Prophets* [Philadelphia: Fortress Press, 1987], p. 42).

2. See Chapter 1 below.

3. E.g. A.S. Rose, 'The "Principles" of Divine Election', in J.J. Jackson and M. Kessler (eds.), *Rhetorical Criticism: Essays in Honor of James Muilenburg* (Pittsburgh: Pickwick Press, 1974), pp. 43-67, who argues that 1 Sam. 16 'is formulated in the categories of thought, and with literary features similar to those of Wisdom Literature' (pp. 43-44); or W.E. March, who investigates the functions and meanings of לכן, in 'Laken: Its Function and Meaning', in Jackson and Kessler (eds.)., *Rhetorical Criticism*, pp. 256-84. Some of the articles seem to have little connection with rhetorical criticism, e.g. E.J. Hamlin's account of 'The Liberator's Ordeal' (pp. 33-42). Perhaps rhetorical criticism is even wider than Muilenburg realized. See Chapter 1 below.

4. J.L. Wilson, *A Rhetorical-Critical Analysis of the Balaam Oracles* (PhD thesis, Southern Baptist Theological Seminary, 1981). Thus he says, 'The sonoric value of the words are [*sic*] inseparably united with the meaning of the word and of the context'. He regards the labials and velars as 'dark letters' and the dentals and palatals as 'bright letters' (p. 23). On p. 35 he says,

> It was shown that sound patterns may affect the mood and emphasis of the content; rhythm may be established if one uses more than one method; parallelism can aid in clarifying the message; the 'old rhetoric' can enable the reader/critic to discern the structure of the poem; and attention to imagery and irony is important in understanding the text.

The main stimulus for it has come from the many scholars who have noted regular structures in Old Testament passages.[1] These range from a single verse (or less) to a whole book (or more).[2] Many of these are stimulating and seem to throw new light upon the meaning of a passage.[3] Most of them, however, it seems to me, are not put forward with sufficient scepticism. I shall illustrate what I mean in Chapter 1 by means of the following:

1. An outline of contemporary structural studies of the kind that I am interested in.
2. A critique of such studies in general terms.
3. Detailed scrutiny of specific works dealing with the structure of biblical texts.
4. Theoretical remarks concerning the objectivity of the results of structural studies.

From this I shall draw some conclusions about a more secure way to proceed in structural studies. In the second part of the book I shall attempt to apply these conclusions to a consideration of the structure of the book of Zechariah. There will be different types of unit in focus:

On p. 151 he concludes that the use of velars and sibilants expresses the invulnerability and strength of Jacob–Israel. This is an interesting thesis but to test it would require another full length volume. I did produce a computer program to enable me to investigate the frequency of various types of consonant in each verse of Zechariah, but it soon became plain that there was no room in this work for such a study.

1. E.g. J.M. Gibbs, a former colleague in Bangalore, who discovered many chiastic structures in different parts of the Bible. See the bibliography and treatment of the Psalms in Chapter 1 below. I am also indebted to Jonathan Magonet, whose study of the book of Jonah (*Form and Meaning: Studies in Literary Techniques in the Book of Jonah* [Sheffield: Almond Press, 1983]) is the most satisfactory and illuminating structural study I have yet seen. L. Alonso-Schökel, J.P. Fokkelman, J.R. Lundbom, W.L. Holladay, P. Auffret and P. Lamarche have all provided great stimulus, even though I have had to disagree with their results in many places.

2. Discoveries of small chiasmuses are numerous. Attempts to identify the structure of large works come from, e.g., J.P. Fokkelman (*Narrative Art and Poetry in the Books of Samuel. I. King David* [2 Sam 9–20 & 1 Kings 1–2] [Assen: Van Gorcum, 1981], and *Narrative Art in Genesis* [Assen: Van Gorcum, 1975]) and J.R. Lundbom (*Jeremiah: A Study in Ancient Hebrew Rhetoric* [Missoula, MT: Scholars Press, 1975]).

3. For example Lundbom's observation of the correspondence between Jer. 1.5 and 20.18, in *Jeremiah*, pp. 28-30.

1. Small individual units (with or without suspected redactional additions or adjustments).
2. Larger units, for example, chs. 1–8, 9–11, 12–14, and 1–14.

In order to avoid circular argument in deciding upon individual units, these will be established, in Chapter 2, with reference to main line Old Testament studies, taking particular note of form-critical criteria and the scholarly consensus. In the following two chapters I shall examine the internal structure of individual units, and then the structure arising out of the relation of these units to one another.

The final section, Chapter 5, summarizes results obtained and estimates their reliability. It is hoped that this will make some contribution to the debate about how structural studies ought to be carried out, and that at least some future results will carry more conviction.

Chapter 1

INVESTIGATING STRUCTURE: IN SEARCH OF A RELIABLE METHOD

In his Presidential Address, at the 1968 annual meeting of the Society
for Biblical Literature, James Muilenburg read a paper entitled 'Form
Criticism and Beyond'.[1] In it he paid tribute to and identified with
Gunkel and those scholars who had built upon his work, but then went
on to point to some limitations which he believed must be met by a
different type of study. This has come to be known as rhetorical criticism. He argued that there had been a tendency to stress the typical
and representative features of a text to the extent that the individual
and unique features had been obscured. What is needed is to take form
and content together as part of an integral whole. He insisted that the
form-critical method need not be applied in a formalistic way, so as to
ignore or even denigrate personal and psychological factors, nor need
it be hostile to aesthetic and artistic studies.[2] Muilenburg went on to
formulate a 'canon':

> a responsible and proper articulation of the words in their linguistic
> patterns and in their precise formulations will reveal to us the texture and
> fabric of the writer's thought, not only what it is that he thinks, but how
> he thinks it.[3]

According to Muilenburg the two main concerns of the rhetorical
critic are as follows: 'To define the limits and scope of the literary
unit'. This will give understanding of a writer's intent and meaning,
and will show, for example, how a major motif is resolved within

1. *JBL* 88 (1969), pp. 1-18; reprinted in T.F. Best (ed.), *Hearing and
Speaking the Word* (Missoula, MT: Scholars Press, 1984).
2. L. Alonso-Schökel makes the same point in his 'Hermeneutical Problems of a
Literary Study of the Bible', in *Congress Volume: Edinburgh 1974* (VTSup, 28;
Leiden: Brill, 1975), pp. 1-15.
3. 'Form Criticism', p. 7.

a unit. In this connection he mentions 'inclusio' as a well attested feature of Hebrew writing (cf. Jer. 3.1–4.4):

> To recognize the structure of a composition and to discern the con-figuration of its component parts, to delineate the warp and woof out of which the literary fabric is woven, and to note the various rhetorical devices that are employed for marking, on the one hand, the sequence and movement of the pericope, and on the other, the shifts or breaks in the development of the writer's thought.[1]

In particular this means noting the way individual strophes (Muilenburg defends the retention of this term) are both marked off and grouped together.[2] In this connection Muilenburg mentions: turn-ing points or breaks or shifts, the use of particles, vocatives, inclusio, questions at points of climax, repetition of keywords.[3]

This address was in no sense a new beginning. Muilenburg himself had written articles with this perspective,[4] and he referred back to much older writers, such as E. König, Bishop Lowth and E. Sievers, together with more recent writers up to U. Cassuto, Cross and Freedman, G. Gerleman and W.L. Holladay, who had shared his concerns.[5] Nevertheless, the article seems to have acted as a stimulus to 'rhetorical criticism'. In 1974 a book by this name was published as

1. 'Form Criticism', p. 10.
2. He gives various examples of turning points or breaks in Hebrew poetry, and argues that particles play a major role in revealing 'the rhetorical cast of Semitic literary mentality' ('Form Criticism', p. 13). He claims that the deictic and emphatic particle *kî* is important in this respect. This has been dealt with in 'The Linguistic and Rhetorical Usages of the Particle *kî* in the Old Testament', *HUCA* 32 (1961), pp. 135-60. Examples given include Isa. 32.2; 34.5a, 6c, 8a; Ps. 95.3, 7; 1.6; Jer. 4.6b, 8b; 5.6c.
3. 'Form Criticism', pp. 13-17.
4. E.g. 'The Linguistic and Rhetorical Usages of the Particle כי in the Old Testament', and 'A Study in Hebrew Rhetoric', in *Congress Volume* (VTSup, 1; Leiden: Brill, 1953), pp. 97-111.
5. E. König, *Stilistik, Rhetorik, und Poetik* (Leipzig, 1900); R. Lowth, *De sacra poesi Hebraeorum praelectiones academicae* (1753); E. Sievers, *Metrische Studien* (1901, 1904–1905, 1907); F.M. Cross and D.N. Freedman, *Studies in Ancient Yahwistic Poetry* (Missoula, MT: Scholars Press, 1950); G. Gerleman, 'The Song of Deborah in the Light of Stylistics', *VT* 1 (1951), pp. 168-80. At this time Holladay had already produced some articles on the book of Jeremiah: 'Prototype and Copies: A New Approach to the Poetry-Prose Problem in the Book of Jeremiah', *JBL* 79 (1960), pp. 351-67; and 'The Recovery of Poetic Passages of Jeremiah', *JBL* 85 (1966), pp. 401-35.

a tribute to James Muilenburg.[1] One of the central features in rhetorical critical studies has been the discovery of 'chiasmus' in virtually all parts of the Old Testament.[2]

Chiasmus was noted by J.A. Bengel as long ago as 1742,[3] but the greatest impetus to this in modern times seems to have come from Nils Lund who, in 1942, produced his book *Chiasmus in the New Testament*.[4] His writings contain patterns typical of those represented in structural studies today, for example, on Ps. 3.7-8:[5]

> Save me
> O my God
>   For thou hast smitten
>   all my enemies
>   On the cheek bone;
>   The teeth
>   of the wicked
>   Thou hast broken
> To Yahweh
> The salvation

This example, like several other short ones, is free from elements of selection and subjective characterization and seems to me to be quite convincing. In other words, Lund has simply put down what is there

---

1. Jackson and Kessler (eds.), *Rhetorical Criticism*.

2. For a long list of patterns claimed in both biblical and extra-biblical literature, see *Chiasmus in Antiquity* (ed. J.W. Welch; Hildesheim: Gerstenberg, 1981), pp. 287-352.

3. *Gnomon Novi Testamenti* (Tübingen), quoted in N.W. Lund, 'The Presence of Chiasmus in the Old Testament', *AJSL* 46 (1930), p. 104. Other scholars who pointed to chiastic structures include J. Jebb, *Sacred Literature* (T. Caldwell and W. Davies, 1820); T. Boys, *Key to the Book of Psalms* (London: L.B. Seely & Sons, 1825); and J. Forbes, *The Symmetrical Structure of Scripture, or the Principles of Scripture Parallelism Exemplified in an Analysis of the Decalogue, the Sermon on the Mount, and Other Passages of the Sacred Writings* (Edinburgh: T. & T. Clark, 1854). Jebb noticed the structure of Zech. 9.5 formed by Ashkelon—Gaza—Ekron—her [= Ekron's]—Gaza—Ashkelon. See the treatment of this section in Chapter 3 below.

4. Chapel Hill: University of North Carolina Press, 1942. He had previously produced several articles including 'The Presence of Chiasmus in the Old Testament', pp. 104-26 and 'Chiasmus in the Psalms', *AJSL* 49 (1933), pp. 281-312.

5. 'Chiasmus in the Psalms', p. 288.

in these two verses, and the correspondence is plain. Patterns found in most other sections are plausible but not all are compelling. In subsequent studies, it seems to me, many scholars have assumed Lund's work to be a solid basis and have built more speculative work on it. They should have given more attention to checking their foundations. Lund himself was aware of the charge of subjectivism that might be levelled at his method and pointed to objective checks such as the 'prevalent parallelism, rhythm, or general sense of the passage in question'. He argues that 'chiasmus as a new instrument. . . need not supplant, but rather will supplement, parallelism and rhythm'.[1] This is accepted in the present study.

Despite the caution expressed by Lund, it seems to me that he did not carry out his studies rigorously enough. This may be illustrated by considering his analysis of some of the Psalms and by comparing his results with those of other scholars.

Lund presents Psalm 15 as follows:

1.	A		Vocative and Repeated question: 'Who shall dwell. . . ?'
2-3a.	B		Two lines each concerned with deeds then words
			Last line only is negative
3b		C	*Not* he doeth to his fellows/evil
			And a reproach/*not* he has taken against his neighbours
4	B'		Two lines each deeds and words [questionable]
			Last line only is negative
5		C'	His money/*not* he putteth out on interest
			And a bribe against the innocent/*not* he taketh
	A'		Answer to the opening question [but not phrased so as to correspond exactly to the question, e.g. 'Whoever does this shall dwell with Yahweh']

Lund comments on the fact that there is chiasmus in B' but not B, and concludes: 'Evidently it was not felt to be necessary to have every feature in the two strophes parallel'.[2] We might as easily have drawn the conclusion that the chiasmus was incidental or unconscious.

Other patterns that Lund detected in the Psalms are (using English verse numbers) shown in figure 1. Where available the patterns

---

1. 'Chiasmus in the Psalms', p. 286.
2. 'Chiasmus in the Psalms', p. 292.

claimed by J.M. Gibbs,[1] R.L. Alden,[2] J.T. Willis, and P. Auffret are given below Lund's.[3]

It is obvious that there are many substantial differences between these outlines. This does not mean that none of them can be right—after all there *may* be a washing powder that really does wash whitest of all— but it does suggest that scholars need to interact with one another and be prepared to demonstrate that their own scheme is more likely to be 'correct' than any of the alternatives. In this study I am assuming, as the scholars working in this area seem to do, that we are concerned with the plan in the mind of the author(s) and/or redactor(s). It is therefore not possible for us, as it would be for structuralists, to claim that the text allows all these patterns to be regarded as genuine.

Psalm 1	1	2	3	4	5	6a	6b
	A		BC	C'	B'	A'	
[Alden	A^1	A^2	B	B	A^1	A^2]	
[Auffret	a	B		b	A		
Also:	I	II		II'	I	II	II']
[Willis	A			B		A	B]

Psalm 2	1	2	3	4	5	6	7a	7b	8	9	10	11	12
	A	BCD	E		F	E'			A'		B'	C'	D'
[Gibbs	a	b	c	d	e	f	g	f'	e'd'	c'	b'	a'	]
[Alden	A^1	A^2		B^1		B^2	B^2		B^1		A^1	A^2	]
[Auffret	A		B			B'					A'		]

1. 'Chiastic Psalms' (Private circulation, 1971).

2. 'Chiastic Psalms: Mechanics of Semitic Poetry in Psalms 1–50', *JETS* 17 (1974), pp. 11-28.

3. Ps. 1: Lund, 'Chiasmus in the Psalms', pp. 294-95; Alden, 'Chiastic Psalms', p. 14; Auffret, 'Essai sur la structure littéraire du Psaume 1', *BZ* 22 (1978), pp. 41, 44-45; J.T. Willis, 'Psalm 1—An Entity', *ZAW* 91 (1979), pp. 381-401. Ps. 2: Lund, 'Chiasmus in the Psalms', pp. 295-98; Alden, 'Chiastic Psalms', pp. 14-15; P. Auffret, *The Literary Structure of Psalm 2* (JSOTSup, 3; Sheffield: JSOT Press, 1977), pp. 31-32. It is unfair to reduce Auffret's thorough and subtle study to this bare outline, since he points to many other marks of structure. Nevertheless, this is how he presents the structure of the whole, and this is the focus of our present comparison. Ps. 3: Lund, 'Chiasmus in the Psalms', pp. 298-300; P. Auffret, 'Note sur la structure littéraire du Psaume 3', *ZAW* 91 (1979), p. 100. Ps. 4: Lund, 'Chiasmus in the Psalms', pp. 299-302; Alden, 'Chiastic Psalms', p. 15. Ps. 30: Lund, 'Chiasmus in the Psalms', pp. 304-306; Alden, 'Chiastic Psalms', pp. 22-23. Ps. 29: Lund, 'Chiasmus in the Psalms', pp. 306-309; Alden, 'Chiastic Psalms', pp. 21-22. Ps. 58: Lund, 'Chiasmus in the Psalms', p. 311.

Psalm 3	1	2	3	4	5	6	7 (first two words)	7	8
	A		B		B'			A'	+ Praise
[Gibbs	a		b	c	d	d	c...............	b	a]
[Auffret	A		B	B'		A'	B............ ...	A	B]

Psalm 4	1	2	3	4	5	6	7	8
	A	B		C	B'		A'	
[Gibbs	abc	def		g	f' e'	d'	c'	b'a'

As Lund but with more detail]

[Alden   A   B   C   B   A   ]

Psalm 30	1	2	3	4	5	[6	7a	7b]	8	9	10	11	12
	A	B	A'	A	B	gloss			C	D	C'	B'	A'

['Yahweh' and 'Yahweh my God' are used to separate sections]

[Gibbs   a   bc   de   fg   hijk   lm   n   oon   ml   kjih   gf   edc   ba

He notes this as 'probably chiastic']

[Alden   A B^1 B^2 B^3 CD   E   D   C B^1 B^2 B^3 A   ]

Psalm 29	1	2	3	4	5	6		8	7+9b	10	11
	A		B	C	D			C'	B'		A'

[Transposing verses in the interests of a theory that concerns the order of verses must be regarded as precarious]

[Gibbs   abc   de   f g^2 h (+ v. 7) g^2 f'e'   d'c'   b'a'

He suggests that vv. 6-7 describe a volcano]

[Alden   A B^1 B^2 B^{3a} B^{3b} 7=B^1 B^2 9=B^{3b+3a} A   ]

Psalm 58	1	2	3	4	5	6	7	8	[9]	10	11
	A	B	C	D		E	D'	C'	gloss	B'	A'

[Gloss supposed to be added by someone who was unaware of the chiastic nature of the Psalm]

[Gibbs   ab   cd   ef   gh   ik   k'i'   h'g'   f'e'   d'   c'   b'a']

Figure 1: *Patterns in the Psalms detected by Lund et al.*

Similar remarks could be made about Lund's other article, 'The Presence of Chiasmus in the Old Testament'.[1] One of the convincing patterns he lays out is Isa. 60.1-3:

---

1. Pp. 109-26.

Arise (קוּמִי)
  shine (אוֹרִי)
    for thy light is come (כִּי בָא אוֹרֵךְ)
      and the glory (וּכְבֹד)
        of Jehovah
          upon thee is risen (זָרָח)
            For, behold, darkness shall cover the earth
              and gross darkness the peoples (לְאֻמִּים)
            but upon thee will arise (יִזְרַח)
          Jehovah
        and his glory (וּכְבֹדוֹ) shall be seen (יֵרָאֶה) upon thee
      and nations shall come to thy light (וְהָלְכוּ גוֹיִם לְאוֹרֵךְ)
    and kings to the brightness (לְנֹגַהּ)
  of thy rising (זַרְחֵךְ)

Even so this may give the impression of greater precision than was intended by the author. The first verb concerned with 'rising' is קוּם whereas the other three are זרח. We might ask why the author did not use קוּמֵךְ in v. 3. Furthermore, 'shine' is not from the same root as 'brightness', but it does share its root with 'thy light' in vv. 1 and 3.

During the past twenty years there has been an increasing flow of articles and books concerned with the structure of literary units. Yet it is still true, as D.N. Freedman said, that 'the study of ancient literary techniques is still in ferment and flux. A common fund of axioms and assumptions and a single sure-handed methodology are yet to be established.' That remark was made in the preface to an important work published in 1981, *Chiasmus in Antiquity*,[1] which attempted to draw together results achieved in various literatures: Sumero-Akkadian and Ugaritic literature, biblical Hebrew (both narrative and poetry), Aramaic (contracts and letters), Talmudic-Aggadic (narrative), the Book of Mormon, the New Testament, and ancient Greek and Latin literature. In addition there is a valuable bibliography of books (but not articles) concerned with structure (although this is often not their prime concern), and an index arranged according to literary reference which gives the patterns detected in the books listed. John Welch shows some concern for objectivity and lists some of the 'objective criteria' which may be observed more or less clearly:

1. P. 7.

repetition
balance
inversion
focus or shift at the centre
density of the parallel forms

He argues that even where these are not clearly in evidence it may sometimes be

> desirable to draw attention to ways in which the text tends toward inverted order, or to focus on a particular sense of balance or symmetry which seems foundational to the text itself. Here it is possible to speak of chiasmus in a looser sense of the term, for chiasmus, like poetical or artistic forms generally, lends itself to a variety of application and arrangements which may on some occasions only approximate to its ideal composition. Where the inversion is less than perfect, some might contend that this is evidence that no inversion was ever intended by the writer at all. Rather, this might better be explained as evidence that the author simply took some liberty with the form... In such instances the analysis becomes much more complex and, depending to a large extent on what is to be proved thereby, may become controversial.

It is not clear how committed to objectivity Welch is, for he says in conclusion,

> In the final analysis, our study ends where it begins: with the ancient text in hand. The features which it ultimately manifests are largely determined by what features the text is observed as manifesting. What a text says, or looks like, or stands for, is fundamentally a matter of what it says to its readers... What one ultimately sees in a text is only limited by, not determined by, potential criticisms which render a view more or less attractive... These remarks...do not purport to prove the validity or importance of chiasmus, for its proof is only in its perception and for that we must turn to the demonstrations below.[1]

This seems to be to give up the hope of D.N. Freedman quoted above. In any case, it seems to me that most scholars interested in structure operate on the assumption that one simply needs to demonstrate a structure by pointing out correspondences that the reader can see. Very little attention is given to what the author might have intended and virtually no space is devoted to considering counter-claims from other scholars, or to explaining why certain correspondences in a text may be ignored. This will be demonstrated below, by considering a

---

1. Welch (ed.), *Chiasmus in Antiquity*, pp. 13-15.

few selected examples from modern articles concerned with structure.

The articles in *Chiasmus in Antiquity* unfortunately, in my opinion, do not go very far towards establishing either particular large scale chiastic structures, or criteria for recognizing structures planned by the author or editor of a text. Some examples are quite persuasive: for example, the Gilgamesh Epic, as presented by Simoons-Vermeer, although it is interesting that R.F. Smith, the writer of the article on Sumero-Akkadian literature, emends her scheme to something more complicated and with a different centre![1] Some of the examples seem ridiculous, for example the Code of Lipit-Ishtar is said to have an A–B–A' structure: Prologue–Laws–Epilogue.[2] Radday's essay on biblical narrative contains some uncertain and, to my mind, irregular patterns. For example, Kings is presented as:

A		Introduction and Rise (1 Kgs 1–2; 2 chapters)
	B	A Single Kingdom: Solomon (1 Kgs 3–11; 9 chapters)
		C The Divided Kingdom (1 Kgs 12–2 Kgs 17; 29 chapters)
	B'	A Single Kingdom: Josiah (2 Kgs 18–23; 6 chapters)
A		Conclusion and Fall (2 Kgs 24–25; 2 chapters)[3]

This does not look particularly regular, nor is it clear that the author/editor thought of 2 Kings 18–23 as a single kingdom matching the kingdom of Solomon.

In the section 1 Kings 3–11 Radday argues for the following pattern:[4]

A B C D E F G H F' E' C' G' B' D' A'.

Apart from the fact that the sections vary in length from five to one hundred and fifty-five verses, this looks like a very irregular pattern. Radday admits that 'deviations from perfect symmetry occur' but argues that the only substantial one is G'. Statistics are used to measure 'deviation from a perfect chiasm', but I do not find this reassuring. It is particularly unsettling that Radday engages in a brief study of the book of Jonah, dismissing 2.2-9 as not integral to the book, without referring to Magonet's study.[5]

---

1.   Welch (ed.), *Chiasmus in Antiquity*, pp. 26-28.
2.   Welch (ed.), *Chiasmus in Antiquity*, p. 20.
3.   Welch (ed.), *Chiasmus in Antiquity*, p. 62.
4.   Welch (ed.), *Chiasmus in Antiquity*, pp. 62-63.
5.   Welch (ed.), *Chiasmus in Antiquity*, pp. 59-61.

The article by W.G.E. Watson is much more circumspect.[1] He first defines in a helpful way the terms he intends to use—hemistich, colon (a single line of poetry), strophe (verse unit made up of one or more cola) and so on—and then gives a brief account of 'Strophic Chiasmus'. The terms he uses are:

1. Pure or mirror chiasmus: abc//cba, where the a's are almost identical;
2. Complete chiasmus: ab//ba (strictly ab//b'a'); abc//cba; etc.
3. Split member chiasmus: a-bc//bc-a; etc.
4. Partial chiasmus: abc//cb; ab-c//ba-c; etc.[2]

As well as straightforward structural chiasmus he notes some other types:

1. 'Skewed chiasmus'—'after the midpoint [it] begins its way back, only to plunge forward briefly once more, and then, in the last line, offers a set of simultaneous balances in several media which psychologically brings us all the way home'.[3]
2. Assonantal chiasmus. This includes (a) texts containing both chiasmus and assonance; (b) texts with a chiastic pattern of root consonants (e.g. Jer. 5.25; 16.6).
3. Semantic-sonant chiasmus. Here one pair of words corresponds because they are similar in meaning; the other pair is similar in sound (e.g. Eccl. 7.1a, משמן טב // טב שם, 'A good name is better than good perfume').
4. Gender chiasmus, which is obtained by the layout of the gender of the nouns used (e.g. Prov. 20.9, 'Young men's glory [f.] is their strength [m.], But old men's splendour [m.] their grey hair [f.]').[4]

---

1. The Society for Old Testament Study Book List found it 'unusually convincing'.

2. 'Chiastic Patterns in Biblical Hebrew Poetry', in Welch (ed.), *Chiasmus in Antiquity*, pp. 118-68 (123-26).

3. Quoting W.L. Holladay, 'Poetic Passages of Jeremiah', *JBL* 85 (1966), pp. 432-33.

4. J. Magonet also refers to gender chiasmus in 'Isaiah 2.1–4.6: Some Poetic Structures and Tactics', *Amsterdamse cahiers voor exegese* 3 (1982), pp. 82-83. He notes Condamin's observation that Isa. 3.18-23 contains groups of nouns, 8 + 5 + 8. The first eight have the genders:

3m. + 3f. + m. + f., and the last: 3f. + 3m. + f. + m.

In addition he lists 'patterns related to chiasmus' as:[1]

1. Alternating chiasmus, i.e. ab//ab which is not chiasmus at all but 'may be significant in considering the development of chiasmus'.

2. Inclusio. Although all chiastic patterns of the form a.../ /...a could be considered as inclusios, Watson says that it is a 'distant form of parallelism' which 'cannot be confused with chiasmus'. Nevertheless, there may well be texts where we are not certain which description is the most apt.

3. Chiastic inclusio. For example, a-b/.../b-a. He also wants to include examples of 'phonological inclusio' (by which he seems to mean the assonantal and semantic-sonant chiasmus mentioned above).[2] This does not appear to be an appropriate name for the latter.

4. Chiastic gather-line. Watson mentions Jer. 23.4 and 23.32 as examples. This gather-line reiterates most of the elements of the poem in reverse order.[3]

Magonet comments, 'It is possible to consider a modified version of this system and discern a pattern to these forms. The first three words have a masculine plural ending, and the second three a feminine plural.' So far so good, but then he makes sense of the middle section by arguing for:

vv. 20-21a   *-îm -ôt -îm* endings, nouns in alphabetical order;
and
v. 21b   construct phrase + single word
              single word + construct phrase.

At this point one must ask what controls are being exercised. For example, three plural nouns are just as likely to look regularly arranged as irregularly (f.f.f.; m.m.m.; m.f.m.; f.m.f.; as opposed to m.m.f., f.f.m., m.f.f., f.m.m.). Further see below.

1. Welch (ed.), *Chiasmus in Antiquity*, pp. 135-36.

2. Assuming that '2.82' means '2.8 (2)'; the referencing is somewhat confusing.

3. Cf. A.R. Ceresko, 'The Chiastic Word Pattern in Hebrew', *CBQ* 40 (1978), pp. 1-10 (2-3). Another example of a gather-line, which *may* be chiastic, seems to me to be Isa. 2.20 which picks up various elements found in vv. 6-8 (idols, silver and gold, work of their hands/made for themselves). Verse 21 is very similar to v. 19 which itself forms the climax to vv. 9-18. According to most scholars vv. 20-21 come from a redactor, and this seems a sensible conclusion. A full treatment of this passage must be given elsewhere. Cf. Magonet, 'Isaiah 2.1–4.6', pp. 79-82. He does not draw attention to this feature.

In dealing with chiasmus in longer passages, Watson recommends some useful criteria:[1]

1. 'Such chiasmus must be *strict*.' Loose chiasmus must be judged against established norms.
2. A whole stretch of text must be involved, not just parts.[2]
3. Repetition of single words is of more value than is the comparison of headings or labels given by the scholar concerned.
4. The basis on which the chiastic structure is posited *must be stated*, whether it is change of speaker, alternation of gender or content.

It seems that this is a useful start, but I shall suggest further safeguards as we proceed. Here I should mention that repetition of *phrases* is likely to be more significant than repetition of *single words*, and common words are less likely to be used to mark structure than rare and distinctive words.[3]

---

1. Welch (ed.), *Chiasmus in Antiquity*, p. 137.
2. Here he criticizes Lund's treatment of Ps. 30 as I have done above.
3. It is interesting to note that one of Watson's examples is Isa. 1.21-26 which was proposed by R. Lack, *La Symbolique du livre d'Isaïe: Essai sur l'image littéraire comme élément de structuration* (AnBib, 59; Rome: Pontifical Biblical Institute, 1973), pp. 164-71, which I noted independently. The two schemes proposed are:

	21	22	23	24	25	26
Lack	A B	C	D	E D	C	B A
Butterworth	a	b	c	d c	b	a

These are in substantial agreement. The rare word 'dross' (סיגים/סיג) occurs in vv. 22, 25 only in the whole of Isaiah. 'Faithful city' (קריה נאמנה) occurs in vv. 21a and 26b, and 'righteousness' (צדק) occurs in vv. 21b and 26b, and this is noted in Lack's arrangement. I have kept his A and B together because the root שפט occurs in vv. 21b and 26a. There is some doubt about the correspondence of vv. 23 and 24b, since no words are repeated, but there is no doubt at all that the turning point comes here, and that this is marked by a heavy formula: 'Therefore, oracle of the Lord Yahweh of hosts, the mighty one of Israel...' Other scholars have also noted and/or accepted this chiasmus, e.g., J.D.W. Watts, who follows Lack, or at least is aware of the work of Lack and Alonso-Schökel on this passage (*Isaiah 1–33* [Waco, TX: Word Books], p. 24).

An Examination of Specific Structural Studies

Having considered recent work on structure in a general way, I shall consider some concrete examples of scholarly work. They are selected with the aim of presenting a cross-section of the work that has been and is being done. So, there are treatments of texts of varying lengths, from one short verse to one large book. In addition there is an example of scholarly interaction. I have not attempted to deal with uncontroversial short verses—I assume that chiasmus has been demonstrated in this area—nor have I chosen an example of work covering more than one book.[1]

1. *John S. Kselman, 'The ABCB Pattern: Further Examples'*[2]

In this brief essay, Kselman adds to results obtained by S. Gevirtz, who noted that the pattern abcb occurs in Gen. 27.29a and Isa. 45.7a, and by B. Porten and U. Rappaport, who discovered (with the assistance of D.N. Freedman) the same pattern in fifteen other short passages. Kselman adds fifteen more examples.[3]

The pattern is not particularly striking in itself, but the fact that it apparently occurs in several places (thirty-two are claimed here) and is recognized by several scholars means that we must take it seriously. For the purposes of this book it is an example of a small scale structure, validated by its frequency.

These examples usually contain four strophes and the elements singled out are either all verbs or all nouns. This removes one possible charge of arbitrariness. Some of the examples seem to be impressive,

1. E.g. J.P. Fokkelman's study of King David in 2 Sam. 9–20 and 1 Kgs 1–2. This is not really a study that extends over more than one book, though it would be surprising if Fokkelman's complete work did not attempt to do this. Another example is Y.T. Radday's 'Chiasm in Samuel', *LB* 9-10 (1971), pp. 21-31.

2. *VT* 32 (1982), pp. 224-29.

3. S. Gevirtz, *Patterns in the Early Poetry of Israel* (Studies in Ancient Oriental Civilization, 32; Chicago: University of Chicago Press, 1963), pp. 43-44; B. Porten and U. Rappaport, 'Poetic Structure in Gen. 9.7', *VT* 21 (1971), pp. 363-69, added Gen. 9.7; Num. 23.7-8; Isa. 28.23; 30.10; 34.1; 42.15; Jer. 22.20; 40.9; and 50.2; D.N. Freedman suggested Isa. 5.5; 44.7; 45.4-5; Jer. 5.3; 11.11-12; 12.7-8; Kselman added Pss. 34.22-23; 46.3-4; 68.10-11; 71.22-23; 72.5-8; 132.13-14; Isa. 29.4; 35.10; 56.1; Jer. 4.15-16; Ezek. 29.4; Amos 9.6; Hab. 1.4; Job 13.23; and Deut. 7.13.

for example, Ps. 72.5-8 has each word at the beginning of a line, and the repeated word, ‏ייר[ו]‏, is significant.[1]

Isa. 35.10 (= 51.11) is very different. It has two word pairs: ‏ברנה‏ ‏ושמחת‏ and ‏ששון ושמחה‏. These are natural word pairs, and according to BDB occur twice and thirteen times respectively. The roots also occur parallel to each other. It seems a mistake, therefore, to say that this example strengthens the case for saying that the pattern abcb is used deliberately.

Several patterns are obtained from words distributed quite irregularly, for example, Ps. 132.13-14 has fifteen words in all; the positions of words chosen for the pattern are 2, 5, 13, 15.[2]

In this last example Kselman notes 'also the chiasmus of b with cb'. This is an unusual way of describing the situation. This could be set out as a bcdcb chiasmus with b-b forming a complete inclusio:

‏אוה‏

‏מושב‏

‏מנוחתי‏

‏אשב‏

‏אותיה‏

This suggests, I believe, that the bcb pattern is unlikely to have been consciously intended by the psalmist.

In Isa. 29.4 Kselman presents a second person singular verb along with three nouns with second person singular suffixes. This is slightly misleading, since there are three other second person singular verbs in the verse. A valid reason for putting the selected words together (which Kselman also mentions) is that they all express the idea of speaking: ‏קולך‏ ,‏אמרתי‏ ,‏תדברי‏. It is true, as Kselman notes, that the full form of the pattern would include the twice repeated ‏מאץ‏ and ‏מעפר‏. Thus we have quite a subtle whole:

---

1.   More accurately 'words' since we have two homographs: 'go down' ‏ירד‏, and 'rule' ‏רדה‏.

2.   Positions and total numbers of words in Kselman's examples are:

1,6,7,12 (15 words)	6,8,13,15 (16 words)	3,8,10,12 (15 words)	3,8,13,16 (20 words)
1,8,16,24 (31 words)	2,5,13,15 (15 words)	3,6,10,12 (13 words)	6,7,10,11 (15 words)
5,7,10,12 (13 words)	3,5,9,12 (14 words)	1,4,8,16 (16 words)	2,5-6,9-10,12-14 (14 words)
3,6,11,15 + 4,8,10,16 (17 words)		3,4,5,6 (7 words)	1,2,3,4 (8 words)

p	And you will be low,
q	from the earth
r	you will speak,

q	and from the dust
p	you will be bowed down (?)
r	(with regard to?) your utterance

s	and it will be like a ghost
q	from the earth
r	your voice
q	and from the dust
r	your utterance
s?	will whisper

It seems to me highly likely that the author intended some sort of pattern here, but abcb does not do it justice and may be quite incidental to the overall effect.[1] In general we may make the following observations.

1. It would be quite easy for a writer to produce the abcb pattern by accident, for it is only necessary to meet the following conditions:

> a. Four comparable items occur in a small unit, i.e. four nouns, four verbs, four identical suffixes etc. Even these do not seem to be enforced too strictly.
>
> b. The second and fourth word are similar (but not necessarily identical).

Neither of these is at all stringent, especially if the repeated word is fairly common,[2] and even more if one has a choice of four items out of five or more.[3]

---

1. The most obvious way of looking at this would be:

> pq-r//qp-r (Watson's partial chiasmus)
> s-qr//qr-s (Watson's split member chiasmus)

This is not very satisfactory, since q and r are kept together in one part and separated in the other, and we should need much more evidence before we could say that this was a recognized pattern. Even so, I think it is more plausible than Kselman's suggestion.

2. E.g. הרים in Ps. 46.3-4; צדקתי/צדקה in Isa. 56.1; אל [פני] ארץ in Amos 9.6, in Kselman, 'The ABCB Pattern', pp. 226-28.

3. A brief examination of the first few verses of Isa. 29, one of the chapters that Kselman refers to, reveals that several have repeated words:

2. The examples are not really all of the same type. They vary in the type of words compared, in the positions of those words in the strophe, in the relationship of the words to other parts of the context. This weakens the cumulative effect of the argument.

3. It may well be the case that Hebrew writers deliberately used the abcb pattern, but the five writers who have claimed to find it have not proved that this is so. They have simply shown that, if one looks at the text in a certain way, this pattern can be seen—or imagined. In other words, there is a subjective apprehension of something that may have had no place in the writer's thoughts, and, in that case, would probably not be significant for the meaning of the text.

A fuller discussion of some of the principles involved in deciding whether a pattern is intended or accidental is to be found below.

I conclude that this article confirms what I asserted above, that the study has been carried out without due regard to the legitimacy of the criteria employed or to possible alternative suggestions that might be made. We go on to consider a rather larger unit: Amos 5.1-17.

2. *J. de Waard, 'The Chiastic Structure of Amos 5.1-17'*[1]

De Waard's article is a good attempt to utilize the methods and results of Old Testament scholarship, and to build on these by giving attention to structure. He thus represents 'rhetorical criticism' as defined by James Muilenburg. The article is particularly suitable for our purposes since his work has been endorsed by several scholars working in the field of prophecy.[2]

v. 1   אריאל (##2,3); שנה (##8,10)
v. 2   אריאל (##2,8); והיתה (##3,6); ח/ואניה (##4,5) (This forms a very tight chiasmus)
v. 3   עליך 3×; first person singular perfect 3×
v. 5   היה (##1,10) cf. vv. 4, 7, 8; המון constr. (##4,8) cf. v. 7.

With so many repeated words and such a variety of patterns, which may or may not have been intended by the author, it is not surprising that we find an abcb sequence here.

1.   *VT* 25 (1977), pp. 170-77.

2.   For example, de Waard's position is accepted without question by N.J. Tromp, 'Amos 5.1-17: Towards a Stylistic and Rhetorical Analysis', *OTS* 23 (1982), pp. 56-84. R.B. Coote also accepts that de Waard discovered the chiastic pattern in Amos 5.4-15. Coote also knows why the writer used this form here: it is at the centre of the centre section of the 'B-stage document' of his theory of redaction (*Amos among the Prophets* [Philadelphia: Fortress Press, 1981], pp. 78-84).

He begins by setting the limits of the passage under discussion and concludes that vv. 1-17 is a rhetorical unit. Reasons given are:

1.   4.4-13 is a rhetorical unit; 5.1 represents a new start with the imperative 'Hear this word...'
2.   5.18-20 is a unit with a clear structure, although it may have a secondary relationship with vv. 1-17. He points to the 'death' theme ('darkness' would be more obvious: vv. 8, 18, 20).[1]
3.   The theme of mourning found in vv. 1-2 and 16-17 encloses the whole passage.

Still, he says, the structure is difficult, and he proceeds to analyse the whole into sub-units.

Verses 1-3 should be taken together; כי (v. 3) does not indicate a later addition, for, semantically, it provides the ground of the *qinah* (lament) in v. 2. In addition, the 3 + 2 (*qinah*) metre is contained in the first two lines of v. 3.

Verse 4 is formally similar to v. 3 ('For thus says Yahweh...') but is best taken as the beginning of a new paragraph because (a) כי can function as a paragraph link; (b) the setting changes from 'war' to 'sanctuaries and exile'; (c) the call to life contrasts with the *qinah*; and (d) v. 4 is integrally connected with vv. 5-6. He presents the following chiastic structure for vv. 4b-6:

a   Seek me and live
 b   seek not Bethel
  c   and to Gilgal do not go
   d   and to Beersheba do not go over
  c'   for Gilgal shall surely go into exile
 b'   and Bethel shall come to nought
a'   Seek Yahweh and live.

The break at v. 3 seems to be justified. We could also point to the fact that in v. 3b 'to the house of Israel' appears to have a double function. It corresponds to בית ישראל in v. 1, and it is echoed in v. 4.

A.G. Auld, in his JSOT Guide to Amos (*Amos* [OTG; Sheffield: JSOT Press, 1986], pp. 50-53), comments: 'De Waard was the first to argue persuasively that Amos 5.1-17 is an example of palistrophe...' He then proceeds to refine de Waard's basic suggestion, and to commend Tromp's further work.

1.   He refers here to J.L. Mays, *Amos* (London: SCM Press, 1969), p. 103.

Scholars have noted its awkwardness in v. 3 and BHS suggests transposing it after אדני יהוה. Structural considerations suggest that MT is right and that the awkwardness is deliberate.

The argument for taking vv. 4-6 together seems, on the contrary, insecure. We note that 'Seek. . . live' is a recurring refrain that appears in v. 14 as well as in vv. 4 and 6. Moreover, v. 4 has 'seek me' after the introductory formula (IF) but vv. 6 and 14 have 'Yahweh' in the third person. This is not a strong argument, but its force is against rather than in favour of considering vv. 4-6 as a unit. A further, more serious problem is that 'Bethel' occurs again in v. 6 thus producing a ragged structure:

a   b   c   d   c   b   a   b

Here, it would be very convenient to accept the LXX's reading בית ישראל. Not only would it remove the ragged structure but it would provide a further inclusio with v. 4. There is no very strong reason for taking this reading and we could not base any far reaching conclusions on it.

If we accept the MT it would seem more logical to see the whole passage like this:

vv. 1-3   A lament and its motivation
vv. 4-5   First exhortation to seek Yahweh and live: no profit in Bethel, Gilgal, Beersheba, Gilgal, Bethel.
vv. 6-?   Second exhortation.
            Bethel represents also Gilgal and Beersheba, and thereby Israel as a (compromised) worshipping community.
vv. 14-?   Third exhortation. . .

De Waard argues that his arrangement confirms the secondary character of the 'list' in v. 6 and refers to Wolff's independent conclusion.[1] Wolff reasons that v. 6 as a whole offers an exegesis of vv. 4-5: its construction is awkward, it is very like 4.6-13, it is restricted to Bethel and it is connected with vv. 8-9. This differs from de Waard's view in taking 'Seek Yahweh and live' as an addition, and in removing v. 7 from its place (to between v. 9 and v. 10, an option rejected by de Waard).

---

1.   H.W. Wolff, *Joel and Amos* (Philadelphia: Fortress Press, 1977), pp. 232-33, 240-41.

This raises the question: which stage of the text's history are we interested in? De Waard seems to assume that the final editor was one who disturbed the structure. Does this mean we are really interested in the purposive editor? Or should we presume that in seeking a coherent stage we might arrive at the words of Amos himself?—or the true canonical text?—or something with more authority at least than our Masoretic Text? In any case the question needs to be addressed. If a structure is discernible in two or more supposed redactional stages we should be interested in both, but the only (almost) certain stage is the final one.

Verse 7 is treated as transitional, preparing for vv. 8-9. Yet this does not prove its independence. It does not necessarily interrupt the flow of vv. 6, 8 unless we can prove that there must follow a characterization of the God whom they are to seek, and not of those who are exhorted to seek. In fact, v. 7 makes good sense where it is:

v. 6   Seek Yahweh...
v. 7   O you who turn justice to wormwood. . .
v. 8   (Seek) him who made the Pleiades. . .

Verses 8-9 is seen in hymnic form; 'Yahweh is his name' occurs in the middle and is often said to disturb its flow. Yet we could as easily take it (as de Waard does) to be the central assertion and focus of these verses.

We must note here that 5.7a is very similar to 6.12. 'Wormwood' occurs nowhere else in Amos, and only six times more in the Hebrew Bible. We ought therefore to consider whether some larger structural arrangement is suggested. Obvious immediate correspondences are:

5.3	declamation	
	[large section on 'seek and live' containing:]	
5.7	turn justice to wormwood	
5.18-20	Woe (to those who desire the Day of Yahweh)	
5.21-23	I hate your feasts and sacrifices	
5.24	Justice	
5.25-27	No sacrifices in the wilderness	
[?6.8?]	[hate, pride, strongholds]	
6.1-3, 4-6	Woe (to those at ease. . .to those on ivory beds)	
6.9	ten men left in a house will die	
6.12	turned justice to wormwood.	

This is not to suggest that any author/editor actually intended this; the matter must be investigated properly. It does confirm that care should be taken to avoid selectivity in pointing to correspondences between one part of a passage and another.

Attention may be drawn to the following repetitions in ch. 5:

הפך	v. 7 '*turn* justice to wormwood'
	v. 8 '*turns* deep darkness into morning' (cf. שפך v. 8)
ל/עלפני הארץ	vv. 7-8
עבר	v. 5 (with the centre of the chiasmus)
	v. 17 'I will pass through the midst of you'
נשא	v. 1; cf. שנא, see below; cf. הקים, v. 2
כרם	vv. 11, 17
שאר	v. 3; cf. שארית v. 15
יוסף	vv. 6, 15
משפט	vv. 7, 15
קרא	vv. 8, 16
ידע	vv. 12, 16
שער	vv. 10, 12, 15
משכיל	v. 13, cf.? כסיל v. 8
רעה, רע	vv. 13, 14

This is not the place to put forward an alternative theory about the structure of this passage. I simply note that we cannot be satisfied with an analysis which leaves so much of the data unaccounted for. A much more wide-ranging and thorough investigation is needed.

Verses 10-12 is considered by de Waard to be a chiastic unit to which v. 13 has been added secondarily. Thus we have:[1]

```
a            no justice in the gate v. 10
    b                oppressing the poor v. 11a
        c
    b'               oppressing the poor v. 12bα
a'           no justice in the gate v. 12bβ
```

This looks fine, but 'in the gate' occurs also in v. 15; 'hate' occurs in both v. 10 and v. 15, as well as in v. 21 (otherwise only 6.8 in Amos). De Waard's solution is to put vv. 4-6 opposite vv. 14-15 and simply to note the secondary relationship among vv. 10a, 12b and 15b 'in the gate'. He does not draw attention to 'hate', nor to 'vineyards' in vv. 11b, 17a. We are entitled to ask about the lack of verbal

---

1. He adds: '. . . when one considers in detail the objects mentioned in this structure a-b-c-b'-a', one gets the following chiastic figure: דבר תמים-צדיק (a-b') and דל-אביונים (b-a')'. This is an interesting observation, which could perhaps be confirmed by a detailed study of chiasmus achieved by recognized word pairs.

correspondence between vv. 1 and 16-17. The word קינה occurs in
v. 1 but not elsewhere, although vv. 16-17 contain מספד (3×) and
אבל. However there is not a single word that is common to both
sections.[1]

In de Waard's final pattern he has:

A vv. 1-3   A' vv. 16-17
    B vv. 4-6   B' vv. 14-15
        C v. 7   C' vv. 10-12 (13)
            D v. 8abc   D' v. 9
                    E v. 8d

On the whole these are fairly evenly matched sections except for C
(v. 7), which is much smaller than vv. 10-13 or even vv. 10-12.

A more convincing explanation of the text as it stands seems to me
to be as follows:

A a   Lamentation over the *house of Israel* (vv. 1-3)
    b   She is fallen, decimated
a   is the *house of Israel*

B a   Thus says Yahweh to the *house of Israel* (vv. 4-5)
    c   *Seek* me and *live*
        d   not *Bethel, Gilgal, Beersheba* (d e f e' d')

B'   c'   *Seek* Yahweh and *live* (v. 6)
    a'?   lest fire...*house of Joseph*
        d'   (lest) devour and...no extinguisher for *Bethel*

Thus a threat has been placed over Israel, and an invitation or
exhortation issued to 'seek Yahweh and live'. There follows a characterization of Israel, in terms which deliberately contrast with the
description of Yahweh (vv. 7, 8-9). Verses 10-12 elaborates on the
sins of Israel; v. 13 seems to be a gloss.

There follows another 'B' section, vv. 14-15, which takes up some
of the words used previously: hate evil—not 'the one who reproves in
the gate' (v. 10); establish justice—do not turn it to wormwood
(v. 7); perhaps Yahweh will be gracious to the remnant (vv. 3, 15) of
Joseph (vv. 6, 15).

---

1. קינה, 8.10 otherwise in Amos, with הפך, which we noted in 5.7, 8. It is also
found in 4.11; 6.12. מספד occurs three times in 5.16-17 but nowhere else—nor the
root—in Amos.

The final verses (16-17) are strange in their lack of verbal correspondence with the rest of the passage. Perhaps they are a later addition from another editor. The content is, however, quite similar to v. 1, and we do have an inclusio here.

In conclusion it would appear that de Waard fails to carry conviction in his presentation because:

1.   He has employed unconscious, imprecise criteria in deciding which correspondences are significant with respect to structure; he has apparently ignored some correspondences completely.
2.   He does not consider *all* the data available, but is selective and apparently arbitrary.
3.   He does not consider alternative theories that might rival his own.
4.   He accepts uncertain emendations to the text.
5.   He offers no rationale for his procedure, nor criteria for estimating the significance of the available data.
6.   He ignores the wider context of the book of Amos, which *might* have a bearing on the passage in question; for example, what is the significance of the correspondences between this passage and others in Amos?
7.   He does not specify which redactional stage he is interested in.[1]

Having looked at examples of work done on texts of one or two verses, and on one whole chapter, we move on to consider work done by two scholars on the book of Jeremiah.

3. *J.R. Lundbom and W. L. Holladay: The Structure of the Book of Jeremiah*

These scholars have made ambitious attempts to determine the structure of a large section of Scripture. Their work was influential in setting the frame of reference for the present work and I believe that they present insights of great value. It is impossible to embark upon a detailed exposition and critique of their work, but it is necessary to

---

1.   At the end of the article there is a reference to J. de Waard and W.A. Smalley, *A Translator's Handbook on Amos* (forthcoming). I have not yet managed to find a copy of this book.

say a little about their methods, criteria and results.[1]

Lundbom's thesis is a response to Muilenburg's call for rhetorical criticism.[2] He appreciates previous work done in literary criticism and attempts to build on it and to go beyond it.[3] He believes that inclusio and chiasmus are the features that control the structure of the book of Jeremiah and presents some persuasive examples, for example, דברי ירמיהו: the first words of 1.1 and the last words of 51.64 which enclose the whole of the book of Jeremiah up to the historical appendix in

---

1. J.R. Lundbom, *Jeremiah: A Study in Ancient Hebrew Rhetoric* (Missoula, MT: Scholars Press, 1975); W.L. Holladay, *The Architecture of Jeremiah 1–20* (Lewisburg, PA: Bucknell University Press, 1976); *idem, Jeremiah*, I (Hermeneia; Philadelphia: Fortress Press, 1986). The introduction to Holladay's Commentary is to appear in volume 2, as is his bibliography. There is surprisingly little cross reference to Lundbom's work, or even his own. He notes both works in the his commentary (p. 125), but he has obviously changed his views of Jeremiah between 1976 and 1986. Although he speaks of inclusios as integrating factors, the detailed results are quite different in a number of particulars. For example, in *Architecture* he wrote about: 2.2-3 = seed oracle; 2.5-37, 3.1-5, 12b-14, 19-25 = harlotry cycle; and 4.1–6.30, 8.4-10a, 13 = foe cycle (pp. 30-34, 35-54, 55-101). In the commentary he talks in terms of: 2.4-9, 3.1-2, 4-5, 12, 14-15, 18b, 19, 21a, 22-23, 24-25*, 4.1-2 = early recension to the north (* = poetic core); 2.1-3, 10-25, 29-37, 3.13, 21b, 4.3-4 = additions in the First Scroll; and 2.26-28, 3.3, 20 = additions in the Second Scroll (pp. 62-77).

He does not seem to offer an explanation of how his two systems are related, although he acknowledges the parallels between 4.5–6.30 and 8.14–10.25 discovered in *Architecture*, pp. 108-109 (Holladay, *Jeremiah*, p. 133 n. 1). It is disconcerting that McKane does not include Lundbom's book, nor Holladay's *Architecture of Jeremiah*, in the bibliography of his commentary.

A book that promises to further our understanding of at least part of the book of Jeremiah, with regard to the structure intended by the redactors, is A.R. Diamond, *The Confessions of Jeremiah in Context: Scenes of Prophetic Drama* (JSOTSup, 45; Sheffield: JSOT Press, 1987). In dealing with the 'Confessions' he considers both 'Typical Form' (which relates primarily to results obtained by form critics) and 'Particular Form' which attempts to present (briefly) the structure of individual sections, noting progression of thought, key words, literary devices such as chiasmus, etc. It is this that I have sought to investigate more rigorously. His interaction with Lundbom and Holladay is surprisingly small. Diamond deals much more fully with 'Redaction', 'Setting', 'Interpretation' and the implications of his exegetical results for the meaning of the parts studied in their historical and literary context.

2. Lundbom, *Jeremiah*, pp. 1-2.

3. Lundbom, *Jeremiah*, pp. 2-16.

Jeremiah 52;[1] 1.5 חצא מרחם, and 20.18 מרחם יצאתי. In the latter case Lundbom says that 20.18 is meant to be read in the light of 1.5. Jeremiah's question, 'Why did I come forth?' has an answer: Yahweh called him before he came forth.[2] Holladay agrees with Lundbom here, though he does not refer to his comment on 'words of' in 1.1. Holladay says that 20.14-18 is the last of Jeremiah's recorded 'confessions' which, 'in its position here, serves as an inclusio to round off the confessions'.

Not all his examples are as attractive as these. For example, he argues that 30.5-6 and 31.22b form an inclusio for the core of the 'Book of Consolation', chs. 30–33.[3] The words which suggest this are זכר and גבר (30.6) and גבר and נקבה (31.22b). The correspondence between these is interesting, and there may well be an intended echo of the 'men acting like women' theme in 31.22. However, there are difficulties in establishing this, for (a) the meaning of the latter is obscure; and (b) the most natural place to look for the beginning of an inclusio would be 30.5b rather than v. 6. If that is so, we need to explain why חרדה is not intended to form an inclusio with מחריד, the final word of 30.10. Perhaps it is a subsidiary inclusio, but if so, it cuts across the one discovered by Lundbom. We might also point to שלום in 33.9 as well as 30.5, and note that there we also find the verb רגז which is used parallel to חרד in 1 Sam. 14.15, and might be considered the recognizable complement of a word pair.

Lundbom himself raises another difficulty, namely that Duhm argued that 31.22b was an appendage. If this were established, it would not necessarily rule out an intended inclusio, but we should have to give the credit for it to an editor.[4]

A further passage where Lundbom's work looks both promising and insecure is 8.13–9.21. The root אסף and the word אין each occur twice in 8.13, while 9.21 ends with the phrase ואן מאסף. This is persuasive—and might be even more so if we included נבל and נבלת in 8.13 and 9.21 respectively. However this might modify Lundbom's

1. Lundbom, *Jeremiah*, pp. 25-27.
2. Lundbom, *Jeremiah*, pp. 28-30; cf. Holladay, *Jeremiah*, p. 563; cf. *Architecture*, p. 20.
3. Lundbom, *Jeremiah*, pp. 32-36.
4. Lundbom, *Jeremiah*, p. 33. Most commentators, however, seem to accept 31.2-22 as Jeremianic (cf. O. Eissfeldt, *The Old Testament: An Introduction* [Oxford: Basil Blackwell, 1965], pp. 361-62).

theory that 'and no one shall gather them' was added to tie together two originally separate poems, apart from the fact that, as Lundbom himself says, 'this has not been put forward as a unit before'.[1]

Pages 31-60 contain numerous other examples of inclusio within the 'Poems of Jeremiah' rather than inclusio in 'the Larger Book of Jeremiah'. He recognizes the problem of delimiting the poems and tries to ensure that this is not done by means of 'the controlling inclusio' but by other criteria, 'some rhetorical, e.g. balancing terms, repetition...and some non-rhetorical, e.g. messenger formula, change of speaker, content, etc.' This is to be appreciated. However, some of the inclusios discovered by Lundbom seem feeble, for example, 5.10-13 is marked only by the very common verb עשׂה, and it occurs in different forms, neither at the beginning nor the end of either verse. It could not be a very forceful demarcation of a unit for a hearer or even a reader of this passage. His next example is 5.26-31 in which an inclusio is formed by 'my people'. His explanation may well be correct, but:

1. There is some doubt about the analysis of Jeremiah 5 into units (v. 26 begins with כי which makes it unlikely to be a self-contained unit, although this does not necessarily nullify the inclusio).
2. 'My people' is not particularly distinctive. In other words the example might give some support to a plausible theory, but it would make a weak foundation.[2]

In dealing with chiasmus[3], Lundbom shows that he is aware of the danger of imposing a modern thought pattern on the text rather than discovering the author's own intention. He therefore proposes only to consider supposed thought patterns that are undergirded by key words. This, again, seems to be a wise proposal. We may ignore chiasmus in single bicola, since they are well established, but also of limited value in helping in our task of determining the structure of a large section. Two slightly larger—and convincing—examples are:[4]

---

1. Lundbom, *Jeremiah*, p. 30.
2. Our confidence is not helped by the fact that Holladay both adopts a different division into units here, (5.20-29, 30-31. *Jeremiah*, pp. 192-201) and ignores the repetition of 'my people'.
3. Lundbom, *Jeremiah*, pp. 61-112.
4. Lundbom, *Jeremiah*, pp. 69-70.

1.   2.27b-28a. The pattern is abcba. Here the outer limits (a) are
     indicated by the phrase 'in the time of their trouble', the next
     ring (b) has the verbs 'arise' and 'save', and the centre (c) is
     'but where are the gods which you made for yourselves?'
     (קומה/יקומו; [ו]בעת רעתם]; and והושיענו/יושיעוך respectively).
2.   4.19c-21. This seems to be a+bc*dd*c'b+a. The correspon-
     ding key words are: שדדה/ו; תרועת/נס; שמעתי/אשמעה; קול שופר.

The most substantial part of the book deals with chiastic poems (of
about four verses or more) and with chiasmus in the larger book of
Jeremiah.[1]

In the latter section Lundbom introduces a new type of chiasmus,
arguing that in chs. 25–26 and 35–36 there is a 'Jehoiakim cluster'
patterned as follows:

a	ch. 25	4th year of Jehoiakim
b	ch. 26	the beginning of Jehoiakim's reign
b'	ch. 35	in the days of Jehoiakim
a'	ch. 36	4th year of Jehoiakim

Both ch. 26 and ch. 35 deal with Jeremiah in the Temple. Lundbom
regards 36.9-32 as a later addition to vv. 1-8, which was intended as
Baruch's signature at the end of an earlier edition of the book.
Similarly a 'Zedekiah cluster' may be detected:

a	ch. 24	after the exile of Jeconiah
b	ch. 27	beginning of Zedekiah's reign
b'	ch. 28	beginning of Zedekiah's reign
a'	ch. 29	after the exile of Jeconiah

Lundbom argues that the two clusters were interspersed because in
this way it was possible to keep ch. 36 at the end, and ch. 24 (which
shows significant parallels to ch. 1) at the beginning of the series.
Chapters 30–33 is taken to be a separate section added later still, and
this may be accepted.[2]

This is, in some ways, an attractive theory, but it does involve quite
a number of suppositions that are difficult to prove. For example:

---

1.   Lundbom, *Jeremiah*, pp. 70-96, 96-112 respectively.
2.   Lundbom, *Jeremiah*, pp. 107-112.

1. There is some *significance for the intended structure* in the fact that these chapters mention the date of the incidents related. If this is so, why is the formula not the same in chs. 26 and 35? A plausible reply might be offered, but it would have to be a guess.

2. There is *significance for the task of relating units to each other* in the fact that chs. 26 and 35 speak of Jeremiah in the Temple. But there are many references to the 'house of the LORD' in the book of Jeremiah, including 28.1, cf. 36.5-6.

3. The formula in 36.9 can safely be discounted in the discussion at this point (cf. 4).

4. Jer. 36.9-32 is a later addition to the text. But 36.8 makes a strange ending for a book—even a first edition.

5. We can safely ignore the parallels between chs. 32 and parts of the chapters in the clusters under consideration (e.g. Anathoth, 29.27).

6. Chapters 27 and 28 should be considered as two separate entities, comparable to 26 and 35, yet they clearly belong together, and there is evidence of some editorial activity in 28.1.

7. Jer. 27.1 should read 'Zedekiah' (which I should accept, but it is not completely certain).

8. Chapter 24 is so similar to ch. 1 that it must have been intended as the first chapter of the clusters, even when they were put together. It is true that there are similarities between chs. 1 and 24—both tell of visions; both have 'What do you see Jeremiah?' (1.11, 13; 24.3); and, we might add, both mention building up, tearing down, planting and uprooting (1.10; 24.6 בנה, הרס, נטע, נתש). Jer. 1.10 also has נתץ and אבד. Nevertheless there is a logical jump here.

9. We may ignore other parallels, such as the promise 'they shall be my people and I will be their God' in 24.7, 31.33 and 32.38.

However plausible each of these might be, none is secure, and the whole series adds up to a shaky hypothesis.

Lundbom, then, has made some very interesting suggestions, but they need to be much more thoroughly investigated. As far as I know he has not attempted to do this.

The same might be said of Holladay's work. His first book only tackles Jeremiah 1–20, so there is more detailed argument. There is also much that seems to me more speculative. He is clearly aware of the difficulty of proving that particular instances of a word are significant for structure. He speaks of

> two kinds of uncertainties that we shall have to face: the first, that often we shall not be able to determine with utter certainty that two or more occurrences of a word (or phrase or whatever) is a significant rhetorical tag; the second, that while we may be able in certain instances to determine with certainty that a given repetition is rhetorically significant, we may still be unable with complete certainty to determine *what that significance is.*

He illustrates the first difficulty by the verb אכל, which occurs four times in 5.17. Holladay believes that these occurrences balance the single occurrence in 2.3, despite the fact that אכל 'is no rare verb, and it appears in...2.7, 30; 3.24'. He believes that the way to a convincing argument is by means of '*many* bits of interlocking data'.[1] That is a possible way forward, provided that they really are interlocking data, that is, pieces of evidence that independently point to the same conclusions. We must not rely on hypotheses that only stand up when, like a card house, they lean against each other. Holladay points to some interesting correspondences, and they seem to be worth following up in a more rigorous way.

The second difficulty is illustrated by the phrases ארור האיש/הגבר אשר in 11.3, 20.15 and 17.5.[2] He suggests three possible ways in which an inclusio might be formed by two of these occurrences, but he does not consider the possibility that Jeremiah did not intend an inclusio at all. If we *assume* that there must be an inclusio, then we shall certainly be able to find reasons to explain its significance. This will not necessarily be 'interlocking evidence'.

Holladay makes use of other types of similarity and contrast. For example, in discussing Jeremiah 2 he points out the changes of person that occur: v. 2 f.s.; 5-10 m.pl.; 16-25 f.s.; 28 m.s.; 29-30 (31?) m.pl.; 33-37 f.s.[3] This pattern does not seem to be very regular;

1. Holladay, *Architecture*, p. 25.
2. Holladay, *Architecture*, p. 26.
3. *Architecture*, p. 36.

various gaps are to be seen; and Holladay has not attempted to *demonstrate* that the changes are significant.

A further problem with Holladay's analysis of Jeremiah 1–20 arises from his main thesis that in chs. 2–3 there is a 'harlotry cycle' which is followed in chs. 4–6 by a 'foe cycle'. However, the material is not so clearly defined as one might hope. The 'harlotry cycle' turns out to be 2.5-37, 3.1-5, 12b-14a, 19-25 where the omissions are almost entirely prose passages. This assumption may be acceptable, but the prose section 3.24-25 is not omitted, and this seems to commit us prematurely to a theory of the redaction history of the passage, viz that 3.24-25 was added so as to form a coherent structure, before 3.6-10 (+ 11-12a), 14b, 15-18, which disrupted the structure. Many scholars regard vv. 19-23 as originally following immediately after vv. 1-5. Holladay wants to include vv. 12b-14a but the grounds he puts forward for doing so are at least partly structural: 'There is a quite lovely chiasmus in the assonances with שוב in vv. 12b, plus 14a and vv. 22...'[1] In attempting to establish a new theory concerning the structure of a book, one needs to have surer foundations and, at least, to respect the scholarly consensus when departing from the received text. In fact Holladay departs from most scholars in arguing that 4.1-4 is not the end of this cycle, but the beginning of the 'foe cycle' (4.1–6.30 + 8.4-10a, 13).[2] His three arguments for this conclusion depend upon spotting inclusios.[3] On pp. 46-47 Holladay had written:

> It is clear that there is much secondary material within chapter 3, and it is difficult to avoid circular reasoning as we attempt to locate the material here that participates in any basic structure, *and* to discern that structure. We must proceed with care.

I think it is clear, even from this very brief critique, that he has not proceeded with nearly enough care.

Holladay's book is a stimulating study, which I have enjoyed reading. He shows himself to be aware of many of the dangers of subjectivity, and the need for safeguards, but he proceeds as if unaware of what he has said. His theory must be regarded as a suggestion that has not been properly tested. In general, his work here confirms our conviction that most structural studies are not carried out with sufficient

1.   *Architecture*, p. 50.
2.   In his commentary he treats Jer. 2.1–4.4 together.
3.   *Architecture*, pp. 55-56.

scepticism, and that scholars are too ready to assume that an intended structure is there, and that our only task is to find it.

So far the results of this examination of specific studies have not been too encouraging. The last example chosen, however, does give some ground for hope that investigations into the literary structure of a passage *may* proceed on surer foundations.

4. *The Structure of Exodus 6.2-8 according to Auffret and Magonet*[1]
There are various examples of scholarly interaction that could have been chosen. For example, J.A. Emerton's essay, 'An examination of some attempts to defend the unity of the flood narrative in Genesis'[2] gives the reaction of an eminent scholar not normally associated with structural studies to at least three treatments that make use of chiastic structures, namely those of F.I. Andersen, G.J. Wenham and Y.T. Radday.[3] Some of his arguments I should certainly endorse. For example, he points to contrivance in dividing up into units and in labelling them, although I think it is a pity that he seems only concerned to defend the traditional documentary division into sources, rather than to ask whether structural studies might throw some light on the activity of the redactor(s) responsible for the text under examination. His conclusion is worth quoting:

> While chiasmus undoubtedly appears from time to time in the Hebrew Bible, not all the examples that have been alleged stand up to detailed examination. It would help the progress of Old Testament study if those who believe that they have found instances were to be self-critical and strict in their methods and to subject their theories to rigorous testing before seeking to publish them.[4]

1.   P. Auffret, 'The Literary Structure of Exodus 6.2-8', *JSOT* 27 (1983), pp. 45-64; *idem*, 'Remarks on J. Magonet's Interpretation of Exodus 6.2-8', *JSOT* 27 (1983), pp. 69-71; J. Magonet, 'The Rhetoric of God: Exodus 6.2-8', *JSOT* 27 (1983), pp. 56-67; *idem*, 'A Response to P. Auffret's "Literary Structure of Exodus 6.2-8"', *JSOT* 27 (1983), pp. 73-74.

2.   *VT* 27 (1987), pp. 401-20; *VT* 28 (1988), pp. 1-21.

3.   F.I. Andersen, *The Sentence in Biblical Hebrew* (Janua Linguarum, Series Practica, 231; Mouton: The Hague, 1974); G.J. Wenham, 'The Coherence of the Flood Narrative', *VT* 28 (1978), pp. 336-48; Y.T. Radday, 'Chiasmus in Hebrew Biblical Narrative', in Welch (ed.), *Chiasmus in Antiquity*, pp. 50-117 (90-100).

4.   Emerton, 'Flood Narrative in Genesis', pp. 20-21.

Another instance of structural treatments of the same text would be those on the Tower of Babel story by J.P. Fokkelman[1] and Isaac M. Kikawada.[2] I believe that the same points an be made from examining work done on any of these passages.

I have chosen to discuss work on a different passage. Exod. 6.2-8 is an especially useful text to consider, since we have in print two treatments by scholars at the forefront of structural studies and the comments of each scholar on the other's work. Auffret also refers to a suggestion of A.M. Besnard.[3] In addition, this is a passage which I analysed independently before these essays appeared. An examination of these three independent enquiries may therefore give us some insight into the reliability of the methods employed.

Auffret draws attention to various words and phrases, namely: God (vv. 2, 7, 7); (I am) YHWH (vv. 2, 3, 6, 7, 8); told (אמר + אל/ל) (vv. 2, 6); to Abraham, Isaac and Jacob (vv. 3, 8); know(n) (vv. 3, 7); swore (oath) (vv. 4, 5, 8); (give) land (vv. [4], 5, 5, [8, 8]; Israelites 5, 6); Egyptians, bondage etc. (vv. 5, 6, 7).

He also characterizes each verse or part verse according to its content: Y(HWH), O(ath), C(anaan) or E(gyptians). This seems oversimplified: v. 3, containing Abraham, Isaac and Jacob is assigned to Y, while that part of v. 8 containing the same three names is assigned to C.[4]

Auffret argues that ברית, vv. 4, 5, is correctly translated 'oath' and appeals to P. Weimar's *Untersuchungen zur priesterschriftlichen Exodusgeschichte*.[5] Even if that is so the actual phrases used in vv. 4-8 are different (נשאתי את ידי, v. 8; ואזכר את בריתי, v. 5; הקמתי את בריתי, v. 4) and it needs to be proved that the author saw these as matching and balancing each other.

He further affirms that Besnard was right to put v. 4 to correspond to v. 8abα since 'the recollection of the oath to give the land where the Fathers were sojourners squares with the promise to give it to the Israelites as patrimony'. I should like to know why we may disregard

1. *Narrative Art in Genesis* (Assen: Van Gorcum, 1975), pp. 11-45.

2. 'The Shape of Genesis 11.1-9', in Jackson and Kessler (eds.), *Rhetorical Criticism*, pp. 18-32.

3. *Le mystère du nom* (Lectio Divina, 35; Paris: Cerf, 1962), pp. 54-56.

4. 'Literary Structure', pp. 46-47.

5. (Forschung zur Bibel, 9; Wurzburg, 1973), pp. 104-106.

the correspondence of 'Abraham, Isaac and Jacob' where the actual names are repeated, and claim correspondence where different terminology is chosen.

Auffret comments that 'the inclusion of the whole by the phrase "I am Yahweh" (vv. 2, 8) is obvious' and that 'since the same phrase can also be seen in direct speech in v. 6, we can suppose that there is a correspondence of v. 2 with v. 6...as of v. 6 with v. 8'.[1] But why is it permissible to ignore the fact that 'I am Yahweh your God' occurs in v. 7? This must surely cause confusion to a reader who is meant to see a strong connection between vv. 2, 6 and 8 by means of the phrase in question. In addition the actual similarity to which Auffret draws attention in vv. 2 and 6 is not a striking one: 'And he said to him'—'Say to the Israelites'. The verb is one of the most common in the Old Testament, it occurs first as part of a stereotyped formula which occurs frequently to introduce a prophetic message, and the preposition is not even the same (ל/אל).

Auffret proceeds from here to construct an intricate pattern which may, I think, be represented as follows:

		Y			(v. 2)
Y	O	C+E	O	Y	(vv. 3-6a)
		Y			(v. 6a: does double duty)
	E	Y	E		(v. 6b-7)
C		O		C	(v. 8abα)
		Y			(v. 8bβ)

Those who are convinced that Auffret's characterization of these verses is correct may persevere with the rest of his analysis. It seems to me that his theological conclusions are basically right, [2] but that his literary analysis is artificial and precarious.

Magonet's criticism of Auffret is very brief and restrained,[3] concentrating on his 'forced translation' (a description I should endorse): 'and if it was not by my name YHWH that I made myself known, I nevertheless swore by the oath I took with them...', and the loss of

1. 'Literary Structure', p. 49.
2. 'Thus, if Yahweh, moved by Israel's distress in Egypt, decides to reveal himself by freeing it, it is by faithfulness to his oath which he remembers. Then we see that the two stages, oath to the Fathers and revelation of the Name to Israel are joined together'.
3. 'A Response', pp. 73-74.

the 'central location and significance of the "redemption" of the people'. The latter seems to me the most serious weakness in Auffret's analysis.

Magonet, in his own essay, acknowledges his indebtedness to Nehama Leibowitz who argues, in her commentary on Exodus,[1] for a chiastic structure to this passage. She indicates three concentric rings as follows:

1bβ + 8bβ (I am YHWH); 3 + 8aβbα (Abraham, Isaac, Jacob); 4 + 8aα; 5 + 7

This leaves, as the centre, a section with three verbs. Leibowitz suggests that, together with the first part of v. 7, they form a sequence ('I shall release—rescue—redeem—take') that reaches its climax in the fifth expression: 'I shall be your God'.

Magonet accepts this overall structure but investigates the middle section further. He proposes a slightly different climax:[2]

> I AM THE LORD
> and I will bring you out from under the burdens of the *Egyptians*
> *and I will deliver you from their bondage*
> and I will redeem you with an outstretched arm
> and with great judgments
> and I will take you to me for a people
> and I will be to you a God
> and you shall *know* that I AM THE LORD your God

It seems to me that the weakness of this is that around the centre we have two pairs of statements which, apart from being pairs, have nothing obvious in common. Moreover, the mention of 'Egyptians' (literally 'Egypt'), which has already been appealed to for structuring, can only confuse by being introduced here if it is not supposed to be significant. It may be that at this point we are trying to press the evidence too far. Otherwise the analysis seems to me cogent and attractive.

Magonet's simplified structure of the whole is:[3]

---

1.   *Studies in Shemot: The Book of Exodus* (2 vols; Jerusalem: 1976), pp. 116-17; noted in Magonet, 'The Rhetoric of God', pp. 57-59, 67 n. 5.

2.   'The Rhetoric of God', p. 62.

3.   'The Rhetoric of God', p. 64.

<pre>
        Covenant (Patriarchs, Land)
              Freedom
                    Freedom
                          Redemption
                    Covenant
              Freedom
        Covenant (Land, Patriarchs)
</pre>

I do not know how this can be tested. It seems artificial to separate 'Redemption' from the 'Covenant' which follows it, viz. 'You shall be my people...'

My own attempt at structuring, before meeting the work of the scholars considered here, resulted in this pattern (see below):

<pre>
a   b   d   e   **a**   **e   f   a**   e   d   b   a
        c   c
</pre>

The phrase 'I am Yahweh' forms an inclusio around the whole, and also around the central section. The climax at the centre is the promise 'I will take you to me for a people, and I will be your God' which also forms part of the content of Genesis 17 where 'El Shaddai' occurs for the first time. In the centre e is used again to take up what has been promised and to make this climax even stronger.[1]

The basic structure of the outer sections is abde edba, with the addition of the covenant in the first part to frame the two important elements: the Land of Canaan and the Egyptian bondage.

a   I am Yahweh
b   I appeared to **Abraham, Isaac and Jacob**
        (as El Shaddai not Yahweh)
c   I established **my covenant**
d   *to give to them* **the land** of Canaan
        the land of their sojourning...
e   I have heard the cry of the children of Israel
        whom **the Egyptians** *keep in bondage*
c   and I have remembered **my covenant**

---

1. This is, of course, an explanation of the purpose of the structuring which cannot be proved; it seemed and seems plausible to me.

a	I am Yahweh
e	and I will **bring you out** *from under the*
	burdens of **the Egyptians** and I will deliver you
	from *their bondage*
	and I will redeem you…
f	AND I WILL TAKE YOU TO ME FOR A PEOPLE
	AND I WILL BE YOUR GOD
a	I am Yahweh
e	who **brought you out** *from under the burdens*
	of **the Egyptians**
d	and I will bring you to **the land** which I *swore*
	to give to
b	**Abraham, Isaac and Jacob**
	and I will *give it to* you for a possession
a	I am Yahweh

Having seen Magonet's analysis it seems to me that I missed the build up of 'I will' verbs in the centre of the unit, and therefore underestimated the emphasis placed on my section f. I shall, in future, want to make clear the progression from 'bring out from under the burdens of the Egyptians' (via 'deliver', 'redeem' and 'take') to the central promise 'I will be your God'. The focus on Yahweh as the mover in this series of promises is not allowed to be disturbed even by the normal form of words: 'you shall be my people'. Yahweh says, 'I will take you to me for a people'.

The interaction promised by the publishing of these essays together turns out to be disappointing. The reactions are too polite and do not address the question why the results obtained do not agree with each other. Or if they *do* agree, despite appearances to the contrary, this is not demonstrated.

Before attempting to sum up our conclusions we shall do two things: (a) attempt a control experiment by testing out the scholarly methods we seem to have encountered so far on a chapter made up of verses randomly selected from the book of Isaiah, 'Isaiah 67'; and (b) make some basic remarks about the probability that a particular regular structure is accidental or 'intended'.

Theoretical Considerations

The Structure of 'Isaiah 67'

Below is a chapter consisting of verses from the book of Isaiah. It was formed by picking numbers from a hat. The chapter was selected by choosing from numbers 1 to 66; the verse was selected from numbers 1 to 37. Where the number drawn from the hat exceeded the number of verses in a particular chapter, the latter number was subtracted from the former (more than once, if necessary) so that an existing reference was obtained. There may well be objections to this procedure from the point of view that it is not a 'purely random' number. From our point of view this is not significant: we simply need to know that the chapter has not been put together with any consistent principle of arrangement.

The chapter formed in this way was then examined to see if the sort of criteria used to establish structure in current studies could be used to argue for some sort of order in a literary unit that we *know* has no planned structure.

The following 'chapter' was obtained:

1 = 13.4	2 = 53.9	3 = 58.3	4 = 37.3	5 = 18.3
6 = 28.5	7 = 29.14	8 = 52.9	9 = 39.8	10 = 29.2
11 = 1.3	12 = 28.13	13 = 15.6	14 = 52.11	15 = 12.5
16 = 66.16	17 = 6.4	18 = 64.4	19 = 17.14	20 = 4.1

קול המון בהרים דמות עם־רב
קול שאון ממלכות גוים נאספים
יהוה צבאות מפקד צבא מלחמה   1

ויתן את־רשעים קברו ואת־עשיר במתיו
על לא־חמס עשה ולא מרמה בפיו   2

למה צמנו ולא ראית ענינו נפשנו ולא תדע
הן ביום צמכם תמצאו־חפץ וכל־עצביכם תנגשו   3

ויאמרו אליו כה אמר חזקיהו יום־צרה ותוכחה
ונאצה היום הזה כי באו בנים עד־משבר
וכח אין ללדה   4

כל־ישבי תבל ושכני ארץ
כנשא־נס הרים תראו וכתקע שופר תשמעו   5

ביום ההוא יהיה יהוה צבאות לעטרת צבי
ולצפירת תפארה לשאר עמו   6

לכן הנני יוסף להפליא את־העם־הזה הפלא ופלא   7
ואבדה חכמת חכמיו ובינת נבניו תסתתר

פצחו רננו יחדו חרבות ירושלם   8
כי־נחם יהוה עמו גאל ירושלם

ויאמר חזקיהו אל־ישעיהו טוה דבר־יהוה   9
אשר דברת ויאמר כי יהוה שלום ואמת בימי

והציקותי לאריאל והיתה תאניה ואניה   10
והיתה לי כאריאל

ידע שור קנהו וחמור אבוס בעליו   11
ישראל לא ידע עמי לא התבונן

והיה להם דבר־יהוה   12
צו לצו צו לצו קו לקו קו לקו
זעיר שם זעיר שם
למען ילכו וכשלו אחור ונשברו ונוקשו ונלכדו

כי־מי נמרים משמות יהיו   13
כי־יבש חציר כלה דשא ירק לא היה

סורו סורו צאו משם טמא אל־תגעו   14
ואו מתוכה הברו נשאי כלה יהוה

זמרו יהוה כי גאות עשׂה   15
מידעת זאת בכל־הארץ

כי באש יהוה נשפט ובחרבו   16
את־כל־בשר ורבו חללה יהוה

וינעו אמות הספים מקול   17
הקורא והבית ימלא עשן

פנעת את־שׂשׂ ועשׂה צדק בדרכיך יזכרוך   18
הן־אתה קצפת ונחטא בהם עולם ונושע

לעת ערב והנה בלהה בטרם בקר איננו   19
זה חלק שוסינו וגורל לבזזינו

והחזיקו שבע נשים באיש אחד ביום ההוא   20
לאמר לחמנו נאכל ושמלתנו נלבש
רק יקרא שמך עלינו אסף חרפתנו

Despite the fact that there really is nothing planned about this selection of verses, we can still produce a pattern that has the appearance
of a regular structure. We may denote a chiastic structure as follows:

```
a        קול v. 1                    (or קול 2×, cf. בפיו, רב vv. 1-2)
  aa       רב v. 1
    b        חדע v. 3
      c        משבר v. 4
        d        כנשא v. 5
          e        עם, העם, עמו vv. 6, 7, 8   (or dd ביום v. 6
                   בינח נביו v. 7                e...עמ vv. 6-8
                                                 dd' בימי v. 9)
            f        לאריאל v. 10
                     והיתה
                     תאניה
                     ואניה
                     והיתה
                     כאריאל
          e'       תתבנג, עמי v. 11
    c'       ונשברו v. 12
      d'       נשאי v. 14
  b'       מ/ודעת v. 15
  aa'      ורבו v. 16
a'       מקול v. 17                  (or רבו, קול vv. 16-17)
```

We have not used vv. 18-20, and should presumably regard them as the work of a later redactor. We could perhaps even argue that the יקרא in v. 20 is intended to correspond with the הקרא of v. 17.

In addition to this verbal pattern, we might note that vv. 1-4, 10-13, and 16-17 have (or can be regarded as having) a judgment or lamentation tone, whereas vv. 5-9 and 14-15 are more related to salvation, hope and promise.

On the basis of this experiment we may conclude:

1. A mechanical plotting of similar words means nothing. We must take account of the overall thought of a passage. In other words, our account of the structure of a passage must be confirmed by independent form- and literary-critical conclusions.

2. Coincidences occur. One of the most striking here is that at the centre of our overall chiasmus we have a chiastic verse.[1]

---

1. While carrying out some exploratory calculations I discovered that chs. 1–33 and 34–66 contain 642 verses each. Using the old fashioned way of doing addition, the tens and units columns of the sum of the verses in each chapter are also equal! I do not know whether this is coincidence or not—if I did it would prove *something*.

3.   This impressive looking structure has been produced by ignoring other words which occur twice or more. For example 'Hezekiah' occurs in vv. 4 and 9, and if anything ought to be significant for the structure, this would surely be one of the most obvious candidates. We have actually ignored ידע in v. 11 although it is actually related to תחבנו! We have also ignored עשׂה in vv. 2, 15 and 18; ראה in vv. 3 and 5; הרים in vv. 1 and 5; and several others.

4.   Common words are of minimal value in indicating structure. In any passage several verses long there are bound to be repetitions. Only if a word has some additional distinctive feature can it be taken to be significant.

Notice that, if we were determined to carry through the theory that this chapter has a chiastic structure, we might argue that not only is there an overall chiasmus from v. 1 to v. 17, but there is another one superimposed on this just before the centre (v. 10):[1]

```
p                ויאמר. . .חזקיהו. . .יום (2×) v. 4
    q                        עמי v. 6
        r                    העם v. 7 (but any other 'centre' could be chosen)
    q'                       עמו v. 8
p'               ויאמר חזקיהו. . .יום v. 9
```

We have to ignore יום in v. 6. On the other hand, we could point out as a supporting argument, the correspondence between the whole world (תבל, ארץ) in v. 6 and Jerusalem (twice) in v. 8.

Clearly there is much that can mislead us here, and our aim will be to find methods of ensuring that an apparent structure was actually planned by the author or editor. No doubt there is a certain amount that statistics could do. For example, we might deduce that since the word עם occurs x times in 1,284 verses in the book of Isaiah the probability is that in any 20 verses it will occur y times. Since I have little competence or confidence in this kind of statistics, more sophisticated methods must be left to others. I believe that we shall obtain

---

1.   This is sometimes claimed to give added weight to arguments for an elaborate structure, e.g. in his treatment of the Tower of Babel story, Fokkelman argues for a parallel *and* a concentric symmetry (which, incidentally, have a different centre); *Narrative Art in Genesis*, pp. 11-45.

surer results by looking at the meaning of the passage in question and asking about the sequence of thought, the purpose of the arrangement and so on.

Structure and Probability

Many works on structure seem to assume that any regular structure that is discovered is likely to be significant and intended by the author/editor. It has been demonstrated above, that coincidences are quite likely to occur. We may make some further remarks on the probability that a regular structure is intentionally so.

1. Given a unit in which we detect four elements aabb, there are only three distinct ways of arranging them:

aabb   abab   abba   (bbaa, baba, baab are the same)

It is obvious, then, that wherever two pairs of elements can be discovered there is a one in three chance of finding a chiastic abba structure. If it is absolutely clear that the a's and b's are intended to correspond to each other, then we should still say that the author had a concern for structure. If, as is often the case, the correspondence of the a's and/or the b's is doubtful, then the proposed chiasmus is likely to be worthless.

2. If we find aabbcc, then there will be twelve distinct combinations. I list them below, together with ways of arguing that they form regular structures.

1	aabbcc	Three parallel pairs (= bbaacc etc., aaccbb)
2	ababcc	Two parallel pairs (Put ab = x → xxcc)
3	abacbc	Two chiasmuses with corresponding centres
4	abaccb	Basically bccb with the first b also made the centre of a chiasmus
5	abbacc	Chiasmus plus a parallel pair
6	abbcac	Similar to 4: abb(c)a(c)
7	abbcca	Inclusio with two parallel pairs
8	abcabc	Repeated three line sequence
9	abcbac	Chiasmus abcba with centre repeated
10	abcbca	Chiasmus ayya (y = bc)
11	abccab	xccx (cf. 2 above)
12	abccba	Chiasmus

Thus it is more difficult to produce an arrangement which is in no sense chiastic than it is to produce a chiasmus of some sort. Moreover, the arrangements that are not chiastic may still be regarded as regular. With this ingenuity available, it is *impossible* to produce a passage that is not 'regular'.

3. It often arises in a passage of several verses (say about ten or more) that there are several repeated words, phrases, or ideas (as was the case with 'Isaiah 67'). We have seen that careful selection of those that we deem to be significant makes it possible to argue for a regular structure. We may also note that it is possible to claim two or more superimposed structures, thus giving the impression of a greater concern for structure, rather than regarding it as confused or conflicting evidence. I cannot attempt to produce a comprehensive theory concerning the probability that a supposed structure was intended to be regular, but it *is* possible to demonstrate that regular structures may be seen where none were intended. Here are some examples of random sequences (again pulled from a hat):

1. dceabdbacae. This may be regarded as ce + abdba + ce (ignore d or note that it corresponds to the centre) or xbdbx (where x is a complex idea containing a, c and e).
2. ddabcaaeecb. Ignore the first part,[1] and we have a beautiful, ready-made chiasmus with a centre formed by two parallel pairs: bcaaeecb.
3. cbecdeaaadb → chiasmus bdaaadb with a very powerful centre, plus cece superimposed over the first half (before the centre).
4. adbcaadbcee → a + xaax + ee (where x = dbc).

I should draw at least four conclusions from this brief experiment and investigation.

1. Great care must be taken in characterizing the elements that we label a, b, etc. If we are keen to find a structure, there are many ways of ensuring that we do.
2. Structures that are 'nearly regular' must be treated with a great deal of reserve. This means that 'partial' and 'split-member' chiastic structures outlined by Watson[2] must be treated with much greater scepticism.

---

1.   If we adhered to the units as given we should avoid this particular mistake.
2.   'Chiastic Patterns', pp. 124-25.

3. We should seek confirmatory evidence of some sort, including the purpose and/or effect of the supposed structure.
4. Superimposed structures should not be posited unless there is strong independent evidence for this intention.

Conclusions

In considering the work done by scholars on literary structures, my purpose has been to throw light on the question: how can we discern the structure, if any, intended by the author or editor of the text in question?

We have examined several examples of work done in this area, including independent work on the same text by different scholars. In the latter case we have been concerned to ask why the analyses differ, and whether the differences are significant or whether they point to basically the same insights. If our aim is to discern the author/editor's intention then the results obtained by different investigators ought to agree in essence.

It seems to me that the same basic conclusions have been forced upon us throughout this present chapter. They may be summarized as follows:

1. Repetitions of the same word or root may be used by a writer to indicate a correspondence between one part of a unit and another. But:

   a. There may be other reasons for repetition.
   b. Very common words have little significance in this regard.
   c. We should not, without good reason, accept some words as significant, while ignoring others.
   d. It should be possible to suggest the reason for a writer's arrangement.
   e. Alternative theories need to be considered.

2. A writer might well have had in mind connections between one part and another, progressions of thought, similar type of content, and so forth, which are not reflected in the use of identical words or roots. We may indeed acknowledge that thematic connections such as the above are more important than merely identical words. Yet it would be strange for a writer to avoid using certain words more than once, if he wanted to draw the reader's attention to the correspondence. There is certainly scope for further research in this area, but at

present, most structural studies do rely on key words and phrases. Moreover, in seeking to discover thematic connections we must be aware of the subjective nature of the task and the probability that several different rationales could be suggested for any particular unit. There is a strong danger of reading our own structures into the text when we supply the headings or labels for the sections to be compared.

3. Allusions to other parts of the OT may sometimes be detected, and this may help us to discover connections intended by the author/editor.

4. Techniques discovered in several different passages may be regarded as more secure than those found only once or twice.

5. There are many individual features of a text and its parts that might be noted, for example, gender and number of nouns, part of speech, conjugation, theme, mood, and so on. The chance that some of these will form regular patterns by accident is sometimes high, and should be recognized.

6. It seems, therefore, that a reasonable procedure in seeking to analyse biblical texts would be to:

- a. Establish the text form and its divisions independently of structural considerations, before attempting to define the structure of particular sections.
- b. Examine *all* repetitions, and discard those that seem to be insignificant. This should be done without regard to a suspected structure in the unit.
- c. Estimate the likely importance of the repeated words that remain. Whole phrases are the most likely to be used to establish structure. Rare words, words used in characteristic ways, clusters of related words, are also likely to be used with a particular purpose. 'Technical terms', that is words which are specially related to the subject matter of the section, may be repeated simply because it is impossible not to repeat them.
- d. Consider the conclusions of scholars in various branches of OT research—especially those who have not been primarily concerned with structure—and compare conclusions concerning the overall meaning and emphasis of the unit.

e. Attempt to explain the purpose(s) of the writer(s)/editor(s) in presenting material in this particular way.

f. Investigate the unit under discussion in its context, to check that any proposed structure is consistent with the relationships that its members have with features elsewhere in the book or section of a book.

As explained in the Introduction I shall attempt to follow my own guidelines as we investigate the book of Zechariah. Chapters 2–4, therefore, consist of the following. Chapter 2: a decision regarding the divisions of the text that we shall investigate, based on traditional form-critical and literary-critical work, and with regard to the scholarly consensus. Chapter 3: an investigation of individual units, examining first the words that occur two or more times in the unit in question, with regard to their appropriateness to be used to indicate structure. The structure discerned will be discussed, taking into account points d, e and f above. Chapter 4: an investigation of individual units seen in relation to the rest of Zechariah 1–8 and/or 9–14. The same pattern will be followed as in Chapter 3.

Chapter 2

THE DIVISION OF THE BOOK OF ZECHARIAH

The first task in approaching the book of Zechariah will be to specify those divisions which may plausibly be considered to be units. These will be different in nature; for example, 2.10-16 is intended to form a unit in connection with 2.5-9, but not on its own. Verses 10-16 may have been added by a redactor and the resulting unit 2.5-16 would then be a secondary unit. This being the case we need to investigate 2.5-9, 2.10-16 and also 2.5-16. An analysis of the whole will, of course, cover the two individual sections and it will not usually be necessary to present a separate table for every small unit.

We shall investigate those divisions of the text which are agreed by the majority of scholars, noting points of substantial disagreement. The criteria used in determining these divisions will be largely form-critical in nature.[1]

The text of Zechariah does not present great problems, despite the fact that there are several very obscure passages.[2] In other words, we

1. The main sources for this preliminary investigation are the books and commentaries by Amsler, Baldwin, Beuken, Chary, C. Jeremias, Lamarche, Mason, C.L. and E.M. Meyers, Mitchell, Otzen, Petersen, Petitjean, Rignell, Rudolph, Sæbø, R.L. Smith, and Willi-Plein. Others are consulted where there is a particularly disputed passage

2. It is generally agreed that Zech. 1–8 is well preserved. For example, D.L. Petersen (*Haggai and Zechariah 1–8* [London: SCM Press, 1985]) only finds it necessary to offer emendations to the MT in 1.4; 2.11-12; 3.2, 5; 4.2, 7, 9; 5.6; 6.3, 6-7; 7.13; 8.6, 16 (p. 125). The only serious problem in these concerns ch. 6 (pp. 263-64); in 8.16 אמת is omitted; in 5.6 he reads עונם for עינם; the others change the forms but not the words found in the text (by adding ב or מ; changing a person: 'I' for 'he' and vice versa; omitting a *daghesh* from *he mappiq*). It would not affect our enquiry greatly if we accepted these; conversely it does not matter greatly if we are wrong in keeping the MT in all these instances.

The case of Zech. 9–14 is more difficult, and corruption is often suspected.

usually know what at least the consonantal text was even if we cannot understand exactly what it means. We shall accept the MT unless there is strong support from the versions for an alternative reading. We shall not allow structure to determine either the division of the text or a textual reading.[1]

Zechariah 1–8

1.1-6: Introduction

Despite the fact that this section shows many signs of being redactional it is intended in its present form as an introduction to the words of Zechariah, and is, in any case, too short to subdivide. Even if Mowinckel is right in thinking that there is a core which came from the prophet himself it is impossible to isolate this. The whole section seems to have been composed for its present position rather than elaborated after the book was compiled.[2]

1.7-17: The First Vision plus Oracles/Teaching

The vision is dated 'On the twenty-fourth day of the eleventh month...in the second year of Darius' and consists of a man riding on a red horse among the myrtle trees, with horses of three different colours behind him. Zechariah asks about them and the angel who spoke with him says he will show him what they are. The man

---

A.T. Jansma (*An Inquiry into the Hebrew Text and the Ancient Versions of Zechariah 9–14* [Leiden: Brill, 1949], p. 58), for example, lists 23 references where the versions give a better sense than the MT in the context. But even here, as W. Rudolph says, 'die Schwierigkeiten liegen . . . weniger im Zustand des Textes als in seiner Deutung' (*Haggai—Sacharja 1–8—Sacharja 9–14—Malachi* [Gütersloh: Gerd Mohn, 1976], p. 165). He feels compelled to emend the text in 9.13, 15, 16, 17; 10.2, 5; 11.15; 12.5; 13.5; 14.6, 18. Of these, only 10.5 is among the 23 references mentioned above. We need to be cautious about uncertain or obscure readings, but feel that it is better to err by being too accepting of the MT than the reverse. The most detailed textual discussion is to be found in B. Otzen, *Studien über Deuterosacharja* (Copenhagen: Prostant apud Munksgaard, 1964), pp. 231-72 and M. Sæbø, 'Die deuterosacharjanische Frage: Eine forschungsgeschichtliche Studie', *ST* 23 (1969), pp. 115-40 (122-32).

1.   There are several places where it is tempting to choose a particular division or reading because it yields a pleasing structure, e.g. 'their iniquity' instead of 'their eye' in 5.6. See also p. 72 n. 2 below.

2.   See Chapter 3 below.

standing among the myrtle trees (presumably still on his horse) gives the explanation.

Verse 11 is noteworthy in that the expression 'the angel of Yahweh' is introduced, and the horses answer him (!)[1] although he has not asked them anything. 'The angel of Yahweh' is here not equivalent to Yahweh, whom he addresses (v. 12).[2] Then Yahweh answers 'the angel who talked with' Zechariah (v. 13). This is the end of the main vision. In vv. 14-17 the angel commands the prophet to proclaim a message concerning Judah and Jerusalem and the nations. It is possible that this is redactional.[3]

We must ask whether in vv. 11-13 we are to think of one or two angels. The fact that one asks a question and the other receives the answer suggests only one. It is also possible that 'the angel of Yahweh' has been introduced as an alternative title for the 'man standing among the myrtle trees' (v. 11).[4] In any case we have to reckon with the possibility that both vv. 14-17 and (less plausibly) vv. 11-13 are redactional. Several scholars regard the first vision as extending from v. 7 to v. 15, with an addition, vv. 16-17, made by means of 'Therefore'.[5]

---

1.   I do not think there is any intended similarity with the story of Balaam's ass here. Perhaps we are meant to supply a rider for each of the other horses, as on the red horse (so, e.g., Calvin, *Zechariah and Malachi* [repr. Carlisle, PA; Banner of Truth Trust, 1986 (1849)], p. 31, who says 'So I understand the passage; for extremely gross is the idea that the horses spoke'! Cf. Petersen, *Haggai and Zechariah*, p. 145). Or perhaps this is just a detail of the picture that the writer does not consciously think about.

2.   Unless, perhaps, those scholars are right who say that v. 12 is a later insertion, cf. C. Jeremias, *Die Nachtgesichte des Sacharja: Untersuchungen zu ihrer Stellung im Zusammenhang der Visionsberichte im Alten Testament und zu ihrem Bildmaterial* (Göttingen: Vandenhoek & Ruprecht, 1977), p. 116.

3.   The fullest discussion is given by A. Petitjean (*Les oracles du Proto-Zacharie* [Paris: Gabalda, 1969], pp. 53-88), who concludes that vv. 14b-17 form a literary unity. See the treatment of Zech. 1.1-17 below.

4.   Most assume, without discussion, that the angel is the same. E.g. Petersen, *Haggai and Zechariah*, p. 145; C.L. Meyers and E.M. Meyers, *Haggai, Zechariah 1-8* (AB; Garden City, NY: Doubleday, 1987), 'probably the same', p. 115.

5.   E.g. S. Amsler, A. Lacocque and R. Vuilleumier, *Commentaire de l'Ancien Testament. XI.c. Aggé, Zacharie 1-8, Zacharie 9-14, Malachie* (Delachaux & Niestlé, 1981), pp. 60-61, 64-65, R. Mason, *The Books of Haggai, Zechariah and Malachi* (Cambridge: Cambridge University Press, 1977), p. 37, L.G. Rignell (who

2.1-4: The Second Vision
This section is clear and well-defined, although its two parts are
introduced differently: ויראני יהוה in v. 3 is quite striking and similar
only to 3.1 (ויראני). It would make the vision meaningless to remove
vv. 3-4.

2.5-9: The Third Vision
The vision is clear in extent and meaning, although it is difficult to
explain why 'another angel' is introduced in v. 7.[1]

2.10-16: Exhortation and Promise
This is marked off from the preceding section not only by its opening
הוי but, more surely, by the difference in form and content. It is an
address to the exiles of Judah exhorting them to escape from Babylon
(v. 7) and elsewhere (vv. 10, 12), coupled with a promise that the
nations will have to let them return and dwell in Jerusalem.

It is no longer necessary to discuss whether the section begins at
v. 7 or v. 10, but scholars still disagree over how to divide the
section. Horst argues for two oracles: vv. 10-13 + 14-16 (17), which
correspond with each other from the point of view of rhythm.[2] Each
has a protasis (vv. 10a + 11/14) and a longer apodosis (vv. 12-13/15-
16). They contain distinct ideas which complement each other. Both
consist of a prophetic (vv. 10-11/15-16) and a divine (vv. 12-13/14)

---

argues that לכן does not introduce what is really the consequence of the preceding)
Die Nachtgesichte des Sacharja (Lund: Gleerup, 1950), p. 50 and C. Jeremias,
Die Nachgesichte. He notes that while three visions end with the meaning, the other
five visions have a word from God added (1.14-15; 2.8b, 9; 3.7; 5.4; 6.8), p. 12.
He seems to assume rather than to argue that vv. 16-17 were a later addition.
W.A.M. Beuken argues that it is wrong to separate v. 16 from its original connection
with vv. 14-15, but he does regard v. 17 as an addition (*Haggai–Sacharja 1–8*
[Assen: Gorcum, 1967], pp. 242-44). Rudolph comments: 'Die Ruckbeziehung auf
V.12-15 ist so deutlich, dass kein Grund besteht, die beiden Verse [16-17] von der
Vision abzutrennen. . . zumal da der Anfang von V. 17 deutlich macht, dass immer
noch der Dolmetscherengel redet' (*Haggai*, p. 79).

1.   Amsler comments that the 'other angel' allows the interpreting angel to stand
aside a little from the scene: 'il parle mais n'agit pas lui même.' It underlines the
distance between divine secrets and that which is revealed on earth (*Commentaire*,
p. 71).

2.   T.H. Robinson and F. Horst, *Die zwölf kleinen Propheten* (Tübingen: Mohr
[Paul Siebeck], 1964), pp. 210-11, 224-25.

word. Marti, Haupt, Sellin and Meyers opt for a threefold division: vv. 10-11, 12-13, 14-16 (17).[1] K. Elliger[2] proposes something different: vv. 10a + 11 + 12a + 13a, 14, 15-16(17). Beuken[3] has these subsections: vv. 10-13, 14-15, and 17, with v. 16 as a later explanatory gloss. Rignell[4] proposes a different understanding of the chapter: 2.5-11 is the extent of the third vision, with subsections vv. 5-9 and 10-11; 2.12-17 consists of three units: vv. 12-13, 14-15 and 16-17.

In the face of this disagreement the only safe way forward is to treat vv. 10-17 together. In their present form, despite the diverse material of which they are composed, vv. 10-17 form a coherent section. An exhortation is introduced very emphatically by הוי הוי plus the imperative המלטי (v. 11). The basis for this is given in v. 12, introduced by כי. Verse 13 follows smoothly: the phrase 'then you will know that Yahweh of hosts has sent me' presumably refers to the same 'me' as in v. 12 (see the excursus below for the interpretation of this passage). We find new imperatives in v. 14, which leads into an expression of one of the central assertions of the book of Zechariah: 'dwell in the midst...shall be my people.' Verse 15b repeats 13b with אליך added. The chiasmus formed thereby is obvious. On the other hand v. 15 speaks of the salvation of many nations rather than their judgment, and may be due to a later redactor.[5]

As stated in the introduction to this chapter, we must consider the whole of 2.5-17, since vv. 10-17 build on vv. 5-9. It may also be fruitful to investigate connections between this section and the first three visions.

1.   K. Marti, *Das Dodekapropheton* (Tübingen: Mohr [Paul Siebeck], 1904), pp. 404-408; P. Haupt, 'The Visions of Zechariah', *JBL* 32 (1913), pp. 107-22; E. Sellin, *Das Zwölfprophetenbuch* (Leipzeig: Deichert, 1922), pp. 469-72, 490-93 (quoted in Petitjean, *Les oracles*, p. 92). C.L. and E.M. Meyers argue that vv. 10-11 expand the third vision; vv. 12-13 develop the second, and vv. 14-17 deal with the first vision. I hope to throw some light on this suggestion below.

2.   *Das Buch der zwölf Kleinen Propheten* (Göttingen: Vandenhoek & Ruprecht, 1982), pp. 110-11.

3.   *Haggai–Sacharja*, pp. 317-30.

4.   *Die Nachtgesichte*, pp. 72-99.

5.   But, as the Meyers' remark, the concept [of all the nations] also occurs in 4.14 and 6.5 (*Haggai, Zechariah*, p. 168). Salvation for the nations is also envisaged in 8.22-23, although it is not expressed quite so clearly.

2.17: Injunction to silence

This verse stands apart from both preceding and succeeding verses, although it is entirely appropriate here, as has been recognized by Petitjean, Rudolph and others. The proposed actions of Yahweh have been outlined. All flesh should remain in awed silence because he has roused himself and the earth will no longer be left at rest. We shall include it with the preceding section for convenience: it is too short for any other course of action.

3.1-10: The Fourth Vision

This vision is unique in several ways, as C. Jeremias (among others)[1] has shown. It begins with וירא֫ני (but cf. 2.3); it is the only vision of a historical person rather than symbolic persons and things (notwithstanding the addition of Zerubbabel to Zech. 4); 'the angel who talked with' Zechariah plays no part, but only the 'angel of Yahweh' (vv. 1, 6) or simply 'the angel' (v. 4); Zechariah himself asks no questions but makes a suggestion directly to those concerned in the vision (v. 5); the meaning of the vision is given implicitly (vv. 2, 7; cf. 1.9; 2.2 etc.). Jeremias also mentions the fulness of detail and liveliness of the presentation, which is approached only otherwise by 2.5-9, and comments on the change that the omission of 3.1-7 makes to the structure of the series (see below). Finally, Joshua is linked with Zerubbabel in ch. 4, where he does not seem to be so prominent as he is here (but see 6.11).

These points do not conclusively prove the work of another hand, since it is not possible to predict the range of variations that a particular writer might employ—certainly not on the basis of the sample of Zechariah's work available to us. Still, it is necessary for us to bear in mind the possibility that 3.1-7 is from a later writer.

The case for treating vv. 8-10 as redactional is stronger. Verse 7 forms a satisfactory conclusion to the vision account; v. 8 opens with an imperative, appropriate to the beginning of a new section, and introduces elements not mentioned previously, but which are taken for granted: the men 'of good omen' who sit before Joshua and the 'stone of seven eyes/springs'. Petitjean regards vv. 8-10 as part of an original cycle of oracles. Verse 10 itself is a rather traditional

---

1. *Die Nachtgesichte*, pp. 201-203.

promise attached to vv. 8-9 by means of ביום ההוא נאם יהוה, and is probably secondary to the oracle.[1]

We need only to examine vv. 1-10, but must bear in mind the possibility of a redactional addition in vv. 8-10.

4.1-14: The Fifth Vision

This unit presents an untidy appearance. The angel shows great reluctance to give any information to the prophet; twice he responds to his questions by 'Do you not know what these are?' (vv. 5, 13). In vv. 11-12 the prophet asks two questions before receiving an answer, and it is not immediately clear which question has been answered. Does the angel refer to the olive trees of v. 11 or the branches of the the trees (v. 12), not mentioned in the original vision account (vv. 2-3)? Or have they both the same significance? Here, as in other places, there seems to be deliberate delay in giving an interpretation in order to heighten the tension felt by the hearers or readers (cf. 1.9).[2]

The answer to the question of v. 4 is further delayed by an address to Zerubbabel (vv. 6a-10a) which includes an introductory sentence spoken by the prophet, hardly compatible with the form of the whole. In v. 10b we find the answer, without any awareness, apparently, that there has been any interruption. In a book teeming with introductory sentences we should expect at least 'And the angel said. . .' I therefore agree with virtually all scholars that 4.6a-10a is a secondary passage.[3] It is possible that v. 12 is also redactional.

For the purpose of this study we must examine the section as a whole, and also the two separate sections vv. 1-6a + 10b-14 and vv. 6a-10a. The reconstruction of the NEB: 4.1-3, 11-14, 4-5, 10b; 3.1-10; 4.6-10a is much too precarious for our purposes. There is nothing to be gained by dividing vv. 6a-10a into two sections between vv. 7 and 8.[4]

---

1. *Les oracles*, pp. 161-89.

2. See, e.g., Zech. 5.5-6a; 6.7 (?); 7.4–8.17.

3. Rignell regards the interruption as a deliberate device of the author; the Meyers' opt for 'the author himself, or less probably a disciple' (*Haggai, Zechariah*, p. 242).

4. One suggestion worth considering perhaps, is that vv. 6a-10a might have affinities with Haggai. See Petersen, *Haggai, Zechariah* and Meyers, *Haggai, Zechariah, in loc.*

5.1-4: The Sixth Vision

This section is clear and self-contained, despite some repetition in vv. 3-4.

5.5-11: The Seventh Vision

The opening ויצא plus the command to 'lift up your eyes and see' a new object of attention coming forth seem to confirm that this is to be regarded as a separate vision. The prophet asks two questions, 'What is it?' (v. 6) and 'Where are they taking it?' (v. 10). Both are necessary for the vision to be intelligible.[1]

6.1-8: The Eighth Vision

Commentators have for a long time recognized the similarity between the first and last visions.[2] Both involve horses of different colours patrolling the earth; both speak of being at rest, though they use different words and in a different sense. In both, the form consists of *vision–question–answer–further action in the vision* (1.8, 9, 10, 11ff.; 6.1-3, 4, 5-6, 7-8). There is no doubt that these verses form a distinct unit.[3]

6.9-15: The Report of an Oracle

The difficulties of this passage are well known (see below).[4] Nevertheless, as a unit it has coherence. There is some repetition in vv. 12-13, 15a (בנה [את/ב]היכל יהוה), and v. 15a is similar to 2.13b, 15b (וידעתם כי יהוה צבאת שלחני אליך/אליכם). Verses 9-14 form an obvious chiasmus (Heldai, Tobijah, Jedaiah, Josiah/crown/priest) as will be shown below.[5] There is disagreement about the subdivision of

---

1. Rudolph notes that some commentators (Keil, Nowack, Rothstein and Bic) regard this section as a continuation of 5.1-4 (*Haggai*, pp. 118-19). It will be convenient to present repeated words for 5.1-11 in one table, and it will be easy to see whether there is any support from our method for this view.

2. See, e.g., C. Jeremias, *Die Nachtgesichte*, pp. 110-38.

3. The only reasonable variant of this view is to regard v. 15a as the conclusion to the vision (see below).

4. Petitjean, *Les oracles*, pp. 268-70.

5. The Meyers' mention this as 'another example of envelope construction' (*Haggai, Zechariah*, p. 338). Petersen notes the similar envelope technique in this section and in 4.6a-10a (*Haggai, Zechariah*, p. 273). He says here: 'We have already observed that the author/editor of Zech. 1–8 is an accomplished literary architect'.

this section. Many exegetes regard it as a literary unity with certain redactional elements (vv. 13a, 15b) and the end of the preceding vision (v. 15a). Horst distinguishes three main parts (vv. 9-13, 14 + 15a) within the section;[1] Rignell has two parts: vv. 9-12 and 13-15.[2] Petitjean argues for two principal parts, vv. 10-12 and 13-15ac (i.e. 15a, b), which have been given the form of a literary unity by the addition of vv. 9 and 15b (i.e. 15a).[3]

Different answers have been given concerning the connection between this section and other parts of the book: a prophetic action to be seen as a fitting sequel to the whole series of visions, a transitional passage leading to chs. 7-8,[4] or a completely new start to the second major division of the whole book.[5] A. Koehler regarded this as a prophetic commission at the close of the visions.[6] A. van Hoonacker argued that the 'ideal scene' here described is analogous to the visions, and belongs with them.[7] Other scholars would also confirm this view; the reference to Joshua in both 3.1 and 6.11, and the new beginning in 7.1 show that the section 1.7–6.15 is a redactional unit.

Although no modern scholars, as far as I am aware, would consider this the start of a new major section in the book of Zechariah, it is formally more similar to 1.1-6 and 7.1–8.23 than the preceding section. It may therefore be worthwhile to look for connections between 1.1-6 and 6.9-15, with or without chs. 7–8.

7–8: Prophetic Response to a Question

These chapters must be treated together, however we may choose to divide them up. The question about fasting (7.3) is not answered until 8.18-19, and the final verses 8.20-23 are very similar to 7.1-2. The incident of the people of Bethel sending to 'entreat the favour of Yahweh' becomes a sign of what 'many cities' (v. 20) and even 'many

---

1. *Die zwölf kleinen Propheten*, p. 237.
2. *Die Nachtgesichte*, pp. 240-42.
3. *Les oracles*, pp. 271-303, esp. 301-303.
4. P.D. Burkius, *Gnomon in Duodecim Prophetas Minores* (Heilbronn, 1753), pp. 526-27, quoted in Petitjean, *Les oracles*, p. 268.
5. E.g. Didymus, *In Zachariam*, (6.9–8.15), and S. Jérôme (6.9–10.12), mentioned in Petitjean, *Les oracles*, p. 268.
6. *Weissagungen Sacharjas erste Hälfte Cap. I-VIII* (Erlangen, 1861), p. 108, mentioned in Petitjean, *Les oracles*, p. 269.
7. *Les douze petits prophètes* (Paris: Gabalda, 1908), pp. 628-29.

peoples and strong nations' (v. 22) will do (vv. 21-22). The chiastic structure is therefore immediately obvious,[1] although the distance between the extremities might suggest later additions to the original chiasmus. This means it might be profitable to suppose an earlier literary unit: 7.1-3 + 8.18-21 (22?, 23?) and to determine the literary nature of subsequent treatment.

Most commentators divide ch. 7 into vv. 1-3, narrative, followed by oracular material: vv. 4-14,[2] or vv. 4-6 + 7-14,[3] or vv. 4-7 + 8-14.[4] Verses 4-7 are introduced by 'And the word of Yahweh came to me' as in 8.1, 18, whereas 7.8 reads '... to Zechariah'. It is possible, therefore, that v. 8 is redactional and that v. 9 originally followed v. 7. If this is so then the division vv. 4-6 + 7-14 is logical. However, we are also interested in the structure of the text after v. 8 was inserted. In other words we want to know whether the redactor helped to create or to destroy a planned structure. It is even possible that he did both. We must therefore consider vv. 4-14 with and without v. 8.

---

1.   Nevertheless I can only find one example of a commentator past or present who has apparently noted this. C. Stuhlmueller, in his brief *Rebuilding with Hope: A Commentary on the Books of Haggai and Zechariah* (International Theological Commentary; Grand Rapids: Eerdmans, 1988), says: 'The editor formed a carefully crafted unit of chs. 7–8 and then stitched this finale harmoniously into place. The question about fasting (7.3-5; 8.18f.) and the role of foreigners (7.1f.; 8.22f.) constitute an envelope around the other material in the final two chapters.' Even the Meyers', who show considerable concern at times for structure, and compare these chapters with Hag. 1–2, content themselves with pointing out the similarities between 8.18-23 and 7.1-6 and the implication that thereby chs. 7–8 are given their own literary integrity, *Haggai, Zechariah,* pp. 442-43. Petersen makes no attempt to introduce chs. 7–8 as a whole, despite the fact that he also notes 8.18-23 as an answer to 7.3. R.L. Smith says that 'the arrangement of the materials in chaps. 7 and 8 is rough' and that they can best be divided into three broad sections: 7.1-6, the question about fasting; 7.7-14, reiteration of the words of the former prophets; 8.1-23, a Decalogue of promises, *Nahum–Malachi* (WBC; Waco, TX: Word Books, 1984), p. 220. A little later he comments that there are superscriptions at vv. 18, 19, 20 and 23 which indicate 'separate collections that have been put together' (pp. 238-39). Even Beuken, who devotes much space to chs. 7–8 (pp. 15-19, 118-83), does not offer a full explanation of their structure.

2.   E.g. Petitjean.

3.   E.g. Amsler, Beuken, Meyers, R.L. Smith.

4.   E.g. Petersen.

Chapter 8 readily divides into ten short oracles by means of the phrase 'Thus says Yahweh': vv. 2, 3, 4, 5, 6, 7-8, 9-13, 14-17, 19, 20-22, 23. Longer introductory formulae are found in vv. 1 and 18. It is very doubtful whether these were originally independent, and even if they were, they are too short for our purposes. There is broad agreement as to how these are to be grouped together: vv. 1-8 + 9-17[1] (or simply 1-17);[2] and vv. 18-23.

The main sections to be investigated in chs. 7–8 are: 7–8; 7.1-3 + 8.18-23; and 7.4-14 + 8.1-17.

Having considered the individual sections of chs. 1–8, we must obviously consider these chapters as a whole. In addition chs. 1–6 form a clear major unit, and we must examine these chapters together, bearing in mind the possibility that 6.9-15 might need to be detached.

Zechariah 9–14

The divisions are much less clear in the second part of the book of Zechariah, and much more difficult to describe from a form-critical point of view without prejudging certain issues.

We may say at the outset that at least three large sections need to be investigated: chs. 9–11, 12–14 and 9–14. These are marked off by the heading מַשָּׂא, and recognized as major divisions by all scholars.[3]

In dealing with smaller divisions of the text we shall opt to deal with too large rather than too small a section.

9.1-8

This section is a clear unit despite the severe problems which beset its detailed interpretation. This is not to deny that it may have an important connection with the following verses (see below). Verses 1-7 all contain references to a foreign city or people, but v. 7 suddenly introduces an unexpected message of salvation for the Philistines. We should consider the possibility that this is redactional.

Some[4] would treat vv. 9-10 with the first section, and v. 8 does

---

1. E.g. Beuken, Petitjean, R.L. Smith.
2. E.g. Amsler, Meyers, Petersen, Rudolph.
3. This does not rule out structures that may cut across this major division, as the situation with 11.15-17 and 13.7-9 shows.
4. E.g. E.G. Kraeling, 'The Historical Situation in Zech. 9.1-10', *AJSL* 41 (1924–25), pp. 24-33; quoted by P.D. Hanson, in *The Dawn of Apocalyptic*

prepare for it to some extent. Nevertheless, the opening imperatives and the new theme that is introduced (the coming king and the peace which he ensures) indicate that we should regard this as a new section.[1]

The last line of v. 8 is strange but need not be taken as a later addition, or even a comment by the prophet himself.[2]

9.9ff.

The imperative גילי begins a new section which consists of vv. 9-10 according to most commentators.[3] Nevertheless the גם of v. 11 presupposes what has gone before (בת ציון, f.s.) so that vv. 9-10 are to be thought of as a subsection of a larger whole. In v. 12 אסירי may be a catchword (see below) and this would be supported by the imperative שובו. There is no *necessary* connection between the prisoners of v. 11 and v. 12. Verse 13 is attached to v. 13 by כי, which could be redactional, but seems more likely to be an integral part of the prophet's message. Verse 14 continues the image of the weapons of Yahweh: Ephraim is the (implied) arrow in Yahweh's bow in v. 13, and in v. 14 'his arrow' goes forth like lightning. A problem arises over the referent of 'them' in v. 14 and again in v. 15. The most consistent interpretation would be to take it to mean the people of Judah in both cases.[4] These verses, therefore, prepare for v. 16.

(Philadelphia: Fortress Press, 1975), p. 293. R.C. Dentan and J.T. Cleland ('Zechariah 9–14', in *The Interpreter's Bible* [ed. G.A. Buttrick; Nashville: Abingdon Press, 1956], VI, pp. 1092-96) treat vv. 1-12 together as 'an oracle composed during the siege of Tyre. . . in 332 BC'.

1.   Hanson, *The Dawn of Apocalyptic*, pp. 292-324, argues that 9.1-17 must be seen as a unity, since it is based on underlying 'ritual conquest and royal procession traditions, upon which the early apocalyptic literature drew so heavily' (p. 295).

2.   See, e.g., Hanson, *The Dawn of Apocalyptic*, p. 320. T. Chary comments: 'Le crescendo s'achève avec le v8' (*Les prophètes et le culte à partir de l'exil* [Paris: Desclée, 1954], p. 161).

3.   All the commentators listed at the beginning of this present chapter, who deal with Zech. 9-14, take it in this way. G.A. Smith treats vv. 9-12 together remarking only that 'it is possible that this oracle closes with v. 10.' T.T. Perowne (*Haggai and Zechariah* [Cambridge: Cambridge University Press, 1888]) takes vv. 9-17 to refer to the coming of the king but without justifying this division or interpretation (pp. 113-18).

4.   So most commentators, e.g. Rudolph, *Haggai*, pp. 183, 187-88; P. Lamarche, *Zacharie 9–14: Structure littéraire et messianisme* (Paris: Gabalda,

However we might understand the details they are a prophecy of salvation.

The ביום ההוא of v. 16 does not begin the sentence but I shall entertain the possibility that it might be redactional.[1] Verse 17 seems to be a comment on what has gone before and forms an apt conclusion to the section. Zech. 10.1 begins with a new imperative and subject matter. I shall therefore deal with the divisions vv. 9-10 and 11-17.[2]

1961), pp. 48, 50-51. If we were to take 'them' to mean the enemies of Judah, this would involve taking גנן (*hiphil*) in a negative sense 'surround' rather than 'cover, defend', and this would be contrary to the meaning in Zech. 12.8. The only other instance is Isa. 31.5, parallel to הציל, פסח and המליט!

1. Most commentators accept vv. 16-17 as an integral part of the text. Sæbø ('Die deuterosacharjanische Frage', pp. 193-207) considers vv. 13-16a and 16b-17 together. Otzen has an unusual view. See p. 73 n. 1 below.

2. This again is agreed by most scholars. Lamarche considers 9.11–10.1 to be a unit on the basis, it seems, of a chiastic arrangement in 9.17b–10.1. So he puts:

> a Grain shall make the young men flourish
>   and wine the maidens
>
>   b Ask of Yahweh rain
>   in the time of spring rain
>
> a' Yahweh makes flashes of lightning
>   he gives showers of rain to them
>   to each one vegetation in the field

Lamarche says: 'Si l'on entend respecter le texte. . .l'on doit simplement constater que l'exhortation à demander la pluie sert de pivot littéraire à une double description de la prospérité agricole' (*Zacharie 9–14*, p. 49). He refers to Deut. 11.13-15. We may agree with him that van Hoonacker was wrong to place 10.1 before 9.17b in order to make a chronological improvement: ask for rain first and the picture of prosperity follows. But Lamarche is not justified in ignoring the form-critical observations made above. From our point of view it would simply be begging the question to employ structural arguments (which in any case look rather tenuous) in order to divide up the text. If there is any true insight in Lamarche's view it needs to be allowed to appear when we consider the larger unit of Zech. 9–11 (or at least 9.1–11.3).

Lacocque differs from Lamarche in treating 9.11-17 together. He notes a double chiastic structure between vv. 11-12 + 16-17 (abcddcba) and vv. 13-14 (abba) (Amsler *et al.*, *Agée, Zacharie, Malachi*, pp. 160-61).

Baldwin follows Lamarche's division, noting that 'there are differences of opinion as to where this section (9.11ff.) should end, but as 10.2b leads into the "shepherd" theme the break has been made at the end of 10.1.' Since the 'flock of his people' has already occurred in 9.16, this is not a strong argument.

10.1ff.

As argued above 10.1 must be regarded as the start of a new unit.[1] Verse 2 is joined to v. 1 by כי and by subject matter: the contrast between Yahweh and other supposed sources of supernatural help. Verse 2b is fittingly joined to 2a by על כן.

Where the section ends is a matter of considerable disagreement. A connection between v. 2 and v. 3a is made by the word רעה, but the use is different, even formally contradictory (על הרעים: אין רעה), and it seems best to regard it as a secondary catchword continuation. Mason[2] admits this as a possibility, but thinks that the change of speech from first to third person in v. 3b is more weighty. One suspects that Lamarche and Baldwin opt for 10.2-3a because an exact structure can be seen 'between the outworking of retribution and the wrong done'.[3] A crucial question is whether פקד, used with the opposite meaning in v. 3a and 3b, is due to the intention of the prophet or whether we have another catchword association. The theme of the verse also changes from judgment for the shepherds to salvation for the flock. These considerations together make the division at v. 3a reasonable. On the other hand, Yahweh is referred to

Sæbø, who gives a detailed analysis of the form of chs. 9–14, divides this section into verses: 9-10, 11-12, 13-16a, 16b-17; he then takes 10.1-2 and 3-12 together. His divisions are too small for us to analyse but we note his results.

1. The connection between 'rain' here and the 'waterless pit' of 9.11 seems, on the face of it, to be too subtle to be a significant guide to structure (Lamarche, *Zacharie 9–14*, pp. 49-52), although R. Mason ('The Use of Earlier Biblical Material in Zechariah 9–14: A Study of Inner Biblical Exegesis' [dissertation, King's College, London, 1973, pp. 68-72) makes a good case for seeing here rich allusion to traditions such as Jer. 2.13; Isa. 49.9-10; Gen. 37.24. Cf. G. Gaide, *Jérusalem, voici ton Roi (Commentaire de Zacharie 9–14)* (Lectio Divina, 49; Paris: Cerf, 1968), p. 73. Otzen, *Studien*, pp. 216-18, takes Lamarche as his starting point and produces his own structure:

9.16	'positives' Hirtenbild
9.17–10.1	'positives' Fruchtbarkeitsmotiv
10.2a	'negatives' Fruchtbarkeitsmotiv
10.2b-3a	'negatives' Hirtenbild.

I investigate this in Chapter 3, as part of the consideration of 9.1–11.3.

2. *Zechariah 9–14*, p. 96.

3. Lamarche, *Zacharie 9–14*, p. 54; J.G. Baldwin, *Haggai, Zechariah, Malachi* (London: Tyndale Press, 1972), p. 172.

in the third person in vv. 1, 3b, and 5b, with divine speech only in v. 3a before v. 6; the thought of the passage progresses logically and the close conjunction of אפקוד and כי פקד (10.3) is striking. The only safe way forward is to treat vv. 1-3a as a possible sub-unit within the larger context.

Virtually all commentators agree that at least the remaining verses of ch. 10 must be kept together, and many would make the next break after 11.3.[1] Perowne[2] makes the division vv. 1-5, 6-12, but without giving explicit reasons. The section 6-12 forms a coherent unit with regard to subject matter: the restoration of the fortunes of Israel, its gathering from among the nations, and the passing away of those nations' prosperity. The inclusio גברתי[ם], vv. 6, 12 is too striking to miss: the *piel* occurs otherwise only in Eccl. 10.10 in the Old Testament. Nevertheless, in the absence of convincing form-critical marks[3] we shall not treat vv. 6-12 as a separate section. If the division is warranted it should become evident from the analysis of vv. 1-12.

11.1-3

There are some connections between this section and the preceding one: judgment of a nation outside Israel, shepherds, specific mention of Lebanon (as in 10.10). On the other hand, the opening imperatives, the direct address to Lebanon, the fact that the doors are opened not to let the expanding nation of Israel in, but rather fire to destroy, and the particularizing of concern to Lebanon and Bashan, suggest that נאם יהוה (10.12) ends the previous section and that 11.1-3 is a separate unit. However, it will not affect my analysis if we consider together

1. E.g. Mitchell, who takes 10.1–11.3 together (H.G. Mitchell, J.M.P. Smith and J.A. Bewer, *Haggai, Zechariah, Malachi and Jonah* [ICC; Edinburgh: T. & T. Clark, 1912], pp. 286-302); Chary (*Les prophètes et le culte*, pp. 178-79), although his argument is partly based on the structure of the whole; Rudolph (*Haggai,* pp. 192-200), who regards 11.1-3 as an independent song, but notes that 11.3a refers back to 10.3a. Mason considers 10.3-12 and 11.1-3 separately, but argues that the latter 'is fittingly placed here since it links with the promise of the preceding oracle that Lebanon would be included within the territory of the people of God (v. 10) and the recurring catch-word "shepherds". . .' Similarly R.L. Smith, *Nahum–Malachi*, p. 267.

2. *Haggai and Zechariah,* pp. 118-20. Perowne regards ch. 10 as a continuation and expansion of the promises made in ch. 9.

3. See Sæbø, 'Die deuterosacharjanische Frage', pp. 214-29.

10.1–11.3,[1] and note the difference that would result by excluding 11.1-3. Zech. 11.1-3 must also be considered separately.

11.4-14 + 15-17

Despite the acute problems of interpretation, there is no dispute about the fact that vv. 4-17 belong together, and that the section falls into two unequal parts: vv. 4-14, 15-17. The word עוד in v. 15 makes the connection explicit (see also below on 13.7-9).

12.1–13.6

The word משׁא which begins both 9.1 and 12.1, coupled with דבר יהוה and נאם יהוה, make this the clearest possible beginning of a new section. Most modern commentators see it as extending to the end of 13.1. Yet 13.1 does introduce the theme of cleansing, not explicitly stated in 12.1-14, and this is continued in a different way in 13.2-6. The והיה ביום ההוא of 13.2 reads strangely after 13.1 ביום ההוא, and it may be that v. 1 was added after vv. 2-6 had been placed in their present position. On the other hand the same phrases occur frequently throughout the section: והיה ביום ההוא (12.3, 9; 13.2, 4). ביום ההוא (12.4, 6, 8, 11; 13.1). Several commentators subdivide the passage somewhere in the middle: after v. 7, 8, or 9.[2] It seems that the most likely place is between vv. 9 and 10, where a new theme, compassion and mourning, begins. The best solution for us is to consider the following units: 12.1-14; 12.1–13.1; 12.1–13.6. This means that the main analysis will be carried out on the last (inclusive) unit.

13.7-9

This section, in its present place, is a clearly defined unit: poetry bounded by prose, with a consistent theme, different from both 13.1-6 and 14.1ff.; it begins with an imperative and reaches a fitting climax in v. 9. The only question is whether it originally belonged in a different place, viz. after 11.4-17.[3] There is no harm in investigating

---

1.   This does not mean giving support to Lamarche's division 10.3b–11.3, which will be considered below.

2.   Verse 7: Otzen, G.A. Smith; v. 8: Mitchell, R.L. Smith; v. 9: Baldwin, Mason, Perowne; Willi-Plein treats vv. 4-11 and 12-14 together, regarding ביום ההוא as a leitmotif (pp. 57-58).

3.   Mason, Mitchell, Rudolph, G.A. Smith. The view of Keil that 13.7–14.21 forms a complete section which is an expansion of 12.1–13.6 is interesting and may

11.4-17 + 13.7-9 as a unit. A negative result would not be surprising, but if these combined units were to exhibit a clear unified structure it would strengthen the case of those who advocate rearrangement.[1] We should also investigate the whole of 11.4–13.9. Assuming that 13.7-9 was given its present place for intelligent reasons, its relation to the preceding sections must be of interest.

14.1-21

It is as obvious that this section must be treated a whole as it is that it shows signs of being added to. This is true even if vv. 16-21 are an independent unit. The theme of the whole is the universal reign of Yahweh, which involves the defeat of Jerusalem by her enemies (v. 2), the defeat of the enemies (vv. 3, 12-15), and finally their worshipping Yahweh in Jerusalem (v. 16). With this are combined several eschatological and even apocalyptic motifs. So numerous are the introductory formulae that almost any verse from v. 4 (or even v. 2) onwards could be deleted as a later addition!

The most obvious break occurs after v. 15, as nearly all commentators acknowledge. Those who subdivide further usually do so after v. 5 and/or v. 11.[2]

It remains for these results to be summarized:

be considered later. It has not found modern supporters as far as I am aware.

1. We might still have to entertain a counter-claim that the unit was deliberately split by the author or editor.

2. Verse 5 and v. 11: R.L. Smith; Gaide has an unusual arrangement: vv. 1-6, *La dernière nuit*; 7-15, *Le jour sans déclin*; those who make no division except after v. 15 include Baldwin, Lacocque, Lamarche. Willi-Plein again has a novel suggestion: vv. 1-9, 10-19, 20-21.

Summary of Results

Main investigation (computer results)[1]	Subsidiary investigation and notes (R = Redactional)
1.1-6	
1.7-17	vv. 11-13 R?? 14-17 R? 16-17 R?
2.1-4	
2.5-17	vv. 5-9, 10-16, 17 well defined
3.1-10	vv. 1-7, or 8-10, or 1-10 R?
4.1-14	vv. 1-6a and 10a-14 taken together; 6aβ-10aα R v. 12 R?
5.1-4	
5.5-11	
6.1-8	
6.9-15	vv. 13a, 15a, b R??
7.1–8.23	Separate sections: 7.1-3, 4-6/7, 7/8-14; 8.1-8, 9-17, 18-23 ?? Try 7.1-3 + 8.18-23 7.4-14 + 8.1-17
1–8[2]	
1.1-6 + 6.9-15 + 7.1–8.23	
9.1-8	v. 7 R?
9.9-10	
9.11-17	
10.1–11.3	11.1-3 separate section. Also 10.1-2??
11.4-14 + 15-17 + 13.7-9	
12.1–13.6	Division after 12.7/8/9/11?
14.1-15 + 16-21	Further subdivision vv. 5, 11?
9–11; 12–14	
1–14	

---

1. Separate sections are dealt with in Chapter 3.
2. The sections from this point onwards are covered in Chapter 4.

Chapter 3

THE STRUCTURE OF INDIVIDUAL SECTIONS
OF THE BOOK OF ZECHARIAH

In this chapter we shall consider those units marked off for separate treatment by our previous investigation. For this purpose a table is given containing *every* repeated word in the section, and they will be discussed individually so as to decide, before we allow structural considerations to intrude, which might be deemed to be relevant as marker words. As the study proceeds we shall be able to omit very common words from the table and the discussion.

Zechariah 1

Repeated Words in Zechariah 1.1-6 + 7-17
Figure 2 shows that 57 words occur twice or more in Zechariah 1. We might be tempted to discount many of these simply because they are common throughout the book (entries 5, 6, 7, 8, 14, 16, 19, 21, 22, 27, 28, 32, 42, 49). However we should then have removed 'Yahweh of hosts', 'word/speak', 'land' and 'Jerusalem', which might be significant in some way, perhaps in providing background emphasis. It is also possible for a common word to become significant by being in a prominent position, or a part of a significant phrase, none of whose members need be significant in themselves (cf. 'What is that to us? See thou to that'). We must therefore examine each occurrence individually, although it will not be desirable to give detailed comment on every word. Numbers 1-12 are all concerned with providing an introductory formula for the two parts of the chapter. The root דבר, however, should not be dismissed without a closer look.

13. נביא is found in vv. 1, 7 as part of an introductory formula, but in vv. 4-6 the plural refers to the prophets who proclaimed God's warning to the fathers.

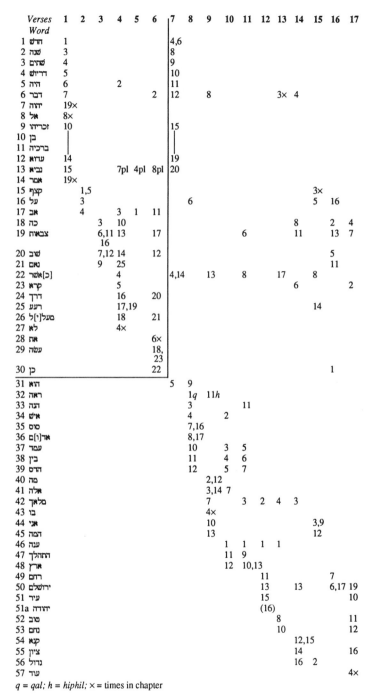

Figure 2: *Zech. 1.1-17: Word numbers of words occurring twice or more*

14. אמר is a common word here, throughout Zechariah, and in the rest of the Hebrew Bible. There is nothing in its use here to make it significant. We may discount it, together with the following items, for similar reasons: 16, 22, 27, 28, 31, 41, 43 (for 15 see 54 below).

17. אב plays an important part in vv. 1-6 (only).

18. כה always occurs as part of the introductory formula, 'thus says Yahweh (Sebaoth)'. This phrase must be considered.[1]

19. צבאת. The heavy emphasis in v. 3 on 'Yahweh Sebaoth' suggests that this title has special significance for Zechariah. It seems to be entirely appropriate for this chapter with its 'holy war' atmosphere.

20. שוב is important in vv. 1-6: the fathers were exhorted to turn but refused; a new offer is made 'return to me and I will return to you'. Then at the end of this chapter Yahweh reports that 'he has (re)turned to Jerusalem'. Is this a prophetic perfect?[2]

21. נאם occurs only as part of the formula 'oracle of Yahweh (Sebaoth)'. It is not important in itself.

23. קרא is used only three times: in v. 4 to refer to the 'calling' of the former prophets to the fathers—without success. There is a contrast with this in vv. 14, 17 where the prophet is told to call (to an unspecified audience, cf. Isaiah 40, especially v. 6) with a message of comfort; the complaint 'How long?' is answered at last (v. 14, cf. v. 12), the nations will be punished and (v. 17) Jerusalem will be blessed.

24. דרך is used twice here, vv. 4 and 6, paired with מעלל[י]ל,[3] to describe ways/doings of the fathers and probably, in v. 6, those of

---

1.   Several scholars give attention to this feature, which is, of course, an important object for form-critical study. See e.g. Meyers, *Haggai, Zechariah*, pp. lii-liii.

2.   Baldwin aptly comments: 'The words *I have returned to Jerusalem* would recall Ezekiel's vision of the departure of the Lord from the Temple (10.18-19; 11.23) and of His return (43.5). His presence is a pledge that the Temple will be finished' (*Haggai, Zechariah, Malachi*, p. 100). This seems a better understanding than that of Rudolph, Petersen and others who translate by a present tense ('Ich wende mich. . .', Rudolph, *Haggai*, p. 72; 'I am returning. . .', Petersen, *Haggai and Zechariah*, p. 137) or the slightly unnatural explanation of Meyers that 'Yahweh's presence is to be manifest' now that temple building has been resumed, as in Haggai, cf. Zech. 1.7 (*Haggai, Zechariah*, pp. 122-23).

3.   It is generally agreed that וממעליכם, the *qere* with *mem* restored, is the best reading here. The word remains in the table with or without the *mem*, or even if we accepted the *kethib* (from מעליל, which is not otherwise attested) since it is so similar in sound. See, e.g., Rudolph, *Haggai*, p. 66; Petersen (who, however, has some confusing printing errors), *Haggai and Zechariah*, p. 127.

Zechariah's contemporaries. Otherwise it occurs only in Zech. 3.7 ('If you will walk in my ways...') and 9.13 ('I have bent Judah as my bow'). The latter seem to have no relevance to ch. 1.

25. רע (adj) is used of both 'ways' and 'doings' in v. 4; in v. 15 רעה occurs in the difficult phrase 'and/but they helped for evil'.[1] The meaning seems to be that the nations helped Yahweh to express his anger in action but went beyond what he intended (a little) with evil result. The connection between these occurrences, if any is intended, can only be that the evil in both cases was the ground for God's wrath.

26. See 24 above. The difference between the *kethib* and *qere* in v. 4 does not affect the meaning. The word occurs nowhere else in Zechariah.

29. עשה is, of course, a common word, but it occurs infrequently in Zechariah (1.6, 6; 2.4; 6.11; 7.3, 9; 8.16; 10.1). No plausible connection between these can be suggested.

30. This should be ignored: כן and לכן are different and too far apart to be connected.

32. ראה only occurs in vv. 8-9 in ch. 1, but twenty times elsewhere in Zechariah. The first occurrence describes *what* the prophet saw (*qal* form); in the second the angel says 'I will cause you to see' what these things signify. The 'seeing' is thus of two types, and the use of the verb twice makes this clear.

33. הנה, vv. 8, 11; also 2.1, 5, 7, 13, 14; 3.8, 9; 4.2; 5.1, 7, 9; 6.1, 12; 8.7; 9.4, 9; 11.6, 16; 12.2; 14.1. This is used in drawing attention to most of the major items in the visions of Zechariah 1–6, with הנני in 2.14 and 3.8 to introduce what Yahweh is about to do (both with בוא, *qal* and *hiphil* participles). It is not used everywhere, or uniformly, but there are other indications that הנה is not used lightly or carelessly. הנני is used at the centre of Zechariah 7–8 (8.7), and again in close proximity to בוא (*hiphil*; 8.8); the verb שכן is also found in 2.14 and 8.8. The last of these is obviously a key point in Zechariah.

---

1. Rudolph: '...Völker, die, als ich kurze Zeit zürnte, des Bösen "zuviel taten"'. He keeps the same verb, in opposition to Sellin and others, but understands it in this sense by analogy with the arabic *gzr* (*Haggai*, pp. 72-73). One way or another, RSV's 'they furthered the disaster' cannot be far wrong. Further see Rignell, *Die Nachtgesichte*, pp. 49-50.

34-39. These are all concerned with the description of Zechariah's vision: the man, the horses and the myrtle trees. They do not connect with any other part of the vision. The description 'standing between the myrtle trees' occurs as a set formula three times—rather oddly in v. 8 where the man is riding on a horse! Does this indicate a later extension of the use of the formula? It has some affinity with the other formula used: 'the angel who spoke with me' (see below).

40. מה may be ignored: two occurrences in a single verse. The repetition seems to be a way of delaying the answer to Zechariah's question (cf. the more elaborate delay and heightened suspense in 4.5, 13).

42. מלאך needs to be noted, despite the fact that its use here is confined to vv. 9, 11, 12, 13 and 14, where Zechariah's conversation is described. Elsewhere it is found in 2.2, 7, 7; 3.1, 3, 5, 6; 4.1, 4, 5; 5.5, 10; 6.4, 5; 12.8. Apart from a brief communication between Yahweh and 'the angel who spoke with me' in v. 13, the angel stays with Zechariah throughout and is referred to explicitly, in all visions but the third and sixth, as 'the angel who spoke with me'. In the latter we find simply 'And he said to me...' In the fourth vision Zechariah has no conversation with 'the angel who spoke with me', but sees 'the Angel of Yahweh' (as in 1.11-12). It is possible that there is evidence of a second author's or an editor's work here.

44. אני is emphatic in v. 9 and v. 15b, but refers to the angel in the former, and to Yahweh in the latter. It seems safe to ignore it.

45. המה. No connection is discernible between the two occurrences of this common word.

46. ענה begins vv. 10, 11, 12 and 13 in the question and answer section of the vision. These instances give a certain continuity and serve to mark it off as a separate entity.

47. התהלך occurs in vv. 10-11 in the same sense: the horses go to 'patrol' and then report that they have 'patrolled' the earth. Otherwise in Zechariah the *hithpael* of the verb is found in 6.7 (3×), and in 10.12. The last occurrence does not seem to be related to the others and an emendation יהללו is sometimes proposed.[1] The other instances are in the vision which corresponds most closely to this one, namely the eighth and last: the chariots and horses patrol the earth and set God's Spirit at rest (6.8).

---

1.   With partial support from one Hebrew manuscript, LXX and Syr.; Otzen, *Studien*, p. 252 (who considers it unnecessary) and Jansma, *Zechariah 9–14*, p. 92.

48. ארץ only occurs in vv. 10, 11 (2×). It signifies the whole earth. However it does not seem significant for our purposes, except that the repetition lays emphasis on the fact that the whole earth is in view. The last occurrence is part of the phrase 'all the earth'.

49, 52, 53. רחם seems to be an important root, vv. 12 (*piel*), 16 (plural noun), and 7.9 (plural noun), 10.6 (*piel*). Verse 16 represents the direct answer to the specific question in v. 12, 'How long will you not have compassion...?' If we exclude vv. 14-17 or vv. 16-17 from the original prophecy we are left with the rather vague answer (דברים נחמים) in v. 13. Despite the distance between רחם and נחם the roots do constitute a word pair. Both occur in vv. 16-17. נחם is joined with טוב both times it occurs, a word which is surprisingly rare in Zechariah (8.19; 9.17; 11.12—'appointed times of good', 'how good it will be' and 'if it seems good to you'). נחם also occurs in 8.14, 'and I did not relent' and 10.2, 'the dreamers...give empty consolation (הבל ינחמון)'.

50, 51, 55. ירושלם (vv. 12, 14, 16 [2×], 17 [+ 36×]) is confined to the end verses where it is introduced as a separate concern by the question 'How long?' The distribution otherwise is interesting (2.2, 6, 8, 16; 3.2; 7.7; 8.3 [2×], 4, 8, 15, 22; 9.9-10. 12.2 [2×], 3, 5, 6 [2×], 7, 8, 9, 10, 11; 13.1; 14.2, 4, 8, 10, 11, 12, 14, 16, 17, 21), but the significance of this must be considered later. ציון is in 1.14, 17, 2.11 [2×], 14, 8.2, 3, 9.9, 13 only. In 1.12-17 it seems that 'Jerusalem' is repeated simply because it is the subject under discussion. The same is true of 'cities of Judah', 'my cities' and 'Zion' (vv. 14, 17). However it is noticeable that all three words occur in v. 17 producing great emphasis. Other references to what has gone before are seen in טוב in association with נחם (cf. v. 13). (Perhaps also בחר is intended to recall בחרים of v. 16 [?].) We note also the *qere* of the IF (cf. vv. 4, 14). This last verse might be regarded as an editorial 'gather line', which aims to sum up the whole chapter and bring it to a satisfying climax. See also 57 below.

52, 53. See above.

54, 56. קנאה is used parallel to קצף in a forceful way. גדול is not distinctive in itself, but is associated with these two other important words. See below.

57. עוד v. 17 (4×). This is given a prominent position and strong emphasis through repetition. It cannot have a structuring function within this chapter, but we note that the word occurs in the phrase

'again choose Jerusalem' both here and at the end of the section
2.10-16.[1] This strengthens the evidence for the hand of an editor with
a concern for structure at work in the early chapters of the book.

Application of Results
Assuming that it is valid to look for structuring in terms of repeated
words, we have now at least removed one source of subjectivity, for
we have considered all repeating words and I have provided reasons
(which may not be universally accepted but can at least be examined)
for retaining some and excluding others as possible pointers to structure. The words which remain are at least reasonably manageable.
They are:

> 1 + 2 + 3 + 4 + 5 + 6 + 9 + 10 + 11 + 13 (sing.) = IF, giving the date
> in terms of the reign of Darius, mentioning 'Zechariah ben Berechiah
> ben Iddo, the prophet' in full
>
> 6   דבר
> 13   נביאים (plural only)
> 15   קצף (גדול 56 + קנא 54 +)
> 17   אב
> 18 + 14 + 7 + 19 = IF כה אמר יהוה צבאות
> 20   שוב
> 23   קרא
> 24   דרך
> 25   רעע
> 26   מעל[י]ל
> 32   ראה
> 33   הנה
> 42   מלאך
> 46   ענה
> 47   התהלך
> 52   טוב
> 53   נחם
> 54   קנא
> 56   גדול

We may now consider the sections 1.1-6 and 1.7-17 separately,
aiming to combine the results of this discussion with those of traditional biblical scholarship.

---

1.   See Chapter 4 below.

The Structure of Zechariah 1.1-6

Verse 1 is an introduction to the prophecy of Zechariah, which is not, however, so separate from the following prophecy as usual. The date is given. This is special in that it is the first occurrence.

Verse 2 fits well as a summary of the present situation and its cause. In form it emphasizes as strongly as possible the wrath of Yahweh, in having the root קצף as an inclusio for this short verse.

Many commentators regard this as an addition to the text,[1] but, if that is so, it seems to have been done in connection with vv. 14-15. See below.

Verse 3 starts again. The prophet is not given a direct message for himself but for the people (ואמרת). There follows another summarizing verse for the future: 'Turn to me and I will turn to you'. There is the strongest possible emphasis on 'Yahweh of hosts'. This title also occurs in v. 4 in a very similar context.

Verse 4 takes up ideas used already:

עַל אֲבוֹתֵיכֶם, cf. v. 2 אֶל תִּהְיוּ כַאֲבֹתֵיכֶם

הַנָּבִיא v. 1 cf. ,קִרְאוּ אֲלֵיהֶם נְבִיאִים הָרִאשׁנִים and

v. 3 וְאָמַרְתָּ אֲלֵיהֶם

כֹּה אָמַר יְהוָה צְבָאוֹת, cf. v. 3

וְאָשׁוּב, cf. v. 3 שׁוּבוּ ,שׁוּבוּ

This is expanded with מַדְרְכֵיכֶם הָרָעִים וּמַעַלִילֵיכֶם הָרָעִים and the negative result is given:

שׁוּבוּ אֵלַי, cf. v. 3 וְלֹא הִקְשִׁיבוּ אֵלַי

Perhaps קשׁב is chosen for its similarity with שׁוב. It occurs otherwise only in 7.11 וַיְמָאֲנוּ לְהַקְשִׁיב. It is also similar in sound to קצף (v. 2.##1,5)

---

1. E.g. Amsler *et al.*, *Agée, Zacharie, Malachi*, p. 56, who regards it as placed there to indicate an important element in Zechariah's message. There is now a more positive appraisal of 1.2 than is evident in older commentaries (e.g. Mitchell *et al.*, *Haggai, Zechariah, Malachi and Jonah*, pp. 109-10). Petersen notes that the verse sits loosely in its present position, but also feels that it does at least three things: summarizes past relationships between Yahweh and Israel; establishes a link between generations; allows for a distinction between various generations and their relationship to Yahweh (*Haggai and Zechariah*, pp. 129-30). Rudolph is emphatic that the verse (a 'Hinzufügung') should be kept, and links it with v. 15 (*Haggai*, p. 66). The Meyers' see it as connecting the three parts of Zechariah (1.1-6; 1.7–6.15; 7–8) (*Haggai, Zechariah*, p. 92).

The result then is a series of widening circles, with the detail gradually increasing. The whole is bound together by a large number of repeated words.

Verse 5 takes up the theme of fathers and prophets with two rhetorical questions. They are seen to be transient. This prepares for v. 6, the final word about the effectiveness of God's word spoken through the prophets. The form is again a rhetorical question and the prophets and fathers both occur.

Verse 6b may be part of the report that began in v. 4. The opening suggests that it is more likely to be a report of what happened as a result of Zechariah's preaching, than that the fathers actually repented. But it may be that שוב is not used in the same sense as in v. 4—hence the Jerusalem Bible's: 'This reduced them to such confusion. . .' It is possible, in any case, that 'they' did 'return', but not so completely that a further appeal would be out of place.

The content of v. 6b exactly sums up what the preaching message has sought to convey: 'as Yahweh of hosts purposed [זמם, only elsewhere 8.14-15] so he has done'.

The question arises here: 'Does "they returned" refer to "the fathers" or to Zechariah's hearers?'[1] Rudolph notes that v. 6b is abrupt in following a historical reference to the fate of 'the fathers'.[2] It does not affect our analysis too much from a literary point of view.

The pattern which emerges, taking virtually all the material into account is:

---

1.   The older commentaries generally take v. 6b to refer to the response of 'the fathers', since there is no new subject specified (cf. e.g. Mitchell *et al.*, *Haggai, Zechariah, Malachi and Jonah*, p. 113; Marti, *Das Dodekapropheton*, p. 400). This is preferred by Petersen (*Haggai and Zechariah*, p. 134) and others. Petitjean, after rejecting the argument of Nowack and Sellin, that v. 6b contradicts v. 4, nevertheless opts for the alternative understanding that this refers to Zechariah's contemporaries (*Les oracles*, pp. 47-51); also Mason (*Haggai, Zechariah and Malachi*, p. 33) and Meyers' (*Haggai, Zechariah*, p. 96). Hag. 1.12-14 is a good parallel for this latter view.

2.   He also believes that the rest of Zechariah 1–8 knows nothing of a conversion on the part of the prophet's hearers. His solution is to emend the text so as to read two imperatives: 'Return, and say. . .'

$4a^1$ as your fathers
b^1 to whom prophets called
c^1 thus says Yahweh of hosts
d^1 Return
e^1 from evil ways and doings
f^1 (cf. d?)   did not hear or turn (an ear)
                  (oracle of Yahweh)
$5a^2$ fathers where?
b^2 prophets forever ?
$6c^3$?   my words and statutes
b^3 which I commanded prophets
a^3 overtook fathers

d^2 they returned
g^1 (f?) (c?)   as Yahweh of hosts purposed *to do* to us
e^2 according to our ways and doings
g^2 so *has he done* with us

This seems to have a clear logic about it, and some apparently clear patterns emerge, e.g. abcba in vv. 5-6a. This is a logical subsection and seems likely to be intended as a chiasmus. The overall thought is consonant with the layout given.

Following the same notation for vv. 1-3, we could add:

1b   the prophet
$2a^0$ your fathers
$3c^{-2}$ thus says Yahweh of hosts
d^{-1} return to me
c^{-1} oracle of Yahweh of hosts
d^0 I will return to you
c^0 say Yahweh of hosts
$4a^1$ your fathers. . .

This presents us with a very tightly structured whole.[1] Virtually every

---

1. We might ask whether Beuken's view that 1.3-6 has the form of a Levitical sermon (cf. 2 Chron. 30.6-9; *Haggai–Sacharja*, pp. 84-115, esp. 91-92) makes any appreciable difference to this investigation. I am unable to accept his thesis as a whole, but it is quite possible that Zechariah or his editor(s) did base some of their writing on traditional forms. Would this mean that regular patterns would be produced unconsciously? In principle we should hope to be able to detect an under- lying pattern and its modification, and to form some opinion of original author and later redactor. However, in practice the evidence that reaches us is capable of too many different reconstructions for this to be done precisely. We must maintain our primary interest in the structure intended by the writer(s), irrespective of his/their

word is made to contribute to the overall effect. If those scholars are right who argue for the work of one or more editors here, then we must be ready for some artistic editing.[1]

For further treatment of this section in relation to the whole chapter, see below.

The Structure of Zechariah 1.7-17

There are signs that this passage has been worked over.[2] The transition from v. 7 to v. 8 is not smooth: 'the word of Yahweh came to me saying, I saw...'; neither is that from v. 9 to v. 10, where the man who stood between the myrtle trees answers without having been asked. 'The angel who spoke with me' is introduced abruptly and it is not clear whether he is meant to be 'the man who stood between the myrtle trees' (cf v. 11 'the angel of Yahweh who stood...' with vv. 12-13 'the angel of Yahweh said...' and 'Yahweh answered gracious...words to the angel who spoke with me'). Verses 16-17 are often regarded as additions to the original text. See Chapter 2 above.

The intended structure of vv. 8-13 is not easy to determine. There are two important focuses: v. 11, where the information is given that the earth is at rest, and v. 13, where the angel receives comforting words which are explained in vv. 14-15. The section falls formally into two sections, each beginning with a question, and may be represented thus:

Question		*Answer*		*Leading to*
9	What?	10	Sent to patrol earth	11 Report: earth at rest
12	How long?	13	Comforting words	14-15 Viz. wrath to jealousy

sources, but try to be aware of the possibilities that Beuken's researches open.

1. H.-G. Schöttler concludes that 1.1-6 is a constructed literary unity: '... ein einheitlicher Text im Sinne der Literarkritik. Die Unebenheiten dieser konstruierten Textfolge sind somit form- und redaktionsgeschichtlich zu erklären und nicht als literarkritische Signale zu werten' (*Gott inmitten seines Volkes: Die Neuordnung des Gottesvolkes nach Sacharja 1–6* [Trier: Paulinus-Verlag, 1987], p. 48).

2. But see Rudolph, *Haggai*, p. 79, who says of the many 'more logical' readings proposed: 'Dabei wird übersehen, dass eine visionäre Schau ihre eigenen Gesetze hat und nicht überall mit der logischen Elle gemessen werden darf. Ich habe deshalb keinen Anlass gesehen, etwas zu ändern'.

It is clear that to delete v. 12 would spoil this pattern. We note also that the two key words, רחם and נחם, of vv. 12 and 13 are not taken up until vv. 16 and 17 respectively. It is possible that they are used in the latter verses to form a chiasmus and emphasize further vv. 14-15. These would already be recognized as a climax by the parallel and contrast: קצף becomes קנאה for Jerusalem; קצף for Jerusalem becomes קצף for the nations (cf. also טוב vv. 13, 17; and יהוה צבאת vv. 12, 14a, 16, 17).

The pattern for the speakers during this section may be represented as follows (where Zech. = Zechariah; As = the angel who spoke with me; Ay signifies the expression 'angel of Yahweh' ; Mm = man standing among the myrtle trees; Y = Yahweh; H = horse(man) + horses?/horsemen?).

9	Zech.	to	'my lord'	(Mm?)	
	As	to	Zech.		
10	Mm	to	(Zech.)		
11			H	to	Aym
12				Ay	to Y
13				Y	to As
14-15	As	to	Zech.		

It seems impossible to draw any far-reaching result out of this, but it seems to confirm that the unit cannot end before v. 14 (and therefore probably v. 15). Verses 14-17 have the form of oracles, but vv. 14-15 are more closely related to the vision in that 'the angel who spoke with me' is the speaker. Speeches are a common feature of the vision in any case, and the whole of vv. 8ff., would reach an unsatisfactory end at v. 13.

Verses 16-17, on the other hand, could be detached without causing a hiatus, and it may be that Rothstein, Sellin, Petitjean, Rudolph and others are right in separating them. Rignell argued that Zechariah himself added vv. 16-17 when the visions were first written down.[1] Beuken argued that לכן in v. 16 indicated an announcement that belonged with the motivation of v. 15.[2] This seems to me to be right, for *someone*, whether author or redactor, intended it that way. Who is to say that it could not have been Zechariah? I do not think that v. 15b already provides a satisfactory explanation for the menace of

1. *Die Nachtgesichte*, pp. 57-59.
2. *Haggai–Sacharja*, pp. 242-43.

v. 15a:[1] it seems to need a further explanatory word.

Various verbal links can be noted between vv. 16-17 and the preceding passage: רחם vv. 12, 16; ירושלים vv. 12, 14, 16, 17; ציון vv. 14, 17; עיר vv. 12, 17; נחם vv. 13, 17; טוב vv.13, 17; קרא vv. 14, 17 (כה, vv. 14, 16, 17, is not a significant word but it does not recur in the rest of the section and is worth comparing with 8.1-8); צבא vv. 12, 14, 16, 17 (only).

The structure of v. 14b recalls v. 2 where קצף sandwiches the rest of the verse; 14b is also chiastic on its own:

If we include v. 15a there is a slightly larger chiasmus produced:

קנאתי לירושלם ולציון קנאה גדולה
וקצף גדול אני קצף

Up to this point the meaning is ambiguous; for קנאה can mean 'anger'; v. 15a, therefore, brings relief from the considerable tension that has been built up through this chapter. The hearers have not been able to rejoice up to this point, but here it becomes clear that God's anger *now* is directed towards the nations, and the קנאה of v. 15a is *zeal for* Jerusalem, not *anger towards* it. This, therefore, forms a climax, if not *the* climax for the chapter.

We note here also the close similarity between this and 8.2,[2] both in words and form:

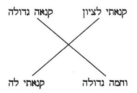

This is the start of God's declaration to act which stands at the heart of chs. 7–8. Thus additional importance and emphasis is indicated.

---

1. Contra Amsler, 'Zacharie', p. 65.
2. See below on Zech. 7–8, and on Zech. 1 in Chapter 4.

The most striking result of excluding vv. 16-17 is that we have
an inclusio with v. 2 (קָצַף, קֶצֶף) formed by קוֹצֵף, קֶצֶף and קָצַפְתִּי.
Otherwise in Zechariah the root occurs only in 7.12 (קֶצֶף) and 8.14
(בְהַקְצִיף), and it is therefore capable of acting as an important marker
word for the whole of Zechariah 1–8. We noted that v. 15 strongly
links the roots קצף and קנא (קִנְאָה קִנֵּאתִי), and these two forms also
occur in 8.2 but nowhere else in Zechariah. We therefore look forward to more illuminating results in dealing with chs. 7–8. We must
also note in v. 15 that הַשַּׁאֲנַנִּים is directly related to וְשֹׁקֶטֶת in v. 11 by
both meaning and context, and that in the use of פוץ in v. 17 we have
an unusual sense (only Prov. 5.16 otherwise) which reminds us of
עזבו לרעה, v. 15.

The Structure of Zechariah 1.1-17
The composition of this chapter according to traditional biblical critical methods is clear. There are two separate sections dated about three
months apart: an oracle and a 'night vision' plus oracle; and possibly
there are additions in one or both sections.

It seems improbable that two independent sections have simply been
placed side by side so as to form a literary unity. It seems more likely
that the overall structure which was indicated most strongly by קצף
and קנאה is due to some editorial additions or modifications—possibly
by Zechariah?[1] On the other hand it seems unlikely that vv. 14-15 can
be detached from vv. 7-13, and we are on safer ground in suggesting
that v. 2 is an editorial expansion. This conclusion has been reached
by perhaps the majority of modern commentators, but usually without
suggesting any constructive purpose with regard to the literary
composition of the book.

Petitjean[2] argues that the correlation between the themes of קנאה
(v. 14b) and alliance–election (v. 17b) together with the correspondence between 1.14b -17 and 8.2-8 establishes the unity of this section.
He believes that the former has been modelled on the latter, and
v. 14a added to introduce it. This implies an original oracle that
ended at v. 13 which does not seem satisfactory, but further consideration must be given after looking at ch. 8.

The most reasonable theory of composition seems to me to be this:

1.   Cf. Mason, *Haggai, Zechariah and Malachi*, pp. 35-36.
2.   *Les oracles*, pp. 75-88.

1. The two oracles belong together. Verses 2-6a speak of the anger of Yahweh against the fathers, and demand a response of the present generation.

2. Verse 6b reports the repentance called for and this prepares the way for the message given in the second vision.

3. Verse 15 brings what was begun in v. 2 to a close by means of a strong inclusio, and vv. 16-17 expand and elaborate on the message of comfort given in vv. 14-15, picking up significant words from vv. 12-13 where an urgent question is asked, but only a general answer is given.

It would be possible to argue for a redactor's hand somewhere here. The most likely verses to come from such a person would be vv. 2 and/or 16-17. Whoever it was who finished our chapter, he seems to have improved on the original version. The whole is very neatly bound together, and we may expect to see signs of artistic structuring as we proceed to the succeeding chapters.

Zechariah 2

Figure 3 gives all repeated words for Zechariah 2. It is convenient to include vv. 1-4, 5-9 and 10-17 in a single table since the units are short, and since we decided above to investigate vv. 5-9 and 10-17 both separately and together.

Zechariah 2.1-4

This unit is clearly defined by the introductory formula (the first five words of v. 1 and v. 5 are identical) and by the content. The distinctive repeated words are, in my judgment, nos. 1-2 (?), 3-4, 7-10, which we may label as follows:

a. נשׂא (?) 1.#1 and 4.##17,27. Otherwise it occurs only in 2.5; 5.1, 5, 7, 9 (2×); 6.1, 13.

b. ראה (?) 1.#4 and 3.#1.

c. [ה]ארבע 1.#6 and 3.#3. This indicates the correspondence between the two halves of the unit.

d. קרן 1.#7, 2.#11, 4.##9,25,28. This is the main subject of the unit.

Verses / Word	1	2	3	4	5	6	7	8	9	10	11	12	13	14	15	16	17
1 משא	1			17, 27	1												
2 ראה	4		1		3	10											
3 ארבע[ה]		6		3							9						
4 קרן	7	11		9,25 28													
5 אמר		1,8		1,6,7		1,5		1,8									
6 אל		2,9		29		6		2,5				9			4,18		
7 מה		6		2													
8 אלה		7,10		3,8 20													
9 זרה		13		11, 32													
10 יהודה		15		13, 31													
11 בוא				4,19										7			
12 ארץ				30						4							
13 עין	3				2							18					
14 ראה (2	4		1)		3	10											
15 איש/אדם			15	5				_13_									
16 הנה				4		1							2	6			
17 יד				6									5				
18 מדד				8		7											
19 ירושלם						9		11									
20 כמה						11, 13											
21 מלאך		(3)					2,6										
22 דבר							3	4									
23 יצא							5,8										
24 ישב								10			4						
25 רב								12							3		
26 תוך								15	11					9	12		
27 היה									2,10				7		8		
28 כבוד									9			7					
29 הוי										1,2	1						
30 נאם										6,14				10			
31 יהוה										7,15		4	12	11	5,15	2	5
32 כי										8		1, 13	1, 11	5	14		6
33 ציון											2			4			
34 בת											5			3			
35 צבאות												5	13		16		
36 שלח												8	14		17		
37 גוי												10			2		
38 שלל												11	8				
39 נגע												14, 16					
40 ידע													10		13		
41 שכן														8	11		
vs תוך								15	11					9	12		
41 קדש																8	9

Figure 3: *Zech. 2.1-4 + 5-17:*
Word numbers of words occurring twice or more

e. מה־אלה, 2.##6,7, 4.##2,3, indicates the correspondence between the two halves of the unit. We note also the word אלה on its own, which introduces the answer to the question each time.

f. זרה, 2.#13, 4.##11,32, describes the action of the horns on Judah. Note also 'Israel and Jerusalem' in v. 2, and 'land of Judah' in v. 4. ישראל is odd here. Is there a play on words שרה/זרה? (Cf. 'Jezreel' יזרעאל in Hos. 1.4? Cf. also חרש/חרד 3.#4, 4.#21).

The use of נשא is strange. The first occurrence is a quite normal introduction (as in 2.5; 5.1). The second, 'the horns that scattered Judah so that no man raised his head', is more striking. The meaning could be that no one in the nations gave any help, or that no one in Israel offered any resistance.[1]

We might ask whether any connection is intended with v. 1: the prophet can at least raise his eyes! On the face of it, this would not seem to be well-founded, since raising the head and raising the eyes have different connotations. Moreover, Zechariah lifts up his eyes to see the horns, but not the smiths. But see below.

The third occasion is also odd: 'the horns which raised the horn'. This seems to be the earliest passage in which 'horn' stands for '*a* power' rather than simply 'power'. The emphasis produced here, makes use of an established metaphor.[2]

The pattern resulting from a mechanical arrangement of letters as above is:

$$a^1 \; b^1 c^1 \; d^1 \; e^1 \; d^2 \; f^1 \; // \; b^2 \; c^2 \; e^2 \; d^3 \; f^2 \; a^2 \; e^3 \; d^4 \; a^3 \; d^5 \; f^3$$

v.1	a^1	I lifted up my eyes
	$b^1 c^1 + d^1$	I saw four horns
v.2	e^1	What are these? These are
	d^2	the horns that
	f^1	scattered Judah. . .
v.3	$b^2 c^2 + (d)$	Yahweh caused me to see four (smiths)

---

1. D.R. Jones's interpretation is similar to the second of these: 'a figure of complete humiliation and subjection', *Haggai, Zechariah, Malachi* (London: SCM Press, 1962), p. 62; cf. C.F. Keil, *The Twelve Minor Prophets* (Edinburgh: T. & T. Clark, 1871), II, p. 241.

2. E.g. Ps. 75.5-6, 11; cf. 'Horn', *ISBE*, II, p. 757.

v.4	e^2				What are these (coming to do)? These are
	d^3			the horns that	
	f^2				scattered Judah
	a^2		so that no one		
			lifted up his head		
	e^3				these (have come to terrify. . . cast down)
	d^4			the horns (of the nations which)	
	a^3		lifted up		
	d^5				the horn (over the land of)
	f^3				Judah to scatter it.

This is not an obviously regular pattern, but it does seem to be unusual in a number of ways. When Zechariah asks, 'What are these coming to do?' the angel first repeats, 'These are the horns which scattered Judah' and adds, 'in such proportion (כפי) that no one raised his head'. The following comments seem plausible:

1. The author emphasizes, by repetition, the horns and their scattering of Israel. This is confirmed in v. 4 by the, strictly speaking, redundant 'which lifted up the horn against Judah to scatter it'.

2. The actual answer to Zechariah's question is delayed and this increases the tension of the reader. The same feature is even more strongly noticeable in Zechariah 4.

3. The author enjoys plays on words and 'lift up the head' with 'lift up the horn' is a little artistic indulgence. There may, therefore, be a play on words between these instances and the opening 'I lifted up my eyes'.

4. The author builds up his pictures gradually, linking one element to the next. We noted this also in 1.2-6.

5. There is a singular lack of emphasis on 'the smiths'. In the interpretation of the vision the word is not repeated at all, whereas 'horn' occurs three more times. Perhaps the intention is to avoid drawing attention to the instrument by which Yahweh will deliver his people.

We need to look out for these features elsewhere in the book of Zechariah. If they occur, then our tentative conclusions will be confirmed. We must note if they occur in original prophetic material or editorial additions, or both. This may give us further insight into the composition of the book.

Possible patterns

There is no point in treating b and c separately since they only occur together. I will therefore replace them by the letter B. There ought probably to be a letter to denote the whole phrase 'These are the horns that scattered Judah', which occurs in identical form in v. 2 and v. 4. I will use the expression F(d, f) for this purpose, where d stands for 'the horn' or 'horn' (i.e. the word used to refer to 'the powers' or 'power') and f stands for the 'scattering of Judah (etc.)'.

I will also put xd to denote a word corresponding to d but different from it. In principle this involves a subjective element; in the case before us the four horns must in some sense correspond to the four smiths.

I shall use the same superscript number for identical words or phrases. This yields the pattern:

$$a^1$$
$$B^1(d^1)$$
$$e^1$$
$$F^1(d^1, f^1)$$
$$B^2(xd)$$
$$e^2$$
$$F^1(d^1, f^1, a^2)$$
$$(a^2)$$
$$F^2(d^1, f^2, a^3, d^2, f^2)$$

This pattern seems to be true to the original emphasis of the passage. We are, to some extent, sacrificing a^1, a^2 and a^3 as important elements for the overall structure, but this would seem to be justified. The 'lifting up' motif retains some importance in binding the whole together. But the most important focus must be on the meaning of the horns, and the above diagram shows this quite clearly. There appears to be something similar to 'the growing phrase' noticed by J. Magonet in his study of Jonah.[1]

In effect the pattern is a twofold one:

What are these?	Answer: These are. . .
What are these?	Delay by recap: These are. . .
	Answer: These are. . .

---

1. *Form and Meaning: Studies in Literary Techniques in the Book of Jonah* (Sheffield: Almond Press, 1983), pp. 31-33, 40.

If we were to put the emphasis on 'the horns that scattered Judah', we should arrive at a slightly different structure:

> I saw four horns
>> horns that scattered Judah. . .
>
> . . . see four contra-horns
>> horns that scattered Judah
>> (contra-horns) are to terrify and cast down
>> horns that scattered Judah

This demonstrates the way that the climax of the passage comes not right at the end but at the pivotal point of a chiasmus—for this does give us an off-centre chiasmus. This also would seem to be faithful to the intention of the writer. We should not, therefore, think that the schemata that we use to demonstrate the intended patterns in the book of Zechariah are necessarily adequate, or 'correct' or 'incorrect'. In this short passage we are fortunate that the meaning is clear, and the points of emphasis can be seen without detailed analysis. It is valuable to see, therefore, that a close consideration of structure, such as we have undertaken, actually does confirm and bring into relief, the features that we should probably note intuitively. Repeated words cannot simply be treated statistically or mathematically. The syntax and meaning have to be taken into consideration. Nevertheless, the fact that we have considered all repeated words has removed the objection to structural studies that only the convenient correspondences are noted. We have been able, in this section at least, to account for all repetitions. This includes the 'technical' word 'horn' which we might think would be bound to occur more than once:[1] we have seen that the 'technical' word 'smith' does not do so, and that 'horn' occurs far more frequently than is necessary.

Zechariah 2.5-17 (5-9 + 10-17)
In dealing with Zech. 2.5-9, 10-17 and 5-17, the neatest way to proceed is to consider the significant repeated words in the sections 2.5-9 and 10-17, and then to consider the whole section together.

Zechariah 2.5-9
Zech. 2.5-9 is less clearly a self-contained unit than vv. 1-4 since it is followed by material which is not a direct account of a vision, but

---

1. Cf. Magonet, *Form and Meaning*, pp. 16, 116.

which has some connection with the vision itself. Nevertheless, v. 9 forms a fitting ending, and v. 10 starts a new section with the thrice repeated הוי (also found in v. 11).[1] Verbal connections between vv. 5-9 and 10-17 are very few: words 15-16 and 23-27. The number of repeated words is not great, nor are the words particularly distinctive. We may ignore אמר, כמה[2] and אל. מדד, which occurs as הֶבֶל מִדָּה and לָמוֹד, may also be ignored. ראה, vv. 5-6 only. This is an important word in describing Zechariah's visions—both the outward appearance to the prophet (v. 5 and most references) and something further within the vision. This may be of two kinds:

1.   One of the characters goes to see something (2.6).
2.   The prophet is made to see (*hiphil*) the significance of a vision or a particular feature (1.9; 2.3).

רָאָה (3.4; 6.8) in the sense of הִנֵּה, will be considered below. 4.10a refers to those who despise the day of small things; they will see that which the plummet in the hand of Zerubbabel signifies. The word is important also in 9.5, 8, 14 and 10.7 (not elsewhere). However, it does not seem to have any structuring function in 2.5ff.

ירושלם (only) occurs in vv. 6 and 8; ציון occurs in vv. 11 and 14.[3]

דבר, מלאך and יצא are closely connected together. Two different angels are involved, but each one 'goes forth' (יֹצֵא). One (presumably the 'other angel') says, presumably to the angel הַדֹּבֵר לִי, 'Run and speak (דַּבֵּר) to this young man...'—presumably the man with the measuring line. The purpose of this may be to enhance the message that comes as the climax of this section, by delaying it. The increase in the number of angels involved may also serve this function.[4] The words do not help to structure the unit as a whole.

תוך occurs in two pairs: בתוכה vv. 8-9, and בתוכך vv. 14-15. See below.

---

1.   See Chapter 2 above.

2.   The exact significance of this may not be clear, but there is no problem about the meaning of 2.7.

3.   It is appropriate that 'Jerusalem' is used of the physical city, and 'Zion' when the concept of God's people is prominent. However, we cannot put too much weight on this, since 'choose Jerusalem' occurs in v. 16. The same applies to the idea that this terminology separates original author and editor.

4.   The only other suggestion I have found is that it is to enhance the authority of the message.

היה occurs twice in an emphatic construction in the form of אהיה, which probably recalls Exod. 3.15. The beginning of v. 9 looks as though it might be a new repetition of the covenant promise: 'I will be to her...'

הנה occurs in vv. 5, 7 to introduce a new feature in the series of visions. Its first occurrence introduces 'a man and in his hand a measuring line' (v. 5). This is then explained by means of a question and answer; הנה reappears to introduce a new element: two angels 'go out' and meet. The 'other angel' says to 'the angel who spoke with me', 'Run and tell that young man[1] that:

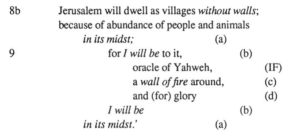

8b	Jerusalem will dwell as villages *without walls*;		
	because of abundance of people and animals		
	in its midst;	(a)	
9	for *I will be* to it,	(b)	
	oracle of Yahweh,		(IF)
	a *wall of fire* around,		(c)
	and (for) glory		(d)
	I will be	(b)	
	in its midst.'	(a)	

The structure of vv. 8b-9 is easily seen: even if this is not accepted as an undisputable chiasmus, it is an important centre with a double-layer inclusio. The correspondence between פרזות and חמות אש does not show up on the list. Perhaps the lack of verbal correspondence is deliberate, so that the chiasmus is not made less distinct; this may only be regarded as a plausible speculation. 'I will be' is emphatic, as is seen by אני in v. 9a, and אהיה in v. 9b, which are both, strictly speaking, unnecessary.

---

1. Keil, after an involved discussion (*Twelve Minor Prophets*, pp. 242-5), concludes that:

1. the man with the measuring line is the angel of Yahweh.
2. 'another angel', i.e. 'the angel who spoke with me' meets him.
3. the man (angel of Yahweh) tells 'the angel who spoke with me' to give the message about Jerusalem to 'that young man' (i.e. Zechariah).

I think that the more usual interpretation is likely to be right, for: this is a rather complicated understanding; 'another angel' would not naturally mean 'the angel who spoke...'; it is odd that in a passage where the word 'angel' is used freely, the 'angel of Yahweh' should be described so obscurely; it seems sensible to assume that the message is relevant to someone who is engaged in measuring Jerusalem. It would be quite in order according to this interpretation to think of 'another angel' as the angel of Yahweh (who appeared in ch. 1).

Zechariah 2.10-17

Here we may ignore words 6 and 29-30 but must consider the other words (from 28 to 41, plus 15 and 25-26)

This section begins with a call (הוי הוי) to the exiles (2nd pl.) to flee from the north, for Yahweh scattered them (abroad) as the four winds of heaven. The next verse reinforces this appeal (הוי once only) by calling to Zion (2nd f. sing.) who dwells with the daughter of Babylon.[1]

It is worth noting the probable parallel between fleeing from ארץ צפון, (which may have mythological overtones, as the dwelling of the gods), and Yahweh's rousing himself from his holy dwelling (ממעון קדשו), vv. 10, 17. Perhaps בבל also adds to this.

A feature of this section is the number of motive clauses introduced by כי (v. 10b already, and vv. 12a, 12b, 13a, 14b, 17b). Verses 12-16 depend on what has been said in vv. 10-11.

ציון, vv. 11, 12 and 14, is used instead of Jerusalem as the prophecy changes from judgment to salvation. In both cases an appeal is made to Zion. No other significance is obvious.

בת, vv. 11, 14. Both verses address Zion directly, but בת occurs with בבל in the former. Is it possible that בת בבל (v. 11) and בבבת (v. 12) are meant to resonate? Zion dwells with בת בבל but is actually בבבת עינו. From a structural point of view we may say that v. 11 and v. 14 are perhaps parallel.

יהוה צבאות occurs only three times, always in connection with the שלחני.

גוים and שלל. The nations are the object of God's judgment in vv. 12-13, although the word itself only occurs in v. 12. Those who spoiled become spoil to their servants. In v. 15 they become part of God's people. שלל is a quite distinctive word, which is also similar in sound to שלח.

נגע. These two occurrences are too close together to have any structuring function.

שלחני, 12.#8, 13.#14, 15.#17. The form is the same each time except that the second is in pause. Unfortunately the meaning of the first occurrence is obscure. Presumably in the other two we are meant to understand that the speaker is 'the angel who spoke with me', who was to run to the young man in v. 8 (see above). In v. 12 he

---

1.   The emendation to המלמו יושבי את is attractive but makes little difference for our purposes, and is only possibly supported by LXX.

is sent to 'the nations that despoiled you'.

The second and third occurrences are as part of the phrase 'know that Yahweh has sent me to you' which is also found in 4.9b and 6.15b. Both are passages which amplify visions. This, therefore, is clearly a major concern of the editor of at least Zechariah 1–6. The change of person of the addressee from second masculine plural to second feminine singular presents no great difficulty: in vv. 12-13 the prophet has the people of Zion in mind; in vv. 11, 14-15 he addresses the personified Zion.

הנה. As mentioned above, this word occurs alone in vv. 5 and 7. In vv. 13-14 we find כי הנני plus a participle, announcing what Yahweh is about to do. These two pairs of verses do not seem to be closely related, but in the latter case the repetition serves to connect the two verses. This makes it more likely that the author/editor who compiled this section did not intend a break after v. 13. This, in turn, makes it more likely that we really have an intended chiasmus in vv. 13-15.

היה is found in two forms: אהיה (v. 9) and והיו (vv. 13, 15). In v. 13 it seems not to be significant, but a similar construction occurs in v. 15, which perhaps implies a special emphasis on the contrast between the nations' becoming spoil for their enemies and becoming a people for God.

ושכנתי בתוכך 14.##7, 8,15.##11,12. This phrase forms a frame for another important motif in Zechariah, והיו לי לעם (cf. 8.8b; 13.9b), and is found in slightly different form (ושכנתי/ושכנו בתוך ירושלם) in 8.3, 8. The rest of the verse adds the thought that not only Israel but many nations will be joined to her. This is found at the end of both ch. 8 and ch. 14.

Let us look first at what *seems on the surface* to be the clearest part of the section: vv. 13-15. They may be set out as follows:

```
a          For behold I. . .
  A            and you shall know that Yahweh of hosts has sent me
a+         Sing. . .for behold I. . .
    B            and I will dwell in your midst
      C              and many nations shall join themselves to Yahweh
                     on that day, and they shall be to me a people
    B            and I will dwell in your midst
  A            and you . . . know that Yahweh of hosts has sent me to you
```

We notice that A and B are introduced as part of a fuller statement, but are repeated 'neat' at the end (a gather-line?) The fact that we can set down this tidy pattern does not, of course, prove that the writer intended it to be read in this way. However, it may be argued that the phrases considered are certainly significant for the following reasons.

1. They are whole phrases that do not occur elsewhere, except that שׁכן בתוך occurs in 8.3, 8 as another significant and apparently structuring phrase.

2. There are no other repeated words which intervene to distract from this pattern.

3. בתוכה is repeated twice in vv. 8-9.

4. A plausible suggestion can be made as to how an editor might have constructed or augmented this section.

13	contains כי הני and שׁלחני. . .וידעתם.
14	contains כי הני either from the original author or from an editor with a nice sense of structure.
14	also contains the promise ושׁכנתי בתוכך, which has affinities with the covenant promise 'I will be their God and they shall be my people' (cf. 8.3-8).
15a	extends the promise to the nations. It may well come from an editor.
15b	encloses this promise in two distinctive repeated phrases, which address Zion rather than the nations just mentioned. They must be intended as balancing vv. 13 and 14, whether they come from a later editor or not.

However, this is not the whole story, for we note that the two occurrences of 'and you shall know that Yahweh of hosts has sent me (to you)' look more like the conclusion of a section than an envelope. Moreover the imperatives in v. 14a are more at home at the beginning of a section, and we have comparable imperatives in v. 10.#3 and v. 11.#3.[1] It seems more likely, therefore, that we should see the whole passage in this way:

Part 1

10	*Ho! ho! Flee* from the land of the north
	For I scattered you as the four winds of heaven
11	*Ho! Zion! Escape* O dweller with the daughter of Babylon
12 IF	
	(after glory sent me to the nations who *despoiled* you
	for who touches you touches the apple of his eye)
13	*For behold* I will. . .they. . .*spoil* for their servants
	AND YOU SHALL KNOW THAT YAHWEH OF HOSTS SENT ME

---

1.   Cf. Chapter 2 above.

Part 2

14   *Sing* and *rejoice* O daughter of *Zion*
              For *behold I* am coming
                     and I will dwell in your midst (oracle of Yahweh)
15   and many nations will join themselves to Yahweh. . .
                     and THEY WILL BE TO ME FOR A PEOPLE
                     and I will dwell in your midst
                            AND YOU SHALL KNOW THAT YAHWEH OF HOSTS SENT ME. . .

Part 3

16   And Yahweh will inherit Judah his portion in the holy land
         and will again choose Jerusalem

This would seem to be true to the overall sense of the whole of
vv. 10-16. It enables us to see the key points more clearly:

| Flee. . . | Nations (spoilers) to be spoil. . . | You will know. . . |
| Rejoice. . . | Nations to join themselves. . . | You will know. . . |

Notice also that v. 16 forms a nice contrast with vv. 10-11: the
unclean land of the north/Babylon—Judah/Jerusalem, holy/chosen.
The final phrase in v. 16 also links this with the first vision (see
below, Chapter 4). Finally, we note that the general injunction in
v. 17 is completely appropriate here: there is a connection between
the land of Judah (made holy by Yahweh) and his own holy dwelling;
and the verse serves to re-emphasize the universal scope of his
jurisdiction. It is because he is Lord over all flesh that the things
spoken of previously can be proclaimed.

Zechariah 2.5-17

There are some words that are only repeated when we consider
vv. 5-17 together.

עין. The first occurrence is in the introductory formula 'and I lifted
up my eyes' (v. 5), which seems to have no connection with 'the
apple/pupil of his (my?) eye' in v. 12.

יד vv. 5, 13. 'In his hand a measuring line' occurs in a salvation
prophecy for Jerusalem: it will become much greater in extent. 'I am
waving my hand. . . ' is part of a judgment prophecy against
Jerusalem's oppressors. The word 'hand' does not seem to have any
particular significance in itself, nor does it seem to be related to v. 5.

ישׁב, vv. 8, 11. Jerusalem, which now dwells in captivity in
Babylon, v. 11, will dwell as פרזות, villages without walls. We should

probably connect this also with שׁכן, vv. 14-15 (also 8.3, 8; ישׁב also occurs in 1.11; 3.8; 5.7; 6.13; 7.7 [2×]; 8.4, 20-21; 9.5-6; ?10.6; 11.6; 12.5-8, 10; 13.1; 14.10-11), especially since both words are found in 8.1-8. This, as we have already noted, has strong links with the present chapter. The words are used for the people and Yahweh respectively, except that שׁכן is used of the people in 8.8. All the other repeated words are confined to vv. 10-17.

כבוד vv. 9, 12, is an important theological word, which occurs nowhere else in Zechariah. Does v. 9 help to explain the author's intention in v. 12?[1] At this stage we can only say that כבוד is *prima*

---

1.   אחר כבוד שׁלחני is one of the most difficult phrases to interpret in the whole of Zechariah. There is no warrant for altering the text in the ancient versions, and certainly no agreed consensus, so we are bound to keep the MT and to try and make sense of it. The main lines of interpretation have been as follows.

אחר = 'after' in a temporal sense, either as a preposition (e.g. Mitchell *et al.*: 'after the glory [vision] he sent me', *Haggai, Zechariah, Malachi and Jonah*, p. 142) or as a conjunction (e.g. Petitjean: 'Car ainsi a parlé Jahvé Sebaôt, après que la Gloire m'eut envoyé.' He takes כבוד without article or suffix to be a divine appellative, *Les oracles*, p. 117).

Or = 'with'. So R.B.Y. Scott, 'Secondary Meanings of אחר', *JTS* 50 (1949), pp. 178-79; M. Dahood, 'Chiastic Breakup in Isaiah 58.7', *Bib* 44 (1963), pp. 292-93. This is difficult to substantiate.

כבוד = 'glory' meaning the divine presence, or the revelation of the divine glory to the prophet in a vision.

Or = 'heaviness'. Chary (*Les prophètes et le culte*, p. 70) takes this sense, translating אחר as 'with', and obtains the sense: 'with insistence he sent me'. Baldwin finds this most convincing, but both choices are questionable, and the final result is doubly uncertain (*Haggai, Zechariah, Malachi*, p. 109).

שׁלחני. Is the subject of the verb 'he' meaning Yahweh (as at the beginning of the verse) or is כבוד the subject? If it is the latter, then כבוד would have to stand for Yahweh in some sense: Yahweh in his glory. This would give a satisfactory meaning, especially soon after v. 9b: 'I will be in your midst for glory'.

We must also ask to what expression 'to the nations' is attached. Is it 'Thus said Yahweh of hosts' or 'sent me'? The latter is more natural, but if this is right, then who was sent to the nations? It could not have been Zechariah, so perhaps we should think of one of the angels. 'The angel who spoke with Zechariah' is a possibility in 4.9b; but 6.15 seems to refer to Zechariah himself unless we take this verse to be a continuation of 6.8. All in all the latter seems to me to be the best solution.

For a full discussion and list of solutions offered see Rignell, *Die Nachtgesichte*, pp. 84-89; Petitjean, *Les oracles*, pp. 109-19. See also P.R. Ackroyd, *Exile and Restoration* (London: SCM Press, 1968), p. 180.

facie the most likely word to be used to indicate structure, and some correspondence between v. 9 and v. 12 might be intended.

I will adopt a method of proceeding that does not build on the results obtained for vv. 5-9 or 10-17, but treats these verses as one whole unit. We may find confirmation of previous conclusions, or we may be forced to go back and look again. Zech. 2.5-17, as a whole, may be set out as follows:

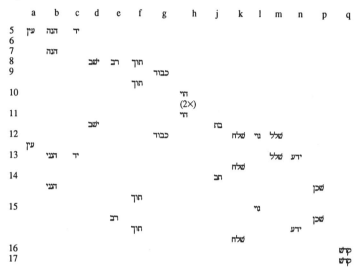

Writing these down mechanically we obtain:

a b c b d e f g f g f h h h d j g k l m a b c m n k j b p f l e p f n k qq
5   7 8   9 10 11   12   13   14   15   16f

We may make the following observations:

1. It is unlikely that the author/editor composed this section by means of algebra. The letters are simply a means of forming hypotheses concerning the plan he had in mind. A repeated word may occur a second time because the first occasion sets off conscious or unconscious associations. The word is not likely to be very significant for the structure if this is the case. A word, therefore, is to be regarded as more important if the second occurrence is:

  a.   Not directly connected with the first.

    b.   A choice from several possibilities—the more unlikely the choice, the more likely it is that the author wants to make a deliberate connection with the first occurrence.

    c.   An important part of a new section.

2. This number of repeated words gives scope for a huge number of possible arrangements. We are forced, therefore, to take the following actions:

    a.   Accept the phrases which must be related to each other (whether as part of a chiasmus, or as a common refrain, or as something as yet undefined), for example, nk, pd.

    b.   Discard the least likely candidates (a, and probably c, e and j).

    c.   Account for the most likely candidates, viz. d, f, g, h, l, m, q. (This leaves b, b' as a doubtful case. We considered that it might be significant in vv. 13 and 14. There, however, it was used identically in the phrase כי הנני; in vv. 5 and 7 the differences make it unlikely to be used even as a short term structuring word).

    d.   Keep in mind and refer always to the text and its meaning and direction.

3. Verses 16 and 17 have no verbal links with the rest of the section; v. 17 is different in nature and was almost always regarded as a later addition by older commentators. This view has now been seriously challenged.[1] The verse has a liturgical feel to it, and is similar to Isa. 2.22 and Hab. 2.20. Must we also think of v. 16 as such? The phrase ובחר עוד ירושלם occurs identically in 1.17 and this points to the hand of the final editor, always allowing for minor additions after the last main redaction.

We thus arrive at the following pattern:

---

1. See, e.g., Rudolph, *Haggai*, pp. 91-92. He argues that this is not a 'nachträglich angefügte liturgische Formel', against Elliger and others, and supporting Chary, Beuken and Petitjean. Rudolph draws attention to the connection between vv. 14 and 17, and we ask why we have not noticed this. The answer is that the idea of dwelling is expressed by שכן in vv. 14-15, but מעון is used in v. 17. The idea of Yahweh rousing himself from his dwelling and coming to dwell with his people in Jerusalem is probably clear enough to be spotted without verbal similarity, and therefore counts as one of those features of the text which our method alone will miss. The words are a recognizable word pair, as far as our evidence goes.

(b)	(b)	d	f	g	f	hhh	d	g-k-l-m	(b')	m	nk	(b')	pf	l	pf	nk	(qq)
5	6	7	8	9		10-11		12		13			14		15		16-17

Possibilities. dfgfd...g. This is not plausible because of the gap between the second f and d; it is much more likely that dfgf hhh dg represents the author/editor's intention. If we regard the first two f's as a preparation for the second two in vv. 14-15, then dg hhh dg represents a chiastic structure of some sort.[1] This is plausible because of the prominent position of the identical form בתוכה at the end of v. 8 and v. 9, and because ישב and כבוד are both important in this context. We need to ask whether this helps to explain the meaning and/or composition of the text. Following up this lead we note the similarity between the ideas expressed in the climax to v. 9, ולכבוד אהיה בתוכה, and in vv. 14b-15b.

We note that hhh dg represents the first three verses of the supposed editorial addition, or at least elaboration of what has gone before. After a general prophecy concerning the material well-being of Jerusalem that is to come, there is an indication of how this is to be brought about. Jerusalem will *dwell* as unwalled villages (v. 8)...but to bring this about the one who *dwells* with the daughter of Babylon must escape (v. 11). It is unfortunate that the meaning of אחר כבוד (v. 12) is so obscure but it is probable that it has some connection with לכבוד in v. 9.[2] It is interesting that v. 8 has פרזות whereas פרשׂתי occurs in v. 10: the contrast between being spread abroad because of God's blessing and scattered because of God's judgment is striking.

Verse 12 looks like an attempt to tie together the two parts of the whole section (vv. 5-15) since אחר כבוד is immediately followed by שלחני, and several other words which seem to be significant in what follows (viz. גוים, שלל, cf. בבבח). The overall structure of vv. 10-15 could, moreover, be more clearly seen with v. 12 omitted; we should simply need to replace אליהם by הגוים השללים אתכם or a similar phrase.[3]

---

1. In Watson's terminology this is split member chiasmus (Welch [ed.], *Chiasmus in Antiquity*, pp. 124-25). He expresses it ab-c // c-ab; we simply have a stronger centre. Examples offered are: Judg. 1.15; Isa. 13.21b; 27.11b; 43.15; 60.2b, 20; 64.1a; Hos. 4.9; Hab. 2.1; Pss. 7.16; 15.3b; Job 10.5; 19.9.

2. See p. 106 n. 1.

3. G.A. Smith apparently omits v. 12. R.L. Smith (*Nahum–Malachi*, p. 196) claims, without giving references, that Watts and Ackroyd move 2.12-13 to follow 2.4. Actually the latter only says that '[2.12f.] links closely to [2.1-4]' (*PCB*, p. 647).

Perhaps we should note the repeated נגע as a point of emphasis.

This leads to the question of how we regard the last part of the above string. The most obvious possibility may be represented like this:

k <u>l</u> m—m nk <u>pf l pf</u> nk

However, we have seen above that nk is likely to be a concluding formula rather than part of an envelope. We must, therefore, take a larger section together and may depict the structure as:

d f g f <hhh d g k b' l m—m nk> <b' pf l pf nk>

This suggests that vv. 10-17 are to be thought of as a *supplement* to vv. 5-9. Its basic form consists of two sections ending with the refrain nk. The first of these picks up the d and g (ישב and כבוד of vv. 8b-9); the second makes use of f (בתוך/ה/ך]; also vv. 8b-9).

This seems to be more than merely a subjective apprehension of patterns which had no place in the thoughts of the writer, for we have examined *all* repeated words, and have tried to minimize subjectivity by considering the distinctiveness and function of each one. We may be able to confirm this if we discover similar method elsewhere in Zechariah, or even in other parts of the Old Testament.

If this reasoning is sound, it suggests that the editor responsible for the final version of chs. 1–8 *supplemented* the visions reports, with a concern to produce a regularly structured whole. This would agree with our conclusions for ch. 1.[1]

Zechariah 3

The word numbers of words occurring twice or more in ch. 3 (omitting only על, אל and אמר) are given in figure 4. We have seen evidence in chs. 1–2 for the view that the text as we have it is the result of two separate processes. We have not yet found strong evidence to enable us to decide between an author-plus-later-editor or an

---

1. It is interesting to compare Schöttler's account of how 2.10-17 was formed: 11; 10a + 12a + 13; 14; 15a + 16; 17; plus two 'textkritische Glossen': 12a, 15ab; and a 'formelhafte Glosse' 12b (pp. 84-85). I believe that the progression of thought and the logical structure I have suggested should make this sort of detailed form-critical analysis virtually impossible to accept.

original-draft-revised theory. In considering this chapter we have to bear in mind that:

1. The majority of commentators believe vv. 8-10 to be an addition to the original text.[1]
2. many scholars believe that this fourth vision is an addition to an original series of seven.[2]

The word ראה may be omitted from consideration, since the uses ('And he caused me to see' and 'See!') are very different and quite far apart.

It is noticeable that יהוה צבאת occurs only at the end of vv. 1-7, and (with נאם) in vv. 9-10, that is at the climax of this whole section. All the other words can be seen to have a specific function in the construction of these verses.

The first notable repeated words are 'Joshua the high priest' (1.##3-5, 8.##3-5). 'Joshua' alone occurs in vv. 3, 6 and 9. In v. 8 the expression introduces a new section and so only rounds off the first section indirectly. However, with Joshua the high priest are included 'your companions who dwell before you, who are men of מופת (sign, wonder, "good omen"?)'.[3] Some correspondence with מפתח (9.#12)

---

1. Petitjean, as usual, gives a full discussion (*Les oracles*, pp. 161-206). He believes that J.W. Rothstein (*Die Nachtgesichte des Sacharja* [Leipzig: Hinrichs, 1910], pp. 87-89) showed that vv. 1-7 were originally an independent pericope, before they were introduced into their present context. Scholars supporting this theory include Sellin, Elliger, Rignell, Eichrodt, Eissfeldt, Rudolph (who also regards vv. 8b and 10 as secondary to vv. 8-10; *Haggai*, pp. 98-103). Mitchell (following Marti) treats vv. 6-10 together but regards v. 8b as a gloss (*Haggai, Zechariah, Malachi and Jonah*, pp. 154-56). Petersen calls vv. 6-10 'The Responses' (*Haggai and Zechariah,* p. 202), regards v. 8 as intrusive and designed to support Zerubbabel against Joshua (pp. 208-14). Beuken holds a novel view: 1-5 + 8-10 are a literary unity, into which vv. 6-7 have been inserted (*Haggai–Sacharja*, pp. 282-303). This is connected with his view that Zechariah comes from a 'Chronistic milieu'.

2. E.g. Horst, Elliger, Chary, C. Jeremias. Many recognize that it forms a unity with the fifth vision. E.g. Beuken (see note above), Amsler (*Agée, Zacharie, Malachi*, p. 58).

3. The word means 'wonder, sign, portent' (BDB, p. 68), here signifying a 'sign or token of a future event' presumably the coming of 'my servant, צמה', cf. Isa. 8.18. Joshua's companions are almost certainly also priests (cf., e.g., Amsler, *Agée, Zacharie, Malachi*, p. 83, Mitchell, *Haggai, Zechariah, Malachi and Jonah*, pp. 147, 155-56).

Verses Word	1	2	3	4	5	6	7	8	9	10
1 ראה	1			13						
2 יהושע הכן הגדול	3-5							3-5		
3 יהושע			1			4			7	
4 עמד	6.11		6	4	16		25			
5 לפני	7		7	5				9	6	
6 מלאך	8		8		14	2				
7 יהוה	9	6.10			15	3	3		17	4
8 צבאת							4		18	5
9 שׂטן	10.14	4.8								
10 נער		5.9								
11 לבש			3	17	12					
12 בגד			4	8	13					
13 צואה			5	9						
14 עון				16					21	
15 שׂים צניף טהור על ראשׁ				7-11	2-6					
16 הלך							7.23			
17 שׁמר							10f.,18			
18 נתן							21		5	
19 רע								7		8
20 אישׁ								11		7
21 הנה								15	2.13	
22 אבן									3.9	
23 אחד									10.25	
24 פתח									14f.	
25 נאם									16	3
26 יום									24	1
27 חתת										10.13

Figure 4: *Zechariah 3: Word numbers of words occurring twice or more*
(omitting על אמר and אל)

may be intended here. In any case note that the chapter is divided into two very logical subsections by these marker words:

1-7	And he showed me Joshua the high priest. . .
8a	Hear now Joshua the high priest You and your *companions* who sit before me. . . . . . they are *men* of מופת
8b-10	. . . they will call, a *man* to his *companion*, under vine and under fig tree.

This gives preliminary support to the division recognized by most scholars, as noted above. It would be possible to divide the chapter into vv. 1-5 (*about* Joshua) and vv. 6-10 (*to* Joshua) as Keil does.[1] Structural, as well as form-critical considerations suggest that the primary division in the final writer's mind was vv. 1-7, 8-10. This is not to deny further subdivisions or the new element in v. 6.

There seems to be some significance in the use of the expressions לפני and עמד:

1a	Joshua was *standing before* the *angel* of Yahweh
1b	the opposer/accuser was *standing* at his right hand to oppose/accuse him
3b	Joshua (in dirty garments) was *standing before* the *angel*

This forms a self-contained section on its own through the three word inclusio. The last phrase is unnecessary to the sense, and the editors of *BHS* want to delete it.[2] They have certainly noted the phrase as a mark of some sort.

In vv. 4-7 we have the following situation:

4a	And he (the angel) said to those who were *standing before* him (Joshua) (Joshua has his clothes changed)

---

1. See, e.g., Meyers, *Haggai, Zechariah*, pp. 178-79, 222-24 (vv. 8-10 are a 'Supplementary Oracle'); Rudolph, *Haggai*, pp. 93-94, 99-100 ('ein weiteres Heilswort').

2. This is of course characteristic of their approach: what Muilenburg might have called 'form criticism and not beyond'. *BHS* wants to delete (or at least note as 'prb add') several other phrases that we have thought to be significant, notably 'and you shall know that Yahweh of hosts has sent me' in 2.13, 15; 4.9 and 6.15;. . .ים in 10.11 (from 9.4 mistakenly); ומלאך יהוה אמר in 3.3, 5; ומשב is regarded as a gloss in 9.8.

5bβ   And the *angel* of Yahweh was *standing*. . .(dittography from what
             follows?)

7b   And I will give you מהלכים among these who *are standing*

This situation may be represented as follows:

1-3	Sja	(Joshua standing before the angel)
	Ssj	(Satan before Joshua)
	Sja	
4-7	Spj	(People standing before Joshua)
	Sa	(Angel standing)
	Spj	

The participles (which they all are) form genuine inclusios and (again)
divide up the section logically. Verses 1-3 describe the scene and
Yahweh's intention; vv. 4-7 describe the symbolic vindication of
Joshua (and therefore Jerusalem).

Verses 1-3 have the root שמן once and the noun three times; also the
verb נער twice. These repetitions seem to be for emphasis and not to
indicate structure. Two words לבש and בגד occur in vv. 1-3 and 4-8
(both words once each in vv. 3, 4, 5). This does not interfere with the
division but links the two parts together. Within vv. 4-8 we find the
following pattern:

4aβ	Take off the garments (בגדים), the filthy ones, from upon him
4bα	And he said to him
	See I have taken away from upon you your sin
4bβ	and clothe (הלבש)[1] you with rich apparel
5aα	And I said[2]
5aβ	Let them set a turban, a clean one, upon his head
5bα1	and they set the turban, the clean one, upon his head
5bα2	and they clothed him with garments
(5bβ	and the angel of Yahweh was standing)

---

1. Is this an imperative or an infinitive? The Septuagint reading καὶ ἐνδύσατε
αὐτον represents הלבישו אתו which would be more natural if we assume that 4bβ
follows directly from 4aβ, or if we put 4bα in parenthesis. The imperative with אתך
does not make good sense.

2. This is usually emended to 'And he said' followed by an imperative. This is
supported by Vulg. and perhaps Syr. and Targ. The LXX has καὶ ἐπίθηκαν which
is evidently to be understood as an imperative in view of the ἐπέθηκαν following.

There appears to be some textual corruption, and it is not clear whether 4bβ should be construed as:

1. Yahweh's continuing declaration of his action (which seems to be the meaning of the MT).[1]
2. A continuation of the narrative: 'they clothed him in rich apparel'. This has not yet been commanded and may be considered premature. It also requires a major change in the text.
3. A continuation of the imperative: 'and clothe him',[2] which makes the best sense, especially if we are prepared to move 4b to the end of v. 5.

The present text is the most difficult and we should retain it. This gives us the following pattern:

(-) $a^1b^1c^1d^1$	הסירו הבנדים הצאים מעליו
	ויאמר אליו ראה
(-) $a^2d^2b^2$	העברתי מעליך עונך
(+) $a^3d^3b^3$	והלבש אתך מחלצות
	ואמר
(+) $a^4b^4c^2d^4$	ישימו צניף טהור על ראשו
(+) $a^4b^4c^2d^4$	וישימו הצניף הטהור על ראשו
(+) $a^3(d^3)b^1$	וילבשו בנדים

This strange section exhibits the following characteristics:

1. The two negative actions 'taking off filthy clothes' and 'taking away sin' are put first. One is a physical action and one is a 'spiritual' one.
2. The reports of the two positive physical actions (putting on a clean gown, and 'garments') are put together last.
3. In the middle are the anticipations of these two actions spoken by Yahweh (and 'I' ?).
4. בנדים forms an inclusio for this section (b¹) within the עמד/עמדים already mentioned.

The remaining part of vv. 1-7 (viz. vv. 5bβ-7) is again enclosed by עמד (5.#16) and העמדים. A symmetry is again noticeable:

---

1. GKC 113z, infinitive absolute with 2 m. sing. object as in 4bα. This would represent the continuation of a finite verb.
2. GKC recommends והלבשו אתו ('with Wellhausen, after the LXX'); see above.

Thus says Yahweh of hosts,

p   If you will walk (הלך) in my ways

  q   and if you will keep my charge (שמר משמרתי)

    r   then also you will judge my house

  q   and you will also keep (שמר) my courts

p   and I will also give you access (?) (מהלכים)

Such unusual words are used that it is unlikely that the resulting structure is accidental.

The remainder of ch. 3 does not show a structure obviously similar to anything we have met before. The phrase ומשתי את עון הארץ ההיא is obviously a further interpretation of העברתי מעליך עונך (4bα). There are extra ingredients which are unexpected: 'I am bringing my servant "the branch" (צמח)', 'the stone which I have set before Joshua', and 'upon one stone with seven עינים I am inscribing its inscription'. All three are introduced and given some emphasis by הנה. The stone is mentioned again in ch. 4 and the 'branch' in chs. 4 and 6. There seems at least to be a deliberate intention to link these symbols with each other and with the cleansing action of Yahweh on Jerusalem's behalf.[1]

It remains to ask whether we have ignored significant marker words. The only possibilities are the following

לפני, vv. 8-9. As Joshua stood before Yahweh, and Satan before Joshua, here Joshua's companions dwell/sit before him, and Yahweh puts a stone before him. It does seem to be indicative of significant relationships throughout the chapter.

עון, vv. 4, 9, serves to link the interpretation in vv. 8-10 with the preceding vision. As previously, a key word is taken up by the final editor.

נתן is used in vv. 7, 9 with מהלכים and (strictly speaking, as in MT, שבעה עינים). There may be some linking function: both have the first person singular *qal* perfect with Yahweh as the speaker, and both are addressed to Joshua.

אחד occurs in two different forms, which makes it unlikely to be a marker word, despite its prominent position at the end of v. 9.

אבן, פתח, יום and תחת are too close together to be significant for the overall structure.

---

1. Cf. esp. 13.1.

We have discovered a carefully constructed whole with clear inclusios and chiastic arrangements, even though the sense is not always entirely clear, and the arrangement does not always seem to us the most logical. There seems to be a sensitivity to the sounds of words, and it might be worthwhile to give more attention to this aspect of the text. (E.g. נער–יער, עין–עון, מפתח–מופח)

My primary concern is not with the question of authorship of the book of Zechariah. If it were, then I believe the evidence we have uncovered in looking at the structure of ch. 3 would be worth a more thorough investigation. It seems to me that the method of the writing employed in vv. 1-7 and 8-10 is remarkably similar to that which we saw in chs. 1–2.

Since we have now discovered evidence of a concern for structure in three out of three chapters, the chances that chs. 1–8 are carefully constructed are increased. If the editor who arranged the final form of chs. 1–8 was responsible for chs. 1–14, then we should expect to see signs of his hand there too. If we do not find this then it becomes more likely that we have two independent works that have been joined together at a later date. We might find evidence of a different type of sectional and/or overall editing.

Zechariah 4.1-6aα, 6aβ-10aα, 10aβ-14

As previously a table of words occurring at least twice in the chapter is given (figure 5). The centre section, Zech. 4.6a-10a, is, in precise terms, 4.6.#5-10.#12.

Virtually all scholars regard the middle section of this chapter as a parenthesis, and most agree that it was inserted by a later editor.[1] It has strong connections with other editorial sections (cf. 2.13, 15; 6.15), so we have here a clear example of an editor's work. We

---

1. The Meyers' (*Haggai, Zechariah*, pp. 265-72) regard it as having been added by the prophet himself, or (less probably) by a disciple; Beuken finds a core of original material in 4.1-3 + 4-5 + 6a + 10b + 6a-7, to which were added in this order: vv. 8-10a; 11 + 13-14; 10b moved to its present position; 12 (*Haggai–Sacharja*, pp. 259-63, esp. p. 264). This cannot be more than an interesting theory from the point of view of the enquiry we are engaged in. Petersen treats vv. 6a-10a as a later interpolation, and in addition makes the novel suggestion that v. 12 was added in order to 'cloud what was a rather clear picture of divine dependence' (*Haggai and Zechariah*, pp. 236-37).

Verses / Word	1	2	3	4	5	6aα	6aβ	7	8	9	10aα	10aβ	11	12	13	14
מלאך	2			4	2											
דבר	3			5	3	6n			2n							
עור	5,8															
אמר		1,6		2,7	5,12	2,4	10,18		5				2	3	1,3,8	1
אל		2		3	6	3	8		4	13			3	4	2	
מה		3		8	9			ם			ם		4	5	6	
אתה		4						2								
ראה		5,7								7						
מנורה		9											10			
(נר)		16,21														
זהב		10												13,16		
(כל)		(11)											19↓			9↓
גלה		12	6													
על		3×	3,8										8,11	15		7
ראש		14,24						11								
שבעה		3×									13					
שנ(/ת)ים			1										5	(6),11		3
זית			2										6	8		
אחד			4,7													
ימין			5										9			
שמאל			9										12			
ענה				1	1	1							1	1		
אלה				9	11						14	7			7	2
אדון				10	14										10	8
ל(ו)א				7,13		11,13										4,9
ידע				8					8					5		
המה				10							17					
זה						5			5							
יהוה						7,19		3	10		16					
זרבבל						9	6		2	12						
כי						15			9	1						
צבאה						20			11							
מי								1		2						
אבן								10		9						
חן								13f.								
יד										1,6	11			10		
כל-ארץ													19f.			9f.

Figure 5: *Zech. 4.1-6aα, 6aβ-10aα, 10aβ-14:*
Word numbers of words occurring twice or more

hope therefore to gain some insight into his methods.

Even a cursory glance at the table of recurring words suggests that there is a difference between the outer and middle sections. Few words are repeated in both apart from very common ones.

Zechariah 4.1-6aα and 10aβ-14

המלאך הדבר בי, vv. 1, 4, 5. The second and third instances seem to be part of a literary device to delay the answer to a question and to heighten the tension. 'Angel' does not occur elsewhere in the chapter, not even on its own. The other part of the delaying phrase is 'And he said to me, "Do you not know what these are?" And I said to him, "No, my Lord."' (vv. 5, 13). The answers come in vv. 10 and 13. The first is immediately after the oracular insertion, where the phrase שבע אלה makes it clear that the explanation is to be of the seven נרות and not the two olive trees. As noted above, the explanation שבעה אלה עיני יהוה could also refer to the stone set before Joshua with שבעה עניים in 3.9.

אמר, אל, על, לא may be ignored as common words.

מה should probably be retained. It helps to characterize the outer sections as dominated by the question 'What?', and even makes a contrast with the middle section where 'Who?' is found in vv. 7, 10.[1]

כל occurs in the expression כל הארץ in vv. 10 and 14 but may be ignored in v. 2.

ראה is one of only three words occurring in the outer and middle sections which could possibly be thought to be significant for the structure. We must keep it.

שמאל, ימין, אחד, זית, שנים, שבעה, זהב, נר, מנורה. These are all used in the description of the vision. Most of them recur in order to explain the meaning of the vision. They may be regarded as 'technical terms'. However, this does not mean they may be discounted completely. For example, the expressions '(one) on the right and (one) on the left' involves some apparently unnecessary repetition which may therefore be significant.

ראש is used in the description of the details of the lampstand in v. 2, while in v. 7 the feminine form ראשה, unique in the Hebrew Bible, is used in apposition to אבן. There does not seem to be a connection between these instances.

---

1. The English translation 'whoever' in v. 10, which is certainly appropriate, should not obscure the fact that מי occurs twice.

המה, ידע, אדון, אלה, ענה. These all occur in connection with the delaying tactics of the author of the outer sections. It is true that ידע occurs also in v. 9b as part of the important phrase 'and you will know that Yahweh of hosts has sent me', but it is difficult to show any significant connection between this and the outer sections.[1] None of them, therefore, seems particularly important for our purposes.

This leaves the expression כל הארץ (vv. 10, 14 only). It occurs as the last element in each of the two informative answers of the angel, which marks it as an important element in the vision.

The Sequence of Thought in the Outer Sections of Zechariah 4

In vv. 1-3 Zechariah is asked what he sees and describes two main items:

1. A menorah with a bowl on top having seven lamps, each with seven lips.
2. Two olive trees (right and left of the bowl).

It is only Zechariah's description which informs the reader of the contents of the vision.

Verse 4 contains Zechariah's question, 'What are these?' The question is vague, and the reader will presumably expect an explanation of both features. However, we actually find:

1. A delaying counter-question.
2. A prophetic oracle.
3. An explanation of 'these seven' only.

This necessitates a further question about the olive trees (v. 11) which is explained in v. 14 after the second delay: 'Do you not know...' (v. 13). They are the two בני היצהר. Still another question is attached to v. 11: 'What are these two branches...and the two golden pipes...?' This looks like a secondary addition. Without it the answer in v. 14 refers unambiguously to the two olive trees. With it, the answer is not clear.[2] Could the 'two sons of oil' be both the olive trees *and* the two צנתרות הזהב 'from which the gold is poured out (?)'? It

---

1. A contrast between the prophet's present ignorance and the future knowledge of the people might be conjectured. It seems to be too tenuous to entertain seriously.

2. This is agreed by most commentators. Petersen regards it as deliberate obfuscation (see above).

seems unlikely, but we need to ask why this strange verse has been inserted, and whether the connections it has with other parts of the book are significant: ביד (v. 10a); זהב (v. 2; 6.11; 13.9; 14.14). The structure may be set out as follows:

Description of the Vision	
('angel who spoke with me' prominent)	
Seven lamps. . .	D1
Two olive trees	D2
Questioning (ambiguous; assumed to be about '7')	Q1
Delay	
Counter-question	CQ
Long interruption	[. . .]
Answer	
Answer to Q1 (with respect to the '7')	A1
Question (about the '2' ; elaborated)	Q2
(Wording of v. 11b very close to v. 3)	
Delay	
Counter-question	CQ
Answer to Q2 (with respect to the '2')	A2

This is not a surprising result. Rather, it confirms that our method does reveal and confirm patterns that could be detected by the more traditional methods of OT scholarship. We have not relied on subjective labelling, nor the selection of certain words as significant at the expense of others. This is the pattern that is actually there in the text, and it seems very likely that the author intended it.

We may ask about the purpose of the insertion. Why was it inserted? Why was it inserted *here*? Could it have been by the author himself? These questions will be taken up after discussion of the middle section itself.

Zechariah 4.6aβ-10aα

The words occurring twice or more may be summarized as follows.

מי occurs in 7.1 and 10.2. We cannot make much of this, but see above (מה).

זו may be ignored. The first instance begins a sentence which makes it prominent, but the second is simply an adjective 'this house' (9.5).

יהוה occurs once on its own as part of the stereotyped expression

דבר יהוה, which may be discounted. יהוה צבאות occurs twice, the first time to close the pithy oracle of v. 6b, the second time as part of the important oracle of v. 9b (cf 2.13, 15; 6.15b).

זרבבל occurs in vv. 6, 7, 9 and 10, and is clearly the most distinctive single word in the section. See below.

כי occurs three times, and is used in three different ways. It may be ignored.

אבן occurs twice: האבן הראשה, 7.10-11; האבן הבדיל, 10.8-9. The relation of these to each other is not clear.[1] The more obvious understandings of 'top stone' and 'plummet' should probably be retained. The second of these may still be chosen specially to correspond with the first.[2]

חן only occurs in 7.13-14, and therefore does not count as a repeated word from our point of view.

יד occurs with זרבבל to form a strong inclusio for the oracle of vv. 9-10aα: 'the hands of Zerubbabel' occurs right at the beginning, and 'in the hand of Zerubbabel' right at the end. The other occurrence belongs with the first: 'The hands of Zerubbabel. . . and his hands. . .' Note that it is ביד that occurs again in v. 12.

The *structure* of this somewhat obscure section is fairly clear. The oracle of vv. 9-10 is introduced by a weighty introductory formula.[3]

---

1. G.R. Driver translated 'the stone (called) Possession' and 'the stone (called) Separation' ('Babylonian and Hebrew Notes', *WO* 2 (1954), p. 22). This links and contrasts the two instances. Petersen (*Haggai and Zechariah,* pp. 237-42) has 'the former stone', meaning a stone taken from the former Temple and used in the rebuilding (based on R. Ellis, *Foundation Deposits in Ancient Mesopotamia* [1968]), and 'the tin tablet'. For further suggestions see Petitjean, *Les oracles,* pp. 230-36; Meyers, *Haggai, Zechariah,* pp. 246-49, 253-54.

2. Amos 7.7-8 uses the word ענך, and other possible references to a plummet occur in 2 Kgs 21.13 and Isa. 28.17 (משך/אלה). It is obvious that we do not know what was the *normal* expression for a plummet. We do know that the word אבן occurs twice.

3. Petitjean moves it to the beginning of the insertion, resulting in an original oracle of vv. 8 + 6a-7 + 9-10a (*Les oracles,* pp. 263-67; [not 4.8-10a, 6b-7; and not pp. 263-68; as in Meyers, *Haggai, Zechariah,* p. 250]). See esp. pp. 239-40. where he analyses principal and secondary introductory formulae and conclusions ('The word of Yahweh came to me. . .'; 'You shall say, "Thus says Yahweh. . . " '; and 'And you shall know. . .') in Zech. 6.9-15 and in various passages in Ezekiel. Cf. 1.1, 7; 7.4, 8; 8.1, 18. We should not assume, however, that 4.9b is simply a concluding formula, despite the fact that Rudolph would like to move it to the end of

This, together with the fact that the oracle is marked off by an inclusio, confirms that we should consider the text that we now have as made up of two main parts.[1]

6		This is a word to Zerubbabel
		Not by might. . . strength, but by my Spirit
		says Yahweh Sebaoth
7		Who are you, great mountain?[2]
		before Zerubbabel למישר
		and he/one will bring forth האבן הראשה
		shouts (תשואות)
8	IF	And the word of Yahweh came to me saying
9		The hands of Zerubbabel founded this house, and
		his hands will finish it
		and you will know that Yahweh Sebaoth has sent me to you
10		For who has despised (בזו + ל) day of small things?
		And they will rejoice
		and they will see the stone, the tin
		in the hand of Zerubbabel

This does not exhibit clear signs of editorial planning. It seems to me to be less tightly structured than any of the sections we have so far considered. As it stands it has no proper introductory or concluding formulae, and must be regarded as dependent upon the outer sections of ch. 4. It has certain ragged features, for example the changes of person are frequent and abrupt; we find: 3 sing. of Yahweh, Zerubbabel and 'whoever' ; 2 m.sing. addressing the mountain; 3 pl. indefinite; 2 m.pl. (2 f.pl. of 'hands' is understandable). Nevertheless, there is a

the section (*Haggai*, pp. 111-12).

1. Petersen and the majority of commentators hold to the two sections mentioned here. Petitjean argues for a unified oracle, after moving v. 8 to the beginning. Amsler has three separate oracles: vv. 6ab, 7, 8-10a (*Agée, Zacharie, Malachi*, pp. 92-95).

2. The mountain has been interpreted as difficulties facing Zerubbabel (van Hoonacker, Rignell, Baldwin); or as personal opposition from Persian (Sellin) or Samaritan (Elliger, Rudolph) sources; or as Joshua the rival to Zerubbabel (Petersen); or as mythical forces (Horst). See Amsler, *Agée, Zacharie, Malachi*, p. 93. Whatever is the case, the purpose of addressing the mountain is to encourage Zerubbabel to believe that God will enable him to succeed in the task to which he has been called, and to make clear to the people that God *has* called him, and his completion of the task will be a sign of Yahweh's involvement through him.

coherence about it. The general principle, 'Not by might...but by my Spirit' sets the context in which the rest is read, and is reflected in the cries of 'Grace, grace, to it', and in the rather low-key evidence of Yahweh's presence, the foundation and completion of the Temple.[1]

Zechariah 4 as a whole

We may now put forward a possible explanation of the text of Zechariah 4 as we now have it. We shall need also to refer to ch. 3. Certain facts may be stated with confidence.

Zechariah 3 is different from the other visions. It is thought by most commentators to be later than the basic material of Zechariah 1–8. It introduces a historical individual, Joshua the high priest.

The outer sections of Zechariah 4 present two individuals. These can naturally be understood to be Joshua and Zerubbabel, who are mentioned in the book of Zechariah only rarely:

Joshua	3.1-10; 6.9-15
צמח	(3.8) (6.12)
Zerubbabel	4.6aβ-10aα.

Without these passages the identification would be obscure. This raises the question when the oracle about Zerubbabel was inserted into the narrative. Most commentators have assumed it to be one of the latest additions to the text, and we have found some evidence to support this, in that it does not seem to be constructed or inserted with quite so much care as the sections previously examined. This is, however, little more than an impression. Beuken is unique in regarding the original oracle as 4.1, 2a, 2b-3, 4, 5, 6a + 10b, 6a-7[2] From our point of view this is not of primary importance.

These two chapters of Zechariah contain the two central visions of the series. The position seems to be significant, as does the mention of Joshua and צמח in 6.9-15, at the very end of the series of visions.

---

1. It is interesting that the word for 'finish' is from the root בצע which means to 'cut, break off, gain by violence'; the meaning 'finish' occurs otherwise only in Isa. 10.12; Lam. 2.17. This may or may not be significant: the violence that Zerubbabel will commit will be to finish the Temple. I should not put any weight on this conjecture.

2. Beuken, *Haggai–Sacharja*, pp. 258-70, esp. 263-64. This is largely based on a form-critical comparison of ch. 4 and 5.1-4.

It is probable that Zechariah 4 was compiled in at least two stages.[1] The texts that we may consider to be redactional units are:

1. The final text as we have it.
2. Verses 1-6aβ + 10aα-14.

Verse 12 may have been absent from 2 and even 1 at some time. It is not clear what it is meant to add (clarification or confusion?); it does pick up one expression, ביד, from the middle section of the chapter, although it refers to the two צנתרות (which must have some connection with the two olive trees) rather than simply Zerubbabel; and it is used in the sense of 'beside' and not 'in the hand of'.

The final redactor intended the readers to note, not only the promises from Yahweh to the effect that he will restore Jerusalem, but that:

1. Joshua the priest has a special function in Yahweh's purposes.
2. Zerubbabel either is 'the Branch' or represents him.
3. Zerubbabel will finish the Temple.
4. The people will know that Yahweh has sent someone to them.[2]

We have already strayed, inevitably, into the proper subject matter of Chapter 4, since chs. 3 and 4 must be interpreted together with 6.9-15. Accordingly I defer further discussion.[3]

---

1. This is the view of most scholars and is assumed here, although I do not think we have very much evidence of the sort of literary construction that might be received in a vision. Our main concern is to understand the significance of the structure.

Opinions vary about this. Petersen regards these verses as pro-Zerubbabel against Joshua, and since ch. 4 as a whole regards the two as on a par, it was necessary to insert vv. 6a-10a at this point. The Meyers' believe that 6b-10a was placed here deliberately to separate the two parts of the vision, and this emphasizes its importance; it was added early by Zechariah or (less probably) a disciple; since Zerubbabel's title and patronymic are consistently omitted, unlike Haggai, we must assume that Zechariah's view was that a Davidide would only become king again in the future, after Zerubbabel's time.

2. See on 2.5-17 above.
3. See the section on Zech. 3 in Chapter 4 below.

Zechariah 5.1-4 + 5-11

It is convenient to present one table (figure 6) displaying references to repeated words in both 5.1-4 and 5-11, since they are short sections and, like the second and third visions, they have much in common.

Zechariah 5.1-4

This sixth vision (V6) has some obvious parallels with the third (2.5-9)[1] as can be seen in the use of several words.

'Its length... and its breadth' (v. 2). This seems to be an unusual addition. It is not mentioned in v. 1, and we are not told how Zechariah knew the measurements. It recalls 2.6 'to measure Jerusalem, to see what is its breadth and... length'.

'Abide [but לון, not ישׁב] in the midst of his house' (v. 4) recalls 2.8-9. 'multitude of men and cattle in the midst' and 'glory in the midst'. These and other parallels will be investigated in Chapter 4 below.

The repeated words function as follows:

ראה (1, 2 [2×]) is used three times instead of one because the common device of question and answer is used. Whereas previously Zechariah has questioned the angel, here the angel questions him (cf. Amos's first two and second two visions Amos 7.1-9, 8.1-3).

מגלה עפה occurs twice only: once in the description of what the prophet saw, and once in his answer to the angel's question. One wonders whether the question is in order to impress the phrase more clearly upon the hearers.

---

1.   There is a difference of opinion among scholars, as mentioned previously, as to whether Zech. 3 should be counted as one of the visions in the cycle. This makes for a discrepancy in labelling them. We regard Zech. 3 as the fourth vision (V4), since this is how it is presented in our received text, and therefore we have VV1-8. There is also a difference in the way that scholars see the correspondence of the visions to one another. A. Jepsen ('Kleine Beiträge zum Zwölfprophetenbuch III', *ZAW* 61 (1945–48), pp. 95-114 [97], quoted in K. Seybold, *Bilder zum Tempelbau: Die Visionen des Propheten Sacharja* [Stuttgarter Biblestudien; Stuttgart: KBW, 1974], p. 35) gave the following scheme (in my own system of labelling):

I	II	III	V (Zech. 4)
VIII	VII	VI	

We shall be considering these claims in Chapter 4.

Verses / Word	1	2	3	4	5	6	7	8	9	10	11
נשא	(2)				7		4		1,14		
עין	(3)				9	10			2		
ראה	4	5,8									
הנה	(5)						1		4		
מגלה	6	9									
עפה	7	10									
אמר		1,6	1		etc.						
אמה		13,16									
יצא			5	1	1,12	7			7		
כל			8,11 16			11					
גנב			12	8							
כמה			14,19								
נקה			15,20								
נשבע			17	11							
ביח				7,10 16							
תוך				(15)			9	7			
יצא			5	1	1,12	7			7		
מלאך					2					3	
דבר					3					4	
אמר		1,6	1		5	1,4,8		1		1	1
אל		2	2	6,9	6			6,13		2	2
נשא	2				7		4		1,14		
עין	3				9	10			2		
ראה	4	5,8			10				3		
מה					11	2					
זאת					13	5,9	5	2			
איפה						6	10	8	16	10	
כל			8,11,16			(11)					
ארץ			9			12			18		6
הנה	5						1		4		
עפרח							3	12			
אשה							6		6		
תוך				15			9	7			
השליך								4,9			
כנף									9,11f.		
בין									17,19		
טן											8,12

Figure 6: *Zech. 5.1-4 + 5-11:*
Word numbers of words occurring twice or more

There may be some similarity intended between עפה and איפה

The next words do not seem to be significant: אמר and אמה, and we shall ignore them.

יצא is a common word in Zechariah; it is normally used of the angels but here the usage seems to be more significant, both in vv. 1-4 and 5-11. 'The curse that goes forth over the face of the whole land' is obviously related to 'This is the ephah that goes forth...this is their eye (?) in all the earth', however the strange expression, עינם, might be understood or emended.

גנב only occurs here in Zechariah. Why is this word chosen? And why should it be linked with him who swears (falsely)?[1]

The phrase כל הֹ[participle] מזה כמה נקה is unusual, but occurs twice only, close together, in v. 3. It may be repeated for emphasis, but is unlikely to have any structuring function. נקה occurs nowhere else in Zechariah.

נשבע occurs only here. We may ask whether it is in any way related to the 'sevens' and 'seventys' that abound?

Lastly בית is found three times (all v. 4). Is there an intended contrast between the house of the evildoer and the house of the LORD?

Note that this occurs in the phrase: 'the house of him who swears by my name...to falsehood!' The punchword comes as a surprise: the sentence cannot be understood or guessed without this.

This small unit therefore has two clear parts:

> Vision (vv. 1-2)
> Interpretation (vv. 3-4)

Within these sections there is a certain emphasis (by repetition) on the main elements:

> Vision: Flying scroll
> Interpretation: Goes forth, (house of) thief and he who swears (falsely),
>   be purged (נקה)

In addition there are connections with other sections:

> 'length and breadth' (with vision 3)
> 'in the midst' (with visions 3 and 7)

---

1.   Baldwin interprets it to represent actions with a human and divine reference: 'He who wrongs his neighbour and he who disgraces God', *Haggai, Zechariah, Malachi*, p. 127.

We may set out the situation as follows (capitals signify the second time a similar word or idea occurs):

1   And I returned[1]
       and I lifted up my eyes
       and I saw
       and behold
          a flying scroll

2   *And he said to me*
       WHAT DO YOU SEE?
    AND I SAID
       I SEE
          A FLYING SCROLL
          its length 20 cubits and
          ITS BREADTH 10 CUBITS

3   AND HE SAID TO ME
       This is the curse that goes forth
       over the face of all the earth/land (cf. 5:(5-)6)
          for every stealer from this like it will be purged
          AND EVERY SWEARER FROM THIS LIKE IT WILL BE PURGED

       IT WILL GO FORTH
    (oracle of Yahweh of hosts)
          and will come to the house of the stealer
          and TO THE HOUSE OF THE SWEARER IN MY NAME FALSELY
          AND WILL LODGE IN THE MIDST OF HIS HOUSE
             and will (completely) destroy it
             its timbers
             AND ITS STONES

It can be seen from this, as from the table, that there are virtually no verbal connections between parts of this section that are more than a verse apart. The unit builds up by a simple formula of repetition plus new element. This pattern in itself links it with the second vision, Zech. 2.1-4 (see above). However, we noted there also a more obviously regular overall pattern.

We have discovered evidence of a concern for structure in all the visions and their attached oracles that we have so far examined. As well as noting similarities in method, we have discovered variations. Unfortunately we have no reliable instrument for helping us to decide how great a variation in method may be expected from a single writer

---

1. Or 'again'; cf. Zech 4.1.

or editor. We shall consider this question later, but it is likely that a satisfactory solution must be left to a later occasion, and probably to others.

Zechariah 5.5-11
The vision falls naturally into the following sections:

5-6	Introduction—
	Lift up eyes
	this is the ephah that goes forth (emphasis goes forth)
	this 'their eye' in all the earth/land
7-8	Lid lifted
	woman in ephah;
	wickedness
	woman pushed in
	lid pushed on
9	Eyes lifted
	two women going forth Spirit/wind in wings
	lifted ephah
10-11	Question and answer.

Note that יצא is used in three different ways: of the angel (v. 5a), the ephah (vv. 5b, 6) and the women (v. 9) who took it away. This is probably partly to produce a particular preponderance of sibilants and glottal stops. Also the letter *taw* is introduced with it (e.g. יוצאת). The word also links with the preceding vision (5.3, 4)

זאת is used many times, including 7bα. Is it a mistake here? Or deliberate multiplication of these sounds? Cf. also איפה (though עפה, v. 1 is not used in vv. 5-11).

נשא is also used in three different ways: of eyes (vv. 5, 9), of the lid of the ephah (v. 7) and of the ephah itself (v. 9).

We are bound, then, to take notice of יצא and נשא. Other duplicate words and phrases are as follows.

המלאך הדבר בי, vv. 5, 10. Verses 10-11 form a new section in which the prophet again engages in dialogue with the angel. Thus vv. 5-6 and 10-11 are comparable. It is not the case that no interpretation is given in vv. 7-9, but no questions are asked.

נשא עינים וראה, vv. 5-9. The forms are different here, but we have already noted that v. 9 is the beginning of a subsection and thus comparable to 5b. נשא alone also occurs in vv. 7 and 9b. The first occurrence is near the beginning of vv. 7-8. In this pericope a new subsection seems always to start with a lifting up. In 9b נשא helps to form an inclusio for v. 9 and indeed for the whole of the vision proper, vv. 5b-9.

עין occurs in the phrase 'lift up the eyes' (vv. 5, 9) but also in v. 6, 'this is their eye in all the earth', referring to the ephah. If it can be established that this makes sense then the correspondence with 4.10b ('the eyes of Yahweh which range through the whole earth/land') is striking. The arguments, however, for emendation are strong: עֵינָם involves a small change, is found in one manuscript and is supported by LXX and Syr.[1]

The best analogies for the meaning 'appearance' seem to be Lev. 13.55, '(if) the diseased spot has not changed its eye' (BDB also suggests emendations in vv. 5 and 37), Num. 11.7 (2×), 'its appearance was as the appearance of הבדלח' and 1 Sam. 16.7 'man sees לעינים'. If we adopt this reading in Zechariah 5 it is not certain what 'their' refers to. The most likely explanation seems to be that it is an indefinite third person plural, referring to the inhabitants of the land.

Another possibility worth exploring is whether we might translate as 'This is what they see', meaning that the only thing that the inhabitants of the world (or land) can see is the ephah.[2]

It is not an easy task to decide between these alternatives. It seems to me that 'this is their iniquity. . .' is not as obvious as it might seem, since 'wickedness' is explicitly applied to the *woman* in the ephah, rather than to both of them together. The best plan seems to be to keep the MT, as the most difficult alternative, and to understand it to mean that this is how Yahweh sees the inhabitants of Judah and Jerusalem: an ephah with wickedness in. The demand for a just ephah (eg. Deut. 25.14-15; Amos 8.5; Prov. 20.10; Lev. 19.36; Ezek. 45.10; Mic. 6.11) may be in the background. The meaning of the vision does not seem to be greatly affected by which emendation is adopted but עינם would make for a closer link with 4.10b: the eyes of Yahweh range over all the earth and this is what they see. We need also to bear

---

1. See, e.g., Rudolph, *Haggai,* p. 118.
2. The emendation שׁוֹיָנָם from the verb עין might even be suggested, although it occurs otherwise only in the *qere* of 1 Sam. 18.9. We should not, of course, be able to make use of this proposal to decide on the intended structure of the passage.

in mind the frequent—and frequently problematical—use of the word עין throughout the book of Zechariah.[1]

If עונם is adopted we have different links with ch. 3; in v.4 'and he said "See, I have taken away your iniquity from upon you"' is often regarded as an addition to the text. It would be consonant with results so far to discover the hand of our final editor here, and to suppose that he had an artistic and theological purpose in making the addition. In v. 9 עון is linked with ארץ which is important in ch. 5 (vv. 3, 9, 11 as well as in v. 6).

אבן occurs only in 3.9 (2×); 4.7, 10; 5.4, 8; (9.15-16; 12.3) and is an important word in most of these references. The problem is that it is used in several different senses and it is difficult to know how to relate them, or whether one should try. The higher our view of the theological/artistic ability of the editor/author of Zechariah, the more likely it is that the correspondence is intended. In 3.9 the stone has seven 'eyes' whose significance is not clear, but it is linked with removing iniquity from the land. In ch. 4 Zerubbabel brings forward האבן הרשאה which is connected with the same complex of events: the completion of the temple as a sign that Jerusalem had been cleansed and God again dwells within her; Zerubbabel also has in his hand האבן הבדיל.

Zech. 5.4 refers to the fate of the house of the thief and the false swearer: unlike the Lord's house which is finished off with the headstone, this is consumed with its timber and even its stones. In 5.8 the ככר עפרת of v. 7 becomes אבן העפרת: that which keeps iniquity shut in so that it can be removed from the land.

זאת occurs frequently: vv. 5, 6 (2×), 7, 8 and thus supplies a sibilant and ת five times. In v. 7 the usage is unusual, and is likely to be deliberately chosen, or else a mistake.[2]

איפה, vv. 6, 7, 8, 9, 10 (note א, פ), is a 'technical term' and would be expected to repeat, though not necessarily five times.

ארץ occurs in vv. 6, 9, 11 each time with a different sense.

הנה begins two of the subsections noted, vv. 7, 9.

---

1. For further suggestions see Meyers, *Haggai, Zechariah*, pp. 297-98.
2. The LXX reads και ιδου, and we should expect והנה in Hebrew. Rudolph (*Haggai*, p. 118) assumes this is a valid meaning, appealing to A.S. van der Woude (*JEOL* 18 [1964], pp. 308-309). GKC 136d² assumes that 'אשה אחת' is in apposition to זאת depending on הנה', cf. Exod. 32.1; Ezek. 40.45 and GKC 126aa.

עפרת (cf. איפה: פ and guttural), vv. 7, 8, forms an inclusio for this subsection.

אשה, v. 7, is possibly intended to resonate with רשעה.

תוך, vv. 7-8 אל/בתוך האיפה is not a striking phrase but תוך has already proved to be a significant word.

שלך, v. 8 (twice). Should we compare the important שלח already considered: the Lord had sent his angel/prophet but pushed wickedness into an enclosed space? Under the terms of reference of this study, we must regard it as insufficiently grounded. Nevertheless, there do seem to be many more correspondences than might be expected, and there may be scope for a more rigorous investigation of this feature in further work on Zechariah.

כנף three times, only in v. 9. Note the פ and guttural-like *kaph* sounds.

בין cannot be considered to be significant, v. 9 (twice).

כון appears twice in v. 11. There seems to be conscious alliteration here again with כ or ח (or ע) and נ (מכנתה to שנער).

What patterns are to be found here? Verses 7-8 look like the most promising starting point. The Meyers' take this to be a 'compact chiastic unit'.[1] The actual words make the following pattern:

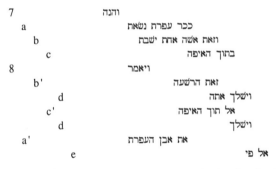

It is not obvious that this is a 'planned structure', despite the fact that it forms a rather elegant pair of chiasmuses with a similar centre, with an inclusio around:

---

1. Pp. 299, 303-304. They note the envelope formed by the leaden cover or stone, and the woman in the middle.

The sequence of thought may be represented as follows:

7   And behold (introductory formula)
                a lid of lead was lifted
                   And *this* (= 'behold' ? See note above):
                   one *woman* sitting in the midst of the ephah[1]
8   And he said (introduces the interpretation = climax)
                      This is *wickedness*
                      [new element but related to the preceding]
                   [Now further action is described]
                      And *he put* her into the midst of the ephah
                      [her original position]
                   And *he put* the stone of lead on its/her mouth
                   [its original position]

This is slightly confused *formally* by the correspondence between the phrases זאת אשה/זאת הרשעה and the repetition of וישלך. However the sense is not confused, and this seems the most logical arrangement. The first part (v. 7) leads in two steps to the identification of the contents of the ephah as 'wickedness'. A further two steps return the ephah to its original state, and in doing so suggest that the problem is being dealt with.

At the end nothing has changed except that we now know:

1.   What is in the ephah.
2.   That wickedness is contained forcibly and deliberately.

Turning to the preceding verses we note that the section is controlled by the verb 'go forth' (יצא) and the question and answer structure. The word 'this' (זאת) which is combined alliteratively with the feminine singular of יצא in its first two occurrences, then adds an obscure new element. Thus we have:

---

1.   The addition of 'one' is rather odd. The best explanation for it seems to be as a preparation for and contrast with the 'two women' who appear shortly, cf. Meyers, *Haggai, Zechariah*, p. 301. They offer the paraphrase 'there was this one woman'. It is not clear why a woman should symbolize wickedness. Suggestions are: that there is a connection with Gen. 3 and/or Gen 6.1-4; that women are connected with menstrual uncleanness; that there is a special connection with idolatry (cf. the women and the Queen of heaven, e.g. Jer. 44.15-19). A full discussion of this outside the bounds of our enquiry, but it seems to me that the fact that two women take away wickedness rules out these suggestions. Perhaps it is simply that 'wickedness' is a feminine noun, as Baldwin suggests, *Haggai, Zechariah, Malachi*, p. 129.

IF	And the angel who spoke with me went forth
IF	And he said to me, Lift up now, your eyes and see
Q1	What is this thing that goes forth
Q2	And I said, What is it?
A1	And he said, This is the ephah that goes forth.
A2	And he said, This is their eye in all the earth.

'What is it?' implies a question about the meaning of the ephah (cf., e.g., Josh. 4.6 מה האבנים האלה לכם). At any rate, the angel understands it in this sense, even if his reply is not as precise as we should wish.

The opening formula contains the phrase 'the angel who spoke with me' which does not occur again until the final section (vv. 10-11) and therefore forms a suitable introduction to the whole of vv. 5-11.

The centre of the chiasmus contains no significant words, yet it forms the pivotal point between description and interpretation.

The final word, ארץ, occurs in vv. 9 and 10 so that we have a *possible* resonance between 'in all the earth', 'between earth and heaven' and 'land of Shinar'. However, this is by no means clear.

The final section begins with the prophet doing what he had been told to do in v. 5, lift up his eyes and see. In v. 5b it formed an introductory formula *and* an integral part of the chiasmus from v. 5b to v. 6. Here we find that the verbs 'lift up' and 'go forth' again figure prominently. The word 'wings' occurs three times in four words, possibly giving prominence to the word חסדה which might remind the reader of חסד and contrast with the רשעה in the ephah.

The final words are difficult to understand and it seems quite likely that the text is corrupt. However, in the absence of an agreed restoration, we should accept the text as it stands.

הוכן is a normal *hophal* of כון, which, being masculine singular, would naturally refer to the house rather than to the ephah: 'And it will be established or ready'.

והניחה as it stands is a *hophal* third person feminine singular of נוח: and it will be caused to rest (there upon its foundation [מכנתה]). This does not seem to be too difficult. The similarity of sound between the three words mentioned above is probably intended to correspond in some way to the forms of כנף found in v. 9.

The structure of these verses is not so clear as that of the previous two subsections. Nevertheless the sequence is clear:

9   And I lifted up my eyes and I saw
               And behold
               Two women going forth
                   and the spirit was in their wings
                       and they had wings
                           as the wings of a stork
                       and they lifted up the ephah
                           between the earth and the heavens

10   And I said to the angel who spoke with me
                   Where are they taking the ephah?
               And he said to me
                       To build for it a house in the land of Shinar
                           and it will be established
                           and it will be made to rest there
                       upon its established place

I am not confident about discerning exactly what the author had in mind in this final part. Nevertheless there is strong evidence throughout vv. 5-11 of a concern to shape the account in an artistic way.

In attempting to sum up the results of this section of the enquiry, I put forward the following conclusions:

1.   We have considered all repeated words and discovered that they fit into a logical progression of thought. It is unlikely that anyone could produce new data or interpretations that would refute these findings.

2.   It is likely that there are features of the unit that have not been properly investigated because the method used only deals with repeated words, not with similar sounding words (although we could not fail to notice some as we proceeded).[1]

3.   There are different ways of presenting the details of the unit, which do not necessarily contradict each other, but it is impossible to be sure of what the author had in mind in terms of structural patterns.

4.   There is a concern for structure in virtually all the material we have so far investigated in the book of Zechariah.

---

1.   I may also have missed correspondences of concept or context, where these are not indicated by identical vocabulary.

Zechariah 6.1-8

This section forms an easily recognizable self-contained unit: the eighth and final vision of Zechariah the prophet. The only words common to vv. 1-8 and 9-15 are בין, נשׂא (vv. 1, 13) and שׁניהם (vv. 1, 13), so that there is no point in combining these two tables.

A look at the table of repeated words (figure 7) reveals that there are very few distinctive words. The only serious candidates are:

1. The colours of the horses (vv. 2-3, 6-7), which belong together with 'four', 'chariots', 'go forth' and 'horses'. These point to the fact that the description given by the prophet in vv. 1-3 is closely matched by the explanation in vv. 5-6 + 7.#1.

2. ענה + אמר. 'Then I answered and said to the angel who talked with me, "What are these, my lord?"', which is immediately followed by 'And the angel answered and said to me, "These..."'. This can only, at most, strengthen the obvious link between vv. 4 and 5.

3. רוח, which is used first of the 'four winds of the heavens', and secondly of 'my spirit'. There may well be an intended resonance here, but it is impossible to build a theory on this single repetition (with different forms).

4. ארץ צפון (6, [2×]). The first occurrence is in the explanation (vv. 5-6 + 7.#1) of the purpose of the four chariots; the second two are in vv. 7-8 which describe the fulfilment of that purpose.

5. The *hithpael* of הלך. This occurs in v. 7 only, where there is further repetition:

    + (אמר +) בארץ + הלך (*hithpael*) + הלך (*qal*)
    + בארץ + הלך (*hithpael*) + הלך (*qal*)
    + בארץ + הלך (*hithpael*)

    This gives the reader ample time to realize that the same phrase was used in the first vision.

The structure of the unit is, in general, clear.

1-3	Vision described (four chariots and different coloured horses)
4	Question about the vision
5-6	Vision explained (in terms of the purpose of the chariots)
7-8	Progress in the vision: Intention carried out; purpose achieved

Verses Word	1	2	3	4	5	6	7	8
ראה	4						6	
ארבע	6		(6)		6			
מרכבה	7	1,5	1,5					
יצא	8				9	5,10,14	2	7
הר	11-13							
סוס		3,7	3,7			3		
שחור		8				4		
לבן			4			9		
ברוד			8			13		
אמץ			9				1	
ענה				1	1			
אמר				2	3		7	5
אל				3	4	6,11,15		4,8
מלאך				4	2			
דבר				5				3
ב				6		2		
אלה				8	5			
אדון				9	12			
רוח					7			13
ארץ					14	7,16	6,10,12	9,14
צפון						8		10,15
הלך/התהלך								4,5,8,9,11

Figure 7: *Zech. 6.1-8: Word numbers of words occurring twice or more*

There is an obvious link between v. 6 and v. 8, which makes it possible to divide the unit up as vv. 1-5 + 6-8, or simply to regard v. 6 as transitional.

In more detailed terms we have:

1	IF	And I returned (or 'Again' see below on 4.1; 5.1)
		And I lifted up my eyes
		and I saw
		and behold[1]
		four chariots (יצאות)
		from between two mountains
		(and the mountains were mountains of bronze)
2-3		with the first chariot: red horses
		with the second chariot: black horses
		with the third chariot: white horses
		with the fourth chariot: ? horses (ברדים אמצים)
4		And I answered[2] and said to the angel. . . me
		What are these אדני?
5		And the angel answered and said to me
		These are the four רוחות of heaven
		יצאות from presenting themselves before
		אדון כל הארץ
6		that with black horses יצאים אל ארץ צפון
		the white יצאו אל אחריהם
		the ברדים יצאו אל ארץ התימן
7		and the אמצים[3]—יצאו
		and they sought to go to patrol the ארץ
		and he said Go, patrol the ארץ
		and they patrolled the ארץ[4]

1. This formula is identical to that used for the sixth vision, and makes use of all elements used in introducing the visions. See Meyers, *Haggai, Zechariah*, p. 317.

2. He has not been asked anything, cf. 1.9. He is presumably responding to what he sees.

3. Petersen calls this 'resumptive', but deletes the first occurrence (*Haggai and Zechariah*, p. 263). A more normal reading would be to accept the Syriac, which omits 'strong' in v. 3, and changes 'red' to 'strong' in v. 7 (accepted by S.R. Driver, *The Minor Prophets: Nahum, Habakkuk, Zephaniah, Haggai, Zechariah, Malachi* ([The Century Bible; Edinburgh: T.C. & E.C. Jack, 1906], pp. 209-210). This is also neater, but there is is still a question why the order is changed (the first becomes last).

4. This is feminine plural, whereas the verb forms before this are masculine. I cannot find an explanation of this: it may simply be anomalous, as is fairly common

8   and he called out to me[1]
                     and he said to me
         See
             the ארץ צפון אל ארץ יצים have set my Spirit at rest
             בארץ צפון

There seems to be some corruption here. Rudolph's solution is probably the neatest: he keeps אשר בה in v. 6, and assumes that the chariot
with red horses, named first in v. 2, together with a singular verb, is
described as going to the east. It is possible to keep the MT 'by
translating v. 3 '...dappled horses; [all] mighty ones'. Then v. 7
refers to all the horses as 'mighty ones'.[2] It is tempting to make the
text more regular, but it requires quite a lot of emendation, and there
are irregularities elsewhere in Zechariah. We must reckon with the
possibility that the changes in the pattern are deliberate.[3]

Note that probably the most distinctive word in this section is אמצים,
which occurs nowhere else in Zechariah (except that the same root is
found in 12.5). It is further emphasized by its position as the last word
of the first section (vv. 1-3), and as the first word of the third section
(vv. 7-8). This is at least a possible purpose of the word in the text as
we have it, and gives reason to be cautious about emending it.[4]

Let us ask about the other irregularities. Why, for example are the
red horses not mentioned again? A possible answer is that they are not
needed (since we can work out where they go from information given
about the others), and their omission puts into greater prominence the
horses who 'go forth to the north' and who bring the chapter to a

in the Hebrew Bible. Perhaps, however, it recalls the opening of the vision where the
focus was initially on the (feminine) chariots. Cf. Meyers, *Haggai, Zechariah*, p. 327.

1.   BDB, p. 277; 'he called me out/forth' would be a more natural grammatical
translation (cf. Judg. 4.10, 13; 2 Sam. 20.4-5) and the Meyers' adopt it (*Haggai,
Zechariah*, p. 328): 'the prophet is to be fully alert and ready to hear the statement
that follows'. Perhaps; though nothing in previous usage has prepared us for this
understanding. On the other hand, this type of address has not occurred before.

2.   Rudolph, *Haggai*, pp. 122-23. The main reason for this is that the first word
of v. 6, אשר, indicates that something has dropped out of the text before it. See also
Meyers, *Haggai, Zechariah*, pp. 316, 320-22; Jeremias, *Die Nachtgesichte*,
pp. 126-30; W.D. McHardy, 'The Horses in Zechariah', in *In Memoriam P Kahle*
(ed. M. Black and G. Fohrer; BZAW, 103; Berlin: Töpelmann, 1968), pp. 174-79.

3.   Although we must admit here that the case for emendation seems stronger
than for retaining MT.

4.   A line may still have been dropped out of the beginning of v. 6.

close. We note also that it is only the north-going black horses who have the participle of יצי. However this might be explained, it has the effect of emphasizing them further, and of making them suitable to stand for all those who 'go forth'. Thus, in v. 8b, we assume that since the most important and difficult task has been accomplished (the north being the home of the gods, and the most feared enemies of Israel), then God's Spirit must be at rest in the whole earth too.[1]

The structure of the passage may be described in the following way. The plural participle יצאים/ות is apparently one that controls the overall shape. It occurs right at the beginning of the description of the vision, along with the four chariots, and also at the end of vv. 4-5, where we find:

1. The prophet's question and the angel's explanation of (presumably) the four chariots.
2. The phrase אדון כל הארץ, which we noted right at the end of Zechariah 4, and which also forms a climax here.

In addition יצאים, together with ארץ צפון, forms an envelope for the final section. We have noted the difficulties in the text and the uncertainty that results from this. Nevertheless, the text that we have presents a regular and logical pattern. The change from feminine to masculine plural participle is striking, as is the avoidance of the participial form between vv. 6a and 8bα. Setting this out we have:

יצאות	+	four chariots
chariot	+	horses[1-4(5?)]
יצאות	+	four רוחות; Lord of all the earth
יצאים	+	horses[2] + ארץ צפון
יצא	+	(horses)[3-4(5)]
יצאים	+	ארץ צפון. . .ארץ צפון

In addition to this, note the two threefold repetitions: 'mountains' and 'patrol the earth', which occur just after the first יצאים and just before the last. Also that רוח occurs at the centre of the very small chiasmus formed by ארץ צפון in v. 8. We leave these as observations, since we cannot prove that their positioning is significant.

It seems fair, though over-simplified, to represent the structure of

---

1. Baldwin mentions 'sinister associations' as in Jer. 1.14; 4.6; 6.22; Ezek. 1.4, etc. (*Haggai, Zechariah, Malachi*, p. 131); Petersen speaks of the north as the 'land of exile, punishment and imprisonment', *Haggai and Zechariah*, p. 271.

the passage as follows (with Y/Y' = יצאים/יצאות; D = description; c = chariots; h = horses; r = רוח; ṣ = צפון; e = [whole] earth; P = 'go...patrol'):

Y(c)
  D(c + h)
Y(r; e)   (Here we remember that c → r)
Y'(ṣ)
  P(e)
Y'(ṣ)   (Here we might even put 'Y'[ṣrṣ]')

In the next chapter we shall consider briefly connections between the major sections of Zechariah. However, it is convenient to discuss the most obvious one here, namely the correspondence between the first vision and this one.

Verse 1 is full of words that have been used in previous visions: ואשב; ואשא עיני ואראה והנה; יצאות; הר (3×). The impression given is of a culmination of what has gone before. The four chariots recall the four horses of the first vision (note also the similarity between מרכבות and רכב in 1.8). The fact that we have noted an apparent awareness of *inclusio* and *chiasmus* in the editor of Zechariah strengthens this impression.

In vv. 2-3 the colours are specified, as is the case in ch. 1, but the actual colours are different:

Ch. 1   red, red, sorrel(?) (שׂרק), white
Ch. 6   red, black, white, dappled grey(?) (אמצים ברדים [ברדים?])

This is very puzzling, and I do not know of a convincing explanation for this variation (cf. the odd changes of name in 6.10, 14, where Heldai and Josiah are replaced by חלם and חן respectively [see below]).[1]

'The angel who talked with me' (v. 4) occurs in 1.9, 14; 2.2, 7; 4.1, 4, 5; 5.5, 10. 'What are these my lord?': 1.9 and 4.4 only. We may also note the phrase 'and I (etc.) answered' (ענה), 1.10, 11, 12, 13.

התיצב (v. 5) is used only here in Zechariah. One wonders why the writer does not use עמד, which occurs in 1.8, 10 and 11, as well as six times in Zechariah 3, and also in 4.14. No certain answer can be given. It does form a nice contrast with the *hithpael* of הלך.

התהלך (v. 7) occurs as mentioned above, three times in 6.7. It is found also in 1.10-11 (The only other occurrence in Zechariah is at 10.12).

---

1.   See on 6.9-15 below.

הניחו (v. 8). For some reason the author does not use the same word for 'being at rest' in 1.11 (ישבת ושקטת).

It is clear that the editor/author intends the reader to notice the correspondence between the first and last visions, and most scholars comment on this. It also seem clear that he misses some good opportunities! And we must assume that he was not concerned to produce a highly complicated correspondence with no loose ends.[1] In this section, we have again discovered a concern for the structure of an individual unit, and for the overall pattern of 1.7–6.8.

Zechariah 6.9-15

The table of words that occur twice or more can be found below in figure 8.

Verses / Word	9	10	11	12	13	14	15
לקח		1	1				
טוביה		6				4	
ידעיה		8				5	
בוא		9,13,19					2
הוא		12			1,6		
צפניה		17				8	
עטרה			5			1	
כהן			11		14		
צמח				11,14			
בנה				15	2		3
היכל				17	4	10	4
כסא					12,16		

Figure 8: *Zech. 6.9-15: Word numbers of words occurring twice or more*

---

1.   See on Zech. 1 in Chapter 4 below.

Repeating words that are distinctive may be set out as follows:

10.##6,8,17	צפניה ידעיה טוביה	
11.#5	עטרות	
11.#11	כהן	
12.#11	צמח	
12.#14	צמח	
	[בנה] היכל	12.#17
	[בנה] היכל	13.#4
	כסא	13.#12
13.#14	כהן	
	כסא	13.#16
14.#1	עטר[ו]ת	
14.##4,5,8	צפניה ידעיה טוביה	
	היכל	14.#10
	[בנה] היכל	15.#4

Virtually all the distinctive duplicate words here fit into two interlocking chiastic patterns (marked by word reference numbers on the right or left). I have omitted only לקח, בוא and הוא, but even these can be seen to serve some purpose (see below). This makes the irregularities all the more striking. Why should חלדי have become חלם? And if it did, why was it not changed back, since the correspondence between v. 10 and v. 14 is obvious? How could יאשיה have become חן and not be changed back when both are called בן צפניה? Only the Syriac supports the emendation in each case.[1] For our purposes the three identical names repeated in vv. 10 and 14 are sufficient to establish a prima facie case for an inclusio. The two repeating words that follow are important (עטרות and כהן) though here again is a puzzle: why are there 'crowns' and why should they (?) be put only on the high priest's head? For us, the emendation proposed by *BHS* and several scholars (viz. to read 'crown' and 'Zerubbabel...' in v. 11 and then make Joshua stand at his right hand [cf. LXX] in v. 13) are out of bounds. Verses 11 and 14 both have the plural crowns, and there is no support for 'Zerubbabel' in the versions, but v. 14 has a singular

---

1.   Rignell, *Die Nachtgesichte*, pp. 234-236. Petitjean (pp. 289-96) argues that originally vv. 10-12 and 13-14 were separate. He calls them 'une pièce prophétique ancienne' and 'le morceau complémentaire qu'il y ajoute'. We are not primarily concerned with the pre-history of the text and my remarks on these verses stand.

verb, so perhaps the best solution is to repoint עֹטֶרֶת in v. 14,[1] and possibly also in v. 11.

There are other awkward features in this passage. The verb בוא occurs three times in v. 10 in such a way as to throw the verse out of balance:

10   Taking[2] from the exiles (מֵאֵת הַגּוֹלָה)
            from (מ) Heldai and
            from (מאת) Tobiah and
            from (מאת) Jedaiah
              (and you shall come, you yourself, on that day
              and you shall come [to] house of Josiah ben Zephaniah)
              who have come from Babylon (or where they have come. . .)
11   And you shall take. . .

Most commentators smooth this out, but the ancient versions confirm a similarly rough text.[3] Moreover, it is intelligible, and should be kept. The verb 'take' serves to keep this section together as one element; the verse stresses the ideas of 'taking' and 'coming' in connection with the exiles.

The passage continues with the completion of the command. It is at last specified what is to be taken: gold and silver, to be made into crowns and put on the head of 'Joshua ben Jehozadak, the high priest'. We have not yet reached a point that could be called a satisfactory end

---

1.   This is the Meyers' solution: '. . . supported by the LXX and Peshitta; an old Phoenician reading may underlie the text'. They complicate matters by translating in v. 11: '. . . make crowns. You will place [one] on the head. . . ' and in v. 14: 'The [other] crown. . . ' (*Haggai, Zechariah*, p. 336). This seems less satisfactory. Rudolph takes וֹ to be a singular ending (in both verses) as in Job 31.36, 'I would bind it on me as a crown', and quotes several other authorities (*Haggai*, p. 128). Petersen (*Haggai and Zechariah*, pp. 272-75) regards the change to the singular in ancient texts as an attempt to avoid the difficulty and reads MT as 'crowns' and as the more difficult reading. He points out that this is in accord with 'the diarchic situation envisioned in 4.1-5, 10b-14'.

2.   This seems best understood as an imperative. The infinitive absolute followed by perfect is well attested in this sense, e.g. Deut. 1.16; 2 Sam. 24.12; cf. GKC 113 aa-gg (Petitjean, *Les oracles*, pp. 272-73). Lipiński regarded it as an abnormal imperative, ('Recherches sur le livre de Zacharie', *VT* 20 [1970], pp. 33-34), but this seems unnecessary.

3.   Even though LXX regards the proper names as appellatives: παρὰ τῶν ἀρχόντων καὶ παρὰ τῶν χρησίμων αὐτῆς καὶ παρὰ τῶν ἐπεγνωκότων αὐτὴν. See Petitjean, *Les oracles*, pp. 271, 274-78, 296.

to the unit, and must take the next verse as part of the original account. Some commentators, including Petersen, take vv. 12-13 to be a separate oracle inserted into vv. 9-11 + 14. It is difficult to find a parallel to a symbolic action of this kind without some sort of explanatory word.[1] It consists of an oracle with a weighty introductory formula and an oracle about 'a man: צמח (is) his name'. 'He will branch up מתחתיו, and he will build the temple of Yahweh.' This oracle is addressed to Joshua and informs him about someone else. It is conjectured that the original text may have been different,[2] but we have no warrant for adopting an emended reading here.

Verse 13 looks as if it could have been added by an editor. It begins by repeating, almost word for word but with emphasis, the last part of the previous verse, before adding new material:

	and he will build the temple of Yahweh
13	And he (is the one who) will build the temple of Yahweh
	And he (is the one who) will bear honour
	and he will sit
	and he will rule
	upon his throne (אל כסאו)
	and there will be a priest
	by his throne (אל כסאו)
	and there will be peace between the two of them.

Verse 14 would have formed a fitting end to our supposed 'original account', with or without v. 13. It mentions the crowns again and the people whose names were specified earlier. What was taken *from* (*with*) the exiles, becomes a remembrance *for* them (ל four times).

1. Petersen does not seem to address this question (*Haggai and Zechariah*, pp. 272-81), although he regards the writer/editor as 'an accomplished literary architect' and vv. 12-13 as 'a carefully constructed oracle' (pp. 273, 278). Stuhlmueller offers Isa. 20, Jer. 28, Ezek. 3.22-27 and chs. 4–5. In the first an oracle was certainly delayed but it was given; Jeremiah was commanded not only to 'make yoke bars' but to give a message to the envoys who had come to Jerusalem (27.2-11); Ezekiel is a special case, hardly comparable to Zech. 6.9ff. However, the examples do illustrate the variety of communication in the OT, and warn us against demanding analogies for everything we seem to find.

2. There is no widespread agreement on this question. Full discussion would involve questions about the historical situation of the time, and in particular what hopes surrounded and what happened to Zerubbabel. These matters are covered in most commentaries, e.g. Amsler, *Agée, Zacharie, Malachi*, pp. 106-110; Meyers, *Haggai, Zechariah*, esp. pp. 350-64.

Their names are still recognizable, but two have been changed to words connected with dreaming (cf. Ps. 126.1?) or strength,[1] and grace (cf. Zech. 4.7). It is tempting to say that in v. 10 the words גולה and בבל, and possibly בן צפניה emphasize the exile, but v. 14 contains hints of deliverance from exile, including the fact that יאשיה בן צפניה has become חן בן צפניה. If חלדי means 'mole', then it is worth changing![2] If the text stopped at v. 14a it would seem incomplete, so we must probably reckon with the whole of v. 14 as our supposed original ending. This gives the following pattern:

```
10      Take. . .
        Tobiah. . . Jedaiah. . . ben Zephaniah
11      Take
            crown(s)
11-12           high priest. . . branch. . . branch up. . . build temple
(13?            build temple. . . throne. . . priest. . . throne. . . peace)
14          crown(s)
        Tobiah. . . Jedaiah. . . ben Zephaniah
            in temple
```

The final word 'temple' would be a connection with the climax of v. 12, and it would make more sense to think of our 'original' without v. 13. If this was the case, then we can understand the probable aims of the editor who added vv. 13 and 15. He doubled the phrase בנה ההיכל (by adding 13.#4 to 12.#17) and matched it by adding the same at 15.#4 (14.#10 was already in place). Within this he used the phrase אל כסאו twice (in different senses), framing the second occurrence of כהן consciously or unconsciously.

Verse 15aα (i.e. 15.##1-5) has the effect of adding a second climax which refers to the future: those who are far off (like the named individuals used to be) will come (cf. v. 10), and they will build the temple. This is similar to the contrast between the men who come to seek the favour of Yahweh in 7.2 and the peoples, inhabitants of many cities, and strong nations who will come in the same way in the future (8.20-23). We have good reason to see the hand of the final redactor

1. This is based on root I 'be healthy, strong', which is only found twice: Job 39.4; Isa. 38.16. It seems odd that it is so readily assumed to point to the meaning of חלם. See Meyers, *Haggai, Zechariah*, p. 340, for further discussion.
2. Noted by D.R. Jones (*Haggai, Zechariah, Malachi*, p. 93).

in this verse, as is also shown by the refrain following: 'you shall know that...sent me to you'.

Zech. 6.15b is odd. The phrase normally introduces another clause; here it stands alone and must be translated 'and this will happen/come to pass if...'[1] What could be the reason for this? The answer might be that the writer wants to end with reference to שמע בקול (which he does in emphatic form), perhaps to correspond with the שמע in 1.4 (otherwise only 3.8; 7.11, 12, 13 [2×]; 8.9, 23). This would confirm again that we have the work of the final editor in v. 15.

It is possible that an allusion to Isa. 6.9 is intended: Isaiah was one of the former prophets whom the fathers refused to hear. However, the finite verb (imperative) precedes the infinitive in Isaiah, and this weakens the contact between them. Nevertheless, שמע is used surprisingly little and at significant points in the book. The Israelite failure to hear in the past was the reason for their downfall. When restoration comes, the same command is set before them, to hear[ken to the voice of] the Lord speaking to them. The sense in 6.15 and 7.11-13 is 'to obey'.

This discussion has led us into the sort of conjecture that we have, for the most part, tried to avoid. However, it seemed to me worthwhile to imagine what might have been the case, *without emending the text*, since we were faced with what seemed a plausible superimposed chiastic structure, something that we had reason to regard with scepticism in Chapter 1.[2]

It is interesting to compare the results of form-critical investigation carried out on this text, and Schöttler's treatment may be taken as the most recent example. He regards the original text as:[3]

> vv. 9, 10bβ, 11 and 13a.
> vv. 12, 13b and 14aαb represent the main editorial reworking.
> v. 15b belongs with 1.1-6 as part of the redaction of the whole vision cycle. Later glosses are:
> vv. 10a, 14aβ; then 10bα; then 15a.

---

1. Nevertheless it is accepted by scholars generally, e.g. Rudolph (*Haggai*, pp. 122, 126), who includes it with vv. 1-8 + 15a but regards it as redactional, and based on Deut. 28.1. Cf. Chary, *Les prophètes et le culte*, pp. 108-109.

2. See pp. 57-59.

3. *Gott inmitten seines Volkes*, pp. 150-63.

In principle this does not look significantly different from my own enquiry and results. It *is* different, in that:

1. I have not put such confidence in form-critical criteria.
2. I have not so much been concerned with separating the editors and deciding their order and dates, as with the purpose and methods which have produced the final text.
3. I have, for the most part, been concerned to find a basis from which to work that would be agreed by the majority of scholars, so that the method which I am trying to establish might not rest on the conclusions of one individual scholar.
4. I have departed from normal practice in this section because of a particular phenomenon (superimposed chiasmus)[1] that seemed to demand explanation (i.e. my treatment of this section is atypical; Schöttler's is typical).
5. I have worked on the assumption that when a redactor makes an alteration or addition, then at least he thinks there is a good reason for it. This explains some differences, for example, the assigning of v. 15a to the status of later gloss in Schöttler's analysis above.

We must consider this section in conjunction with other parts of Zechariah in Chapter 4, but we have, I believe, some significant discoveries to take forward to that chapter: an editorial reworking (I still have not proved that it is a different editor) of 6.9-15, a concern to tie this in with the introduction to the whole of Zechariah 1–6 and links with the final editing of chs. 7–8.

Zechariah 7–8

This section is so large that it is advisable to eliminate common words before presenting a table. I shall therefore, after some preliminary remarks, discuss all repeated words and their function first, then give the table, and finally discuss the possible structures that emerge.

Preliminary Observations

The general structure and movement of these chapters are clear. They begin with a group of men who come to 'entreat the favour of

1. See pp. 57-59.

Yahweh' (חלה פני יהוה) and to ask a question about fasting: should they go on fasting in the fifth month as has been the custom for so many years? This is countered with a question about their motive in fasting (not only in the fifth but also in the seventh month). The answer to the question comes only at the end of ch. 8: the fasts of the fifth, and seventh, and also the previously unmentioned fourth and tenth months[1] will become 'seasons of joy and gladness, and cheerful feasts'. This, then, already forms an inclusio around the intervening material. But there is a further inclusio of the whole when the phrase 'entreat the favour of Yahweh' reappears twice (vv. 21-22). A climax is achieved in vv. 20-21: not only the inhabitants of Bethel, but many cities will go to entreat the favour of Yahweh; this is further enlarged in vv. 22-23'many peoples and strong nations' will also come, even ten times the number of Jews will come from outside, since they have heard that 'God is with you' (v. 23, cf. 8.3). There may be further intentional correspondence between the picture of Jerusalem in the centre of many people and cities, and with many inhabitants, in vv. 6-7, and Jerusalem as the centre, in effect, of the world in vv. 20-23.

Within these two inclusios we have a further one formed by mention of the appeal of the former prophets: 'Render true judgments...not devise evil in your heart...' (7.9-10), and the renewed appeal in 8.16-17.

Repeated Words and their Function

שׁנה is used as follows: 7.1 in dating the oracle; 7.3, 5, referring to the period of the exile during which the fast has been kept. The word is not taken up at the end, although there is some contrasting resonance between the years of exile and the seasons of gladness to come (v. 19). This is not concrete enough to lay any weight on.

ארבעה occurs in dating the oracle in 7.1, 'fourth year...fourth day' and (רביעי) in adding the fourth month in the reply in 8.19. We may ignore this.

היה דבר יהוה אל זכריה occurs in 7.1 and 7.8. It is the most important of a number of introductory formulae in this section. Thus v. 8 is marked off as a new beginning. It forms a contrast with the previous reference to the words of Yahweh by the 'hand' of the former

---

1.   This again is reminiscent of the 'growing phrase' (Magonet) noted in 2.1-4 above p. 98 n. 1.

prophets and the present word. Since Zechariah is here spoken of in the third person it is probable that this belongs to the latest editorial stage. Most scholars consider this to be clumsy, since 7.9-10 represents the words of the former prophets (7.7) to the fathers (cf. 7.11), and not a word via Zechariah to his contemporaries.[1]

'The word of Yahweh of hosts was to me' is found in 7.4; 8.1, 18. The first of these introduces the off-putting reply (vv. 5-7) which delays the answer to the question put to the prophet; Zech. 7.9-14[2] elaborates on the lack of concern the Israelites have shown to obey Yahweh and reports the result of it. Zech. 8.2ff, on the contrary, is concerned with the imminent action of Yahweh which will reverse the state previously depicted. The phrase 'Thus says Yahweh of hosts' (7.9.##1-4; 8.2.##1-4, 4.##1-4, 6.##1-4, 7.##1-4, 9.##1-4, 14.##2-5, 19.##1-4, 20.##1-4, 23.##1-4) occurs frequently in this section and with obvious emphasis. The last occurrence of the phrase, 8.18, introduces at last the answer to the question in 7.3. Again, 'Thus says...hosts' is frequent (three times in five verses).

Thus we have a division into major sections, and both continuity and emphasis achieved by these phrases. This conclusion is in accord with that reached by literary-critical methods, as is the observation that 7.8-14 may be due to a redactor. What is not usually suggested is that the insertion may be for purposes of balance or structure.[3]

חדש only occurs in vv. 1 and 3. It is not even used in 8.19 and may be discounted.

---

1. See, e.g., Rudolph, *Haggai*, p. 142; cf. p. 160 n. 1 below.

2. This may or may not be an editorial addition. It certainly is closely related to the forms and message of earlier prophets. See, e.g., Petersen, *Haggai and Zechariah*, pp. 288-91, who also, however, argues that vv. 9-10 are not a 'pale copy of prophetic speech' but 'vigorous prophetic discourse'. Cf. Beuken, *Haggai–Sacharja*, pp. 124-38; Chary, *Les prophètes et le culte*, p. 123.

3. Even the Anchor Bible does not entertain seriously the possibility that Zech. 7–8 as a whole might be put together artistically; cf. e.g. p. 307, where 7.9-10 is compared with 8.16-17. Chary (*Les prophètes et le culte*, pp. 117-18), considers the literary structure of chs. 7–8, but apart from noting the correspondence between 7.2-3 and 8.18-19, his comment consists of little more than a division into units with form-critical notes. He describes 8.20-23 as added by the redactor of the whole book (i.e. Zech. 1–8) but does not notice the link with 7.2. See pp. 70-71 in Chapter 2 above.

שלח has previously been significant and must be considered here, although the uses seem quite different: '...Bethel sent...' (7.2); 'they refused to hear the torah and words that Yahweh had sent' (7.12); 'I sent every man against his fellow' (8.10).[1]

איש is not a promising word, but there is some correspondence (not exact) between 7.2 and 8.23, and the expressions in 7.9 and 8.16 (איש את רעהו), 7.10 (איש אחיו), 8.10 (איש ברעהו) and 8.17 (איש את רעת רעהו) are similar and somewhat distinctive. Even 8.10 is comparable (ואיש משענתו בידו). All are used distributively. However 8.4 is different—unless a contrast is intended between 8.4-5 and 10. Zech. 7.9-10 and 8.16-17 occur in passages that are similar in other ways.

חלה את פני יהוה is clearly an important phrase, as noted above.

כהן. The people come to ask the priest a question, but receive their answer from the prophet Zechariah, who also addresses the priests. They are not heard of again.

בית occurs at 7.3 and 8.9 ('house of Yahweh'), 8.13, 15, 19 ('house of Judah') and 8.13 ('house of Israel'). The word is not distinctive in itself, and the use of the different phrases does not seem to be significant. For example, the 'house of Yahweh' is not mentioned in 8.20-23, where it would be entirely natural.

נביא occurs four times. Men from Bethel come to ask a question of 'the priests...and the prophets'. It may be an editorial addition or an afterthought, but it makes the point that they have heard previously 'by the hand of the former prophets' (7.7, 12) but not taken notice. Zech. 8.9 refers to the promises that they have been hearing from the prophets more recently, that is, since the founding of the second temple. Thus the word is used to express a contrast already evident in the sections noted.

חמישי, together with the noun and verb צום, and other ordinals, form the inclusio referred to above.

עשה is normally a common word. Here its use may be significant. The questioners ask, 'Shall I...as I have done?' The answer in 7.9 draws attention to what they should have done; 8.16 makes this clearer by introducing a command which would have been sufficient on its

---

1. In the text we received רגם מלך is treated as one word, and so the repetition does not show up. There does not seem to be any obvious correlation between this name and 'King Darius' in v. 1. It is surprising, however, that in 1.1 and 7, Darius is not called 'king'.

own. Thus the word supports the correspondence suggested between
7.9-10 and 8.16-17.

זה is used in different ways: 'these many years' and 'these seventy
years' (7.3, 5) on the one hand, and 'the remnant of this people' (8.6,
11-12) on the other. The first two refer to the same period. Only the
last three need to be noted, taken together with שארית and עם.

כל is too common to plot. We may note the phrase את כל אלה in
8.12, 17, but there seems to be no arguable connection between its use
in these two references.

עם. We have noted the phrase 'remnant of the people'. In the middle
of these references the word is used twice in a favourable sense (עמי
and היו לי לעם) in 8.7-8. There is a contrast between the stern address
to 'all the people of the land' in 7.5 and the promise to '(many)
peoples' in 8.20, 22. The word is used, therefore, in accordance with
the movement of the chapter. The people of the land have not acted as
God's people; nevertheless the remnant are to be his people again in
Jerusalem and many others are to be brought in.

ארץ. The theme of land is set out in the address to 'all the people of
the land', 7.5. Whereas the pleasant land (ארץ חמדה) was made
desolate (הארץ נשמה...לשמה) 7.14, Yahweh will bring his people
מארץ מבוא השמש and מארץ מזרח, 8.7, and the land will (again) give its
increase, 8.12.

כי, in 7.5-6, means 'when'. Otherwise it is used in the sense of
'because' (or possibly 'if') (8.6) or 'for' (8.10, 12, 14, 17). It seems
that we can ignore it.

צום and שבע must obviously be kept, as noted above.

אני, although not distinctive in itself, draws attention to itself by its
emphatic use, occurring three times at the end of a phrase, and once,
in the important covenant promise, at the beginning.

(7.5) הצום צמתני אני
(8.8) ואני אהיה להם לאלהים
(8.11) ועתה לא כימים הראשנים אני
(8.21) ולבקש את יהוה צבאת אלכה גם אני

The use with ראשנים helps to form a contrast between the sections
describing the former time (7.4-7, 8-14) and the new situation that is
coming about (8.1-17). There does not seem to be any obvious
connection between the first three occurrences and the last.

אכל and שתה occur together, and only in v. 6, as part of the prophet's off-putting reply, justifying his sermon before he gives an answer.

קרא, 7.7, 13 (2×), 8.3. The first of these refers to words which the Lord 'called by the hand of the prophets...' The second and third refer directly to this, which is not surprising if 7.8-14 is an editorial addition, as suggested above.[1] The last reference, Jerusalem shall be called (*niphal*) 'city of truth', does not seem to connect with the others. We should plot it but there seems little hope of finding the usage significant in terms of structure.

יד, 7.7, 12; 8.4, 9, 13. For the first two see above. The last two occur in the phrase 'let your hands be strong' which form an inclusio for vv. 9-13, one of our obvious self-contained sub-sections. Zech. 8.4 has the old men sitting with staffs in their hands; it does not seem likely that a play on words is intended with either of the other two uses, though it may just be possible. It is better to consider the phrases 'by the hand of the former prophets' and 'let your hands be strong' separately. The *hiphil* of חזק is also found in 8.23 (2×); only 14.13 elsewhere in Zechariah.

ראשון. See אני above.

ירושלם occurs most significantly in the phrase ושכנתי/ושכנו בתוך ירושלם, 8.3, 8, which forms an inclusio for the material between the statement of Yahweh's purpose for Jerusalem (8.1-2, where the root קנה occurs three times, and the statement 'They will be my people...').

Thus there is a clear parallel between 8.3a and 8a:

> I will return to Zion and I will dwell in the midst of
> Jerusalem
> I will bring them and they will dwell in the midst
> of Jerusalem[2]

Otherwise Jerusalem is mentioned because it is a central concern of the whole chapter. The highest concentration of references is, naturally, in 8.1-8 (vv. 3 (2×), 4, 8 + 'Zion' vv. 2, 3); it also occurs in 7.7, 8.15, 22.

---

1. In other words this is the sort of link we should expect to see made by a redactor, especially one with a grasp of the whole unit.

2. We recall here the significance attaching to בתוך in Zech. 2.5-9 + 10-17.

יָשַׁב, 7.7 (2×), 8.4, 20, 21, looks hopeful. The first two references
are participles expressing the fact that in former (good) times
Jerusalem and also the Negeb and Shephelah were inhabited.
Zech. 8.4 speaks of old men and old women *again* (עוד) sitting in the
streets of Jerusalem in the age to come; 8.20 and 8.21 speak of the
inhabitants of other cities who will go up to Jerusalem. Perhaps we
may discern some movement from past (Jerusalem with its own
people) to present (virtually uninhabited) to future (even people
settled permanently elsewhere will come to Jerusalem). However they
do not come to dwell in Jerusalem, and the usage in 8.4 is different, so
we probably should not consider יָשַׁב as a structuring word. Still we
ought to plot it.

עִיר, 7.7, 8.3, 5, 20, occurs in the same locations as יָשַׁב and similar
remarks apply to it.

שׁפט, 7.9 (2×), 8.16, occurs in passages which seem to be parallel.[1]
Each time the phrase used is שׁפט משׁפט, and אמת occurs in close
conjuction in each case. There are no other instances of שׁפט in
Zechariah.

אמת occurs with שׁפט, as stated above (actually twice in v. 16,
though the second of these is often deleted as dittography. This does
not seriously weaken the impression that the sections are intended as
parallel). In addition אמת is found in 8.3, 8 which have already been
noted as the beginning and end of a major subsection. Note that the
second of these occurs outside the inclusio (8.3a, 8a), which itself
leads to the climax expressed in 8.8.##6-12. 'Truth' then is at the
heart of God's requirements for his people, and truth is what he will
achieve in the city and in his relationship to his people.

אז 7.9-10, should be considered with רֵעַ (see above under אִישׁ).

אל-תחשבו בלבבכם ...[רעת] occurs only in 7.10 and 8.17. חשׁב occurs
nowhere else in Zechariah (and לבם only in 7.12; 10.7 [2×]; 12.5; לבב
does not occur elsewhere).

נתן only occurs in 7.11; 8.12 (3×), which do not seem to be
connected: 'they gave a stubborn shoulder' compared to the coming

---

1.   This is recognized by many commentators, including Petitjean. He presents a
comparison of 7.7, 9-10 and 8.16-17 (*Les oracles*, p. 413) stating that, 'Les deux
péricopes présentent la même structure: une phrase introductoire, suivie de quatre
commandements. Dans les deux codes, les deux premiers préceptes sont formulés à
l'impératif, les deux derniers au "vétitif" *'al* + jussif.'

days when vine, heavens and earth shall give their various blessings.

שמע occurs in 7.11, 12, 13 (2×) (all referring to the Israelites refusal to hear) and 8.9 (which occurs in an exhortation of comfort to those who have been hearing the words of the prophets). Thus the word concentrates attention in 7.11-13 on this single motif, and 8.9 describes a contrasted situation.

שים, 7.12, 14. In 7.12.##2-4 there is some alliteration (שמו שמיר משמוע) which is similar in some ways to v. 14 (ומשב וישימו ארץ־חמדה לשמה). It is difficult to evaluate the significance or purpose of this with any certainty, but it recalls our discussion of Zech. 5.5-11.

קצף, 7.12, 8.14. See on Zechariah 1 above. The only other chapter in which this root occurs is ch. 1 (v. 2 twice, v. 15 three times). In 1.14 we also find קנאתי לירושלם ולציון קנאה גדולה, which is very similar to 8.2b, קנאתי לציון קנאה גדולה וחמה גדולה קנאתי לה. Thus we need to consider whether there is an intended connection between these contrasting but similar words. חמה does not occur elsewhere in Zechariah.

כן, 7.13, 8.13, 15, does not seem to be significant in any way for our purposes.

גוי, 7.14, 8.13, 22, 23. The first two refer to Judah's being scattered/a curse among the nations. The last two refer to the nations coming to Jerusalem. From being scattered among the nations Judah will cause an unscattering of the nations themselves. We must plot the word, although it is not immediately evident whether it is used in structuring the chapter.

שוב, 7.14, 8.3, 15, is a common but significant word in passages such as the present one. The first reference is interesting: 'And the land was made desolate after them with respect to/preventing going out/over or returning'. Does it mean the land was shut behind them so that they were prevented from returning from exile? This seems better than RSV's rather weak 'so that no one went to and fro'.[1] Zech. 8.3 has 'I will return to Jerusalem' and v. 15 has 'Thus I have returned I have purposed...to do good...' which may simply mean, 'Thus again I have purposed...' We cannot lay much stress on these references, therefore, but I will plot them.

---

1. RSV presumably means that all normal life was suspended; cf. possibly Ps. 121.8, יהוה ישמר צאתך ובואך. So Rudolph: 'ohne Verkehr' (*Haggai*, p. 141). Driver refers to Ezek. 35.7, והכרתי ממנו עבר ושב, which is certainly similar to the present context, but equally ambiguous.

נשמה/לשמה, 7.14. These words from the same root make the climax of 7.8-14 very clear: והארץ נשמה...ארץ חמדה לשמה, preparing the way for the picture of blessing that replaces it in the verses immediately following.

קנא, 8.2.##5,7,11.[1] See קצף above.

שׁכן בתוך. See ירושלם above.

הר, 8.3.##14,17 only, is used of Jerusalem to emphasize the results of Yahweh's dwelling in her midst. It is not relevant for our purposes since the two instances are so close together.

עוד, 8.4, 20, does not seem to be significant.

זקן occurs only in 8.4.##7-8 in masculine and feminine plurals, once each. We need not plot it.

רחוב 8.4, 5 (2×), seems to be used to tie together and emphasize the picture portrayed in 8.4-5. The boys and girls playing in the streets balance the old men and women sitting in the streets. We need not plot this word, nor ילד, 8.5.##4-5.

רב, 8.4, 20, 22. The last two occurrences are identical forms, referring to 'the inhabitants of many cities' and 'many peoples' who will 'come' to Jerusalem in the days that are to come. We need not plot it but can consider it along with בוא.

יום 8.6, 9 (2×), 10, 11, 15, 23. 8.6, 10 and 23 have the expression בימים ההם/ההמה; 8.10 seems to mean 'these' (present) days; ימים האלה does occur in 8.9, 15. In other words there are references to the present or former days in 8.9-11 and 15, and to those that are to come in vv. 6 and 23. The form ההם occurs only in vv. 6 and 10. There does not seem to be any clear indication of structure in this usage. It does confirm the fact that the section 8.9-17 has a strong emphasis on the present and even the past, despite its obvious concern with the future. It does not seem possible that the phrases in question are pointers to structure.

בעיני + נפלא, only 8.6 (2×). This verse is isolated from the others by the introductory formula. The exact significance of the *niphal* of פלא is uncertain: does it mean 'to be wonderful' in the sense of 'almost impossible' or 'to be desired, approved'. The verse may be taken to imply either:

---

1. קנא is found otherwise only in 1.14, 12, 15. There it balances קצף, 1.2 and 15 (3×) which occurs otherwise only in 7.12; 8.14.

1. 'Just because it seems impossible to the remnant of the people, should it seem impossible to me also?'
2. 'Surely it seems a wonderful thing to happen to the remnant of this people. . . it also seems so to me' (i.e. our aims are the same). The only possible structural use of this phrase seems to be as a frame for the next expression.

שארית העם הזה, 8.6, 11, 12. This expression should be noted.

גם, 8.6, 21. There is some parallel between the phrases גם בעיני and גם אני but it does not seem striking enough to be significant. In the first Yahweh is the speaker, the second is spoken by people from the nations around.

נאם, 8.6, 11, 17, is not a hopeful word to investigate. In fact, in the first and third references it merely marks the end of a unit already delineated by another introductory formula. Its usage in 8.11 does not seem significant.

הושיע, 8.7, 13, must be plotted. It occurs within each of the inclusios noted in 8.1-13.

בוא, 8.7 (a), 8 (b), 10 (c), 20, 22 (d), is used in very different ways: (a) ארץ מבוא שמש; (b) והבאתי (*hiphil*, Yahweh speaking of the people); (c) וליוצא ולבא (cf. 7.14 מעבר ומשב, but it is not clear whether a connection is intended, probably not); (d) יבאו and ובאו of the foreigners who will come. The correspondence between (b) and (d) has been made clear in other ways (see above). It is probably safe to ignore (a) and (c).

אלהים occurs only at two significant points, the centre of 8.1-13 and the last word but one in ch. 8. 'And I will be their God (God to them)' and 'We have heard that God is with you'. We must accordingly plot this unlikely word.

חזק. We have noted the inclusio formed by this verb (*qal*) in vv. 9 and 13. The *hiphil* occurs twice in v. 23 when once would be sufficient grammatically. NEB's 'pluck up courage' for the first occurrence seems unwarranted.

אלה occurs not only with 'years' (see above) but with דברים, 8.9, 16. We need not plot it.

אדם, שכר, and אין all occur twice in v. 10 and nowhere else. Thus they establish the verse as a self-contained unit, as is already clear from the sense.

שלום ought to be significant: v. 10 'there was no peace from enemies'; v. 12 has 'seed of peace' which perhaps should be emended,[1] although its general import is clear as it is; v. 16 has 'truth and judgment of peace (you shall) judge in your gate'. Perhaps 'truth' has arisen by dittography; v. 19 has 'love truth and peace'. The variety of usage here makes it difficult to connect these instances.

רע, vv. 10, 16-17. See above under איש.

יהודה, 8.13, 15, 19, always occurs with בית. Note also יהודי in 8.23.

אל תיראו, 8.13, 15, is a traditional word of assurance. Combined with חזק it reminds the reader especially of Joshua 1, which is particularly appropriate in v. 13 after אושיע. We shall plot it, although the relation between the two references is not obvious.

זמם is used only twice with contrasting verbs להרע and להטיב, thus unifying vv. 14-15.

אהב, 8.17, 19, only occurs elsewhere in Zechariah in 13.6. In v. 17, 'love no false oath' comes at the end of an exhortation and warning, and immediately before 'all these things (which?) I hate'. In v. 19 the final phrase is a command to 'love truth and peace', two important words from the preceding sections (7.9; 8.8, 10, 12, 16).

הלך is concentrated in v. 21 (##1,7,8,17) and occurs also at 23.#19. There is no doubt that the word is central to the thought of these final verses; נלכה הלוך expresses a long term commitment to worship at Jerusalem; the repeated נלכה in v. 23 confirms the emphasis. Nevertheless there is no clear structuring purpose. It does not occur in 7.2 which is marked out as a parallel to vv. 21-22 by לחלות את פני יהוה. There is a virtual inclusio in v. 21.

אחת may be ignored. We note simply the concern of the writer with what goes on between people within the land; cf. expressions with רע and את.

בקש, vv. 21.#13, 22.#6, occurs as part of the phrase לבקש את יהוה צבאת, which is framed by ולחלות את פני יהוה. Whether this is an intended chiasmus or not, it is a striking one. The centre would be

---

1.   Petersen translates, 'Indeed, there shall be a sowing of peace' (*Haggai and Zechariah*, p. 304), and comments: 'The metaphor suggests that it will happen slowly and require patience, just as does the maturation of seeds in a field' (p. 307). The problem is that the noun clause is apparently incomplete. Rudolph adds משב after שלום and translates: 'Ja, "seither" gibt es die glückhafte Aussaat. . .' (*Haggai*, pp. 141-43). This is conjectural but cannot be too far from what is meant. For a full discussion see Petitjean, *Les oracles*, pp. 395-401.

'(Let me go, even I). And many peoples and strong nations will come'. It seems more in keeping with the thought of the passage, however, to regard the phrase as an emphatic parallel to 'to seek the favour of Yahweh' with the parallel inverted on the second occasion. Setting this out more fully, I think that we have in vv. 20b-22 the following structure:

a		Yet there will come peoples and inhabitants of many cities
		and the inhabitants of one will go to another saying
	b	Let us go
		c	to entreat the face of Yahweh
		c'	and to seek Yahweh of hosts
	b	I, even I, will go
a		And many peoples and strong nations will come
		c'	to seek Yahweh of hosts in Jerusalem
		c	and to entreat the face of Yahweh

For further details see below. Figure 9 gives the table of repeated words that may possibly be significant.

The overall movement of the chapter may be clear, but it is not easy to state precisely where one section goes into the next. The main problems come in connection with v. 8, which looks like a clumsy piece of editing by the final editor (see note above), for v. 9 seems to represent the content of the former prophets' preaching, and v. 11 gives the former response of the people of Judah, not that of Zechariah's hearers.[1]

---

1. Seeligmann says 'one is. . . compelled to assume that this verse is merely an erroneous editorial addition' ('Indications of Editorial Alteration in the Massoretic Text and the Septuagint', *VT* 11 (1961), p. 213). Petitjean notes that even commentators who accept the authenticity of v. 8 can hardly explain it in this context (*Les oracles*, pp. 321-22). Thus Van Hoonacker writes: 'On ne dirait certes pas que la formule. . . serve à introduire des citations d'anciens prophètes' (*Les douze prophètes* [Paris: Gabalda, 1908], p. 639. Elliger thought that vv. 8-10 were an independent unit inserted into the oracle 7.4-7/11-14 (*Das Buch der zwölf kleinen Propheten* [ATD, 25; Göttingen: Vandenhoeck & Ruprecht, 1982], II, p. 137 n. 8). He notes the similarity with the contents of 8.16-17. Petitjean himself (*Les oracles*, p. 322) assumes that 7.8 was put in by a reviser who thought that the following כה אמר יהוה must be the start of the new oracle. Greek manuscript 240 omits vv. 8-9a.

Chapter	7							8							
Verses / **Word**	1	3	5	7	9	11	13	1	4	7	10	13	16	19	22
שלח		2^1				12^{10}					10^{18}				
איש		2^5			9^{12}	10^8			4^{11}		10^{22}		$16^7 17^1$		
חלה + פנים }		2^6 2^8													$\begin{Bmatrix}21^9+ \\ 22^{11}+\end{Bmatrix}$
נביא		3^9		7^8		12^{15}				9^{14}					
חמישי		3^{13}	5^{12}											19^8	
עשה		3^{16}			9^{11}								16^4		
ארץ			5^5				$14^{8,14}$		$7^{9,11}$		12^7				
צום			$5(3\times)$											$19(4\times)$	
שבעי			5^{13}											19^{10}	
אבי			5^{19}							8^9	11^5				
קרא				7^5		$13^{3,7}$			3^{10}						
יד				7^7		12^{14}			4^{13}	9^6		13^{18}			
ראשון				7^9		12^{16}					11^4				
ירושלם				7^{11}					$3^{9,11}4^{10}$	8^5			15^8		22^{10}
ישב				$7^{12,18}$					4^6					$20^9 21^2$	
עיר				7^{14}					$3^{12}5^2$					20^{10}	
שפט					$9^{6,8}$								$16^{11,13}$		
אמת					9^7				3^{13}	8^{13}			$16^{6,10}$	19^{20}	
אח					$9^{14}10^9$										
חשב לבב					10^{11f}								17^{6f}		
נתן					11^3							$12^{5,8,12}$			
שמע					11^8	$12^4 13^{5,9}$				9^7					
שים					12^2	14^{13}									
קצף cf. קנאה↓					12^{18}		$\downarrow$						14^{10}		
גדול					12^{19}			$2^{8,10}$							
גוי							14^4					13^5			$22^4 23^{13}$
שוב							14^{12}	3^4					15^2		
שמם/שמה							$14^{9,16}$								
קנא								$2^{5,7,11}$							
ציון								$2^6 3^6$							
שכן בתוך ירושלם								3^7+		8^3+					
נפלא בעיני									$6^{6f.,14f.}$						
שארית העם הזה									6^8+		$11^6 12^{16}+$				
הושיע									7^6			13^{11}			
בוא									$7^{12}8^1$		10^{13}			$20^7 22^1$	23^{23}
אלהים										8^{12}					
יד + חזק										9^5+		$13^{17}+$			
שלום											$10^{15}12^3$		16^{12}	19^{21}	
רא											10^{23}		16^9	17^4	
יהודה												13^7	15^{11}	19^{15}	
אל תיראו												$13^{15f.}$	$15^{12f.}$		
זמם												14^7	15^3		
אהב														$17^{11} 19^{22}$	
הלך														$21(4\times)$	
חלה את פני cf. בקש														$21^{13}22^6$	

Figure 9: *Zechariah 7–8:*
Verse and word numbers of words occurring twice or more
(superscripts = word numbers)

It would be strange indeed to find such an incompetent piece of work by the editor who has apparently shown such sensitivity and concern for detail in the construction of the final form of the text that he passed on. We note that v. 8 does mark a major transition to the central section of this whole unit. The scene has been set by the description of the men who come to entreat the favour of Yahweh, and by the question about fasting. The unit will end by an answer to the question and a promise that many will entreat the favour of Yahweh. Immediately within this frame we find whole phrases that form a further strong inner frame (משפט אמת שפטו, 7.9; אמת ומשפט ואיש את רעת, 7.10; ורעת איש אחיו אל תחשבו בלבבכם, 8.16; שלום שפטו רעהו אל תחשבו בלבבכם, 8.17).

In view of these facts it seems logical to assume that the final redactor added v. 8 deliberately to mark off this section. Further, it would make sense to understand it in this way:

1.   'And the word...Zechariah'. The redactor reinforces what is said in v. 1 which is interrupted by vv. 2-3 and then continued by the preliminary off-putting reply.
2.   The correct understanding of the tenses and punctuation is: 'Thus Yahweh has said, "Render true judgments...your heart". But they refused...desolate.'

This means that mention of the 'former prophets' in v. 7, followed by an emphatic description of the prosperity of the whole land, is meant to prepare the reader for a fuller message from the former prophets, an account of the lack of response and the consequences (vv. 9-10, 11-12a [ending with 'former prophets'], and vv. 12b-14 [ending with the twice repeated description of the land as desolate]).

We can appreciate why many scholars have regarded vv. 8-10 (or 8-14) as redactional without assenting to negative opinions about the skill with which it has been done. The progression of thought seems to me to be clear and satisfying. If v. 8 does represent a misunderstanding by an editor, then I think we have to think in terms of someone other than the one responsible for the basic shape and direction of the final text of chs. 7-8.

Zechariah 8 begins with another strong introductory formula, which marks a new phase in the prophecy. We are about to hear the *good* news. Before giving the description of Yahweh's return to Jerusalem the writer picks up the theme of wrath (קצף, 7.12) against the people.

```
IF    7.1
A     2          Men of Bethel sent to entreat favour of Yahweh
  B   3              Question about fasting
      4-7            Off-putting reply: fasting for whose benefit?
                     Remember what former prophets said
                     when land prosperous

  IF      8
  C       9-10        Former prophets said, Render true judgments. . .
                      do not devise evil against brother in your heart

   cd      11-12a     They refused to hear words of former prophets

    D       12b-14    Therefore great wrath (קצף) came. . .
                      Land became desolate

      IF 8.1
      de 2                  Thus....'I am jealous with great jealousy and wrath'
         E      3-8a        'I will. . .dwell in midst of Jerusalem
                            Promise of blessing for remnant of people
                            will save from east. . .and west. . .
                            . . .they will dwell in midst of Jerusalem

         F      8b          They my people and I their God. . .

         E      9-13        'Let your hands be strong. . .
                            Promise of blessing for remnant of people
                            . . .were a byword among nations, but now I
                            will save and you will be a blessing
                                Fear not
                            Let hands be strong'

    D      14-15     As I purposed evil when. . .provoked to קצף
                     So now purposed to do good to Jerusalem
                            Fear not

  C    15-17    So now: Render true judgments. . .
                do not devise evil in your heart. . .etc.

 IF  18
 B   19             Fasts will become feasts, so love truth and peace
A  20-23            Many will come to entreat the favour of Yahweh[1]
```

Figure 10: *Overall structure of Zechariah 7–8*

---

of Judah, and turns it into jealousy for Jerusalem (the root קנא is repeated three times, recalling 1.14 where it occurs twice, and its connection with קצף in Zech. 1.2 [twice] and v. 15 [three times]; and the word חמה is introduced). The word קצף itself is not repeated until 8.14.

In 8.3 we have a subsidiary introductory formula which leads into a section enclosed by שכן בתוך ירושלם, and which contains three further introductory formulae. This is the central promise of the whole section, and it leads to its climax in v. 8, with the affirmation of the central covenant promise 'they shall be my people and I will be their God'. After this there follow exhortations concerning the appropriate response to this, along with various further concrete promises.

We note that in 8.3-8a and 9-13 certain features strengthen the overall structure. שארית העם הזה occurs in 8.6, 11 and 12, הושיע in 8.7 and 13. They are arranged serially rather than chiastically, but it is impossible to say whether this is intended or not: they would have to be arranged in some way that looked regular.

Note also that the words תחזקנה ידיכם form an inclusio around vv. 9-13. And, linking in with this, אל תיראו forms a further inclusio for vv. 14-15. The only trouble is that the first one occurs immediately *before* the תחזקנה ידיכם of v. 13. This looks like an effective device for linking and yet marking off separate sections, but I have not been able to prove that its use was recognized. The resulting overall structure is set out in figure 10.

It is now possible to test the security of this result. Have I been selective in my use of specific marker words? Have I ignored important words or phrases that would distract the attentive hearer or reader from this structure? If so, then it would cast doubt upon either the intentions or the competence of the writer. It will be seen from the table that the majority of words that might be considered distinctive are actually accounted for in this outline. Words that are clearly distinctive, and especially whole phrases do, by and large, fall inside corresponding sections and not outside. The only serious possible counter-examples seem to be שלום and the plural גוים. The latter is used in a different phrase, and does not count against the outline. שלום seems to be a special element introduced in the latter part of the section:

8.10   In those days there was no שלום. . .
8.12   But now there will be a sowing of שלום
8.16   Therefore do the things that the former prophets urged—especially
        משפט and אמת—things that make for שלום
8.19   Joyful feasts are coming so love אמת and שלום.

I do not know why it was kept until the end. In any case it seems to perform a logical function as it is used in our text.

The table also reveals other possibilities for strengthening this conclusion: the plural 'cities' is found in only 7.7 and 8.20; אמת is more important than we have allowed for, for it occurs not only in the phrases where it is linked with משפט, but twice in the central section 8.3-8a + b, and with שלום in 8.19. Thus it links together all the important theological words (including צדקה in 8.8b) that describe Yahweh's requirements.

שמע occurs only in 7.11-14 and its matching partner 8.9-13. However, we must regard these as of possible subsidiary value only.

The result has been based on:

1. Divisions of the text decided on form- and literary-critical methods, independent of structural concerns.
2. Consideration of *all* repeating words and phrases, without regard to how they might fit into an overall pattern.
3. The progression of thought of the whole section.

We may therefore claim that this is a secure result, which agrees in the main with the scholarly consensus,[1] but attempts to find a coherent plan in the working of the final redactor. As previously, there is reason to think that he was someone with literary sensitivity, who recognized and used inclusios and chiastic structures with clarity and subtlety.

It remains for us to ask whether he had any further purposes in arranging chs. 1–8 in this way, and whether he even had a hand in 9–14. This we shall do in Chapter 4.

---

1.   S. Mittmann ('Die Einheit von Sacharja', in W. Claasen [ed.], *Text and Context* [Sheffield: JSOT Press, 1988], pp. 269-82) argues for a different structure for 8.1-8 as follows: IF (v. 1), A (v. 2), B (a, v. 2; b, vv. 4-6aβ), C (a, v. 6aαb; b, vv. 7-8). He also sees subsidiary patterns within this, e.g. v. 3 = abba: Zion–Jerusalem–Jerusalem–Zion; vv. 7 and 8 each represent abba. He has not taken adequate note of the whole context of chs. 7–8, and most of the criticisms I have made of their scholars' work in Chapter 1 above also apply to this article.

The Structure of Individual Units in Zechariah 9–14

As we proceed through the second part of the book of Zechariah we shall have in mind the results obtained by Lamarche in his analysis of these chapters. I believe that he has failed to take account of the safeguards that we recommended in Chapter 1, and that, therefore, results largely have to be rejected or modified. I propose to show this by a detailed consideration of his treatment of Zech. 9.1-8, which will be the first unit to be dealt with, and then by a briefer consideration of his work on other sections. I shall also mention other scholars who have followed or reacted to Lamarche to some extent, notably Lacocque and Otzen.[1]

Since Lamarche's book is difficult to obtain I give a brief account of its aims and results. The sub-title of the book, *Structure littéraire et messianisme*, describes its two main concerns. Lamarche believes that, throughout Zech. 9-14, there is a careful ordering of the text. Individual units are seen to have a regular structure of some sort

---

1. Lacocque is sympathetic to Lamarche's work and his results are quite similar. Otzen has one section devoted to structure in his otherwise standard historically oriented work (*Studien*, pp. 213-29), brief indeed, when a large proportion of it is taken up in either outlining and criticizing Lamarche's results or in enthusing about Ed. Nielsen's work on Mic. 4–5 (*Oral Tradition* [London: SCM Press, 1954], pp. 84-93). This causes one reviewer, R. Tournay, to remark that it is a pity he has not read B. Renaud's *Structure et attaches littéraires de Michée 4–5* (*RB* 72 [1965], p. 446). His theory is that these highly structured texts are based on older documents, e.g. Zech. 9–10 'ist sicher *aus kultisch-liturgisches Form-gestaltungen entlehnt*' (his italics; pp. 223-24). I shall discuss his treatment of Zech. 9–10 (after I have considered Zech. 10.1–11.3) but be content with brief remarks on the other chapters. J.D.W. Watts has a brief treatment of the structure of 9.1–11.3 in his *Broadman Bible Commentary. VII. Hosea to Malachi* (Nashville: Broadman Press, 1972), p. 341. He presents the section as

Frame	(9.1-8)	The reclamation of Assyrian provinces
A	(9.9-10)	The king of peace comes
B	(9.11-17)	The Lord returns the captives
A	(10.1)	The Lord provides
B	(10.2-11)	The Lord cares for Judah and Joseph
A	(10.12)	The Lord strengthens his people
Frame	(11.1-3)	The conquest of Lebanon and Bashan.

Some of these headings are not appropriate for the whole unit, and it is not clear why the units marked A or B should be thought to be parallel to each other.

(often chiastic) and the units themselves are arranged in an elaborate chiastic fashion:

A 9.1-8   Judgment and salvation of neighbouring peoples
  B 9.9-10   Arrival and description of the king
    C 9.11-10.1   WAR AND VICTORY OF ISRAEL
      D 10.2-3a   *Presence of idols; judgment*
    C 10.3b-11.3   WAR AND VICTORY OF ISRAEL
  B 11.4-17   The shepherd rejected by the people

    C 12.1-9   WAR AND VICTORY OF ISRAEL
      B 12.10-13.1   Yahweh's representative pierced;
                    mourning and purification
        D 13.2-6   *Suppression of idols and false prophets*
      B 13.7-9   Shepherd struck; people tested, purification
                 and return to God
    C 14.1-15   WAR AND VICTORY OF ISRAEL
A 14.16-21   Judgment and salvation of all nations[1]

If this represents the intention of the author/editor, as Lamarche believes, then we have good reason to interpret the sections marked 'B' as referring to the same person: the shepherd-king, who is Yahweh's representative, and who, through his own suffering, brings about purification for the people. This is obviously very much in harmony with the NT and traditional Christian teaching about the messiah.

Lamarche's interpretation of the meaning of Zechariah 9–14 for its own time is as follows: there was a historical individual, whose contemporaries considered to be a possible messiah. After his death, the author of Zechariah 9–14, who knew the 'suffering servant' poems, continued in his messianic hope for a while. When he realized that the dead prophet might not be the messiah, 'our prophet does not limit himself to this perspective alone; he envisages also, after the messiah's death, and the conversion of Israel, a dynastic messianism (12.8) and a messianic salvation set up by Yahweh the King (14.8ff)'.[2]

Lamarche's book was given a positive, if more or less cautious, welcome by scholars who reviewed it, including Rowley and Emerton. It has been accepted by Baldwin in her commentary, and

---

1. *Zacharie 9–14*, pp. 112-13, cf. Baldwin, *Haggai, Zechariah, Malachi*, pp. 78-79.
2. Lamarche, *Zacharie 9–14*, p. 153

many evangelical scholars have found it congenial.[1] It is therefore worthwhile to examine carefully its method and conclusions.

Zechariah 9.1-8

This section has formidable difficulties and there is a good chance that several corruptions have found their way into the text. Unfortunately there is little agreement on how it should be emended and I shall not entertain any emendation unless it has strong support from the versions. It is possible that some important indication of structure may have been lost through textual corruption, and that restoration of the true text would reveal it. This study, however, is attempting to find a firm basis from which to determine the writer's/editor's intentions with regard to structure. We must therefore be prepared to miss some of these, and leave them to be discovered and confirmed at a later date. On the other hand it is possible that an accidental corruption of the text has produced something that looks like an intentional pattern. It is not likely that this will happen very often, and so there is probably not much danger in sticking to the MT. We may, of course, take additional precautions by noting readings that are especially dubious.

In Zech. 9.1-8 there are no emendations, in my opinion, that can be considered secure enough to be adopted. The only reading of the MT that is seriously in doubt and significant for our purposes is עין אדם in v. 1.[2]

We may be sure that vv. 1-8 form a unit of some sort, and that they contain both judgment (vv. 3-4 of Tyre; vv. 5-6 of Philistia) and

---

1. As well as Baldwin, we may mention R.T. France, *Jesus and the Old Testament* (London: Tyndale Press, 1971).

2. It is probably precarious to accept the MT here. So I shall be careful not to build any weighty theory on it. The most popular emendation is ערי ארם, translating, 'to Yahweh belong the cities of Aram', which ties in well with the mention of Damascus, and the northern cities of Hamath, Tyre and Sidon. However there is no textual warrant for changing 'eye' to 'cities' or 'city', and it is difficult to explain how the easy reading ארם came to be altered to the less likely אדם. Cf. Otzen, *Studien,* pp. 235-36; Baldwin, *Haggai, Zechariah, Malachi,* p. 159; and also Rudolph, *Haggai,* p. 168, who prefers to emend אדם only, translating 'for to Yahweh belongs the eye of Aram'. He notes that LXX, Syr. and Targ. have 'For Yahweh has an eye on man', which is preferable to Elliger's 'To Yahweh is the eye of mankind directed' (p. 76 of 'Ein Zeugnis aus der jüdischen Gemeinde im Alexanderjahr 332 v Chr: Eine territorialgeschichtliche Studien zu Sach 9.1-8', *ZAW* 61-62, [1949-50], pp. 63-115; *Zwölf kleinen Propheten,* II, p. 144).

promise (v. 7b at least, for Philistia; v. 8 for Jerusalem). Verses 1-2 certainly mention Damascus and Hamath in Syria, and the Phoenician cities of Tyre and Sidon, and it seems most likely that the tone of the message is judgment.

This short section is of particular importance because it begins the second part of Zechariah. I shall set out below the words which occur twice or more in this section together with points of contact in other sections of Zechariah, for the following reasons:

1. It is likely that, if there are any intended connections at all between the major units of Zechariah 9–14, then some are likely to involve this section.
2. Lamarche ignores some distinctive phrases that occur here and elsewhere in Zechariah 9–14, and it is convenient to demonstrate this here, where we are dealing in more detail than subsequently with his method and results.
3. It is helpful to consider this section in relation to the whole, in order either to understand its overall function or to establish that it is independent of the rest.

The Structure of Zechariah 9.1-8 according to Lamarche
Lamarche presents the following plan:[1]

a	'Rattachement' of the nations to the Kingdom of Yahweh (1a, 2a-bα)		2 *vers*	Salvation 3 *vers*	
	For Yahweh has seen (1b)		1 *vers*		
					North: 6 *vers*
	b	Motifs of condemnation (2bβ-3)	2 *vers*	Punishment 3 *vers*	
		Punishment (4)	1 *vers*		
	b'	Punishment (5-6a)	2 *vers*		
		Suppression of motifs of condemnation (6b-7a, α, β)	1 *vers*	Punishment 3 *vers*	
					South: 6 *vers*
a'	'Rattachement' of the nations to the Kingdom of Yahweh (7aγ-8a)		$2\frac{1}{2}$ *vers*	Salvation 3 *vers*	
	For Yahweh has seen (8b)		$\frac{1}{2}$ *vers*		

1. *Zacharie 9–14*, p. 42.

We agree on the unit as verses 1-8, and that themes of condemnation, punishment and salvation are found in this section. However, several words of caution must be mentioned.

1. The titles for each section are artificial. Sections a and a' do not correspond nearly as closely as this scheme suggests.

2. The only actual word in common is עין (but see below). Lamarche's 'for Yahweh has seen' depends on accepting a consonantal text that is not quite certain, and an interpretation that is not the most natural, although it does find support in the LXX (and possibly the Syriac and Targum): 'for Yahweh has his eye on men'.[1] He suggests that it may be possible to read the verb עין instead of the noun and appeals to its frequency in Ugaritic. In the OT it only occurs as a *qere* (!) in 1 Sam. 18.9. It is quite possible that an inclusio is intended, but it is illegitimate to confirm the interpretation of v. 1 by appealing to the resulting structure.

3. 'Salvation' is intended in this section, but it is only certain in v. 7. To characterize a and a' in this way is to take a precarious step. However there does seem to be a genuine similarity between 'and all the tribes of Israel' and 'like a clan in Judah'. This, together with the fact that 'Israel' occurs in the northern section and 'Judah' in the southern, lends support to Lamarche's interpretation.

4. The 'verses' or 'lines' that Lamarche records are of unequal length, and the balance and symmetry of the text is not nearly so exact as that of Lamarche's scheme:[2]

Lamarche's divisions and quantification		words/ combinations	words
1a, 2ab	2 *vers*	8	13
1b	1 *vers*	3	7
2bβ-3	2 *vers*	12	13
4	1 *vers*	9	9
5-6a	2 *vers*	18	19
6b-7aαβ	1 *vers*	7	9
7aγ-8a	2 *vers*	17	19
8b	½ *vers*	4	4

5. There is very little to suggest that the writer thought of the sort of divisions that Lamarche sets out. There are almost no significant words that occur in a and a' or in b and b':

1. *Zacharie 9–14*, p. 36. See p. 166 n. 2.
2. *Zacharie 9–14*, p. 42.

a + a'   עין only (ראה is in b' + a')
b + b'   מאזד only (שקלון, עזה and ישב occur only in b')

On the other hand צר and עקרון occur in a + b and b' + a' respectively. This *could* mean that in both halves a place name provides a link over a break (continuity in discontinuity). However, the material linked in vv. 2-3 is very different from that linked in vv. 5-7. We should seem to be resorting to rather desperate conjectures.

When we look at the actual content of vv. 1 and 8, it is difficult to believe that 'The word of Yahweh is in the land of Hadrach' is meant to correspond to 'I will encamp at (? = ל) my house...' One would have expected at least some verbal clue (e.g. ? בביתי).

6. Lamarche links this section with 14.16-21. The possibly significant verbal links between the sections are as follows:

יהודה	9.7; 14.21 (but also 9.13; 10.3, 6; 11.14; 12 (6×); 14.5, 14)
בית	*9.8; 14.20, 21* (but also 10.3, 6, 6; *11.13*; 12 (7×); 13.1, 6; 14.2. Instances italicized refer to the Temple).
מלך	9.5; *14.16, 17* (but also *9.9*; 11.6; 14.5, *9*, 10. Instances italicized refer to Yahweh as king).

This does not inspire confidence. The theme of Yahweh's kingship is, however, important and only found explicitly in 9.9 and 14.9, 16-17, suggesting that further research along these lines might be fruitful.

7. There are several distinctive words and phrases which occur elsewhere (e.g. מעבר ומשב, הכה בים, טים, חוצות). These need to be accounted for. Further, specific nations are mentioned in 10.10-12 (or 11.1) (Egypt, Assyria and Lebanon) as well as in 14.16-21 (Egypt alone). Why should we not put 10.10-12 parallel to 14.18-19?

Although Lamarche does not seem to have considered this sort of possibility, his method implies an answer: the relationship of each passage as a whole to other whole passages matters more than individual repeating words. Thus it is true, as he says, that there is a progression towards universalism. In 9.1-8 the focus is on Israel's near neighbours, with muted promises about salvation outside Israel/ Judah. In 14.16-21, although Egypt is singled out, the focus is primarily upon 'all the nations'.

It should be interesting to see what results my own proposed method leads to in comparison with those of Lamarche.

Repeated Words in Zechariah 9.1-8

יהוה, vv. 1.##3,9, 14.##1,8,15,16. There is an interesting gap between vv. 1 and 14, but it does not seem to be significant for our purposes.

גם, vv. *2*, 7*, 11*, *12*. Otherwise: 3.7##12*,17; 8.6, 21*; 11.8; 12.2; 13.2; *14.14*. Instances marked with an asterisk have a following *maqqeph* with a pronoun. Those italicized are followed by a noun. The word itself is insignificant enough. Does it suggest the work of a redactor, particularly when used at the beginning of a verse? It does not seem possible that it has any structuring function within 9.1-8 or chs. 9–14.

כי may be ignored.

עין, vv. 1, 8. It is tempting to try and make use of this. It has been an important (though sometimes obscure) word in chs. 1–8, and it occurs only at the beginning and end of our section. Elsewhere in chs. 9–14: 11.12, 17##10,15; 12.4; 14.12. (In Zech. 1–8: 2.1*, 5*, 12; 3.9; 4.10; 5.1*, 5*, 6, 9*; 6.1*. An asterisk denotes the expression 'I lifted up my eyes' or similar expressions). Our safest course of action is to keep the MT and to translate 'Yahweh's eye is upon man' (cf. Zech. 12.4; 3.9; 4.10). See p. 166 n. 3 above, and the section on 'eye' in Chapter 4 below.

צר, vv. 2, 3; cf. מצור 3.3. There are no occurrences elsewhere.

מאד, vv. 2, 5, 9 ('very wise', 'writhe exceedingly', 'rejoice exceedingly'). Some sort of progression or contrast may be intended here but it is impossible to demonstrate it. We must ignore the word.

ראה, vv. 5, 8, 14, is a common word in chs. 1–6, but occurs, in the rest of the book, only here and at 10.7.

אשקלון, v. 5.##2,14; עזה, v. 5.##4,13; and עקרון, vv. 5.#7, 7.#14, should be considered together. Verse 5 has a chiastic formation:

Ashkelon—Gaza—Ekron—Gaza—Ashkelon

But Ekron also occurs in v. 7, after mention has been made of Ashdod, and Philistia as a whole. We have met this pattern before.[1]

---

1.   Amos 5.5-6. Zeph. 2.4-7 has the following sequence:

v. 4	Gaza—Ashkelon—Ashdod—Ekron
v. 5	Cherethites/Philistines
v. 7	Ashkelon.

Here it would be reasonable to suppose that the mention of Ashkelon stands for the whole group of Philistine cities. Note also that Gath is omitted also from Zephaniah,

Gath is not mentioned, possibly because it no longer existed, but that is not our particular concern. Thus vv. 5-7 have this structure:

$$a^1 \, a^2 \, a^3 \, a^2 \, a^1 \, a^4 \, A^{1-4} \, B \, a^3$$

Clearly this has a certain regularity, but it is not obviously one intended by the author or redactor of the section. It would be understandable if:

1. Ekron was special in some way, for example the chief of the Philistine cities.
2. Ashdod was to receive special treatment, for example if an especially large number of deportees and/or settlers came from elsewhere. Perhaps Isa. 20.1 and Jer. 25.20 support this. On the other hand we might want to posit a redactor who inserted v. 6a.

ישב, vv. 5.#16, 6.#1 (adjacent words). This is a fairly frequent word in Zechariah. In Zechariah 9–14 it occurs in 10.6; 11.6; 12.5, 6, *7*, *8*, *10*; *13.1*; 14.10, 11.##1,7 (occurrences of the participle 'inhabitants' are italicized). In 10.6 we should perhaps read והשיבותים 'I will bring them back' instead of והושבתים 'I will cause them to dwell'.[1]

There are no other repeated words in Zech. 9.1-8, so it may be worthwhile to ask what words occur in this section and elsewhere up to the end of the next major unit, 11.3. If we do that the following words are included.

and that there are several similarities between Zeph. 3.14-20 and Zechariah, especially 9.9 (cf. R. Mason, *The Use of Earlier Biblical Material in Zechariah 9–14: A Study of Inner Biblical Exegesis* [dissertation, King's College, London, 1973], pp. 140-41), but also other parts of the book. Jer. 47.5, 7 has Gaza and Ashkelon and then Ashkelon. This yields no firm evidence of any understood patterns.

In Zech. 10.10–11.1 we find:

10.10-11	Egypt—Assyria—Gilead and	Lebanon—Assyria—Egypt
11.1		Lebanon

It is *possible* that one form of inclusio was aBa...B (or more elaborately, abCba...C). This may only be proposed tentatively at this stage (see below on 10.1–11.3).

1. Rudolph (*Haggai*, pp.193-94) notes that MT in 10.6 is a mixed form from והשבתים and והשיבותים ('und ich lasse sie wohnen/zuruckkehren'). He reads the latter (against LXX) on the basis of 10.9b, 10a.

חוצות טיט is found at 9.3 and 10.5. The usage is not the same and neither word occurs elsewhere in Zechariah ('streets' in 8.5 is רחבות), although the phrase occurs in Mic. 7.10 and Ps. 18.42 (= 2 Sam. 22.43), 'always as a simile of contempt, ignominious treatment'.[1] Is this meant to indicate the beginning and end of a section? Is 9.3 near enough to the beginning to form an inclusio? The suggestion does not look plausible, but it is interesting that there is an inclusio in 10.6, 12.

אדני, 9.4, 14, occurs nowhere else in Zechariah. Perhaps this unlikely word had some significance (which would never have been noticed once 'Yahweh' was replaced by 'The Lord' in public reading).

והכה בים, 9.4; 10.11 (ים is also found in 9.10.##13,15; 10.11; 14.4, 8.##10,14). The two occurrences of this phrase, apart from being quite distinctive, have several features in common. 'The Lord will smite/hurl(?) her wealth into the sea (והכה בים חילה)' refers to Tyre, but would probably also recall the fate of Pharaoh's host in the Red Sea. It is therefore particularly interesting that in 10.11 we find והכה בים גלים, possibly referring to the 'sea of Egypt' (reading מצרים for צרה). I lay no weight on this unsupported emendation, but Egypt is mentioned in 10.10 and later in v. 11 (by name, and also by means of the expression 'depths of the Nile'). Some correspondence is probably intended, therefore, between 9.4 and 10.11, particularly since the meaning of הכה is different in each case.[2]

In 9.10 we find the idea of the king's dominion from 'sea to sea', while in 14.8 living waters flow from Jerusalem to the eastern sea and to the western sea. This statement is immediately followed by the assertion that 'Yahweh will become king over all the earth'. The thought is comparable in that the seas are used to express the worldwide extent of the king's rule. The victory is won and peace/life is established. The reference in 14.4 seems to be unconnected (מזרחה וימה).

· 1. BDB, p. 376.

2. In 9.4 והכה בים הילה is a *hiphil* of the root נכה (smite) followed by two nouns, one with ב and one without. In Num. 11.33 the same situation occurs, but there the noun with *beth* is the object: ויך יהוה בעם מכה. Here the meaning must be: 'And he will smite its wealth in/into/with/by the sea' if the text is correct. The meaning 'hurl' adopted by RSV and some commentators (e.g. Baldwin) does not find support elsewhere in the OT. In 10.11 we have two accusatives: 'And he will smite the sea (+ ב) waves'. The word does occur elsewhere, plus *beth* before the object (e.g. Exod. 17.6; 1 Sam. 14.31).

אכל, vv. 4, 15. Otherwise only 7.6.##2,7; 11.1, 9, 16; 12.6. In ch. 7 the meaning is literal; in chs. 9–14 it is figurative of destruction.

מלך, vv. 5, 9. There is a strong contrast here: 'the king will perish from Gaza...O Zion, Your king comes to you'. Elsewhere in Zechariah the word is found in 7.1 ('King Darius' in a date formula), 11.6, 14.5, 9, 10, 16, 17 (in which vv. 9 and 16-17 refer to Yahweh as the king). There is an obvious connection between 9.9-10 and these verses in ch. 14.

כרת, 9.6, 10.##1,6. All these refer in some way to the establishment of peace in Israel. The pride of the Philistines, the chariot and the battle bow, will be cut off. Elsewhere the word occurs in Zechariah only in 11.10 (in the phrase 'covenant which I cut') and 13.2, 8 (both referring to judgment).

אלהים, 9.7, 16, is comparatively rare in Zechariah. It occurs in expressions such as 'Yahweh your God' or 'I will be their (etc.) God'. Verse 16, which contains the first type of expression, also reflects the second (כצאן עמו). Verse 7 speaks of Philistia as a remnant 'to our God'. There is no warrant, therefore, for ignoring this word, but rather confirmation that it is significant in Zechariah. Again, the connection is not within vv. 1-8.

יהודה, 9.7, 13. Otherwise 1.12; 2 (4×); 8 (3×); 10.3, 6; 11.14; 12.2-7 (6×); 14.5, 14, 21.

עבר, 9.8.##4,7. Also 3.4 (*hiphil*); 7.14; 10.11; 13.2 (*hiphil*). The unusual expression מעבר ומשב also occurs in 7.14.

שוב, 9.8 (מעבר ומשב), 12.##1,9 ('Return!'—'I will cause to return' [i.e. 'restore']). Also 10.9, 10 ('return', 'cause them to return [from Egypt]'; both used of blessing); 13.7 in chs. 9–14 (see above for chs. 1–8). Zech. 9.12 and 10.9-10 correspond well to each other. I wonder if there is an intentional contrast between the lack of עבר and שוב in 9.8, and the promise of both in 10.9-11, but it is impossible to demonstrate this or to build on it.

In examining repeated words in the section 9.1–11.3, we have discovered some surprising and possibly significant facts.

1. There does not seem to be much correspondence within the section 9.1-8, certainly less than in any of the small sections that we examined in Zechariah 1–8. The only plausible theory of intentional structuring would have to be based on the names of Philistine cities, and the textually doubtful עין (see below).

2.   The most distinctive repeated words occur in two two-word phrases (which strengthens their power to draw attention to themselves), and nowhere else in Zechariah. These must be accounted for.

3.   If these phrases are part of the original text then they are the most likely to be used to link different sections of Zechariah together, viz. 9.3 with 10.5, and 9.4 with 10.11.

Some further observations may be made. In 10.11 there are several words which are found in 9.1-8. They are as follows:

Word number		
1	ועבר	9.8.##4,7
2	בים	9.4 (see words 4-5 below)
3	צרה	(+ 8.10 only)
4-5	והכה בים	9.4
6	גלים	(cf. נָלָּה only 4.2)
7	והובישו	9.5 (+ 10.5; 11.17.##13-14)
8	כל	
9	מצולות	(+ 1.8 only. Listed separately as doubtful in BDB)
10	יאר	
11	והורד	(+ 11.2 only)
12	גאון	9.6
13	אשור	(cf. 9.6)
14	ושבם	9.1 (cf. אלף 9.7)
15	מצרים	(+ 10.10; 14.18, 19)
16	יסור	9.7 (+ 3.4; 7.11)

There are indications here that the end of ch. 10 is the end of a major section. Seven of v. 11's fifteen different words occur in 9.1-8 and both sections deal with Israel's traditional enemies. It is therefore likely that an inclusio of some sort is intended. In addition we note that 10.11 is the sort of verse that a redactor might have produced: a gather-line (though the gathering is not done in strict order). In addition, there is an inclusio formed by ובברתי[ם] 10.6, 12, which directs our attention to חוצות טים[כ/ב] 9.3 and 10.5. This encloses nearly the whole of the remainder of 9.1–10.12. Yet another inclusio now appears likely:

9.10   קשת מלחמה
10.3b-5a   במלחמה   קשת מלחמה   במלחמה[1]

These, however, must be investigated more fully if we are not to fall into the trap of making arbitrary selections from possibly significant words.

Summary

There are few words that occur twice or more in 9.1-8. Moreover, most of the potentially significant words have contacts only outside this section. Within it we have discovered only: עין (with כי, גם, יהוה textual problems), צר (adjacent words), ישב, ראה, מאד (adjacent words), עבר (two words intervening), apart from the Philistine references. There are grounds, therefore, for the following assertions:

1. Verses 5-7 are bound together by a strange inclusio of 'Ekron' and 'Ekron as part of a chiasmus'.
2. ראה might form an inclusio for vv. 5-8, but the word is not very distinctive. *Perhaps* the fact that 'eye' *may* also be used to form an inclusio strengthens the claim of the word 'see'.
3. עין might form an inclusio for vv. 1b-8, but v. 1b is dubious and not really in the right place.[2]
4. I have noted particular connections between 9.1-8 and 10.10-12, and these suggest that we should consider the larger unit more fully. In fact I shall treat 9.1–11.3 together since most commentators continue to this point before making a division.[3]

Before doing that we shall examine the smaller units that make up this section, viz. 9.9-10, 9.11-17 and 10.1–11.3. If we find that they do have an integrity of their own, we shall be inclined to conclude that 9.1-8 is, after all, a self-contained unit. If however, we discover links mainly outside the separate units, we shall have confirmed the tentative conclusions reached in this section.

1. See p. 170 n. 1.
2. However, see Mason, *Zechariah 9–14*, p. 32; Sæbø, 'Die deutero-sacharjanische Frage', p. 161 and n. 6. It becomes plausible if Hamath and Damascus are representative: 'beyond Damascus', 'far north'.
3. See Chapter 2 above.

Zechariah 9.9-17

We shall first consider words which occur twice or more within 9.9-17 before looking at vv. 9-10 and 11-17 separately:

בת, v. 9.##3,6. This is used in the parallel expressions 'daughter of Zion/Jerusalem'. It does not occur elsewhere in Zechariah 9–14.

בן, vv. 9, 13.##9,12. The first of these means 'foal' which is hardly comparable to the normal use in v. 13. Otherwise it only occurs in 10.7, 9 where the fairly rare גבור is found, as in 9.13 (otherwise only 10.5). In 9.13 and 10.7, 9 the form is plural with pronominal suffix.

ישע, vv. 9, 16. Otherwise 8.7, 13 (see above), 10.6, 12.7. Verse 9 contains the unusual *niphal* participle form which refers to Zion's king. *Hiphils* occur in the other references in Deutero-Zechariah. In all cases the agent of salvation is Yahweh.

רכב, vv. 9, 10, '*riding* upon an ass … cut off the *chariot*'. Some contrast is indicated in the use of the root רכב, first as a verb and then as a noun. However, it is not obvious that this was intended by the writer.

כרת (see above on 9.6), v. 10.##1,6, is used in parallel clauses; the first is *hiphil* first person singular, while the second is *niphal* third person singular. It is not clear what the significance of this might be, if any, but it is noticeable that a number of words since 9.1 have occurred close together. It could be that we have some sort of catchword linkage in operation. ונשאר גם הוא, 9.7, and ונושע הוא, 9.9, may well have been noticed in reading aloud.

אפרים, vv. 10, 13; plus 10.7 only. This seems to be the first sign of an interest in the northern kingdom. Each reference is favourable to Ephraim. Zech. 9.13 has 'Judah and Ephraim'; 10.6 has 'the house of Judah/Joseph'.

קשת, vv. 10, 13; plus 10.4. See above on קשת/מלחמה, 9.10; 10.3b-5a.

עד, v. 10.##14,17. This may be ignored.

אסיר, vv. 11, 12. This seems to have no significance for structure. It may be considered as a catchword.

יום, vv. 12, 16.

מלא, vv. 13, 15. קשת seems to be needed for both verbs in v. 13a; v. 15 is obscure and it is impossible to be sure of any intended correspondence.[1]

---

1.   Rudolph has a novel argument: to shoot one arrow (Ephraim) is of little use. He proposes to add אשפה (quiver), omitted by homoioarchton with אפרים, thus

אבן, vv. 15-16. Unfortunately 9.15 is obscure, but the meaning of אבני־קלע is 'slingstones'. It is possible that there is an intended contrast in v. 16 (especially since the same construction is used: אבנ). They will tread down slingstones; they will be stones in a crown.[1]

מה, v. 17.##2,4, may be ignored.

The Structure of Zechariah 9.9-10 and 11-17

The results for this section are quite meagre. Repeating words in vv. 9-10, כרת רכב, בת, ירושלם and עד, do not yield any obvious pattern. In the case of vv. 11-17, despite the appearance in the list of מלא and אבן, nothing can be proved from this collection.

If we consider vv. 9-17 together, the words that stand out are 'save' in vv. 9 and 16, and both 'bow' and 'Ephraim' in vv. 10 and 13. This could be significant, since the movement of this section is:

> 9-10 Promise of peace
> 11-12 ?Continues the promise[2]
> 13-16 How the peace will come about: victory in battle

Any scheme that asks to be taken seriously must account for these corresponding words.

We have again found contact with the rest of the chapter and with ch. 10 in particular. This confirms the decision above (in the summary of results for 9.1-8) that 9.1–11.3 should be considered as a whole.

---

making Ephraim the quiver and not the arrow. This seems to demand too logical an approach of the poet. It seems better to accept Rudolph's explanation of MT: 'I have bent Judah as my bow; I have filled (it) with Ephraim'.

1. Verse 15 is notoriously difficult to translate. The most commonly accepted emendation is דָּמָ[ם] instead of המו (as LXX; 'they shall drink their blood [like wine]. . .', not 'they shall drink, they shall be boisterous'). We should keep MT, which Baldwin (*Haggai, Zechariah, Malachi*, pp. 169-70) makes a good attempt to explain.

2. גם־את *casus pendens* links the verse with v. 9 (cf. I. Willi-Plein, *Prophetie am Ende: Untersuchungen zu Sacharja 9–14* [BBB, 42; Bonn: Peter Hanstein, 1974], p. 9; G. Gaide, *Jérusalem, voici ton roi: Commentaire de Zacharie 9–14* [Lectio Divina, 49; Paris: Cerf, 1968], p. 73). Some older commentators (e.g. Sellin) regarded vv. 9-10 as an insertion, but the connection of vv. 11-12 with v. 8 is difficult. Sellin referred the 'blood of the covenant' (v. 11) to the bloody sacrifices of v. 7a, omitting v. 8 as a gloss (*Das Zwölfprophetenbuch* [Leipzig: Deichert, 1922], pp. 495, 499-501). This over-confident adjustment of the text need not be accepted.

Zech. 9.9-10 is probably the best known and most discussed passage in Zechariah 9–14. Christian tradition has affirmed that Christ fulfilled this prophecy when he rode into Jerusalem just before his arrest and death.[1] Jesus himself seems deliberately to have acted out the prophecy. Since he also referred other passages from Deutero-Zechariah to himself there is considerable interest in the relation that these have to each other. Lamarche connected them by means of his elaborate chiastic structure and argued that together they make up a coherent picture of a shepherd-king messiah. We did not find confirmation of the details of Lamarche's thesis in 9.1-8. The passage is crucial to Lamarche's understanding and interpretation of Zechariah 9–14.

Lamarche analyses 9.9-10 as follows:

    a   Arrival of the king; its/his description (9): 3 *vers*
    a'   Action of the king for peace; his empire (10): 3 *vers*

He rejects the easier reading והכרית, which would have made this interpretation even more sure, and retains the *lectio difficilior* of the MT. This is sound procedure and the descriptions that he gives are accurate. The assigning of the letters a and a' is of doubtful value.

He also suggests a chiasmus in these verses:

    a   Jerusalem
        b   victorious king[2]
            c   ass
            c'   horses
        b'   peace
    a'   all the earth

Set out like this, it looks plausible, and Lacocque remarks, 'with P. Lamarche one will notice the remarkable chiastic parallel in these

---

1. It is, of course, recorded in all four gospels that Jesus rode into Jerusalem on a donkey, Mt. 21.1-11; Mk 11.1-11; Lk. 19.29-40; Jn 12.12-18. Matthew and John have an explicit quotation of Zech. 9.9.

2. The normal meaning of נושע is 'saved'. Although Lamarche translates 'victorieux' he understands it in a passive sense (against LXX, σώζων, and Vulg., *salvator*) 'sauvé' (*Zacharie 9–14*, p. 43). Many commentators, including Lamarche and Rudolph, refer to Isa. 45.21 which speaks of Yahweh as צדיק ומושיע, and argue that certain nuances come from Deutero-Isaiah. Rudolph's 'reich an erfahrener Hilfe', as a translation, seems pedantic (*Haggai*, pp. 177-78).

verses...' [1] It is unfortunately achieved by a discriminating choice of words: 'Jerusalem' also occurs after 'horses'; repeated roots are not accounted for. Perhaps we could improve on this by noting the following.

כרת is repeated twice, and three things are 'cut off': chariot from Ephraim, horse from Jerusalem, battle bow.

Three adjectives are used to describe the king: צדרק, נושע and עני.

Three expressions are used to describe the king's mount: עיר, חמור and בן אתנות.

The word רכב is used of the king riding on his humble ass, and the same root gives the noun 'chariot' which is to be cut off.

Perhaps some resonance is intended between שלום לגוים and ומשלו מים.

It seems that there is a satisfying rhythm and balance to these two verses.

Lamarche treats 9.11–10.1 as a unit[2] and sees the following patterns:

	9.11-12	9.17b–10.1	Strophes of three *vers*
a	v. 11 (נם...)	9.17b	each : promises
b	v. 12a	10.1a	and exhortation
a'	v. 12b (נם...)	10.1b	

Verses 13-17a are regarded as two strophes each with four *vers*:

13aα, β	כי battle,
13aγ, δ	battle
14a	intervention of Yahweh.
14b	intervention of Yahweh

15aα, β	intervention of Yahweh,
15aγ-b	victory
16a	intervention of Yahweh
16b-17a	כי prosperity.

Similar remarks apply to this as to 9.1-8. It is by no means certain that this is the right division or subdivision of the text; the descriptions 'intervention by Yahweh' are vague and link together sections with little concrete in common; words used to mark correspondences are not distinctive (כי and יהוה). There is no attempt to demonstrate

1. Amsler *et al.*, *Agée, Zacharie, Malachi*, p. 156.
2. *Zacharie 9–14*, p. 52.

that this is the intended structure of the editor, for example, by showing that this is a more satisfactory scheme than its possible rivals. Even if 'battle' and 'intervention of Yahweh' are the right way of describing the sections so named, it is by no means clear that the central pattern, xxyy yx'yx", is a regular or pleasing structure. We noted above that the strongest verbal correspondences between vv. 13 and 16 are with vv. 10 and 9 respectively, but these are just outside Lamarche's section.

The same method is used by Lamarche throughout his book, and there seems little point in making the same criticisms for each section. We shall, therefore, confine further criticism to points that are specific to the section in question.

Lacocque's scheme is slightly different here. He takes vv. 11-17 together and sets out the following pattern:

a	11a	blood alliance	a'	15	blood banquet
b	11b	out of the pit	b'	16a	divine salvation
c	12a	the stronghold	c'	16b	God's field
d	12b	promise of prosperity	d'	17	prosperity

Verses 13-14 are an *incise*:

> a   Judah (south)
> b   Ephraim (north)
>   1   Zion (east)
>   2   Yavan (west)
> b' God's lightning (north)
> a' God comes from Teman (south)

This is surely fanciful. There are no words in common between any two parallel sections; 'blood' in v. 15 comes from the LXX; v. 15a is four times as long as v. 11a; the word 'prisoners' occurs in both 11b and 12a but this is ignored; גם at the beginning of vv. 11 and 12b, which Lamarche made use of, is ignored; there is no warrant for taking 'Zion' to represent the east; lightning is apparently associated with the north by appeal to the god of thunder at Ugarit.[1]

There seems to be no way of justifying this plan. Lacocque does not argue his case.

---

1.   Lamarche, *Zacharie 9–14*, pp. 160-61.

Zechariah 10.1-11.3

It remains to look at one final individual section before we consider
the larger whole of 9.1–11.3. The words that occur twice or more in
10.1–11.3 are set out in figure 11.

It is obvious from the layout that, although there are many repeating words, nearly all of them occur quite close together. Exceptions to
this are 5, רעה; 11, וגברתי (which is the strongest marker within
ch. 10); 12, הוביש (cf. possibly 19, שוב; also cf. the *hiphil* of יבש in
v. 6, often emended, with Syr., Targ. and Vulg., to the *hiphil* of שוב).

Few words may be confidently ignored: even 2, 3, 4 (different
meanings), 16 (different roots, and lacking other connections), and 18
(רבו כמו רבו) may possibly serve some function by their repetition.

The result is that we have a remarkably large number of words that
serve to give continuity to this section: מטר is part of a step parallelism, דבר ties v. 2aα-γ together. ענה, in v. 2, describes the Israelites as
afflicted through being without a shepherd, while in v. 6 Yahweh
declares emphatically, 'I will *answer* them'. It is not at all certain that
this was how the writer or editor saw these words, but we cannot rule
it out. פקד is used in contrasting ways in the space of three words, and
serves to change the mood from that of judgment on the nations to
promise for Israel. 'House of Judah' in v. 3, prepares for the addition
of 'Joseph' in v. 6 after the concentrated section concerning מלחמה,
3.#21-5.#6 (plus the root לחם in 5.7). גבור plus כ links vv. 5 and 7: in
both cases the word follows והיו, although the first is singular and the
second plural.[1]

---

1.   The singular in v. 7 is odd and LXX, Vulg., Syr. and Targ. are assumed by
Mitchell (*Haggai, Zechariah, Malachi and Jonah,* p. 300) to have read the plural. It
is just as likely that they took it to be a collective singular with a plural verb (cf. GKC
145.2). Rudolph (*Haggai,* pp. 193-94) follows LXX and translates: 'die von
Ephraim'. The plural would be better from a structuring point of view but we should
keep the MT in the absence of strong evidence to the contrary.

BHS proposes to take ממנו in v. 5 with the last word of v. 4, which requires an
emendation to יִהְיוּ, and makes the connection with v. 5 less strong. However, this
should not be accepted according to the principles I have adopted, even though the
sense is easier, and the change is very small. There is no reason to accept Rudolph's
rearrangement of the text: vv. 3, 5, 4 (*Haggai,* pp. 192, 195-96). Lamarche translates יחדו 'pareillement' which seems acceptable, cf. 1 Sam. 30.24; Deut. 12.22;
BDB, p. 403c 'the one as well as the other'; cf. Otzen, *Studien,* pp. 248-49.

#	Word	1	3	5	7	9	11	1	3
1	מטר	$1^{3,9}$							
2	דבר		$2^{3,10}$						
3	כמו		2^{16}		7^6	8^7			
4	ענה		2^{18}		6^{20}				
5	רעה		$2^{21}\ 3^2$						3^3
6	פקד		$3^{7,9}$						
7	בית		3^{15}		$6^{3,6}$				
8	יהודה		3^{16}		6^4				
9	סוס		3^{19}	5^{13}					
10	מלחמה		$3^{21}\ 4^7$	$5^{6,7}$					
11	גב[ו]ר (piel)			5^2	$6^1\ 7^2$		12^1		
12	יבש (hiph)			5^{11}			11^7		
13	שמח				$7^{4,10}$				
14	לבב				$7^{5,12}$				
15	בניהם				7^8	9^7			
16	גיל/גלל				7^{11}		11^6		
17	קבץ					8^3	10^5		
18	רבב					$8^{6,8}$			
19	שוב					9^8	10^1		
20	ארץ						$10^{2,7}$		
21	מצרים						$10^3\ 11^{15}$		
22	אשור						$10^4\ 11^{13}$		
23	לבנן						10^9	1^2	
24	ים						$11^{2,5}$		
25	ירד						11^{11}	2^{13}	
26	גאון						11^{12}		3^{12}
27	ארז							$1^6\ 2^5$	
28	ילל (noun)							$2^{1,9}$	3^2
29	אדר							2^7	3^6
30	שדד (pual)							2^8	$3^{5,11}$
31	קול								$3^{1,7}$

Figure 11: *Zech. 10.1–11.3: Verse and word numbers of words occuring twice or more (superscripts = word numbers)*

שמח occurs very close to לבם twice, in v. 7, emphasizing and expanding the idea of rejoicing by adding 'their sons'. This latter word is, of course, very common, but in vv. 7 and 9 the identical form occurs. It also reminds us of the twice repeated בניך in 9.13. The same distinctive form אקבצם is found in vv. 8 and 10. שוב occurs in *qal* as the last word of v. 9, and in *hiphil* as the first word of v. 10, where it introduces a small chiasmus, as noted above. Within this it is possible that ארץ is used to draw attention to the contrast between coming back from bondage in the land of Egypt, and spreading out into the *land* of Gilead and Lebanon, through increased numbers. It is not that these connections can be proved, but we cannot rule them out.

The final section, 11.1-3, which we noted as needing separate consideration in Chapter 2, has a high concentration of repeated words. In addition three important words occur in 10.11-12 and 11.1-3. We should also note ירדן, the last word of 11.3, which is similar to ירד.

Taking into account these repeated words, the form-critical results noted in our discussion of the divisions of the text, and the progression of thought in this section, we obtain this plan:

Ch. 10

1	Ask from Yahweh *rain*. . .(expanded)	Exhortation to ask
	rain-showers. . .	Yahweh for rain.
2	For the teraphim *speak* wickedness. . .	Reason: other
	and dreamers *speak* vanity. . .	sources useless.
	Therefore. . . sheep. . . no רעה	Result of trusting other sources
3	Upon הרעים my anger is hot . . .	Yahweh declares saving
	and upon he-goats (leaders) I will visit	intention
	For Yahweh. . . *visits* . . . his flock. . .	Narrator's comment
	house of Judah	
	and make them like proud *horse* in *battle*	
4	From/out of (4×) (Judah) will come/go	(continuing)
	פנה, יתד, *battle bow*, נוגש together.[1]	

---

1. ממנו is taken to refer to Judah by the majority of commentators, including Baldwin who allows that it might refer 'just possibly to the Lord' (*Haggai, Zechariah, Malachi*, p. 174). Should it have the same sense each time it occurs? In other words, does it mean that Judah (or just possibly the Lord) will supply cornerstone, tent peg, battle bow and נוגש? If we accept MT with its final יחדו then the answer is yes. We must then accept the translation 'ruler' in a good sense, as in

5   And they. . . like גבורים in mud of streets
in *battle*. And they will *fight* (לחם)   (continuing)
for Yahweh with them והבישׁ רכבי סוסים

6   וגברתי את בית יהדה. . .בית יוסף . . .save   Yahweh gives a
והשׁבותים for I. . .and they will be. . .   promise to his
for I Yahweh am their God and   people
    I will answer them

7   *And they will be like a* גבור, Ephraim   (continuing?)
and *their heart will be glad*. . .wine
and *their sons* will see and *be glad*
and *their heart* will rejoice in Yahweh

8   And I will signal. . .אקבצם   (continuing)
for I redeemed and they will be as were many

9   And I will sow them[1] among peoples. . .   (continuing)
from afar will remember
and they will live with *their sons* ושבו[2]

10   <u>והשׁיבותים מארץ מצרים</u>   (continuing)
ומאשׁור אקבצם
ואל ארץ גלעד ולבנון אביאם
ולא ימצא להם

(only) Isa. 60.17 (BDB, p. 620; Isa. 3.12 is at best doubtful), and not the normal meaning 'oppressor'. Cf. Amsler *et al.*, *Agée, Zacharie, Malachi*, p. 166; Lamarche, *Zacharie 9–14*, p. 56. If we allow a play on words with 'out of it' then the first two would mean that Judah supplies the leaders; the second two would imply an end to war and oppression. I do not think פנה can be applied in this way to foreign rulers. Even in Isa. 19.13, applied ironically to the princes of Zoan and Memphis, it retains the sense of something good and reliable. Rudolph wants to take יצא with נגשׂ alone and translates the final part of the verse: 'zugleich verschwindet aus ihm jegliche Tyrann' (*Haggai*, pp. 192, 196).

   1.   Verse 9 is difficult, and it is easy to see why many commentators (e.g. Rudolph, *Haggai*, pp. 193, 197-98, and Mitchell, *Haggai, Zechariah, Malachi and Jonah*, p. 292) regard it as an interruption. MT's pointing of ואזרעם (which is confirmed by LXX, Syr., and Targ.; Sæbø, 'Die deuterosacharjanische Frage', p. 68) implies a conditional (cf. Mitchell) or future (Lacocque) tense. The use of זרע is stronger than the more usual זרה, for 'sowing implies a harvest and so conveys hops' (Baldwin, *Haggai, Zechariah, Malachi*, p. 176).

   2.   Vulg. and Targ. confirm MT's 'they will live with their sons'; LXX and Syr. read 'they will bring up their children' (יחיו; Rudolph, *Haggai*, p. 194).

11   ועבר <u>בים</u> צרה והכה <u>בים</u> גלים
    <u>והבישו</u> כל מצולות יאר
    <u>והורד גאון אשור</u>
    ושבט <u>מצרים</u> יסור

12   <u>וגברתי ביהוה</u> ובשמו יתהלכו   (continuing)
    נאם יהוה   Concluding formula

Ch. 11
1   Open your doors <u>לבנן</u>. . . fire devour *cedars*   Call to lament
2   <u>הילל</u> cypress for *the cedar* has fallen   with reasons
    <u>אשר אדרים שדדו</u>
    <u>כי ירד</u> <u>הילילו</u> oaks of Bashan
    יער הבצור
3   <u>קול ילת הרעם</u>
    <u>כי שדדה אדרתם</u>
    <u>קול</u> שאגת כפירים
    <u>כי שדד גאון הירדן</u>

It appears from this that the section progresses by steps:

        1   rain. . .rain
        2   speak. . .speak. . .
                shepherd
        3   shepherds. . .
                visit . . . (3b) visit . . .
                house of Judah
                horse. . .battle
        4   bow. . .battle
        5   והיו גברים. . .battle
                battle [verb]
                הוביש
                horse(-riders)

So far there is no difficulty.[1] Verses 3b-5 are from the narrator in the middle of Yahweh-speech, and we note that it is here that we find the distinctive phrases קשת מלחמה and סים חוצות (see above), and other important words that have occurred previously, for example רכב and סוס. We have already commented upon נגש (v. 4 and 9.8).

---

1.   I have not allowed myself to emend or rearrange the text on the basis of structure, but perhaps it is in order to point out that MT seems more consonant with the writer's method than does Rudolph's rearrangement. See p. 83 n. 1 above. Many older commentators regarded v. 4 as a scribal gloss (e.g. Mitchell, *Haggai, Zechariah, Malachi and Jonah*, p. 289).

It is possible, therefore, to see the hand of an editor here, who wants to elaborate on the word 'visit' in such a way as to relate this whole section to what has gone before. If this is true, did he also want to link in the root גבר that occurs in v. 7, and forms an inclusio? In any case, we note that v. 6, as it stands, begins a new sub-section. It also picks up motifs from vv. 3b-5.[1] Thus we continue:

6	וגברתי. . . house of Judah. . . (Joseph)
	(? הובישׁ) הושׁיב
7	והיו גבור
	be glad. . . their heart
	their sons
	be glad. . . their heart
8	I gather them
9	with their sons
	they will return

It is not clear how we should regard the *hiphil*(s) of ישׁב (י ישׁב). They do not fit neatly into the subdivisions of the text established by form-critical methods. We must at least leave them aside for the moment. Verses 6-9 continue by repeating the elements of strength/might for the house of Judah, and gradually add new emphases: rejoicing (in heart) and posterity, both traditional ways of signifying God's blessing. Then comes the theme of bringing back those who are scattered, expressed in two ways: 'I will gather them' and 'They will return'. It is not easy to represent this diagrammatically in a convincing way, but the progression is clear and logical. There is no need to delete v. 9 as an interruption, although it is not an elegant verse, and may be due to an editor. (See p. 186 n. 1 above.)

There follow, in vv. 10-12, at least two clearly recognizable literary figures: a chiasmus formed by the place names Egypt, Assyria and Gilead + Lebanon; and the second part of an inclusio formed by גברתי. The chiasmus seems to be overweight at the middle, caused by v11a. Many commentators would delete והכה בים גלים from 9.4,[2] but it

---

1. 'House of Judah'; גבר, and just possibly ענה (see above).
2. We have noted two distinctive phrases which occur in 9.3-4 (both referring to Tyre, and close to the beginning of the book) and 10.5, 11. While one might be regarded as mistaken copying, to treat both in this way would be questionable. Those familiar with this section would then see the description of Tyre's silver 'like the mud of the streets' as waiting to be trampled on. The correspondence between Tyre's wealth destroyed in the sea, and the more complete, exodus-like victory of 10.11,

would seem odd for it to have been put in completely by accident. Presumably an editor of some sort thought it belonged here. Three words here are taken up in 11.1-3 ('Lebanon', 'brought down' and 'pride') and we must ask why this should be. Was 11.1-3 composed so as to add on to this existing unit? Or were the words added here so as to prepare for them in 11.1-3? The latter seems more probable. It is difficult to imagine that two independent units both contained all three. This means we have further reason to suggest that an editor has been at work in 10.11a. Note that the words 'gather' and 'return' form an abba chiasmus in vv. 8, 9 and 10, which suggests the work of an (another?) editor. Let us suppose, first of all, that there were two stages in the composition of 10.10-11, viz:

	Stage 1	Stage 2 added:
10	I will cause them to return	
	from land Egypt	
	from Assyria	
	I gather them	
	to land of	
	Gilead and Lebanon	
11		(references to Egypt?)
		הוביש
		brought down
		pride of
	Assyria	
	...Egypt...	

This is not very satisfactory, since והורד גאון אשור is an integral part of the unit. It is better, therefore, to suppose that one person added vv. 10-11 (with the possible exception of v. 11a), and it is natural to give him credit also for 10.12 (since he is apparently aware of structural matters), and 11.1-3.

On this supposition, we can make good sense of this final unit. In form it is a summons to lament, signifying a prophecy of judgment against Israel's enemies. Lebanon is commanded to open its doors for fire to devour its cedars. Presumably the editor thought that Lebanon needed to be conquered, not just to receive people from Israel on a friendly basis. The great trees of Lebanon (cedars, cypresses, cedars

near the end of this section, would also probably not escape notice.

and oaks) symbolizing majesty and pride (as in e.g. Cant. 5.15; Isa. 10.33-34 and especially 2.12-13) are brought down and the writer calls on them to wail (v. 2).

In v. 3 the picture changes while the terminology remains largely the same: this time the רעים wail because *their* glory (אדרת not אדיר, but the similarity is sufficient to establish a connection) is spoiled. The last strophe (3b) is closely parallel to v. 3a:

קול שאגת כפירים // קול יללח הרעים
כי שדד גאון הירדן // כי שדדה אדרתם

Even lions are in trouble when their home is destroyed. There may be an intentional play on words: ירד; ירדן (vv. 2b, 3b).[1]

Conclusions

It appears that Zech. 10.1–11.3 has its own integrity, and that it has been worked over by at least one redactor who attached it to 9.1-8, 9-10. He seems to have had some awareness of structure, but the result is not so obvious (nor, to my mind, satisfying) as we found in Zechariah 1–8. We need to investigate any connections that exist between the separate sections of Zech. 9.1–11.3. In Chapter 4 we shall consider the relation of the whole to the rest of Zechariah.

Post-Script: Otzen on the Structure of Zechariah 9–10

Otzen believes that Zechariah 9–14 is composed of four tradition complexes: chs. 9–10, 11, 12–13 and 14. This, he has argued for, at great length, in the second section of his book.[2] The literary structure he proposes for chs. 9–10 is as follows:

1.   It is odd to find the Jordan referred to here. Perhaps it is to be understood figuratively: 'Die Libanonzedern sind die besten und die Basanseichen die stärksten, genau wie in v. 3 das Jordandickicht den dichtesten Dschungel meint' (Rudolph, *Haggai*, p. 200).

2.   'Der Historische Hintergrund Deuterosacharjas', in *Studien*, pp. 35-212. He believes that chs. 9–10 derive from the time of Josiah, but our concern is with the structure he puts forward.

9.1-8   Israel reconquers territory of Assyria and Egypt
9.9-10   The victorious of the king
9.11-12   The return of the northern kingdom out of exile
9.13-15   The battle against the enemy (Judah and Ephraim)
9.16   'Positive' shepherd picture
9.17-10.1   'Positive' fertility/fruitfulness motif
10.2a   'Negative' fertility/fruitfulness motif
10.2b-3a   'Negative' shepherd picture
10.3b-5   The battle against the enemy (Judah)
10.6-10   The return of the northern kingdom out of exile
10.11a   Yahweh's victorious Epiphany
10.11b-12   The might of Assyria and Egypt is destroyed and that of Israel is
             strengthened

If my criticisms of other work have been valid, then this presentation must be regarded as largely fanciful. The most serious defects are that:

1. It is based on labelling that is subjective, and at times, far-fetched; for example 10.2a has nothing to do with the kind of 'fertility/fruitfulness' pictured in 9.17–10.1; 9.9-10 may be described correctly, but 10.11a can only with great difficulty be made to mean Yahweh's epiphany.[1]

2. Verbal links are not sought, and they often do not exist, between corresponding sections; for example the first and last only have שׁבב, and סור in common; 9.9-10 shares no vocabulary with 10.11a.

3. The sections do not balance one another; for example 9.1-8 does not balance 10.11b-12.[2]

4. Parallels between sections that are not put opposite one another are not accounted for (see the investigation of 9.1–11.3 below).

---

1.   Otzen, *Studien*, pp. 251-52.

2.   It is ironic that Otzen regards it as a virtue that he has not produced a scheme with lines of equal length: 'Wir haben in unser Analyse ganz darauf verzichtet, eine strenge Symmetrie in dem Formalen zustande zu bringen; bei uns stehen recht kurz und ziemlich lange Perikopen in Parallele (s. z.B. 9.1-8 gegenüber 10.11b-12)' (*Studien*, p. 221). It is not clear why this should add weight to his argument, since one would naturally think that members of roughly equal size would balance each other better. Perhaps he has in mind Lund's statement that, after 'analyzing carefully Pss. 1–74. . . neither the length nor number of lines are [*sic*] essential to the strophe, but only the order of the ideas' ('Chiasmus in the Psalms', p. 285). Or perhaps he simply finds Lamarche's scheme suspiciously regular.

Repeated Words in Zechariah 9.1-11.3

Words that are certainly unimportant for structure or that only occur within the individual sections 9.1-8, 9-10, 11-17, 10.1-12 or 11.1-3, have been omitted from the table (figure 12). Several features stand out from this table.

1. The links between different sections are formed by a small number of verses, viz. 9.1-8 with 10.5 and 11; 9.9-10, 13 with 10.3-7 (as noticed in our discussion of the relevant sections above).

2. The three similar-sounding verbs, יבשׁ, ישׁב and שׁוב, seem to connect with each other. יבשׁ is used only of judgment on Israel's enemies (Ekron, horse-riders, depths of the Nile); ישׁב is used to describe blessing (denied and modified in 9.5, 6 respectively), and שׁוב is similar to this. Thus 'returning' and 'dwelling' are important concepts in Zechariah.[1]

3. Zech. 9.9-13 is bound together in a number of ways: the focus on Zion/Jerusalem/Ephraim; קשׁת which links also with 10.3-5, as do שׁים and גבור. Zech. 9.11 plays no part in making these connections; v. 12 only connects with 8.5 and 10.9-10, by means of the verb שׁוב.

4. Zech. 9.13 is also linked with 10.7, by means of אפרים, 'sons' (also 10.9), and גבור.

5. Zech. 9.9 also has links with 10.6-7 in גיל and ישׁע (although we should probably ignore אני/יענו/ואענם).

6. In 9.4 and 11.1 we find אשׁ + אכל (we should probably ignore the obscure reference 'they shall eat' in 9.15).

7. This leaves few words unaccounted for: אדני and עם ('his people', 'the nations') should probably be ignored; ירשׁ ('dispossess', 'new wine') should certainly be ignored. The most significant words must be אלהים and ישׁע. On examination of their contexts, we find a strong connection between 9.16 and 10.6 ('Yahweh their God' and 'save [Israel]').

---

1. Cf. the discussion of 'Jerusalem as inhabited', p. 103; cf. also 1.11 which ends with the striking phrase ישׁבת ושׁקמה. As the message proceeds there is a change from the nations 'dwelling (securely)' to Judah and Jerusalem enjoying this privilege.

Chapter	9									10				11
Verses	**1**	**3**	**5**	**7**	**9**	**11**	**13**	**15**	**17**	**2**	**5**	**8**	**11**	**1**
Word														
שבט	1[13]												11[14]	
חרץ + סים		3[9f.]									5[4f.]			
אדני		4[2]					14[7]							
ירש		4[3]							17[8]					
הכה בים		4[4f.]											11[4f.]	
אש		4[8]												1[5]
אכל		4[9]					15[5]							1[4]
ראה			5[1]		8[13]		14[3]					7[9]		
יבש			5[9]								5[11]		11[7]	
מלך			5[12]		9[9]									
ישב			5[16] 6[1]								6[9]?			
כרת				6[4]	10[1,6]									
גאון				6[5]									11[12]	
סור				7[1]									11[16]	
אלהים				7[10]				16[3]						
עבר					8[4,7]								11[1]	
שוב					8[5]	12[1,9]						9[8] 10[1]		
נטש					8[10]					4[11]				
ציון/ירושלם					9[4,7] 10[5]		13[10]							
גיל					9[1]							7[11]		
בוא					9[10]								10[10]	
ישע					9[13]			16[1]				6[8]		
ענה					9[15]					2[18]	6[20]			
רכב					9[16] 10[2]						5[12]			
סוס					10[4]					3[19]	5[13]			
אפרים					10[3]		13[7]					7[3]		
קשת					10[7]		13[5]				4[6]			
מלחמה					10[8]					3[21]	4[7] 5[6]			
בן pl. + suffix							13[9,12]					7[8]	9[7]	
שים							13[14]			3[17]				
גבור							13[16]				5[2]	7[2]		
(גבר) [verb]												6[1]	12[1])	
יצא							14[4]				4[9]			
עם								16[7]					9[2]	

Figure 12: *Zech. 9.1–11.3:*
Verse and word numbers of words occurring twice or more
(superscripts = word numbers)

Assuming that these observations are reliable we may conclude that the overall structure of the passage is something like this:

9.1-8   Main connections 10.5(-6), 11; 11.1
linked (by שוב, כרת, ראה) with:
    9.9-10   Main connections 10.3-5 + 6? + 7
linked (by קשת, אפרים, ציון) with:
    9.13 (+ 16? ישע) Main connections 10.3-5 + 6? + 7 (?-9, 10)

We have already seen that 9.1-8 contains very few words repeated within it, yet there are quite a number of connections with following sections. There are many obscurities, but the general theme of the section was clear: Israel's traditional enemies are to be judged—and saved.

This accords with 9.9-10, which follows: Israel's saved and righteous king will come, there will be peace, and his reign will extend over the whole world.

The scene changes to the time before this peace is established, and more detail is given about the way victory will come. Verses 13 and 16 link in with what has gone before, vv. 11-12, 14-15 and 17 have few links. There is room for speculation about editorial work here, but the section as a whole holds together well enough.

Zech. 10.1-2 focus on the present situation, and a new feature (but one related to 9.9-10) appears: a concern with the leaders of the community.[1] As we saw above the only significant verbal link with a remote verse here was the word 'shepherd' (10.2.#21, 3.#2; 11.3.#3). This suggests that 10.1-2 is transitional and leads to an important focus upon the question of leadership in 10.2b-4. This confirms the connection between 9.9-10 and vv. 3-5 which has been noted, and gives it point.

Verses 3-5 move on to deal with the future punishment of Israel's enemies and her own blessing (as in 9.[9]11-17, where, however, the element of blessing was more muted). Verses 1-5 form a self-contained section in some sense, and it is plausible to speak of an inclusio formed by גברתי for vv. 6-12. However, it would be misleading to try to represent this by a, b, a' and so on, in the conventional way, since we have noted so many links outside the section, which do not form regular patterns either in series or chiastically.

Zech. 11.1-3 is a closely structured unit, yet it manages to link up

---

1.   Lamarche's plan does not acknowledge the correspondence between 10.2-3a and any of the 'shepherd sections' of Zech. 9–14.

with 9.4 (fire devours) and 10.2ff. (shepherds), and in doing so, to prepare for the shepherd allegory of 11.4ff.

I conclude that 9.1–11.3 is to be thought of as an editorial unity and interpreted as a whole. We need, therefore, to put aside patchwork theories of compililation once and for all.[1]

Comparison with the editorial methods shown in Zechariah 1–8, shows this first section of Zechariah 9–14 to be very different. There is still, apparently, a concern for literary structure, but:

1. The units are not so clearly marked off.
2. The structures are less precisely indicated by repeated words, and so forth.
3. There is much more inter-relationship between different sub-sections of the whole.

P.D. *Hanson's* The Dawn of Apocalyptic

It is of interest to enquire how this result relates to other work in this field. In Chapter 2 we considered the divisions proposed by scholars, mainly on the basis of form-critical criteria. Although we have confirmed the subdivisions of the text and are basically in line with the scholarly consensus, the suggestion that 9.1–11.3 should be kept together as an editorial unit is unusual.

One work that goes some way towards this is P.D. Hanson's *The Dawn of Apocalyptic*,[2] which argues that at least 9.1-17 and 10.1-12 are whole units. Moreover, he regards the writer of Zechariah 10 as having before him ch. 9, which is a similar situation to what I have suggested: a redactor may have been responsible for parts of ch. 10, especially vv. 5 and 11.

Hanson bases his argument on a 'contextual-typological method', claiming that there is a recognizable 'Divine Warrior Hymn' underlying Zechariah 9. This he seeks to demonstrate by appealing to

---

1. However, many older studies were not so much incompatible with, as uninterested in, the conclusions I have drawn. It could be that many of the differences noted do derive from different authors and editors. The real incompatibility is that I have not felt able to prove editorial incompetence.

2. Philadelphia: Fortress Press, 1975. He repeats the same views more briefly in 'Old Testament Apocalyptic Re-examined', *Int* 25 (1971), pp. 454-79, reprinted in *Visionaries and their Apocalypses* (ed. P.D. Hanson; Philadelphia: Fortress Press, 1983), pp. 37-60.

various texts from the OT and other ancient west Asian sources.[1] The pattern he presents for Zechariah 9 is:

> Conflict—victory (1-7)
> Temple secured (8)
> Victory shout and procession (9)
> Manifestation of Yahweh's universal reign (10)
> Salvation: Captives released (11-13)
> Theophany of Divine Warrior (14)
> Sacrifice and banquet (15)
> Fertility of restored order (16-17)

I have two questions in mind: does this holistic approach to Zechariah 9 (and 10) in any way support—or undermine—our own results? And do his sub-divisions confirm or call into question those that we have discovered?

The answer to both questions must be negative. First of all, we note that he employs the same sort of subjective 'labelling' that we discovered in many structural studies. 'Conflict–victory' is a rather general category and it would be difficult to write a salvation prophecy that could not be labelled in this way. The victory element here is not prominent. Verse 8 *might* be correctly translated 'I will stand guard near my house' and mean 'the temple is secured', but the text is difficult, and the 'house' might mean the land of Judah: at any rate some caution is needed before making far-reaching claims. 'Manifestation' seems gratuitous; vv. 11-13 deal with more than 'release of captives' and 'salvation' is the subject for the whole of 9.1–11.3 (the word 'save' occurs not here but in 9.16 etc.). The emphasis in 9.16-17 is not on 'fertility of restored order' but on Yahweh's action on behalf of his people and the pleasantness of having grain and new wine again, traditional signs of blessing. We can only suspect that the plan has been slanted so as to fit the Divine Warrior theory. Moreover, the same criticism could be levelled against the examples he gives in order to establish the pattern. Given the fact that the people of Israel believed that Yahweh intervened in history on their behalf, prayed to him against their enemies, celebrated victories by processions, by worship and by sacrifice (with feasting) in the temple, and looked forward to the time when he would be acknowledged as Lord over all the earth, it is not surprising that certain types of psalm contain the required elements.

---

1. *Dawn of Apocalyptic*, pp. 300-22, esp. 315-16.

Secondly, although the sub-divisions generally conform to the larger established units, they are unsatisfactory in a number of ways. There is no clear principle underlying them; they distract attention away from the concern for peace which is implied in both v. 9 and v. 10, and even more from the surprising element of the humility of Zion's king.

In the case of Zechariah 10, which he calls 'The Divine Warrior Hymn applied to the Inner-Community Polemic', he puts forward a similar scheme:[1]

1-3	(ריב versus leaders)
4-6	Combat–victory
4	Yahweh equips himself with Israel as his host
5-6a	Ritual conquest
6b-10	Salvation: restoration of the scattered people
11	Procession re-enacting the victory of the Divine Warrior over Yamm (= Assyria–Egypt)
12	Victory shout

This, I believe, confirms what was said above. In particular, the titles for vv. 4, 5-6a, 11 and 12 are highly imaginative. I can only conclude that Hanson's attempt to break new ground in this way is a mistake. Similar remarks could be made about the other sections with which he deals.[2]

I. Willi-Plein's Prophetie am Ende

Willi-Plein investigates Zechariah 9–14 from the standpoint of textual, literary and form criticism—and beyond. She concludes that the book forms a coherent unit as we now have it, and presents a diagram[3] to show how the parts of the book relate to the whole. Although the questions she asks and the criteria she employs (e.g. sentence structure and metre, rather than use of vocabulary) are somewhat different from my own, it is interesting to see a certain correspondence in the results:

---

1. *Dawn of Apocalyptic*, pp. 325-34.

2. Zech. 11.1-3, pp. 334-337, 'A Taunt against Foreign Nations Redirected against Israel's Leaders'; Zech. 11.4-7 + 13.7-9, pp. 337-354, 'A Commissioning Narrative transformed into a Prophecy of Doom'; Zech. 12.1–13.6, pp. 354-68, 'An Apocalypse molded by the Inner-Community Struggle', and Zech. 14.1-21, pp. 369-401, 'An Apocalypse structured upon the Ritual Pattern of the Conflict Myth and reflecting bitter Inter-Community Conflict'.

3. *Prophetie am Ende*, p 97.

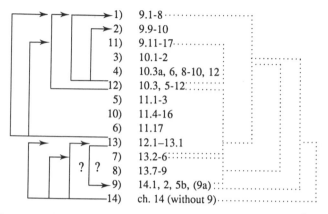

1)	9.1-8	
2)	9.9-10	
11)	9.11-17	
3)	10.1-2	
4)	10.3a, 6, 8-10, 12	
12)	10.3, 5-12	
5)	11.1-3	
10)	11.4-16	
6)	11.17	
13)	12.1–13.1	
7)	13.2-6	
8)	13.7-9	
9)	14.1, 2, 5b, (9a)	
14)	ch. 14 (without 9)	

Relevant to the present chapter is the correspondence between 10.3-12 (only when vv. 5 and 11 are added) and both 9.1-8 and 9-10. Although I do not feel that the pruning of ch. 10, on the basis of form-critical (Yahweh-speech, and analysis into 'Wort + Auslegung', principally) and metrical considerations, is likely to produce reliable results,[1] yet it might be that the work of a different editor would show different characteristics in all these areas. There is slightly stronger reason, therefore, for arguing that an editor added 10.5 and 11, in order deliberately to form links with 9.1-8, 9-10. Willi-Plein would claim to have shown that this editor is different from the original writer, which my own investigation leaves open.

Zechariah 11.4-17 + 13.7-9

Since the brief section 13.7-9 is often related to ch. 11 and even moved to be continuous with it,[2] it is convenient to treat them both together. We shall easily see what words are repeated within 13.7-9 itself.

---

1. Esp. pp. 49-52.
2. So most commentators this century, e.g. Mitchell (*Haggai, Zechariah, Malachi and Jonah,* pp. 314-16), Mason (*Haggai, Zechariah and Malachi,* pp. 110-11), Rudolph (*Haggai,* pp. 211-13), and even Chary (*Les propètes et le culte,* p. 194); but not Sæbø ('Die deuterosacharjanische Frage', pp. 276., q.v. for further details), or Stuhlmueller. R.C. Dentan actually says: '*My shepherd* in this oracle has no connection with the shepherd of 11.15-17' (*IB,* VI, p. 1109)!

Very few words seem likely to be significant. We may immediately dispose of the common words: בו, לו, נאם, כי,[1] על, לא, אשר, את, יהוה, אותו, כל, אל, אם and בין. Other repeated words are as follows.

אמר is a common word but needs to be taken into consideration here. It occurs in the main introductory formula in v. 4, 'Thus said Yahweh my God', as well as in two other types of formula: 'And Yahweh said to me' (vv. 13, 15) and 'And I said' (vv. 9, 12). They each occur in some sort of introductory role and thus have a bearing on the structure. The remaining instances are in v. 5 where the sellers of the sheep 'say "Blessed be Yahweh..."'' and the final part of 13.9, 'I have said "he is my people" and he will say "Yahweh is my God"'. There is a nice contrast between the hypocritical words of the traders concerning Yahweh and the confession of faith of the restored flock.

אלהי, 11.4, 13.9. The use of this is striking and forms an inclusio around the whole section which suggests that we should also see what difference it would make to include 12.1–13.6 in our table. The opening phrase of 11.4 is כה אמר יהוה אלהי while the end of 13.9 has והוא יאמר יהוה אלהי. We have seen that the word אלהים is not frequent in the book of Zechariah. Moreover the forms 'your God' or 'their God' are the normal ones. There could be a deliberate change here in order to get 'my God'.

ראה and צאן would normally be important. In this context they are largely 'technical' words. However, we note them, and particularly the verbal forms of ראה.

צאן הרגה, 11.4, 7, is a distinctive, if cryptic, phrase.

חמל's two occurrences are close together and the second interprets the first.

עוד might be noted since it occurs to mark a new phase of Yahweh's dealings with the people, but the first occurs in an interpretation, the second in a command to symbolic action.

ארץ may be ignored. Its use is different in each of its occurrences.

הנה אנכי should be noted as a strong introductory phrase, vv. 6, 16. Both occur in the theological interpretation of what is commanded.

יד is concentrated in v. 6 (3×) referring to being in the hand/power of another; 13.7 'turn my hand against' is similar enough to consider. אשה את בשר רעותה, v. 9, is similar to איש ביד רעהו, v. 6.

---

1. This word actually assists in forming a distinctive phrase: חרב על, 11.17; 13.7!

כן עני הצאן [ל]כן עניי הצאן must be considered, whether we accept the usual emendation or not, vv. 7, 11. We should also bear in mind the כנעני in 14.21.[1]

לקח is used in conjunction with מקל in vv. 7 and 10. We should probably also consider ואגדע which is also used similarly, cf. v. 10: 'And I took my staff, Grace, and I broke it', and which has a similar sound to ואקח. לקח and מקל may be linked because of their common consonants. The verb is also used with 'the thirty pieces of silver', v. 13, and the implements of a worthless shepherd, v. 15. Thus, in this chapter all references may be taken to be connected with leadership under Yahweh's authority.

שנים and אחד do not seem to be significant here.

קרא occurs in 11.7 (2×); 13.9. No correspondence is apparent: 'Call one "Grace"...', 'Call upon my name...'

נאם and חבל occur simply where they have to occur, vv. 7 (2×), 10, 14. We should consider them along with מקל and so on.

כחד, vv. 8, 9 (2×), 16, is a fairly rare word (nowhere else in Zechariah and only 28 times elsewhere in the OT). The participial forms והנכחדת and והנכחדות are distinctive and both contexts relate to the shepherds' lack of care for the sheep.

שלש, 11.8, 12, 13; 13.8, 9. It is difficult to know how, if at all, these are to be related: 'destroyed three shepherds', 'thirty pieces of silver' (2×), 'the third which remains' (2×). We should probably plot it but not expect much from it. See below on כסף.

נפש and מות occur twice each in a single verse (8 and 9, respectively) and may be ignored.

אכל plus בשר, vv. 9, 16, must be considered. The phrase is used of the sheep who devour the flesh of one another and of the worthless shepherd who devours the flesh of the fat ones of the flock. See כחד above.

גדע, vv. 10, 14. See לקח above.

פרר, vv. 10, 11, 14, belongs with גדע, which it interprets.

כרת is used with ברית in v. 10, but with the meaning 'be cut off' in 13.8. It may be ignored.

עם only occurs in 11.10 and 13.9, but the contexts are worth considering. The first is the striking phrase 'covenant with all the peoples',[2]

---

1. Since it is unlikely that we shall reach agreement on the interpretation of this phrase, I propose to operate with it as an algebraic variable for as long as possible.

2. *BHS* proposes reading העם, but without manuscript support. We cannot accept this, even though it is difficult to understand the MT. Baldwin takes it to refer

the second is also covenantal and refers to the 'my-people-their-God' motif which occurs at important points in Proto-Zechariah. It seems likely that both 11.10 and 13.9 are climax points in the section(s).

הוא is an insignificant word, but seems to be used for special emphasis in this context. In 11.11 we find two occurrences including a non-standard use of ביום ההוא: 'It was broken on that day'. Frequent use of the expression 'and on that day' to denote a future day of fulfilment would lend power to its use here. וידעו...כי דבר יהוה הוא adds further weight and reminds us of the phrase 'you shall know that Yahweh has sent me...' in Zechariah 1–8. In 13.9 the use is different from that in 11.11, but emphatic nevertheless. It is uncertain whether any resonance is intended between the two uses. We should probably plot it.

עין, 11.12. 'If it is good in your eyes' is a very ordinary expression, but, in view of the word's importance elsewhere, we should keep it. In 11.17 there is apparently unnecessary repetition of עין ימינו. Note also 12.4, 'I will open my eyes' (for judgment) and 'strike every horse of the peoples with blindness'. This may, of course indicate that 11.12 and 17 do not correspond with each other or that we need to include 12.1–13.6 together with the present passages.

שכר only occurs in v. 12 (twice) and cannot be used as a marker word.

שלשים כסף occurs only in connection with the receiving and throwing away of the shepherd's wage. It is interesting that in 13.9 השלשית will be burned in the fire and refined as כסף is refined. Some resonance may be intended here.

Most of the other words simply occur together in a single verse: השליך אל היאצר occurs outside יקר (noun and verb) in v. 13. We could claim this to be a regular pattern:

a + b	thirty pieces silver (IF)...throw them to the potter
cc	lordly price...priced by them
a + b	took thirty pieces silver...threw them...to the potter

There is no doubt that the pattern is actually there, but it is doubtful whether it is intentional or significant. Any time a narrator describes a command to do something, and the carrying out of the command, this

to Jewish colonies scattered among the nations (*Haggai, Zechariah, Malachi*, p. 184). S.R. Driver's suggestion is more convincing: 'that "the covenant" which he had (metaphorically) made with the nations that they should not molest Israel was now annulled' (*The Minor Prophets*, p. 257).

structure will result—although not necessarily with a repeated word in the middle.

כהה, יבש, ימין, זרע occur in v. 17 only.

צרף is found in 13.9 only.

שנה, 11.4; 13.7 does not occur in comparable forms.

חרב...על, 11.17; 13.7. This is the expression that most of all draws attention to the similarity between the two sections, and the form רעי confirms it. The verses do not follow each other smoothly, however, and NEB's characteristic rearrangement of the text seems over-confident. It acknowledges that 13.7 is the beginning of a new oracle.

We should also consider אולי, 11.15, and האליל, v. 17, which are both used to describe the shepherd of this section. It is puzzling that two different words with such similar forms and meaning should have been employed.[1] Neither word occurs again in Zechariah.

Words occurring in 12.1–13.6 and in 11.4-17 or 13.7-9

אלהים, see above. The extra occurrences do not seem significant: 12.5, 'Yahweh of hosts, their God', and v. 8, 'like God, like an angel of Yahweh'.

קנה, 11.5 and 13.5, is a fairly distinctive word, but both these references are somewhat obscure. It is difficult to see how they could be related.[2]

נשאר is used of the sheep that are to be left to perish in 11.9, and of the 'families that are left' in the list of those who mourn over the one who is pierced. No connection is obvious. Compare also the word יתר which is found in 13.8 (also 14.16; יֶתֶר, 14.2).

אכל, see above, also occurs in 12.6 of the clans of Judah, who devour peoples to the right and left. The figure used is of fire, not 'eating flesh', and there would not seem to be any connection here.

---

1.   There is no warrant in the version for emending the text. אולי is given in BDB (p. 17) as an adjective, the only example of this form meaning 'foolish'. It could as easily be taken to mean 'my foolish one' (the sense always includes the idea of moral evil). אליל means 'worthlessness, nothingness' (BDB, p. 47) and is character-istically used of idols. Rudolph (*Haggai*, p. 203) suggests emendations, but these are not legitimate for us.

2.   קנה is apparently used of 'buyers' in 11.5, in contrast to the sellers of the צאן ההרגה. In 13.5 the most likely meaning is 'man (i.e. not God) *possessed* me from my youth'. See, e.g., R.L. Smith, *Nahum–Malachi*, p. 280. Many emend the text, e.g. substituting קנא for קנה. See Rudolph, *Haggai*, pp. 266-67.

Chapter	11													13		
Verses / Word	4	5	6	7	8	9	10	11	12	13	14	15	16	17	7	8	9
אמר*	3Y	7				1I			1I	1Y		1Y					19,23
אלהי	4																25
רעה (v)	5	11		1,18	4	3						8	5	2	4,13		
צאן	7			3,7,20										5	15		
צאן הרעה	7f.	(3)		3f.													
עד			4									4					
הנה אנכי			10f.											2f.			
יד			3×												17		
איש ביד רעהו		15+															
אשה . . . רעותה						11+											
[ל]כן עני				5f.				5f.									
לקח				8			1			12		5					
מקל				11			3				3						
נעם				14			5										
חבל				17							6						
כחד					1	7,8							7				
שלש					3				14	13						(11	3)
אכל						10							21				
בשר						13							19				
נרע							6				1						
פרר							8	1			7						
עם +							15										20
הוא								3,13									13,21f.
עין									5					10,15			
שלשים + כסף									14f.	13f.							8
השליך										4,15							
יוצר										6,20							
יקר										8,10							
חרב														6	1		
זרע														8,12			
ימין														11,16			
יבש														13,14			
כהה														17,18			
שלישית																11	3
צרף																	5,6

*Y = Yahweh subject; I = 'and I said'

Figure 13: *Zech. 11.4-17 + 13.7-9:*
Word number of words occurring twice or more
(Common words and those judged to have no significance for the structure have been omitted from the table.)

אשה also occurs, in the plural, five times in ch. 12. We may ignore this.

עין. See above.

אדרת, 13.4, does not seem to be connected with אדר in 11.13.

יהדה and ישראל are linked in 11.14, but not in ch. 12, where יהדה occurs six times, and ישראל only in 12.1.

נער. It is likely that this is the wrong reading in 11.16;[1] even if it is correct, there is not likely to be a connection with נערי in 13.5.

עור represents two different roots: עור (*piel*), to make blind, used of the horses in 12.4; and עור, to awake, 13.7. The former does recall the emphatic use of כהה in 11.17. However, it is impossible to demonstrate a connection between them.

The result of this subsidiary investigation is almost entirely negative. The only plausible verbal connection seems to be via the word 'eye' and the idea of blindness as a punishment.

The table of repeated words for this section is given in figure 13.

General structure of the passages

There is little dispute about the overall structure of these sections. It may be set out as follows:

11.4-17	The prophet as shepherd: part 1
11.4-6	Yahweh commanded me to shepherd the flock of slaughter (v. 6 already contains a theological interpretation)
11.7-14	I did so. (An account of what happened)
7	I shepherded the flock of slaughter (. . . ? . . .) and took two staffs
8	I destroyed three shepherds but became impatient with the sheep and they detested me
9	And I said I will not shepherd. . . let it die
10	And I broke the first staff. . .
11	?? (Something connected with v. 7)
12	And I said Give me my wages. . . They weighed out thirty pieces of silver
13	Yahweh said Throw it to the ?potter?. . . and I threw it in the house of Yahweh to the ?potter?
14	And I broke the second staff. . .

---

1. Rudolph, *Haggai,* p. 203.

11.15-17   The prophet as shepherd: part 2
            Yahweh commanded me to act as a worthless shepherd
            (No account of the prophet's having done so)
            (v. 16 theological interpretation)
            Curse against my/the[1] worthless shepherd

13.7-9   Curse against 'my shepherd'
            (רעי used but a different expression from 11.17)
            (vv. 8-9 theological interpretation with the great promise 'my
            people. . .my God' as the climax)

If I set out the words that might be significant (see the table) it is
possible to construct a formal chiastic unit as follows:

7	a			therefore/thus the poor of the flock
		b		took. . .staffs. . .Grace. . .Union
			c	I shepherded. . .
8				I destroyed. . .
				d ( )
9			c	I will not shepherd. . .
				what is to be destroyed let it be destroyed
10		b		took. . .staff. . .Grace
11	a			thus the poor of the flock

At this stage it makes no difference whether we put 'the poor of the
flock' or 'those who trafficked in the sheep'. If this were to be
accepted we should see at d the turning point of the subsection. This,
in fact, makes good sense: '*But* I became impatient with them. . .' The
main difficulty with it is that we have ignored five words that occur
before 11.11.#6, namely פרר, גדע, בשׂר, אכל and עם. We should also
note that 'I shepherded the sheep' occurs at the beginning and end of
v. 7, forming an inclusio for this.

   If we treat the table with more respect we are bound to conclude
that v. 10 forms some sort of parallel with v. 7 but adds certain new
elements which again occur in v. 14. It is not clear whether v. 11
should be treated with the preceding or succeeding verses. The sense
of the passage clarifies this for v. 11a continues the thought of v. 10,
v. 11 has a closing formula and v. 12 starts with an introductory

   1.   Rudolph takes the י of רעי to be *yodh compaginis*, indicating the construct
state, 'as the following עובי shows'. The reasoning is cogent, but those hearing the
prophecy would presumably first assume that those hearing the prophecy would
presumably first assume רעי meant 'my shepherd'. The phrase following adds to the
enigma of this passage. In 13.7, רעי does mean 'my shepherd'.

formula. This means that we should take vv. 7-11 as a subsection of the narrative, and that the 'poor of the flock' or 'the traffickers in the sheep' are used to form an inclusio for it. 'And they knew...word of Yahweh' is a climax within the section, as we suspected it might be in discussing individual repeated words.

The structure may therefore be set out:

11.4	Thus said Yahweh my God
	Shepherd the sheep of slaughter
11.6	For[1] I will cause each to fall
	hand of his neighbour
11.7	And I shepherded the sheep of slaughter
	לכן עניי הצאן
	I took...staffs...Grace...Union
	And I shepherded the sheep
11.8	I destroyed (כחד) three shepherds...
	BUT mutual hostility (נפשם/נפשי)
11.9	And I said I will not shepherd you...
	בשר...אכל...כחד each...of her neighbour
11.10	I took...staff...Grace...to annul covenant
11.11	it was annulled
	כן עיי הצאן...word of Yahweh
11.12-13	And I said...thirty pieces of silver...potter
11.14	broke...Union...to annul brotherhood...
11.15	And Yahweh said to me
	Again take implements of a shepherd, a/my foolish one
11.16	For behold I am raising up a shepherd in the land
	אכל...בשר...כחד...who

1. The כי of v. 6 is puzzling, since it suggests that the first purpose in the prophet's becoming a shepherd is to do with God's judgment. The best way to approach the problem is to recognize that v. 6 is theological interpretation, rather than an integral part of the parable, and to consider the sheep–shepherd picture as a whole on its own first. The situation is then clarified: become a good shepherd... he does (cf. 'Grace' and 'Union'). He starts to give service to the sheep by removing their bad leaders, but then gives up. We are meant to imagine the prophet within the picture first of all, i.e. as a shepherd with sheep. We should not simply try to by-pass this by interpreting the allegory. Verse 6, therefore, can be understood in this sense: act out this situation because it represents that which I am bringing about in the land.

11.17 Woe to the/my worthless shepherd[1]
       who forsakes the sheep

       a sword against his arm
           and against his   right eye
                    may his arm   be utterly withered
                    may his   right eye be utterly dim

13.7   sword awake against
                    my shepherd and against . . .
                                (oracle of Yahweh of hosts)
                    smite the shepherd. . . sheep scattered
                    (my hand) against[2] little ones
13.8   In whole land two thirds cut off. . . one third left

13.9   I will bring the one third. . . fire . . .
                    refined like silver. . . tried as gold

       He will call on my name and
                    I will answer them
                    I will say. . . my people
       and he will say Yahweh my God

We may now compare this result, which is unspectacular, with what
other commentators have concluded. We can see immediately the
appeal of excising 11.12-13 as a later addition. These verses have no
apparent connection with the rest of the section, and they divide up the
two staffs, vv. 10, 14, which are introduced together. I hesitate to do
this because they are already separated by '. . . it was annulled . . .הצון
כן עןיי' (v. 11). If vv. 11-13 are excluded[3] an important part of the
narrative (whatever it means) is lost, and we must assume that the
editor who added vv. 11-13 was concerned to make an integral link
between his addition and v. 7.

---

1. GKC 901 regards this as a construct state form (also עזבי) rather than a noun
with first person singular suffix. The form seems to have been chosen deliberately in
any case.

2. I do not think that it is possible to take this to mean 'extend my hand over (to
protect)', (Lamarche, *Zacharie 9–14*, pp. 91-92), because: (a) It is too sudden and
too soon a change to salvation from judgment, in the context of this unit. (b) על is
used twice in the preceding half verse to signify hostile action. (c) The instances of
יד אל . . . (*hiphil*) שוב that I can find express stern rather than comforting action,
even if the final goal is restored harmony. Cf. also Amos 1.8; Ps. 81.15.

3. See, e.g., Otzen, *Studien*, pp. 156-62.

If we keep the text as it is, the sub-divisions that we have discerned are similar to those of scholars in general. Even those French scholars who favour a structural approach agree on this.

Lamarche puts forward a more detailed plan, and is followed by Lacocque:[1]

I   IF: Yahweh speech:
   A   Oppressed people are given a last chance, 4-5
   B   If they will not take it, will not spare them any more, 6

II   A'   Good shepherd sent to save the flock, 7-8a
   a   First staff broken, 8b-11
   a'   Second staff broken, 12-14

III   B'   The attempt having failed, Yahweh does not spare them; sends a bad pastor, 15
   b   who brings misfortune on the flock, 16
   b'   and on himself, 17

In 13.7-9 he labels vv. 7-8 a, and v. 9 a' but without clear explanation. He notes the interior parallelism of v. 9b: 'they will call...' // 'I will answer'; and 'I will say...' // 'they will say'; and also the exterior chiastic parallelism, as set out in the plan above.

On the whole Lamarche's plan seems to represent the sequence of thought accurately, except that for 11.6 he adds an interpretation ('If ...') which is not in the text. The letters are not particularly helpful: the headings he gives for vv. 8b-11 and 12-14 seem more related to B than A. It will be of greater interest to examine his view of the overall structure of Zechariah 9–14, which we shall do in Chapter 4.

The Meaning of Zechariah 11.4-17 + 13.7-9

In discussing the meaning of these sections, I hope that certain lines of interpretation may be confirmed and, where certainty cannot be obtained, alternative possibilities may be seen clearly. I cannot tackle

---

1.   Lamarche, *Zacharie 9–14*, pp. 66-71; Lacocque (Amsler *et al.*, *Agée, Zecharie, Malachi*, p. 172), keeps the basic plan unchanged. He also states that, from the point of view of vocabulary, there are two pivotal verses, 7 and 14. They have the following important elements. Verse 7: רעה—'ואראה ponctue tout le morceau'; חבלים; נעם; מקלות; ואקח; לכן עניי הצאן; צאן ההרגה; 'le troupeau';
V. 14: ואגדע; מקלי; חבלים; להפר.
All of these except ואראה and חבלים are also found in v. 10, which suggests that this also should be given pivotal status.

the historical problems raised by this chapter: who the 'three shepherds' were, or even the general era from which this unit came.

We know that ch. 11 is symbolic rather than a real account of a prophetic action, as is proved beyond doubt by the expressions 'destroyed three shepherds' and 'covenant with all the peoples' (even 'people' would be enough).

We know that it refers to a historical situation in which the people (sheep) were oppressed by their leaders (shepherds, buyers and sellers, 'each...his king', and possibly כנענים).[1] Yahweh decides to do

---

1. The vast majority of modern commentators accept the emendation 'for the traffickers of the sheep' for good reasons:

   a. MT is difficult if not impossible to understand; arguments 1 and 3 offered below are invalid, for there are no analogies for these idioms.
   b. It is easy to see how the mistake could have occurred: it only requires the mistaken division of the consonantal text at a stage before final forms were known.
   c. LXX largely supports the emendation: εἰς τὴν Χαναανῖτιν in v. 7 and οἱ Χαναναῖοι in v. 11.

Arguments to support the MT have been:

   a. 'Verily' (= לכן) is a possible translation in v. 7, and this fits well after 'sheep of slaughter', especially if we accept RVm: 'verily the most miserable of sheep'.
   b. The prophet did not shepherd the sheep *'for* the traffickers...' and the sense of MT is better.
   c. כן in v. 11, makes good sense if translated 'thus' or 'of a truth' (RV, RVm, respectively).
   d. It is more difficult to see how MT could have changed to LXX than vice versa, especially when כנעי occurs in Zech. 14.21.
   e. The versions read the same text as MT: Vulg. definitely, Syr. and Targ. probably.

For further details see Rudolph, *Haggai*, p. 202: Sæbø, 'Die deuterosacharjanische Frage', pp. 75-76.

Concerning the meaning of the passage, the points at issue are comparatively minor, as Willi-Plein also notes (*Prophetie am Ende*, pp. 53-56). In v. 7 we have an incidental reference of one sort or another: a further description of the flock as 'poor', or the statement that the shepherd worked for the 'traffickers'. In v. 11 it is a matter of whether the sheep or the traffickers (a) recognized the word of Yahweh, and (b) paid the prophet his wages. On balance I think the emendation is the better choice.

something for the sheep and sends a shepherd, who at first does his job properly, and gets rid of certain bad leaders.

For some reason—almost certainly to do with their lack of response to him—the shepherd leaves the sheep to their fate. Almost certainly, we are meant to assume that they are left in the hands of their leaders.

The failure of the shepherd to bring about a change in the attitude and situation of the sheep leads to the breaking of the staffs נעם and חבלים, which have something to do with a covenant Yahweh has made, and the brotherhood between Israel and Judah. Probably this signifies that there will be disunity between the two parts of Israel, and that they will be at the mercy of other peoples.

We can not be sure of the significance of the thirty shekels, or their ending up with the potter[1] in the Temple. They represent at least the low value placed by either the 'traffickers in the sheep' or the 'poor of the flock' on the services of God's shepherd.

In 11.15-17, we find a new stage in the story. The prophet is commanded to become a shepherd again, but this time he is to be actively bad. For this he is himself to be punished. We are accustomed to reading that Yahweh uses evil instruments for his purposes (cf. Isa. 10.5-19; Hab. 1.5-6) or that he uses Cyrus, 'although he does not know' God (Isa. 45.5), to achieve what he wants. It is quite different to read that a prophet is commanded to do something evil. The closest parallel is probably the ironic speech of Micaiah in 1 Kgs 22.19-23, or Ezek. 20.25-26. The section ends with a totally bleak picture.

In 13.7-9, as we have seen from the parallels, the position is taken up from where it was at the end of 11.17. Are we to assume that the sword is against him because he has not done his job properly? The text does not say this; in fact the emphasis is on the relationship between Yahweh and the shepherd: this time רעי definitely means 'my shepherd', and עמיתי confirms it. A severe double refining process is described at the end of which the relationship between Yahweh and

---

1. The reading אל היוצר has occasioned difficulty. Syr. reads האוצר, the treasury, and it is felt that this is more easily understandable, especially in the light of the בית יהוה before the second mention of the phrase. LXX, 'A, Σ, L and Matt. 27.10 support MT, which should be accepted. There is a difference of opinion as to whether this means 'potter' or 'founder'. C.C. Torrey ('The Foundry of the Second Temple at Jerusalem', *JBL* 55 [1936], pp. 247-60) argued that the word refers to the official in charge of the foundry. Further see Rudolph, *Haggai*, pp. 202-203; Sæbø, 'Die deuterosacharjanische Frage', pp. 78-83.

Word	12.1	12.2	12.3	12.4	12.5	12.6	12.7	12.8	12.9	12.10	12.11	12.12	12.13	12.14	13.1	13.2	13.3	13.4	13.5	13.6
דבר	2															15				
יהוה	3,7			4	9		2	4,18							5	17				
נאם	6			3											4					
ארץ	11		19									2				12,24				
רוח	13									8						20				
אדם	14																			10
שים		3,4				3														
ירושלם ↓		5,17	6	8		23,26	15	7	11	7	5				9					
כל		8	9,11 17	6,17		19			7				1							
העמים +		9	10	19		20														
סביב +		10				21														
יהודה		13		13	3	6	5,17													
ביום ההוא			2f.	1f.		1f.		1f. 11f.	2f.		1f.				1f.	2f.		2f.		
עמם			8,12																	
שרח			13f.																	
גוי (pl.)			18						8											
נכה				5,20																4,10
סוס				7,18																
בית ↓			12			11	14			3		7,13	2		6					11
אמר				1													6	1		1,8
אלוף					2	5														
ישב + ירושלם					7	22	14	6		6					8					
צבאות					10											6				
אלהים					11			16												
אש						8,11														
גדל							9				3									
תפארת							10,13													
בית דויד							11f. 13 14f.			3f.		7f.			6f.					
חזן										9,10										
דקר										15							18			
ספד										16, 18	4,6	1								
מרר										21,23										
משפחה												4×	2×	3×						
לבד												5×	4×	2×						
נשיהם (+לבד)												2×	2×	1×						
נביא																18	3,22	5,8	3	
אב + עם + ילד																	{ 8-10 / 19-21			

Figure 14: *Zech. 12.1–13.6:*
Word numbers of words occurring twice or more

the people is restored. The words of v. 9b are similar to those used in expressing the covenant goal throughout the Bible (Gen. 17.8b; Exod. 6.7; Hos. 1.9–2.1; Jer. 31.33 etc.). We have already seen an emphasis on this in the first part of Zechariah (2.15; 8.8b).

We need to ask whether the editor has a specific purpose in separating 13.7-9 from the previous 'shepherd' passages. It would not be surprising to find this. We shall investigate this in Chapter 4.

Zechariah 12.1–13.6

Figure 14 gives the table of repeating words, from which the following have been omitted: למען, עוד, היה, גם, אנכי. This section must be considered as a whole, for:

1. To subdivide it would produce rather brief passages, particularly 13.2-6, which has very few repeated words that do not also occur in 12.1–13.1.
2. Commentaries disagree on the subdivision (e.g. 12.1-14 or 12.1–13.1).
3. The phrase 'and on that day' (12.3-4, 6, 8-9, 11; 13.1-2, 4) occurs throughout the whole section.

The words in the table seem to be potentially significant, either because of their distinctiveness, or because of their position or use in distinctive phrases. We shall discuss individual words only as we consider the structure and thought of the section.

The structure of the whole is as follows. CF signifies 'Continuation Formula'. It is convenient to give Lamarche's structure,[1] at the same time.

---

1. *Zacharie 9–14*, pp. 78-79, 86-87, 89-90. Lacocque has a different scheme (pp. 181-82). Here is a comparison of the two:

Verses 12:	1	2	3	4	5	6	7	8	9	10	11	12-14	13: 1	2	3	4 to 6
Lamarche	I	a	a'	b		b'	c	c'	C	ab	b'			a'	A	A'
															[ab c	c'b'a']
Lacocque	a		b		c	c'		b'	a'	d				e	e'	d'

I = Introduction; C = Conclusion.

			Lamarche's structure
Ch. 12			
1	IF		Intro
2		Theme of the whole, Jerusalem besieged but victorious over all the nations round about	a
3	I/CF	Jerusalem becomes אבן מעמסה	a'
4	CF	I will strike (נכה) every horse. . .riders. . . I will open my eyes upon Judah and every horse strike (נכה) with blindness	b
5		And Judah will say, 'Jerusalem. . .strength through Yahweh'	
6	CF	Judah a blazing pot to devour. . . Jerusalem will still dwell in its place in Jerusalem	b'
7		And Yahweh will first save tents of Judah. . . so that David and Jerusalem not exalted over Judah	c
8	CF	Yahweh will shield inhabitants of Jerusalem so that feeblest of them (CF) like David. . .	c'
9	I/CF	I will seek to destroy all nations that come against Jerusalem	
10		And I will pour out on. . .David and. . .Jerusalem spirit of חן and תחנונים	a
		they will look to me (with?) the one they *pierced* and I will weep for him as weep for an only child and weep bitterly as for a firstborn	b
11	CF	. . .weeping for Jerusalem as great as for Hadad-rimmon in plain of Megiddo	b'
12-14		Families of the land will weep by themselves (David, Nathan, Levi, Shimeites and their wives)	
Ch. 13			
1	CF	. . .fountain for. . .David and. . .Jerusalem for sin and for uncleanness	a'
2	I/CF	I will cut off names of idols. . .remembered no more . . .remove from the land the prophets and unclean spirit	a / b
3		והיה if a man prophesies. . .father and mother will say not live because speak falsely. . .*pierce* him through	c

(right-brace bracketing a, b, c labelled **A**)

4	I/CF	prophets will be ashamed of visions. . . will not put on אדרת שער in order to deceive	c'	
5		And he will say לא נביא אנכי כי אדם הקנני מנעורי	b'	A'
6		And one will say to him 'What are these מכות. . . ?' and he will say, that which הכיתי in. . . friends	a'	

General Remarks

There are several peculiar features in this passage. 'David' is mentioned six times here (five times in the expression 'house of David'), but nowhere else in Zechariah. The distinction between the house of David and the inhabitants of Jerusalem is found several times. Judah and Jerusalem are mentioned separately as previously (1.12, Jerusalem and the cities of Judah [cf. 2.2; 8.15; 2.16] is simply synonymous parallelism; 2.4, 8.19 and 14.5 mention Judah alone; 8.13 contrasts Judah and Israel; see also 9.7, 13; 10.3, 6; 11.4; 14.14, 21).

The passage also hints at tension between Judah on the one hand, and David and Jerusalem on the other (v. 7).[1] Verse 5 shows Judah thinking of Jerusalem as 'them'. Does v. 2 actually imply that Judah joins the siege against Jerusalem?[2] Literally it is: 'And it/he will also be against/upon Judah in the siege against Jerusalem'. The subject seems to be the 'cup of reeling' since the change from 'I' to 'he'

---

1.   Mason notes the possibility of seeing tension between Judah and Jerusalem in vv. 4, 6 and 7, but feels this was not the original intention (*Haggai, Zechariah and Malachi*, pp. 115-16; in more detail: *Zechariah 9–14*, pp. 213-19).

2.   Those who accept the MT tend to opt for one of two understandings:

   a.   Judah joins the nations in the siege against Jerusalem, e.g. Baldwin (*Haggai, Zechariah, Malachi,* p. 189), E. Cashdan (hesitantly, noting that the Targum, all Jewish and many modern commentators think that Judah is forced into this by the nations; *Soncino Books of the Bible: Zechariah* [London: Soncino, 1967], pp. 318-19), Jones (*Haggai, Zechariah, Malachi,* p. 158).

   b.   'The siege against Jerusalem will also be against Judah', based on Marti's suggestion that היה במצור means not 'to take part in' the siege but 'to be in a state of' siege, as in Ezek. 4.3; see Otzen, *Studien,* pp. 184-85; Amsler *et al., Agée, Zecharie, Malachi,* p. 186.

For various emendations see, e.g., Rudolph, *Haggai,* pp. 217-19; Sæbø, 'Die deuterosacharjanische Frage', pp. 88-92; Mason, *Zechariah 9–14,* pp. 219-20.

(i.e. Yahweh) would be abrupt.[1] Zech. 14.14 is relevant but also inconclusive: וגם יהודה נלחם בירושלם. Does Judah fight *with* or *against* Jerusalem?[2]

Whatever may be the case in v. 2, vv. 6-7 show Judah on the same side as Jerusalem. There are echoes of 2.9 (and 8) in the 'blazing pot' and the 'flaming torch' (cf. also אכל, 9.4, 15; 11.1, 9, 16; see above).

Zech. 12.1-9 forms a unit dealing with the nations who come against Jerusalem; v. 9 forms a logical end to the section with כל גוים הבאים על ירושלם (cf. ואספו עליה כל גויי הארץ v. 3). The word גוי occurs nowhere else in the chapter.

A new element appears in v. 10, the figure pierced by the people (the house of David and the inhabitants of Jerusalem). Again there are obscurities: should we read 'on me whom they have pierced?' as in the MT? The verse continues with 'him', so that Theodotion's reading is logical and understandable. It is not so easy, however, to see how a change from 'him' to 'me' could have been made—unless it was a purely mechanical mistake: the omission of a *waw*. The thought, however, is of a human figure and MT's 'on me' is probably to be understood as a bold expression of Yahweh's suffering through or with his representative.[3] The section extends to v. 14 with an expansion of 'they shall weep for him'. It is interesting that the word for 'pierce', דקר, occurs also at the end of 13.3, and nowhere else in Zechariah. A father and mother will pierce their own son if he is a false prophet. This seems to allude to 12.10, 'as one weeps for an only child...a firstborn'.

---

1.   S.R. Driver mentions the view of Keil that 'it' means 'that which has just been mentioned', i.e. in v. 2, which will fall upon Judah as upon Jerusalem. As he remarks: 'the thought is not expressed at all naturally' (*The Minor Prophets*, p. 262).

2.   The most natural translation is 'against' but the context favours 'with' or 'in'. NEB's ambiguous translation 'Judah too shall be caught up in the siege of Jerusalem' is neat, and passes on the problem to the reader.

3.   There have been many different attempts to reconcile the details. See, e.g., Rudolph, *Haggai*, pp. 217-18; Lamarche, *Zacharie 9–14*, pp. 80-84; Otzen, *Studien*, pp. 173-184. We may at least be confident that some historical figure is portrayed here, someone who was murdered or martyred by the house of David and the inhabitants of Jerusalem (v. 10). It is not necessary for us to try and identify the historical situation, but to describe how it functions from a literary point of view.

Zech. 13.1 introduces the next new element: a fountain for cleansing from sin of the house of David and the inhabitants of Jerusalem. The verse has more in common with ch. 12 than with 13.2-6 (especially 'house of David', the last occurrence) but 'on that day' also links this latter passage with what has gone before. It is clearly concerned with cleansing.[1]

Zech. 13.2-6 is another puzzling passage, but vv. 3-4 seem to confirm that false prophecy is in focus, and that it is at least partly given 'in the name of Yahweh'. Verse 2 also suggests that there might be prophecy in the name of idols; v. 6 suggests the sort of outward form of prophecy seen in 1 Kings 18.

The most noteworthy words are דקר and נכה (also important elsewhere: 1.6; 9.4; 10.11; 13.7). How they fit into a pattern, if they do, is not yet clear.

Smaller sections that exhibit some sort of regular structure are:

12.4	
IF	ביום ההוא נאם יהוה
ab	אכה כל סוס בתמהון
	ורכבו בשגעון
c	ועל בית ישראל אפקח את עיני
b'a'	וכל סוס העמים אכה בעורון[2]

The three rare words here, תמהון, שגעון and עורון occur in Deut. 28.28 as the punishments that will come if the people are unfaithful. Only the middle of these occurs elsewhere in the OT: of Jehu who drives with שגעון! There is a contrast expressed between c and a'b' (open eyes/blindness).

---

1. Mason takes this to mean there will be a 'continuing means of cleansing in Jerusalem. . . a purified temple and cult' (*Zechariah 9–14*, p. 120); Rudolph says that the prophet goes back to cultic ideas, as in Num. 8.7 ('water of expiation') and 19.9 ('water for impurity'), but here it is not prepared—and renewed—by human hands, it is from God and a sign of his favour (*Haggai*, p. 227).

2. This is a quite definite chiasmus. The outer sentences are also similar as a whole (b + particular sign of judgment indicates this). Rudolph deletes the last phrase along with vv. 2b and 3b (*Haggai*, pp. 216-20).

In 12.10 it is worth noting the exact parallelism:

וספדו עליו כמספד על היחיד

והמר עליו כהמר על הבכור

Cf. also v. 11:

יגדל המספד בירושלם כמספד   הדד־רמון בבקעת מגדון

In 13.3 we have:

IF	והיה
a	כי ינבא איש עוד
b	ואמרו אליו אביו ואמו ילדיו
c	לא יחיה כי שקר דברת בשם יהוה ודקרהו
b'	אביהו ואמו ילדיו
a'	בנבאו

Note here the similarity of sound between שקר and דקר, which may well be intentional, although I do not think we should be justified in putting cc as the middle point.

If we consider ודקרהו as the centre of a chiasmus, and part of the larger unit, 12.1–13.6, there are two variations of the abcba...c pattern suggested in 9.5-7. In the case of דקר (= c) it would be reversed: c...abcba; in the case of נכה in 12.4 and 13.6 we have a(bcb)a...a'a". (The only other word common to these two verses is 'house of' which does not seem to be significant.)

The overall plan of this whole section, then, is governed by the introduction and continuation formulae that occur. Within this structure it is possible to recognize smaller regular patterns. If we ask whether there are important words that we have left unaccounted for, and whether they confirm or undermine our conclusions so far, the results are as follows.

רוח occurs as part of the description of Yahweh in v. 1, where it is combined with אדם—and יצר! It is possible that there is some connection between this and the important turning point in v. 10, but I do not think anything can be demonstrated.

שים is repeated twice at the start of the announcement of Yahweh's action on behalf of Jerusalem against the nations. The pattern is:

2.   *I am setting Jerusalem* a cup of reeling
              for *all the peoples around* (+. . . ?)[1]

3. I/CF   והיה ביום ההוא
              I will set Jerusalem a heavy burden
                  for all the peoples, all who carry it as a burden
                      will indeed be lacerated
                      and there will be gathered against her
                  all nations of the earth

4.   . . .

5.   *clans of Judah*. . . Yahweh hosts their God

6. CF   ביום ההוא
              I will set clans of Judah as pot of *fire* among wood
                      and as torch of *fire* among sheaves
                      and will devour on right hand and left hand
              all peoples around (+. . . ?)[2]

It is obviously dangerous to build anything on the obscure sections
marked above. Note, however, that they contain references to Judah
(v. 2, cf. vv. 4, 5, 6) and Jerusalem (vv. 2, 6 [2×]). The resulting
structure is remarkably regular and intricate. We have not met anything like it, in this respect, since Zechariah 1–8. We have to decide
how to regard this. It could represent a kind of inclusio: vv. 2-3 and
v. 6, indicated by שׂים together with 'for all peoples סביב' (vv. 2, 6;
without סביב in v. 3). Within this we should have pairs of important
words to carry forward the thought of the passage, ending with אלוף,
in vv. 5-6. Yet it is more likely that we have two parallel units:

vv. 2-5   I will set Jerusalem. . .for all nations around
vv. 6ff.   I will set tribes of Judah. . .for all nations around[3]

---

1. NEB takes סף, which normally means 'cup', to mean 'threshold', and
produces an ingenious translation: 'I am making the steep approaches to Jerusalem
slippery. . .' It is more likely that the well-established 'cup' imagery is correct, cf.
Isa. 51.17 (כוס התרעלה // כוס המתו; sim. v. 22); Jer. 25.17, 28. There are no other
instances of סף used in this sense, although an emendation to Hab. 2.15 would produce one more.

2. 'Jerusalem will dwell again/continually in its place in Jerusalem'. The second
occurrence of 'Jerusalem' is odd, and could be improved by reading 'in peace', but
there is no warrant for the change. It does not affect the structure.

3. See on 12.1–13.6 in Chapter 2 above. Rudolph, in common with several
scholars, treats the section differently: vv. 2a + 3a + 4a; then 4bα + 5-6 + 8 + 7,
pp. 216-23. Similarly Lutz (*Jahwe, Jerusalem und die Völker* [Neukirchen–Vluyn:

Then v. 5 forms a transition to the second section by linking the tribes of Judah with Jerusalem. This way of looking at the passage agrees better with the way the formulae are employed. Verse 7 reintroduces Jerusalem, mentioning the 'house of David' for the first time. Again a distinctive word, תפארת, is used twice. Judah and Jerusalem are now reconciled. Verse 8 ends the section in the same way that v. 5 did: it mentions the 'inhabitants of Jerusalem' and refers to their strength (although in a different way). The only other word that stands out is גדל, vv. 7, 11. These instances do not seem to be connected.

Lamarche's Treatment of Zechariah 12.1–13.6
Lamarche's results suffer from two opposite deficiencies, which have been noted previously:

1. They do not recognize some of the correspondences noted above.
2. They treat as significant, words and phrases which are insignificant, and which often also occur in places not mentioned by him.

His plan of Zech. 12.1-9 (p. 78) is as follows:

Neukirchener Verlag, 1968], pp. 15 [-20]): 2a + 3a + 4a; then 5 + 6b + 8; then 3b + 4bβ + 6α + 7. Willi-Plein conducts an unusual investigation using the categories 'Aufnahme' and 'Trennung' following Richter (*Prophetie am Ende*, pp. 40-42). She notes the following marks of separation (2b = asyndeton; 3b = change of person; 3b = change in type of sentence; 5b = personal pronoun without reference to the preceding; 10b = introductory or concluding changes in the preceding sentence) and continuity (2a = connecting or backward looking conjunction):

12.1	2b	3b	4b	10b	
12.4	2b	3b		10b	
12.6	2b	3b		10b	
12.7		3b			2a
12.9		3b		10b	2a
etc.					

These are relative terms, and the sense of the actual text is of first importance. Nevertheless, this seems to confirm the subsidiary break at v. 6, and to direct our attention more strongly to v. 4.

1		Introduction	
2	a	Here is what I will make (שׁים) Jerusalem	Assault of all nations repulsed
3	a'	And on that day I will make (שׁים) Jerusalem	Assault of all nations repulsed
4-5	b	On that day: battle	Example of Jerusalem encourages Judah
6	b'	On that day: battle	Judah, in the hands of Yahweh, saves Jerusalem
7	c	Yahweh will save	Judah in the first place
8	c'	On that day Yahweh protects	and exalts. . . David and . . . Jerusalem
		on that day. . .	
9		Conclusion: And on that day	Destruction of all nations that besieged Jerusalem

In vv. 2-3 שׁים is distinctive and worthy of note, but why is כל גוים (vv. 4, 9) not properly accounted for, nor the slightly varying phrases (כל העמים [סביב])? The formula is only taken note of where it is convenient to do so. It occurs, for example, in v. 9 but not v. 10. Lamarche's analysis is not without plausibility: it does trace three phases in the narrative. However, they are neither so distinct nor so exact as he suggests.

Lamarche's plan for 12.10–13.1 is:[1]

12.10a	a	Conversion and return to Yahweh of the house of David and the inhabitants of Jerusalem
v. 10b	b	Mourning
vv. 11-14	b'	*On that day* mourning
13.1	a'	*On that day* conversion and purification of the house of David and the inhabitants of Jerusalem

Similar remarks may be made. 'Conversion' might pass as a description of what is described in 12.10a and/or 13.1, but it is not exact, nor completely accurate. It does, however, seem likely that this section is at least a subdivision of 12.1–13.6 which the author/editor himself had in mind.

---

1. *Zacharie 9–14*, pp. 86-87.

There is greater difficulty when 12.10–13.1 is compared with 13.7-9, 'pierced' and 'struck'. The 'pierced' of 13.3 is ignored and the verse included in vv. 2-6 under the title 'idols and false prophets'. The two instances of נכה in 12.4 are also excluded from consideration.

Zech. 13.2-6 is given as follows (p. 89; I have supplied a, b, c):

2	A		*And it will happen on that day*
	a		Rejection of idols. . .no more mentioned [actually 'remembered']
		b	Suppression of false prophets
3			c	If anyone prophesies and speaks falsely. . .pierced

4-6	A'		*And it will happen on that day*
		c	If prophesy. . .shame. No more tell lies.
		b	Suppression of false prophets
	a		Not mention idols any more

This is not satisfactory for the following reasons.

1. Aab represent two parallel statements in v. 2. The internal parallel is lost in Lamarche's plan. It is actually:

$$\text{אכרית את שמות העצבים \quad מן הארץ}$$
$$\text{ולא יזכרו עוד}$$
$$\text{וגם \quad את נביאים ואת רוח הטמאה}$$
$$\text{אעביר \quad מן הארץ}$$

It seems highly artificial to divide this verse so as to make it balance a rather longer passage at the end of the section.

2. The label in A'a is misleading. 'Idols' are not mentioned, and it is doubtful whether this is the main concern of v. 6.

3. The strong repetition of v. 3 is missed: 'his father[1] and his mother who bore him', which is a heavy phrase (worthy of P!). It is actually used to frame the important word דקר, which Lamarche ignores. This is the most serious oversight of all, since it spoils his whole theory of the structure of at least Zechariah 12–14. For the structure of v. 3, see above.

4. Lamarche notes that the strongest formula occurs in v. 4, and is right therefore to make the main break between vv. 3 and 4. He does not note the similarity, however, between בהנבאו and בהנבאתו[2]

---

1. The change from אביו to אביהו is slightly against this suggestion, but I think the similarity is still too strong to be missed.

2. The latter is usually reckoned to be the result of confusion between *lamedh–aleph* and *lamedh–he* forms, and emended to read as in v. 3 (Sæbø, 'Die

(vv. 3, 4). This means that the reader is invited to see the connection between the two verses. Having seen it, we note the similarity between שׁקר in v. 3, and כחשׁ in v. 4. The two roots occur together in Lev. 19.11-12 (as verbs in v. 11, with חשׁבעו בשׁמי לשׁקר in v. 12) and are likely to have been connected in the mind of our writer. (We note also here two strong allusions to older traditions: Jacob's deceiving the hairy Esau with goatskins, and Amos's statement in 7.14.) The most obvious difference between the two verses is that v. 4 goes on to speak about prophets in the plural, which makes the אישׁ and the singular suffix on the two following words in v. 4 stand out more clearly.

5. Verses 5-6 do not have any obvious connection with what has gone before, and should not be forced into a neat plan.[1] They appear to be a picturesque commentary on v. 4, and they match v. 3 in their conversational style.

Summary

The basic pattern is that given at the outset, which is largely indicated by the introductory and continuation formulae that are used. Within this overall plan there are several small units that exhibit a regular structure (e.g. v. 4). There is a stronger link here with chs. 1–8 than we have discovered so far, not only in the concentration on Jerusalem, which would not necessarily link the writers at all, but in the method of structuring the material. It is not possible, in my opinion, to say that there must be or there could not be an editor who had a hand in both Zechariah 1–8 and Zechariah 12. We may find further evidence in Chapter 4 below.

Zechariah 14

There are 67 words which occur at least twice in Zechariah 14, and we must again eliminate some of them before attempting to produce a table. We may ignore the following words (numbers in brackets denote occurrences in Zech. 14 and in Zech. 1–14 respectively): יהוה

---

deuterosacharjanische Frage', p. 104). It makes no difference to the structure.

1. Lamarche says: 'Les correspondances entre les deux strophes ne sont peut-être pas assez nettes pour qu'on puisse parler de structure à proprement parler' (*Zacharie 9–14*, p. 89). The correspondences seem to be both (even) less clear than he thinks, and more clear—but different.

מן (24, 67), היה, אשר, על, לא, אל (12, 42), כל (6, 48), את (15, 133).

קרב, vv. 1, 3, is interesting. In the first instance it means 'in your midst' from root II; v. 3 contains a noun from root I meaning 'battle'. A pun of some sort might be intended but the difference in pronunciation makes this unlikely. However the word is rare (only 12.1 otherwise in Zechariah: 'the spirit of man within him') and we should plot it.

אסף occurs in vv. 2, 14; otherwise only in 12.3.

גוי (6, 17) is common but must be retained as expressing one of the major concerns of the prophet. We should also consider it along with עם, vv. 2, 18.

ירושלם is similar. It often occurs with 'Judah' and is sometimes referred to by another expression, e.g. העיר, vv. 3, 10.

לחם (4, 9) must be retained.

בית (3, 31) occurs in its absolute plural form in v. 2, which may be ignored, and in the expression 'house of Yahweh' in vv. 20-21, which is surprisingly rare in Zechariah 9–14.[1] We shall plot it.

יצא (3, 24) has previously proved to be an important word and must be retained.

חצי only occurs in this chapter: vv. 2, 4 (3×), 8 (2×); so we must retain it.

רגל + עמד. These occur together in vv. 4 and 12. The latter does not occur elsewhere in Zechariah, and this is obviously one of the likeliest phrases to have a structuring function. The combination, however, is different: עמד על רגליו and ועמדו רגליו.

הר occurs five times in vv. 4-5, once in 4.7, three times in 6.1 and twice in 8.3. If it is significant at all for our purposes it will be for a larger section of the book. See זית below.

זית occurs twice in v. 4 together with הר in the expression 'Mount of Olives'. We may probably ignore it here. Elsewhere in Zechariah it occurs in the vision of the lampstand and the olive trees (4.3, 11-12).

The next group contains words sufficiently rare and/or distinctive for us to plot them: קדם (2, 2), ים (3, 7), גיא (3, 3), נגב (2, 3; otherwise 7.7), נוס (3, 5), מלך (5, 9; vv. 5, 9-10, 16-17), יהודה (3, 22), קדש (3, 6), אור (2, 2), אחד (3, 13), ערב (2, 2); we ignore גדל (2, 13), and מאד (2, 5).

---

1. 'My house' occurs in Zech. 9.8; in Zech. 1–8 the expression occurs only in 1.16; 3.7; 3.9; 7.3.

ארץ (vv. 9, 10, 14; otherwise 37 times) is not certainly to be excluded. We retain סבב (2, 6), ישב (3, 24), שער (3, 5), but may ignore עד (3, 6) and בו (3, 26).

עוד (2, 16) seems to be more significant; the association with חרם in v. 11 and כנעני in v. 21 may confirm this.

זאת does not seem to be significant but its associates may be: וזאת זאת תהיה חטאת מצרים (v. 15), and מגפה הזאת (v. 12), תהיה המגפה (v. 19). These occur at the beginning of vv. 12 and 19, and at the end of v. 15.

נגף is probably one of the most significant words. The verb occurs with the noun מגפה in vv. 12, 18: וזאת תהיה המגפה אשר יגף יהוה את כל העמים/גוים אשר; the noun also occurs twice in v. 15. There are no other instances of this root in Zechariah.

צבא occurs as a verb in v. 12, but only otherwise in the name 'Yahweh of hosts'. We shall retain it.

מקק occurs only in v. 12 (three times). We retain it only in view of its rarity: it is found nowhere else in Zechariah and only seven more times in the Hebrew Bible.

רבב occurs only in vv. 13 and 14 in different forms and may be disregarded.

יד is not promising since it occurs three times, all in v. 13. However, we shall keep it, noting that several times in this chapter a word occurs three times in a single verse: עיר v. 3, חצי v. 4, שער v. 10, מקק v. 12, יד v. 13.

עאר (2, 11) reminds us of Zech. 11.6, cf. 8.10 and 7.10; עלה (6, 6) occurs in a cluster of verses (13-19); סוס (2, 14) has been an important word in Zechariah. We shall retain these three words.

שנה occurs in the expression 'from year to year' and hardly qualifies for the category of words occurring twice or more.

שחה (2, 2), חגג (6, 6) and סכה (3, 3) must be retained.

The last five words must also be retained: משפחה (2, 11; otherwise only in Zech. 12), מצרים (2, 4; otherwise 10.10-11), חטאת (2, 3; otherwise 13.1), סיר (2, 2) and זבח (2, 3; מזבח occurs in 9.15 and 14.21; זבחים occurs in 14.21).

There is general agreement that this chapter may be divided into vv. 1-15 and 16-21. Further subdivisions are sometimes made after v. 5[1] and/or v. 19. There are obvious similarities between this and

---

1. Or v. 6: Gaide calls vv. 1-6 'La Dernière Nuit' and vv. 7-15 'Le jour sans

Word	1	2	3	4	5	6	7	8	9	10	11	12	13	14	15	16	17	18	19	20	21
יום הוא	2		6,8	3	15	2	2,8	2	7				2							1	23
בא	3				19											6		7			9
(קרב)	7		(9)																		
אסף		1												5							
גו/עם		4,19	4									9		8	5			16	7		
ירושלם		6		11				7		8	8		13	4	8	9					4
(יהוה)					18									2							5
לחם (verb)		7n	3,7											3							
עיר			3×																		
בית יהוה		11																		11	20
יצא		14	1					4													
הצי		15		3×				8,12													
יתר		18															3				
עם		19										9									
עמד				1								17									
רגל				2								19									
הר				3× 3,7																	
זית				7,15																	
קדם								11													
ים								10,14													
ניא				19	2,6																
נגב				27					7												
נוס				3×																	
מלך				17					3	25						14	11				
יהודה				18									2								5
קדש				23																7	6
אור						6	15														
אחד							3		11,13												
ערב							13		4												
ארץ								6	3								7				
סבב									1					9							
ישב										10	1,7										
שער										3×											
עד										6											19
זאת										1					15			1			
נגף/מגפה										3,5					3,14			11,13			
צבא										11[verb]						16	13				8,22
מקק										3×											
רבב												7	13								
יד												3×									
רע												12,17									
עלה												13				9	4	5,19	10		
סוס														4					6		
שחה																13	10				
חגג																17,19		20,22	11,13		
סכה																20		23	14		
משפחה																	6	2			
מצרים																		3	4		
חטאת																			3,5		
סיר																				10	3
זבח																				15	11

Figure 15: *Zechariah 14: Word numbers of words occurring twice or more.*

other parts of the book. Zech. 12.1-9 is the closest parallel; 9.11ff. and 10.3b–11.3 are less similar but deal with the the same theme: the war between Jerusalem and the nations.

A table of words occurring twice or more frequently in Zechariah 14 is given in figure 15. Lamarche and Lacocque, who give detailed plans of the structure of the chapter, differ from the scholarly consensus and from each other:

Lamarche			Lacocque[1]			
Zech. 14.1-15			*Zech. 14.1-15*			
1-2aα	a	Lo a day comes. . . booty, enemies	1	A	A day comes Yahweh/booty/nations/war	
2aβ-b	b	Jerusalem taken. . . insecurity	2	B	Jerusalem invested pillage. . .division	
3-5	c	*On that day* (v. 4)	3	C	Intervention of Yahweh	
3		Yahweh goes out			a	against these nations (universalism)
4[-5aα]		Division mountains	4		b	cataclysm Jerusalem
5a[β]		Flight	5a		c	flight of population
5b		Yahweh returns [בא]	5b	D	Entry Yahweh and angels	
6	d	*And. . .on that day* darkness, cold, ice	6		1	Day of light
7a	e	A UNIQUE DAY	7		2	Unique day without evening
7b	d´	*And. . .on that day* light				
8		living water summer as winter	8	D´	Living water. . .Jerusalem 1 general fertility 2 uninterrupted flow	
9	c´	*On that day* (9b) Yahweh king Yahweh unique	9	C´	Yahweh King a´ unique (universalism)	
10a		Land becomes a plain	10		b´	restoration of Jerusalem
10b-11	b´	Jerusalem protected by ramparts; security	11		c´	security
12-15	a´	*And. . .on that day* (13)	12	B´	Plague on the nations rotting of their flesh	
12		Plague against enemy				

déclin'. Lamarche puts a climax following v. 6; Lacocque makes the division after v. 7; Chary is alone in dividing the chapter 1-11 + 12-21 (*Les prophètes et le culte*, p. 231; *Commentary*, p. 210), but he further subdivides after vv. 5 and 15.

1. Lamarche, *Zacharie 9–14*, pp. 100.; Amsler *et al., Agée, Zacharie, Malachi*, pp. 132-33.

13	Enemies' disarray	13	disarray and division
14	Booty	14-15 A'	Judah/war/spoil/nations
15	Plague against animals		

Lamarche calls vv. 1-6 a 'series of misfortunes' and vv. 7b-15 a 'series of victories'.[1] It is doubtful whether the division of the mountains should be described in this way. It seems rather to be a terrifying sign of Yahweh's intervention. We must question the use of the common formula '(and it will be) on that day'. The use of this formula to add two separate sections could easily be mistaken for a deliberate structuring of the final passage. The latter could, of course, be true but it needs to be established by independent criteria. Notice needs to be taken of two further facts.

1. 'On that day' does not occur at the beginning of the sub-sections, vv. 3-5, 7b-8 or 12-15; Lamarche's plan obscures this.
2. In such cases the formula is unlikely to be used for editorial additions, and perhaps more likely to be used in structuring the chapter.

Lacocque comments that 'Lamarche gives a table of the structure of 14.1-[1]5 which shows he has not understood the text in question'.[2] He does little, however, to justify his own plan. Lamarche's plan for the remainder of the chapter is as follows:[3]

| 16-19 | a | Under pain of judgment the remnant of the nations go to Jerusalem to worship: the King Yahweh Sebaoth (2×) |
| 20-21 | a' | Everything is sacred
On that day
    on horses' bells. . .*holy to Yahweh*
    on pots in Jerusalem. . .*holy to Yahweh*
on that day |

---

1. He does not justify this description: he states it and refers to the plan (*Zacharie 9–14*, p. 98).

2. Amsler *et al.*, *Agée, Zecharie, Malachi*, p. 132 n. 2 (where there is a misprint: '14.1-5' should be '14.1-15'. The heading to his own plan reads '14.1-14', but, since he treats vv. 1-15 together in the body of commentary (see esp. p. 205), I assume that this is also a mistake.

3. *Zacharie 9–14*, p. 104

Criticisms made previously apply also to this treatment of ch. 14. For instance, the correspondences are formal, based mainly on introductory formulae; some sections have little content in common (e.g. c and c' in Lamarche's plan); some points of contact are ignored (e.g. king is found in v. 5 [Uzziah] as well as in v. 9; the only other apparently significant word the sections have in common is נגב); the sections ded' encompass some very uncertain text; e cannot be said to be a very satisfying or convincing climax: Yahweh's becoming king is more likely to be at the centre, particularly in view of 14.16-17 which is part of the climax of chs. 9–14, with contacts in 9.1-8 and 9.9-10 especially; formally c looks similar to a'; and a and a' are not similar with regard to introductory formulae or detail.

Before offering my own explanation of the structure of vv. 1-15, I shall deal with vv. 16-19. Lamarche's analysis of this section seems to be more successful, and he summarizes v. 16-19 correctly (Lacocque apparently does not see a particular structure here). He does not, however, deal with all the duplicate words and phrases that abound in this section. It may be set out as follows:

16a	And it will be
	all that remains of all the nations
	that <u>came</u> against (אל) Jerusalem
16b	they <u>will go up</u> year by year
	to worship the King Yahweh Sebaoth
	<u>and to keep the feast את חג of booths</u>
17	And it will be
	whoever <u>will not go up</u>
	from all the families of the earth to Jerusalem
	to worship the King Yahweh Sebaoth
	there will be no rain on them
18	and if a family of Egypt <u>will not go up</u> and not <u>come</u>
	and not upon them
	there will be the plague (with) which Yahweh
	will plague the nations
	who <u>will not go up to keep the feast of booths</u>
19	this will be the חמאת of Egypt
	and the חמאת of all the nations
	who <u>will not go up to keep the feast of booths</u>

There are almost too many inter-relationships and repetitions here. We can say with certainty that:

1. There is a positive prophecy (v. 16) followed by exception clauses (vv. 17-19).
2. There is great emphasis upon:

    > going up to Jerusalem
    > to worship the King Yahweh Sebaoth, and
    > to 'feast the feast of booths'

3. There is stern punishment for those who refuse the opportunity to join with Yahweh's people in worship and feast.
4. Egypt is a representative nation. If she remains hostile as in the days of Israel's bondage in Egypt then she merits and will suffer plague (as previously).[1]

There is one textual difficulty in v. 18a: עֲלֵיהֶם וְלֹא which almost certainly needs emendation. Various solutions are offered.

1. Delete it as dittography from v. 17b.
2. Delete only לֹא with some Hebrew manuscripts, LXX and Syr. This seems to be the best solution.
3. Understand the phrase to mean 'there will not be (rain) upon them (either)'.[2] In this case we should expect 'and' with the verb that follows.

We cannot understand the text to mean that 'if Egypt, however, does not go up. . . the plague which the nations will suffer will not come upon Egypt' since v. 19 associates the nations and Egypt in the punishment that they will undergo.

Verses 16-19 are not completely separate from the preceding verses, 12-15. They still deal with the situation of the war against Jerusalem and Yahweh's victory. Here the reference to plagues both encloses the rest of the material and links with vv. 16-19. Verses 12-15, recognized as a coherent unit, cause us to look at vv. 1-3 (at least) which deal with the nations' battle against Jerusalem. Only vv. 1-2 actually describe Jerusalem's defeat (contrary to Lamarche's

---

1. Lacocque says that since Egypt was not affected by lack of rain it was necessary to mention it separately (Amsler *et al.*, *Agée, Zecharie, Malachi*, p. 214).

2. Most commentators follow LXX and Syr. Rudolph thinks that the Targum is on the right track and so adds: '(so würde) "für sie der Nil nicht steigen"' (*Haggai*, pp. 231, 233).

plan);[1] there are verbal contacts between vv. 1-2 and 14b. The spoil will be divided by the nations whom Yahweh gathers against Jerusalem (vv. 1-2): שללך, חלק, אספתי. In v. 14 the wealth of all nations (which is spoil) will be gathered (חיל, ואסף). The word גוי only occurs in vv. 2, 3, 4, 16, 18, 19).

It seems that Lamarche is right to equate vv. 12-15 with the beginning of the chapter and to point to booty as an important element. But it does not seem reasonable to subdivide vv. 1-3 into three sections.

We may ask whether vv. 1-3 should stand alone. Arguments for this would be:

1. Verses 4-5 deal with geographical upheavals rather than with action in battle.
2. Verse 4 has 'on that day'.

However, also note that:

1. Verses 4-5 would form a suitable prelude to the defeat of the nations.
2. Verse 4 does not begin with 'on that day'.
3. To finish at v. 3 would leave a very inconclusive section.
4. There is verbal correspondence between ועמדו רגליו in v. 4 and עמד על רגליו in v. 12.

Whichever of these alternatives is accepted the material between these two sections concerns geographical events. There seem to be several possibilities for the devoted structural analyst to argue for a chiastic structure:

4-5a	Mount (of Olives) and Valley (of Kidron) *levelled*
10(-11)	Whole land *levelled*—except Jerusalem
5b	flee as in the days of *King* Uzziah
9	Yahweh will become *King* over all the earth[2]
6-8	(As Lamarche)

But if the writer did have a more exact chiastic structure in mind here, the centre is more likely to have been v. 9.

---

1.   Verse 1 could even be taken to be a general summary of the outcome, which stands as a sort of superscription. The spoil (שלל) taken by Jerusalem will be divided in its midst. However, we may assume the more usual interpretation, that it means the spoils taken *from* Jerusalem.

2.   See p. 233 point 6.

In each of these schemes certain words are chosen as significant and others are ignored. Let us now, therefore, try to set out the whole of vv. 1-15. In doing so we shall provide a rather over-literal translation, bearing in mind also that several parts of the chapter are obscure, and probably corrupt.

1	Behold a day is coming for Yahweh
	and spoil will be divided out in your midst
2	And I will gather all nations to Jerusalem for battle
	and city captured, houses plundered, women ravished
	HALF city *go forth* into exile,
	and rest of the people not cut off from city
3	Yahweh *go forth* and *fight* against those nations
	as he *fights* on a battle day
4	And his feet will stand, *on that day*, on *Mount of Olives*
	which is before Jerusalem on the east
	and the *Mount of Olives* will be split in HALF
	eastwards and westwards, a very great valley
	and HALF the *Mount* depart northwards, and HALF southwards
5[1]	And you will flee, *valley of my mountains*
	for the *valley of mountains* will touch the side of it
	and you will flee as you fled
	from the earthquake in days of Uzziah *King* of Judah
	and Yahweh my God will come
	all holy ones with you
6	IF And *it will be on that day*
	there will not be light, precious things and congelation
7	And there will be *one day*
	it is known to Yahweh
	no day and no night
	and it will be evening time
	there will be light
8	And *it will be on that day*
	living waters will *go forth* from Jerusalem
	HALF of them to the eastern sea, and
	HALF of them to the western sea
	in summer and autumn it will be

1. This is the most difficult verse to translate in ch. 14. Despite this there are few probable emendations which are supported by external sources and agreed by the majority of scholars. The addition of the conjunction in 5.#22 is an exception, but makes little difference for our purposes. See Sæbø, 'Die deuterosacharjanische Frage', pp. 110-15.

9	And Yahweh will be *King* over all the earth
	on that day Yahweh will be *one* and his name *one*
10	And all the land/earth shall be turned like the Arabah,
	from Geba to Rimmon, south of Jerusalem
	And she will be high and dwell in her place
	from Benjamin gate as far as the place of the former gate
	as far as the gate of the פנים
	and tower of Hananel as far as the wine presses of the *king*
11	And they will dwell in her
	and חרם will not be
	and Jerusalem will dwell in trust/security
12	And this the PLAGUE. . .all peoples against Jerusalem
	flesh rot while standing on his feet
	eye rot in socket, tongue rot in mouth
13	and *it will be on that day* great panic from Yahweh
	and they will take hold of, a man the hand of his neighbour
	and his hand will be raised upon the hand of his neighbour
14	And also Judah will fight with/against Jerusalem
	and wealth of nations around will be gathered
	gold and silver and garments, in great abundance
15	And thus will be PLAGUE of horse etc. in those camps
	like this PLAGUE

It is plain that vv. 12-15 are marked off by their subject matter:
plague for the enemies of Jerusalem. It is emphasized by the inclusio,
וזאת תהיה המגפה and כמגפה הזאת, the first and last words of this unit. It
is also clear that, from a form-critical point of view, the strongest
introductory formulae are at the beginning of vv. 6, 7 and 13. Other
features also stand out.

1. There is frequent mention of the word חצי, and it is associated
with the directions east-west (vv. 4, 8) and north-south (v. 4). This
seems to be connected with two main ideas: division (vv. 2, 4), and
comprehensiveness (v. 8).

2. There are concrete local and historical references in two places,
vv. 4-5 and 10.

3. In the centre of these verses there is an emphasis on oneness (day,
vv. 6-7; Yahweh and his name, v. 9b; cf. 'whole earth', v. 9
[cf. v. 10a]). There may be an intentional contrast with the division
expressed in vv. 2, 4.

4. Certain verbs perform important functions:

a.   יצא shows a progression from disaster (v. 2b), via Yahweh's going forth (v. 3), to blessing (v. 8).
b.   נוס is given heavy emphasis, occurring three times in v. 5 expressing panic and displacement.
c.   ישב occurs three times in vv. 10-11, expressing Jerusalem's security, and contrasting with the 'flee' of v. 5.

5. There is a contrast between ירושלם למלחמה and ירושלם לבטח (vv. 2, 11).

6. The section concerning the plague, vv. 12-15, which seems to be unnecessary after the prophecy of blessing in v. 11, actually matches (mostly contrasting with) vv. 1-3:

vv. 1-3	vv. 12-14
nations (attack)	nations (punished)
'your' spoil divided	cf. wealth of nations
gather (all nations)	(wealth of nations) gathered
for battle (מלחמה)	Judah fights (לחם). . .
all peoples to Jerusalem	all nations against Jerusalem

The variation in the use of these repeating words is striking.

7. The use of 'king' is interesting: Yahweh as king occurs in the central section, and may possibly be deliberately framed by two other references. In Isa. 6.1-5 I believe we have a contrast intended between King Uzziah who died that year, and Yahweh the king, who was sitting on the throne. Perhaps the reference to King Uzziah here would recall Isaiah's vision, as well as the preaching of Amos (1.1). We recall here that the word 'king' has been used only in 9.5, 9 and 11.6 in Zechariah 9–14. I do not know what significance may be attached to 'wine presses of the king' and it is wise not to speculate.

8. The phrase(s) לא יהיה אור forms an inclusio for vv. 6a-7. This causes some confusion about where the centre of the chapter really is. A plausible solution seems to be to understand 'light' as a means of emphasizing 'one day' by framing it.

It seems impossible to arrange this in a precisely structured whole, but the overall movement and emphasis is clearly seen. This is true despite the fact that the text appears to be corrupt in several places, and there are therefore some uncertainties in this presentation. The centre is vv. 6-9, bound together by the idea of 'one', and by the concentration of introductory formulae, '(And it will be) on that day', vv. 6a, 8a, 9b. The words 'half' and 'go forth' become positive.

Jerusalem is no longer a centre for battle, but the source of blessing. One might disagree about some of the details, but this seems to represent the main intent of the writer fairly and accurately.[1]

As we have seen, vv. 1-15 lead in to vv. 16-19. The section concerns the remnant of the 'nations who came against (or 'come to') Jerusalem'. But they are now transformed into worshippers of Yahweh, and are expected to keep the feast of booths. Yahweh is called 'king' twice (vv. 16-17) and the significant title 'of hosts/armies' is now introduced (v. 12; see below).

The final section, 14.20-21, has a number of contacts with earlier material, though they are mostly difficult to define precisely. For example the bells of the horses recall the plague on the horses in 14.15, and the two references in 12.4 (cf. also perhaps 10.3, 5; 9.10; and even the first and last visions in Zechariah 1–6).

סיר refers first to the pots in the Temple and then to every pot in Judah and Jerusalem.

בית יהוה is infrequent in Zechariah as noted above.

מזבח and מזרק both occur in 9.15.

There do not seem to be any other uncommon words to account for except כנעני. If this reading is correct in ch. 11 then this would indicate that the inconclusive work of the shepherd there is at least finished. The Temple is finally purified: there are no corrupt leaders, no commercial potters(?); the vessels are holy to Yahweh and anyone may come and make use of them. It forms a fitting conclusion to a work that looks beyond the deliverance of the people of Judah and Jerusalem to the deliverance of all nations.

The structure of the final section may be set out as follows:

---

1. I have not clarified the meaning of vv. 6-7. 'There will not be light' should not be understood to contradict v. 7. Baldwin takes it to mean sunlight, and this would be consonant with 'the splendid ones congeal', that is, lose their light, v. 6bβ (*Haggai, Zechariah, Malachi,* p. 203). For further suggestions, see Rudolph, *Haggai,* pp. 230, 232; Sæbø, 'Die deuterosacharjanische Frage', p. 115.

20   *On that day*
            there will be on the horse *bells*
20aβ   holy to Yahweh

                And it will be
                    the *household vessels* in the house of Yahweh
                    (will be) like the bowls before the altar

21   *And it will be*
            every *household vessel* in Judah and Jerusalem
21aα   holy to Yahweh Sebaoth

21aβ   And all sacrificers will come
                    and will take from *them*
                        and boil (sc. sacrifices) in them

                    And there will not be
                        a trader any more in the house of Yahweh
                            Sebaoth
        on that day.

Note that this is not a chiastic structure in the straightforward sense
although there is an overall inclusio, and a chiasmus could be read in
to the section 20a-21a: holy to Yahweh—household vessels—household
vessels—holy to Yahweh Sebaoth. This, however, would confuse the
structure that the sense of the passage implies:

            On that day
                Horse bells will have 'holy to Yahweh'
                Household vessels will have 'holy to Yahweh Sebaoth'
                    Expansion concerning household vessels
                    General expansion illustrating holiness of the Temple
            on that day.

It is interesting to note the 'growing phrase' from 'Yahweh' to
'Yahweh Sebaoth' here twice ('holy to...'; 'house of...').

There are several contacts between this final section and important
earlier statements: v. 6, Yahweh and holy ones; cf. v. 20-21, 'holy to
Yahweh'; v. 11, וחרם לא יהיה עוד, cf. v. 21, ולא יהיה כנעני עוד; v. 12,
צבא used of the nations, cf. יהוה צבאות, vv. 16-17, 20-21 only.

It seems clear that ch. 14 as a whole, despite its uncertain text,
displays a logic and structure that must be presumed to have been
intended by its author/editor(s). The plans of Lamarche and Lacocque,
though they do not do justice to the many links between different parts
of the chapter, are partly successful in showing its main concerns.

Summary of Results

As we have worked through the individual sections of Zechariah, we have observed several recurring features.

1. There is clear evidence of careful structuring in all sections of chs. 1–8. It may be set out briefly as follows:

1.1-6   Redactional but constructed so as to form a coherent and well-structured whole, with strong links with the end of ch. 1.

1.7-17   Signs of some roughness, but well-integrated. Difficult to detach more than vv. 16-17. These last verses may well be redactional, but again show signs of literary ability and a concern to produce a coherent whole (vv. 1-17).

2.1-4   Very tightly and logically structured, although too complicated to represent adequately in one diagram. Effective use is made of repeated words—even technical words.

2.5-17   Verses 5-9 are not so tightly ordered, though there is a probably intended chiasmus in vv. 8b-9. Verses 10-17 contain many distinctive words. It is necessary to give careful attention to the logical movement of the passage in order to discern the structure intended by the editor (or author acting as editor). The first section has been supplemented by the second to produce a regularly structured whole.

3.1-10   The chapter is divided by reference to 'Joshua the high priest'; vv. 1-7 show signs of careful, concentrated structuring, with unusual ordering of actions, chiasmus, and continuity achieved by the verb 'standing'; vv. 8-10 are bounded by an inclusio.

4.1-14   Insertion of vv. 6a-10a seems deliberate; evidence of concern for structure overall and in the outer sections; less strong but still present in the central insertion. Even at this stage it is impossible to miss the connection between the two visions. They, and 6.9-15, must be examined together.

5.1-4   Different type of construction: repetition plus new element. Some similarity to the second vision in this.

5.5-11   Falls naturally into three clear and logical sections, the middle one chiastic; the last one less clear.

6.1-8   Overall movement clear; repetition of important words, apparently controlled by the idea of 'going forth', forming two chiasmuses.

6.9-15   Clearly chiastic; possibly constructed in two stages to form an overlapping chiasmus.

7-8   Very strong, large chiasmus.

2. The clearest, most elaborately structured passages are found in the sections reckoned to be redactional by the majority of scholars. At the least, this points to a different kind of literary activity in describing the visions and in the rest of the presentation.[1]

3. The structuring discernible in Zechariah 9–14 seems different from and less precise than that found in Zechariah 1–8. The small units specified on form-critical grounds yield very little, and it is obvious that there are more contacts outside the units than within them.

4. Negatively, the structures proposed by Lamarche, Lacocque, Otzen and Hanson do not stand up to critical scrutiny. Yet there are signs of a unified plan for these parts of the book:

    a. There are links between the different parts of Zech. 9.1–11.3; there is evidence of progression of thought over long sections achieved in small steps by repeated words.
    b. Zech. 11.4-17 + 13.7-9 contains some very obscure elements, and does not form an obviously recognizable pattern. Yet its overall movement is clear and logical. We have yet to discover the reason for the separation of these two passages.
    c. Zech. 12.1–13.6 contains material more akin to chs. 1–8, in its construction, than anything found previously.
    d. Zechariah 14 shows clear progression of thought; some sort of overall chiastic pattern, and apparently deliberate use of distinctive and repeated words to indicate structure and emphasis.

---

1. It would be interesting to study the difference between work produced by visionaries who describe and explain (or supplement in some way) their experiences. When that is done we may have some clearer ground for saying whether Zechariah could or could not have edited his own dream visions.

Chapter 4

CONNECTIONS BETWEEN SECTIONS OF ZECHARIAH 1–14

In this chapter I shall try and determine whether there are clear links between individual sections of Zechariah. I shall therefore consider each separate section in relation to the whole. It will be necessary to restrict the words picked out to quite distinctive words or whole phrases. It is obvious that a word which would mark out a structure in one connected section, would not necessarily be effective over a longer distance, especially when material of a different kind intervenes between two occurrences.

The plan adopted is to plot the words and phrases that *might possibly* be significant (i.e. that we cannot rule out *prima facie*) in indicating intended connections between individual sections of Zechariah. I shall divide the first part of this chapter as follows:

Connections between: Zechariah 1, 2–8, and 9–14
                       Zechariah 2, 3–8, and 9–14
                       Zechariah 3, 4–8, and 9–14
                       Zechariah 4, 5–8, and 9–14
                       Zechariah 5, 6–8, and 9–14
                       Zechariah 6, 7–8, and 9–14
                       Zechariah 7–8, and 9–14

Chapters 2 and 5 are short enough to consider together in one table but I shall give attention to the separate units as previously. There is a danger to guard against, in that a particular later chapter may have connections with several earlier ones, but none of them seem significant in themselves. As long as we are aware of this, it does not seem necessary to repeat connections with earlier chapters. However, when we come to chs. 9–14 I shall plot words occurring in chs. 1–8.[1] The

---

1. Even this scheme may seem over-pedantic. I have decided against further omissions since it is easier to ignore an unnecessary table than to refer back repeatedly to earlier section for information that would be useful in one place.

second part of this chapter, therefore, contains tables of repeating words as follows:

Connections between: Zech. 9.1–11.3, 1–8, and 11.4–14.21
Zech. 11.4–13.9, 1–8, and 14.1-21
Zech. 14.1-21 and 1–8

In the table below bold type signifies references which probably have some connection; bold italic means a doubtful connection; italic or underlined indicates sections which may have something in common with each other but not with the section being considered.

Connections between Zechariah 1 and the Rest of Zechariah

Verse	Word	Occurrences in 1.1-17	Occurrences in the rest of 1.1–8.23	Occurrences in chs. 9–14
2	קצף	**2** (2×) 15 (3×)	**7.12; 8.14**	
	אב	**2, 4, 5, 6**	**8.14**	13.3 (2×)
3	שוב	**3** (2×), **4, 6, 16**	4.1; 5.1; 6.1; *7.14;* 8.3, 15.2	*9.8*, 12.##1,*9*; <u>10.6.#9?</u>, <u>9.8,</u> <u>10.1</u>; 13.7
4	קרא	**4, 14** 17	3.10; **7.7,** **13** (2×), 8.3	11.7 (2×) **13.9**
	ראשון	4	6.2; **7.7,** **12; 8.11**	12.7; 14.10
	דרך	**4, 6**	**3.7**	9.13;
	רע	**4** (2×), 15.14	**8.14, 17**	
	שמע	4	**3.8; 6.15** (2×) **7.11-13** (4×) **8.9, 23**	
	הקשׁיב	4	**7.11**	
5	חיה	5		*10.9; 13.3;* 14.8
6	עבד	6	2.13, **3.8**	13.5
	זמם	6	**8.14, 15**	
	עשה	*6.##18,23*	*2.4*; 6.11; *7.3, 9*; *8.16*	10.1
8	רכב	8	6.1-3 (5×)	*9.9, 10; 10.5; 12.4*
	סוס	8 (2×)	6.2-3 (4×), 6	*9.10; 10.3, 5 ;* *12.4* (2×) *14.15, 20*
	אדום	8.##8,17	6.2	(14.4 perfect)
	עמד	*8, 10*	*3.1* (2×), *3, <u>4.</u>*	(14.4 perfect)
	<u>עמדים</u>	*11.5*	*5, <u>7</u>; <u>4.14</u>*	14.12

	מצ(ו)לה	8		10.11
	לבן	8	6.3, 6	
9	+ מלאך		(2.7 [אחר])	
	הדבר בי	9, 13, 14	2.2, 7; 4.1, 4, 5; 5.5, 10; 6.4, (5)	
	יהוה + מלאך	11, 12	3.1, (3), 5, 6	12.8
10	שלח	*10*	2.12, 13, 15 4.9; 6.15; 7.2 *12*; 8.10	9.11
	התהלך	10, 11	6.7 (3×)	10.12
11	ישב	11	2.8, 11; 3.8; 5.7; 6.13; 7.7 (2×); 8.4, 20, 21	*9.5, 6;* 10.6; 11.6; 12.5, **6,** 7-8, 10; 13.1; 14.10, 11.##1,7
12	רחם	12, 16	7.9	*10.6*
12	ירושלם	12, 14 16 (2×), 17	2.2, 6, 8, 16; 3.2; 7.7; 8.3 (2×), 4, 8, 15, 22	*9.9, 10;* 12.2-13.1 (12×); ch. 14 (10×)
14	ציון	14, 17	2.11 (2×), 14; 8.2,3	*9.9,* 13
12	עיר	12, 17	7.7; 8.3, 5, 20	14.2 (3×)
12	יהודה	12	2.2, 4, 4, 16 8.13, 15, 19	9.7, 13; 10.3, 6; 11.14; 12.2-7 (6×); 14.5, 14, 21
12	זה שבעים שנה	**12**	7.5	
13	טוב	*13, 17*	8.19	9.17; 11.12
	נחם	13, 17	8.14	*10.2*
14	קנא	**14.#12**	8.2.##5,11	
	קנאה גדלה	**14.##15-16**	8.2.#7	
15	גוי	*15*	2.4, 12, 15; 7.14; 8.13, 22,23	*9.10;* 12.3, 9; 14.2-3, 14, 16, 18,19
16	נסה	16		12.1
17	חפוצינ(ה)	**17**		13.7
	+ בחר ירושלם	<u>17</u>	<u>2.16</u>; <u>3.2</u>	9.17

(Words omitted from this and subsequent sections: אדון (not divine name), אני, אחרי, כה אמר יהוה, הדס, הלך, גדל, בית, בין, ארץ ,כל[1] יום, כן, מעלל, עד, עוד, ענה).

---

1. See Meyers, *Haggai, Zechariah*, pp. 1-1iii.

We first consider the nature of these repetitions.

קצף 1.2 (2×), 15 (3×), which also (and only) occurs in 7.12 and 8.14, must be considered along with: זמם (1.6; 8.14-15) and קנא (1.14; 8.2 [2×]) with קנאה גדלה (1.14; 8.2). Together these form the strongest evidence for treating 1.1-6, 15-17 and chs. 7–8 as coming from the same hand. The general context is similar: they are concerned with Yahweh's anger against his people in the past; with what he purposed to do to them, and with what he will do in the future.

אב is used in 1.2, 4, 5, 6 and 8.14 of 'the fathers'. In 13.3.##8,19 it refers to a man's father.

שוב, in 1.3 (2×), 4, 6 and 16 is used of (re)turning to Yahweh. Zech. 4.1; 5.1, 6.1 and 8.15 do not seem to be significant (= 'again'). The usage elsewhere varies, but refers mostly to returning (physically) to Zion (Yahweh in 8.3; the people in Zech. 9.12–10.10; the MT has 'dwell' in 10.6). An interesting parallel, connecting Zechariah 1–8 and 9–14, is מעבר ומשב, 7.14 and 9.8.[1] The meaning is 'turn (my hand against)' in 13.7.

קרא 1.4, 14, 17; 3.10; 7.7, 13 (2×); 8.3 (Jerusalem called city of truth); 11.7 (2×) (naming the staffs); 13.9. The verb is used in Zechariah 1 and 7.7 of prophetic communication, in 7.13 of reciprocal communication (or rather the lack of it) and in 13.9 of calling upon the name of Yahweh. The remainder refer to 'naming'. There is some additional evidence here that the same editor worked over 1.1-6 and chs. 7–8.

ראשון occurs in 1.4 and 7.7, 12 with reference to the 'former prophets'. This is clearly related to the 'former days' in 8.11. The other references are different: 'first chariot', 'victory first to...', 'former gate'. This confirms what is said above in connection with קרא.

דרך, in 1.4 and 6, refers to the Israelites' evil ways. Zech. 3.7 is related to this: Joshua is charged to walk in God's ways. Zech. 9.13 is completely different. This gives weak support to the view that Zechariah 3 is later than the other visions and may be connected with the redactor rather than the prophet himself.

---

1. The phrase in 9.8 is often deleted as a gloss; e.g. *BHS*. On the other hand, it is accepted by conservative scholars as evidence of the unity of Zechariah. E.g. Baldwin, *Haggai, Zechariah, Malachi,* pp. 68-69; K.L. Barker, 'Zechariah', in *The Expositor's Bible Commentary* (ed. F.E. Gaebelein; Grand Rapids: Zondervan, 1985), VII, pp. 595-697 (596 n. 2).

רע is not a rare word in the Hebrew Bible, but in Zechariah it only occurs in 1.4 (2×), 15 and 8.14, 17. The same may be said of שמע, 1.4; 3.8; 6.15 (2×); 7.11, 12 (2×), 13; 8.9, 23 only. It should be noted that 6.15 is the last verse of the whole of the second part of Zechariah 1–8; the phrase is emphatic and comprises part of the concluding conditional promise. The reference in 8.23 is slightly different, but it is interesting that this also is a final verse and, like 6.15, contains a rare reference to אלהים. Again these occurrences give some support to conclusions reached so far concerning the redactor of Zechariah 1–8.

הקשיב, 1.4; 7.11. These would support our theory, even though two isolated references are of uncertain value in themselves. They both refer to the refusal of the Israelites of old to listen to God.

חיה only occurs in 1.5 in Zechariah 1–8, and then in 10.9, 13.3 and 14.8. There is some similarity between the first two of these: 'the prophets, will they live for ever?' and 'their children shall live and return'.[1] Zech. 13.3 has 'You shall not live. . .' which might conceivably be related; 14.8 'living waters' is quite different. The word is not distinctive enough to build on.

עבד gives us little evidence. There is some affinity between 'my servants the prophets' (1.6) and 'my servant the Branch' (3.8), but the other instances are different ('those who served them', 2.13; 'tiller of the soil', 13.5). However, note once again a connection between 1.1-6 and ch. 3.

עשה. Although a very common word, its occurrence in Zechariah is limited, and its repetition in 1.6 has a certain emphasis. The infinitive occurs in 1.6 and 2.4 referring to Yahweh's action in judging his people and to the action of Yahweh's agents (the four smiths) in judging the people's enemies. 'Make crowns', 6.11, does not seem to be related to this. In chs. 7 and 8 the reference is to what the people have done or are to do. In 10.1 the usage is different: 'Yahweh makes the lightning'. It would be convenient, but also precarious, to claim that this word also connects 1.1-6 with chs. 7–8.

Five of the next words may be taken together: לבן, אדום, סוס, רכב and התהלך. They all have to do with the two visions with horses. The first two occur in Zechariah 9–14, all in relation to battle in some way. שלח, in 9.11, means 'set free'.

עמד is a common verb, but its use here is restricted in certain ways:

---

1. It does not seem to have been picked up by other commentators.

almost all instances are of the participle; they have to do either with an angel 'standing among the myrtle trees' or with 'standing before (the angel of) Yahweh'; they only occur in 1.8-11, 3.1-7 and 4.14; there is therefore an inclusio for Zechariah 3–4, and 4.14 is, as the Meyers' point out, the 'climax to the entire central portion of the visionary section' of Zechariah.[1] It would be plausible to see evidence here, therefore, of the editor's hand. In ch. 14 its use is different ('And his feet shall stand', '[while] he is standing on his feet').

מצולה is a very rare word (12 times in the OT), but the two instances here cannot be linked: 'the myrtle trees which במצלה (glen?)' and the 'depths (מצלות) of the Nile'.

מלאך הדבר בי cannot indicate specific connections between sections since it is so common. However, it does indicate continuity between this vision and nos. 2, 3, 5, 6, 7 and 8. This being the case, it is noticeable that the phrase does not occur in the fourth vision. There we find the מלאך יהוה which adds weight to the supposition that vv.12-13 is redactional and belongs in some sense with ch. 3. This is not a strong piece of evidence on its own, since the expression is fairly common in the OT, and there is obviously some point in having a mysterious lead-up to the naming of the angel as מלאך יהוה, and in putting such a reference in the opening vision.

שלח is an important editorial word in chs. 2, 4 and 6, where it occurs in the phrase '...know that Yahweh has sent me'. The use is somewhat similar in 1.10 in that the horses are sent by Yahweh to patrol the earth. On the other hand there is no emphasis on the fact of a single person's being sent, which would have made a stronger connection with 'sent me' (2.12-13, 15 etc.; see the discussion below). This could have been done, so we assume it was not intended. The same could be said for 7.12 which refers to the 'law and the words sent by his Spirit through the former prophets'. Zech. 7.2, 8.10 and 9.11 represent different usage.

ישב is too common a verb in Zechariah to be considered on its own. Nevertheless, it does occur as part of the phrase 'Jerusalem... inhabited' (2.8; 7.7 [lowlands also]; 12.6; 14.11; cf. also 9.5-6, 'Ashkelon will be uninhabited... a mongrel people will dwell in Ashdod'). The meaning is 'sit' in 3.8, 5.7, 6.13 and 8.4. Zech. 2.11, 'you who dwell with the daughter of Babylon', forms a contrast with

---

1. *Haggai, Zechariah*, p. 275.

2.8. The participle ('inhabitants') is used in 8.20-21, 11.6, 12.5, 7-8, 10, 13.1. The idea of security is implied in 10.6, 14.10-11.

רחם refers to Yahweh's compassion in chs. 1 and 10, and to the people's in 7.9. Taken together with נחם (1.13, 17; 8.19; 10.2) it helps to strengthen the connection of the vision itself[1] with vv. 1-6, 16-17 and also chs. 7–8, and to make it possible to think of a link with ch. 10.

'Jerusalem' and 'Judah' must be considered together with 'city' and 'Zion'. These are concentrated together in 1.12-17 (10×); ch. 2 (11×); chs. 7-8 (16×) in Zechariah 1–8 (only 3.2 lies outside these references and this is connected with the editorial sections by being joined with בחר as in 1.17 and 2.16). In Zechariah 9–14 they are more spread out but still congregate together in chs. 12 (17×) and 14 (16×). We can at least confirm that the editor or editors of both sections of the book has or have a particularly strong concern for Jerusalem. It could be that this distinguishes him or them from the author of the main part of Zechariah 1–8, but their use in 2.1-9 undermines this suggestion. Similar remarks could be made of גוי. See the table above.

זה שבעים שנה is a strong link between the first vision[2] and the concluding collection of oracles in chs. 7–8. Both refer to the period of the exile as one of suffering. In 7.5 an original point is made that, even in their outward penitence, the Israelites' thoughts were not focused on God. Despite this the passage goes on to give a promise of salvation.

טוב is normally a common word, but in Zechariah it only occurs in 1.13 (good words), 17 (cities overflow with good), 8.19 (good seasons), 9.17 ('How good!') and 11.12 ('If it [seems] good...'). Although there is some similarity between the first three occurrences, which would strengthen the link between chs. 1 and 7–8, it must be regarded with caution.

נטה is a fairly distinctive word, but its use in 1.16 and 12.1 is different.

פוץ is remarkable in that it is only found twice, each time with the same *qal* imperfect second feminine plural form. The meaning is similar in that both refer to the scattering of the people of Israel. However, whereas 13.7 speaks of Yahweh's scattering of 'the sheep' in

---

1. Unless those scholars are right who regard 1.12-13 as redactional. However, if this is all we can find, we might reconsider the conclusions reached in Chapter 3 about the construction of Zech. 1.7-17 (see pp. 86-90 above).

2. See previous note.

judgment, 1.17 envisages a scattering that is due to his blessing: 'Again my cities will be scattered—because of good'.[1] It is not clear how much we can make of this. It might be that the editor of 1.17 was aware of 13.7, but we need more evidence than we have so far found.

בחר ירושלם occurs in 1.17, 2.16 and 3.2. The first two instances are clearly redactional. This might mean that the redactor prepared for the statement of 3.2, 'Yahweh has chosen Jerusalem', by the repeated 'will again choose Jerusalem' at the end of the first vision and the next pair of visions. It could, of course, be the case that he was responsible for all three instances. The word in 9.17, בחורים, is completely different and may be ignored.

Summary and Conclusions

Of the distinctive words found in ch. 1 and elsewhere in Zechariah 1–8, the greatest number occur in either ch. 6 or chs. 7–8, but there are some contacts with chs. 2 and 3. In ch. 2 the repetitions are either concerned with Jerusalem, or else occur in the oracular section 2.10-16 (the only exceptions being עשה and גוי). In the case of ch. 3 we have four words linking 1.4-6 with 3.7-10, plus בחר בירושלם and עמד linking 1.8 and 17 with 3.1-7 and 3.2 respectively. The only references outside these sections in chs. 2–8 are שוב in 4.1 and 5.1, which is different from other occurrences and may be ignored; שלח which occurs in 4.9, part of the editorial section; and עמדים, 4.14, which may also be redactional.

The contacts between chs. 1, 6, and 7–8 may be divided as follows:

1.   Zech. 1.1-6 + 10 (11? 12? 13? 14? 15?)-17 dealing with Yahweh's past action expressing his wrath and his future compassion. This has strong contact with Zechariah 7–8 but little with Zechariah 6.

2.   Zech. 1.7-11 dealing with the description of the visions of horses of various colours and riders/chariots. These verses have clear parallels in Zechariah 6 but little verbal contact with Zechariah 7–8.

---

1.   It is better, I think, to keep the meaning 'be scattered' since: (1) it makes for a very effective surprise with מטוב at the end of the clause; (2) the meaning (over)flow is only suggested here and in Prov. 5.16 (BDB, p. 807), where it can equally well mean 'be scattered'; and (3) the picture is consonant with Zech. 2.8.

This strengthens the impression that the writer who gave ch. 1 its final form was the one who also shaped chs. 7 and 8. It is probable that he was responsible also for their position in relation to Zechariah 1–8. It seems plausible to assume that he intended an inclusio.

Can we discern the work of this editor elsewhere in chs. 1–14? To determine this there will need to be strong contacts between editorial sections such as 1.1-6, 15-17, and chs. 7–8 and 9–14. I shall evaluate the cumulative evidence in an excursus, after considering each section of Zechariah in relation to the rest. I shall compare the findings with traditional arguments for the unity of Zechariah.[1]

If contacts are found between these editorial sections in Zechariah 1 etc and others in Zechariah 9-11, we shall conclude that the same editor who did the work we have discovered here was also responsible for the whole book and wrote later than Deutero-Zechariah.

If the contacts are with the main part of Deutero-Zechariah then it will be likely that our editor was Deutero-Zechariah himself. I shall not have proved that he could not have been the original Zechariah, but it will be unlikely in the absence of contacts between editorial sections and 'original' text in Zechariah 1–8.

We have found strong supporting evidence in this enquiry for the view that the final editor of Zechariah 1–8 was responsible for:

1. The final wording and position of 1.1-6 and 12 (15?16?)-17, and other parts that are additional to the visions themselves.
2. The position of the first and last visions of Zechariah 1–6.
3. The position and part of the content of Zechariah 7–8.
4. Possibly some of the content of Zechariah 3.
5. The final form of Zechariah 4.

So far we have found few likely connections between Zechariah 1 and 9–14: עבר + שוב, חיה, רחם + נחם, פוץ, and the concern with Jerusalem and Judah. None of these is particularly strong, and this is in striking contrast to the evidence in favour of a unified editing of chs. 1–8.

Connections between Zechariah 2 and the Rest of Zechariah

There are comparatively few words in Zechariah 2 that have links with other parts of Zechariah and the table for the whole chapter is

---

1. See below after the discussion of chs. 7–8.

given. Some words have been considered in connection with ch. 1: עשׂה ,שׁלח ,ירושׁלם etc., עוד, בחר (see above). An asterisk denotes a reference outside the section signified by the headings below. A super-script number with an asterisk placed against a word denotes the section above in which this word was discussed, thus *[1] refers to the discussion of words in Zechariah 1 and elsewhere in Zechariah.

Verse	Word	Occurrences in ch. 2	Occurrences in the rest of 1.1–8.23	Occurrences in chs. 9–14
			Vision 2 (2.1-4)	
1	נשׂא	1, *4* (2×), *5.1	5.1, 5, *7,* 9.##1,*14;* 6.1, 13	
	עין	1, 5, **12*	*3.9; 4.10;* 5.1, 5, 6, 9; 6.1; 8.6 (2×)	*9.10, 8;* 11.12, *17* (2×); *12.4;* 14.12
	ארבע	*1, 3, *10*	*6.1, 3, 5;* 7.1 (2×); 8.19	
2	מלאך +*[1]			
	הדבר בי	*2, 7*	*4.1, 4, 5; 5.5, 10;* 6.4, (5 + art.)	
	יהוה+מלאך		3.1, (3 + art.), 5-6	*12.8*
	ישׂראל	2	8.13	9.1; 11.14; 12.1
4	עשׂה*[1]	*4*	6.11; *7.3, 9;* *8.16*	10.1
			Vision 3 (2.5-9)	
5	חבל	5		11.7, 14
6	איה	*6*	*5.10*	
	רחב	*6*	**5.2;* 8.4, 5 (2×)	
	ארך	*6*	**5.2*	
7	יצא	*7.##5,8*	4.7; *5.3, 4, 5* (2×), *6, 9; 6.1, 5, 6* (3×), *7, 8;* 8.10	*9.14; 10.4* 14.2-3, 8
8	נער	8		11.16; 13.5
	רב	8, *15	8.4, 20, 22	10.8 (2×); 14.13, 14
	בהמה	8	8.10	14.15
	תוך	8-9, *14-15	5.4, 7, 8; 8.3, 8	

9	אש	**9**	3.2	**9.4; 11.1;** **12.6** (2×); 13.9
	סבב	9	7.7	12.2, 6; 14.10, 14
	כבוד	9, *<u>12</u>	7.11	

The Attached Oracle (2.10-17)

10	יוה	10 (2×), 11		11.17.1
	נוס	10		(נסס 9.16); 14.5 (3×)
	צפון	**10**	**6.6, 8** (2×)	14.4
	רוח	*10*	4.6; *5.9;* **6.5,** **8**; *7.12*	12.1, 10; 13.2
	שמים	**10**	5.9; **6.5;** 8.12	12.1
11	בת	11, **14**		**9.9** (2×)
	בבל	11	6.10	
12	אחר	12	6.6; 7.14	14.8
	שלח*1	**12, 13,** **15**	**4.9; 6.15** 7.2, *12*; 8.10	9.11
	שלל	12, 13		14.1
	נגע	12.##14,16		14.5
13	עבד*1	13	3.8	13.5
	ידע	**13, 15**	4.5, **9**, 13; **6.15**; 7.14	*11.11;* 14.7
14	שמח	14	4.10; 8.19	10.7 (2×)
	שכן	14, 15	8.3, 8	
15	עם	15	7.5; 8.6-8, 11-12, 20, 22	9.16; 10.9; 11.10; 12.2, 4, 6; 13.9; 14.2, 12
16	נחל	16	8.12	
	חלק	16		14.1
	אדמה	16		9.16, 13.5
	קדש	*16*, 17	*8.3*	14.5, 20, 21
	בחר*1 + ירושלם	<u>16</u>	<u>3.2</u>	9.17
17	בשר	17		11.9, 16; 14.12
	עור	17	4.1 (2×)	9.13; 12.4; 13.7

Words omitted (in addition to common words omitted from the previous table): ציון*1, פה, מפני, מדד, מה + כ, *1ירושלם*1, יהודה, יד, זרה, גוי*1, בוא, איה, אחר.

General Remarks

The introductory formula ואשא את עיני וארא והנה occurs at the beginning of Visions (VV) 2, 3, 6, and 8 (2.1.##1-5, with את; 2.5.##1-4; 5.1.##2-5; 6.1.##2-5); שא נא עיניך וראה occurs in V7 (5.5.##7-10). In addition, אישׁוב occurs as the first word of 5.1 and 6.1. These five visions are, therefore, in some sense linked together already, with V7 slightly out of line. In V2 and V8 the introductory formula is followed immediately by 'four', which strengthens the link between them. The angel in view in this chapter is המלאך הדבר בי throughout. See the discussion in chapter 3 above.[1]

The question arises whether the use of נשׂא and עינים together makes both words less effective as markers, or whether they become important by repetition, and thereby noteworthy when used in a different way. It seems to me that the use of the plural in the expression 'lift up...eyes' does not detract from the distinctiveness of the singular as used in Zechariah, or even the 'seven eyes' of the stone placed before Joshua. In discussing the second vision we noted a possible play on words in the different uses of נשׂא, but were unable to establish this suggestion.[2]

The Second Vision
This seems to have no other significant verbal parallels with other major sections of Zechariah, except that נשׂא is in two distinctive phrases in 2.4 ('no one raised his head' and 'lifted up the horns') and also in 5.7, 9 ('lifted the cover of the ephah' and 'lifted up the ephah'). This is striking but it may be only a coincidence. There is no essential correspondence between the ideas expressed, but simply a verbal resonance. See Chapter 3 above and the previous note.

עין is worthy of special consideration in certain references and the distinctive uses here are in 2.13 ('apple of his eye'), 3.9, 4.10 ('seven facets'? and 'seven...eyes of Yahweh') and the obscure 5.6 ('their appearance'?).

---

1.   There is a second angel introduced, of course.
2.   The Meyers' (*Haggai, Zechariah*, p. liii) present a table of correspondences between Zech. 1.17–6.15 and Zech. 7–8, which contains certain entries not represented in my table: Jerusalem inhabited, 2.8, 7.7; Jerusalem protected/secured, 2.9, 7.7 (the expressions used are quite different); (divine anger/wrath should read 1.15; 7.12, which we have noted); holy mountain, 2.17 (מעון קדשׁו); 8.3 (הר הקדשׁ); nations will go to Jerusalem, 2.15 (נלוו גוים רבים); 8.22 (ובאו עמים רבים); Yehud as holy land, 2.16; 8.22-23 (קדשׁ not used in the latter). Some of these seem legitimate, but the hand is overplayed. In any case, they are not compelling enough for us to take special note, since we are concentrating on links which are demonstrably intended by the author/editor. I accept that there may be many other links in mind which cannot, at present, be *shown* to be probable.

'Four' is a prominent number in the first two visions and the last one, although the first vision does not mention the number four, and actually mentions one red horse, then more than one each of red, sorrel and white. This is enough to confuse any neat pattern built on the basis of 'four'. However, we should note that V2 begins with ואשוב ואשא עיני וארא והנה and V6 has ואשא את עיני וארא והנה ארבע ארבע. This might well be strong enough to recall the second vision.

We should note that ירושלם features in the first four visions, together with other related words (עיר, יהודה, ציון) but not at all in the last four where the geographical canvas is wider (even in the case of the fourth vision which centres on Joshua and Zerubbabel. Note 4.10b 'whole earth'.) See below for the phrase 'choose Jerusalem'.

'Israel' occurs in 2.2 in the middle of 'Judah' and 'Jerusalem', where it is often regarded as a gloss. Its use in 8.13 ('house of Judah. . . Israel') cannot be strongly linked with this. The occurrences in Zechariah 9, 11 and 12 are too varied to build on.

The Third Vision
This also has few distinctive words in common with other major sections. 'Length' and 'breadth' are the two best candidates, which link it with the sixth vision. רוחות has a different meaning, 'streets', in 8.4-5.

יצא occurs twice in connection with the two angels who appear in 2.7, which seems unnecessary. The verb also occurs in 5.1-4 (3.#5, 4.#1), and in 5.5-11 (5.##1,12, 6.#7, 9.#7), so that it would make some sort of link between V2 and VV6 and 7. However, the word also occurs seven times in V8 (1.#8, 5.#9, 6.##5,10,14, 7.#2, 8.#7) which is also more than necessary. In the circumstances it seems strange that the verb does not occur in ch. 1. It is possible that the author intended a correspondence between V2 and VV6-8, cf. also *9.

There seems to be no connection between the occurrences of נער, רב and בהמה here, despite the fact that 'man (אדם) and beast' are found together in 2.8 and 8.10.

בתוך is an important word in the sections noted above. It is used in various ways to express Yahweh's favour towards his people in that he will dwell in the midst of them. It suggests links between V2 (2.8-9) with its attached oracle (2.14-15), and with the important promise in 8.3-8. It is more doubtful whether the connection is intended with vv. 6 and 7 (the curse in the midst of the thief's house; and the woman in the midst of the ephah).

One possibility which does not show up in the table is that 'measuring line' is a significant motif (in 1.16 the word used is קוה [hapax legomenon] and not חבל). If so, we should suppose that the editor who added the end of ch. 1 intended a connection with the third vision. However, there is little verbal repetition, so that we could as well argue that this was not a conscious intention. Zech. 11.7, 14, 'bands' or 'union', may be discounted from this discussion.

סבב is not distinctive enough for our purposes. The form in 2.9 is different from the others, and that which surrounds is also different: 'fire', 'her cities', 'peoples' (12.2; 14.14). In Zech. 14.10 the verb form is completely different.

It is of particular interest to enquire whether we can confirm that V2 is intended to be parallel to V6 or V7, and similarly for V3. We may say that such evidence as there is from this method of investigation supports the linking of V2 with V7 ('lift up' only), and V3 with V6 ('length and breadth', 'go forth' [2×], 'in the midst'), but (less plausibly) also with V7 ('where?', 'go forth' [4×], and 'in the midst' [2×]). We should, however, also remember that V2 and V3 are strongly linked by the whole introductory formula והנה ואשא את עיני וארא, so that there are grounds for treating VV2, 3, 6 and 7 together in some sense.[1]

This question is discussed by several scholars. For example, Meyers:[2] the visions are labelled 1-7; ch. 3 is called a 'prophetic vision'. In my terminology they put the following visions parallel:

V1 and V8 (e.g. horses)
V2 and V7 (e.g. internal structure, two parts each)
V3 and V6 (e.g. direct inclusion of oracular material)

Inverse order can be established on stylistic grounds. This establishes the central two as a pair. Stylistic contrast, rather than stylistic correspondence, characterizes these.

The correspondence is also established by the scope of the visions:

V1 and V8: Universal. God's omniscience/omnipotence
V2 and V7: International. Judah, the empires/Yehud, Persia
V3 and V6: National. Jerusalem's territory/self-rule of Yehud
V4 + V5: Jerusalem. Leadership, temple

---

1. Note also that VV1-4 are linked by the phrase 'choose Jerusalem' (1.17; 2.16; 3.2).
2. *Haggai, Zechariah*, pp. liv-lvi.

Although there is some oversimplification, my own investigation supports these general conclusions.

Schöttler's traditio-historical study[1] agrees with this pattern in the final eight-vision cycle, but he has two additional patterns on the way to this:

Stage 1: V5 = middle point; V3 // V7
Stage 2: V4 = middle point; V2 // V7, and V3 // V5
Stage 3: V4 + V5 = middle point; V2 // V7, and V3 // V6

This seems to prove that, if one is flexible enough, one can discern correspondences between all sorts of different units.

Baldwin[2] has V2 // V6, and V3 // V7, and brackets VV2-3 and VV6-7 together giving an overall chiastic structure:

V1	a		A patrol of the whole earth reports
V2	b		The nations meet retribution
V3	b1		Jerusalem has a divine protector
V4		c	The high priest reinstated
V5		c1	Divine resources for high priest and prince
V6	b2		Evil meets retribution
V7	b3		Jerusalem is purified
V8	a1		God's patrols compass the earth

We have found confirmation of the bracketing of VV2-3, 6-7, but must regard the labelling as suspect. For example, we noted that 'Jerusalem' does not occur in V7, but does occur in V2. In VV6-7 it is 'the (whole) land' that is in view (5.3, 6; cf. v. 11). Stuhlmueller[3] reproduces a diagram similar to Baldwin's but thinks the suggestion that VV2-3 parallel VV6-7 'remains problematical'.

C. Jeremias[4] notes that:

1. V2 and V7 (using my notation: he excludes V4 from the original cycle) have a multiple application of the *Grundschema*. VV2, 5, 7 end with the meaning of the vision. The other visions do not.
2. VV1, 3, 6 and 8 end with divine speech.

---

1. See below, pp. 275-78.
2. *Haggai, Zechariah, Malachi*, p. 85.
3. *Rebuilding with Hope: A Commentary on the Books of Haggai and Zechariah* (International Theological Commentary; Grand Rapids: Eerdmans, 1988), pp. 60-61.
4. *Die Nachtgesichte*, pp. 12-13.

The conclusions of these scholars are probably strong enough to claim confirmation of my own results.

There is one interesting point of contact with Zechariah 9–14: in 2.9 Yahweh is for Jerusalem a 'wall of fire around'; in 12.6 the clans of Judah become a pot of fire and a torch of fire to devour the nations around. This is not exactly the same usage, but it is similar enough to be noticed.[1] Other parallels seem too remote to be significant.

The Oracle of Zechariah 2.10-16 + 17
This has obvious links with the sections where the phrase '...know that Yahweh has sent me' occurs. We shall discuss this separately.

Most words in this table either represent different uses or are insufficiently distinctive for our purposes.

הוי means 'Ho!' in 2.10-11, and 'Woe!' in 11.17; נוס means 'escape' and 'flee' (because destruction has come to the city), 2.10, 14.5.[2] בת is very common, but here it occurs in the phrase 'Sing and rejoice, O daughter of Zion, for behold I am coming...', which is similar to 9.9, 'Rejoice greatly O daughter of Zion, shout for joy O daughter of Jerusalem. Behold, your king will come...' The verbs do not overlap at all, but they are often associated with each other elsewhere, and the imperatives, together with the other common words, make quite a strong link between the two passages. Perhaps this example also indicates that it would be useful to do a further study which would treat recognizable word pairs as repeated words.[3]

שלל and נגע are used in similar ways in 2.12 and 14.1, 5. Taking נוס, קדש, חלק, צפון (14.1-5) into consideration might be expected to yield some connection. The general situation is the same, and the 'reversal

1. Cf. Mason, *Zechariah 9–14*, pp. 203-204.
2. Admittedly, there is some similarity between these two ideas, in that in both cases the people are running from a city under attack, but I think the difference is too great to allow us to maintain a connection between these passages.
3. I have not felt able to tackle this in the present study. There are some useful starting points in the works of R.C. Culley (e.g. *Oral Formulaic Language in the Biblical Psalms* [Toronto: University of Toronto Press, 1967]), S. Gevirtz, W.R. Watters (*Formula Criticism of the Poetry of the Old Testament* [BZAW, 138; Berlin: de Gruyter, 1976]; he gives some useful lists of word pairs for Isaiah, pp. 155ff.) and W. Whallon (*Formula, Character and Context* [Cambridge, MA; Harvard University Press, 1969], esp. pp. 140-61); see general bibliography.

of fortunes' theme is noticeable.[1] Nevertheless every word here is used differently in ch. 14 from ch. 2.

שמח. See בח above.

עמי occurs in 2.15, 8.7 and (especially) 8.8; this is also the form in 13.9. שארית העם הזה occurs in the other three references in ch. 8, but a similar idea is expressed in different words in 14.2, יתר העם. In the instances underlined above the plural is used.

נחל is used of Yahweh who 'inherits Judah', 2.16, and of the remnant of this people: 'all these things', 8.12. אדמת הקדש is found in 2.16; אדמתו in 9.16 is comparable, but no more; in 13.5 it refers to the ground. הר הקדש, 8.3, is similar to the expression in 2.16; מעון קדשו, 2.17, is slightly less so. Zech. 14.5 refers to the holy ones; 'Holy to Yahweh' is the inscription on the bells, and applies also to the vessels in the temple (14.20-21).[2] The use of בשר in 2.17 is completely different from all the other occurrences.

עור represents waking from sleep (4.1), 'brandishing' (9.13), blindness (עורון) (12.4), as well as 'stir into action' (2.17; 13.7; *niphal* and *qal* respectively). The last two represent Yahweh's action, but the mode of expression is very different. However, despite these disappointments, there are some clear pointers.

The most striking phrase of this section is 'Then/and you shall know that Yahweh has sent me to you' (2.13, 15; 4.9; 6.15) together with the 'sent me' of 2.12. It is obvious that it is the final redactor of Zechariah 1–8 who is responsible for this phrase, and that he intends it to be noted. It is not only repeated four times, but the first two occurrences frame the promise that Yahweh will dwell in the midst of his people and many nations will be his people (cf. the section in Chapter 2 above on 2.10-17).

צפון is specially emphasized in 6.8 (twice) after being mentioned along with the west and the south in v. 6. The north was traditionally the place from which the enemy came, and the place of other gods. I wonder if we are meant to notice that, in 6.10, the exiles from

---

1.   This partly depends on how 14.1 is understood. Does it mean that Jerusalem will get its own plunder back? The consensus view is that Jerusalem will suffer the humiliation of seeing its enemies divide up the plunder in the city itself (Baldwin, *Haggai, Zechariah, Malachi*, p. 200; Mason, *Haggai, Zechariah and Malachi*, 1977, p. 124; Rudolph, *Haggai*, p. 234).

2.   The Meyers' (*Haggai, Zechariah*, p. liii) put 'holy mountain' as a correspondence between 2.17 and 8.3, but this is not strictly true.

Babylon (cf. 2.11) go to the house of Josiah בן צפניה, the one whose
name mysteriously becomes חן in v. 14. This is speculative. However,
the exiles from Babylon are a visible sign of the fulfilment of the
prophecy in 2.10-11. Both passages, of course, are additions to the
series of night visions.[1]

ארבע רוחות השמים occurs in 2.10, 'I have spread you abroad as the
four winds', and in 6.5, 'These are going forth as the four winds of
heaven'. In other places רוח means 'spirit'. There is presumably a
deliberate reference to this by the one who added 2.10.

בבל occurs in the exhortation: 'Escape to Zion, you who dwell with
the daughter of Babylon' (2.11) and in the reference to '...the exiles
who have arrived from Babylon' (6.10). They are a visible sign of the
fulfilment of the prophecy of 2.11, and the phrase thereby gains in
significance. Both passages, again, are additions to the vision reports.

The most obvious parallel is that between the centres of 2.13-15 and
the whole section Zechariah 7–8: '[many nations]...shall be my
people' and '...they shall be my people and I will be their God'. We
noted above the similar passage in 13.9b. Closely associated with this is
the phrase 'I will dwell in the midst of you/Jerusalem' (2.14, 15; 8.3, 8).

It is noteworthy that the parallels which exist are only brought
about by redactional passages. This adds weight to the view that we
are dealing with an editor different from Zechariah himself. It also
seems likely that we have further evidence of his concern to produce a
logical overall structure. In the original visions themselves we have
discovered few verbal parallels that would link them together. The
introductory formulae cannot definitely be regarded as part of the
original visions.

A look at the table above also reveals a number of words that occur
in 2.10-17 and ch. 14. Most of these are not significant: נוס, צפון, נגע,
ידע, חלק are used differently in the two sections. There is some
parallel between the reversal of plundered and plunderer in 2.13 and
14.1 (שלל) but there is not enough to indicate a conscious attempt to
link the two. The same applies to the mention of קדש in the climax to
2.10-16 and 14.16-21. The only clear link between Zechariah 2 and
9–14 is 2.14.##1-7.[2]

---

1. I have not found support for this suggestion in any commentary and should
not lay any weight on it.

2. Mason (*Zechariah 9–14*, pp. 40-41), draws attention to the similarity

'Eye' in Zechariah

The relevant references are as follows:

2.12	כי הנגע בכם נגע בבבת עינו
3.9	על אבן אחת שבעה עינים
4.10	אלה עיני יהוה המה משוטטים בכל הארץ
5.6	זאת עינם בכל הארץ
9.1	כי ליהוה עין אדם
9.8	כי עתה ראיתי בעיני
11.17	חרב על זרועו ועל עין ימינו
12.4	ועל בית יהודה אפקח את עיני
14.12	והוא עמד על רגליו ועיניו תמקנה בחריהן

Phrases such as 'I lifted my eyes. . .' have been omitted in accordance with previous discussion, although they might still have a part to play in building up an emphasis on 'eyes' and 'seeing'. We saw that the (slightly varying) phrase served to link together visions 2, 3, 6, 7 and 8.

This aspect of the book of Zechariah does not seem to have received the attention which it deserves. Sæbø comments that the use of עין in 9.8 points to Zecharianic sources, where the concept plays a decisive role.[1] He does not elaborate. We cannot undertake a full investigation of these passages, but must concentrate on possible links between them.

First, I shall deal with chs. 3 and 4. In Zechariah 3, the word עין, which is related to the 'stone' set before Joshua, could mean 'eye', 'spring' or 'facet'; the context has to do with cleansing. A fairly obvious translation, therefore, would be:

> For behold the stone which I set before Joshua. Upon?/by? one stone there are seven springs; behold I am opening its openings. . . and I will remove the עין of that land in one day.

The main problem with this is the awkwardness of the translation in 3.9, for it is not clear how the reader would be expected to visualize seven springs related to one stone. This does not seem insuperable, especially if Lipiński is right in understanding 'on a single stone' as an idiom for 'at one and the same time'.[2] Moreover, there could well be

---

between Zech. 2.14 and 9.9, and also Zeph. 3.14-20 (which has the verbs, רנן, שמח and עלז; הריע). See on Zech. 9.9-10 below.

1. *Sacharja 9–14*, p. 161.

2. E. Lipiński, 'Recherches sur le livre de Zacharie', *VT* 20 (1970), pp. 25-30. He says: 'Celle-ci fait en réalité pendant à ביום אהד "en un seul jour", formule utilisé à

an allusion to Moses' bringing water from the rock (Exod. 17.6; Num. 20.7-11).

This seems better, therefore, than the more usual translation 'eyes': '...on one stone seven eyes...remove the guilt...in one day'.[1]

If this is right, it would then make for a strong link with the picture in 13.1, 'On that day there will be a fountain (מָקוֹר) *opened* for the house of David and the inhabitants of Jerusalem for sin and for uncleanness'. Zech. 12.4 would then have double significance: 'I will *open* my eyes' as the basic meaning but resonating with the 'spring' imagery. Also note that an important feature of Zechariah 14 is the מים חיים ירושלם (note the triple rhyme here, which is very noticeable in public reading).

However, we must face the question of the meaning of 4.10b, and its relation to 3.9. The natural interpretation, favoured by most scholars, is that the 'seven' referred to are the lamps of v. 2, about which the prophet has apparently asked. Baldwin objects that this makes the two anointed supply oil to Yahweh, 'an interpretation which is quite untenable'. Her solution is to refer it to the springs of 3.9 and translate: 'These seven are the springs of the Lord; they flow out over the whole earth'.[2]

In the text as it stands, the distance between the question in v. 4 and the answer in v. 10b, makes it possible to think of both 'seven's mentioned previously. Could it be that this was one of the purposes of the insertion? The whole matter is complicated by the different redaction histories that might be proposed. For, if we consider 4.1-6a + 10b-14, the reference is clear and unambiguous. If vv. 6b-10a are added before 3.9 (probably 3.8-10), then the reference is not so clear, but is still unambiguous. When 3.9 is added, with its explicit mention of 'eyes', then the reference is no longer clear.

It seems plausible that the intention of the final editor of Zechariah 3–4 was that the seven 'eyes' and seven lamps should be linked together, and that the ideas of cleansing (3.9, cf. vv. 3-5) and blessing

---

la fin du même verset. Les deux locutions sont presque synonymes: "en même temps", "en un jour" ' (p. 26). Cf. Baldwin, *Haggai, Zechariah, Malachi*, pp. 117-18.

1. Cf. Rudolph, *Haggai*, pp. 98, 101-103.

2. *Haggai, Zechariah, Malachi*, p. 123. If v. 12 is treated as a later insertion, the argument becomes less persuasive. For a useful, open discussion, see R.L. Smith, *Nahum–Malachi*, pp. 203-205.

(seen in the completion of the temple, and suggested by the oil and light in ch. 4) should be seen as a unity.

Zech. 2.12b is interpreted in two main ways.

1.   It continues the prophet's speech, giving a reason for the oracle of Yahweh that is to follow.[1]
2.   It begins Yahweh's speech, and the עינו must be emended to עיני, probably due to the qualms of later copyists who could not allow such a direct anthropomorphism.[2]

The decision is difficult because both v. 12b and v. 13 begin with כי. The meaning, however, is not seriously in doubt. It is probably analagous to Deut. 32.10,[3] and it denotes something precious to Yahweh. Having said all this, I do not think we can claim that this expression makes any clear link with other parts of the book. The passage closest to this is 12.4, which at least refers to *Yahweh*'s eyes, but uses the plural, and in a different expression.

'This is their "appearance"' was the interpretation of 5.6 favoured above. There is some affinity between this and 2.12, in that both passages describe how Yahweh sees the people of the land. However, the expressions are again different, and the interpretation uncertain.

The references in ch. 9 were dealt with above, and there is no clear connection that can be made with any other place. Those in chs. 11 and 14 both refer to God's judgment, and are distinctive in giving special mention to the eye. However, the first is singular (and the eye is specified) and parallel to 'arm'; the second is plural, and associated with 'flesh' and 'tongues'. The first is directed against האליל רעי, the second against the peoples that wage war against Jerusalem. These could still be connected, but the signs are ambiguous, and we must ignore them.

---

1.   E.g. Mitchell, *Haggai, Zechariah, Malachi, and Jonah*, p. 142.

2.   E.g. Petersen, *Haggai and Zechariah*, p. 173; Meyers, *Haggai, Zechariah*, p. 166; Rudolph, *Haggai*, pp. 86, 88; following E. Robertson, 'The Apple of the Eye in the Masoretic Text', *JTS* 38 (1937), pp. 56-59.

3.   בבה only occurs in Zech. 2.12. It is usually related to בבא, meaning 'gate' in *Targ. Esth.* 5.14, or נבב ('perforate'), hence 'opening'; or else an Arabic word yielding 'pupil'; Dozy suggested 'baby' (BDB, p. 93). Deut. 32.10 has a different word, אישון, which signifies preciousness in three out of the five places where it occurs (+ Prov. 7.2; Ps. 17.8).

In conclusion, we may say that 'eye' is a significant motif throughout Zechariah, but its use as a marker for structure cannot be demonstrated, apart from its use to link together the two central visions of chs. 1–6.

Connections between Zechariah 3 and the Rest of Zechariah

Verse	Word	Occurrences in ch. 3	Occurrences in the rest of 1.1–8.23	Occurrences in chs. 9–14
1	יהושע	**1, 3, 6, 8, 9**	**6.11**	
	עמד*1	**1** (+ 5×)	**4.14**	14.4, 12
	כהן + גדול	**1, 8**	**6.11**, 13; 7.3, 5	
	ימין	1	4.3, 11	11.17 (2×)
2	נצל	2		11.6
	אש*2	2		*9.4; 11.1; 12.6* (2×); 13.9
3	לבש	3, 4, 5		13.4
	בגד	3, 4, 5		14.14
4	סור	4	7.11	9.7; 10.11
	עבר	4 (*hiphil*)	7.14	9.8 (2×); 10.11; 13.2 (*hiphil*)
5	ראש	**5.##6,11**	4.2 (2×), 24, *7*; **6.11**	
	שים	5.##2,7	6.11; 7.12, 14	9.13; 10.3; 12.2, 3, 6
7	שמר	7.##10-11,18	7.12 (שמיר)	11.11
	נתן	7, 9	7.11; 8.12 (3×);	10.11; 12.12
8	שמע*1	*8*	6.15 (2×); 7.11, 12, 13 (2×); 8.9, 23	
	הביא	8	8.8	10.10; 13.9
	עבד*1	8		13.5
	צמח	8	**6.12** (2×)	
9	אבן	9.##3,9	4.7, *10*; *5.4, 8*	9.15, 16; 12.3
	אחר/אחה	*9.##10,25*	*4.3* (2×); 5.7; 8.21 (2×)	11.7.##12,15, 8; *14.7* (2×)
	שבעה	9	*4.2* (3×), **10** (8.17 verb)	
	עין*2 (+ נשא)	*9*	*4.10;* 5.1, 5, 6, 9; 6.1; 8.6 (2×)	*9.1, 8;* 11.12, 17 (2×); *12.4;* 14.12
	פתח	9.##14, 15		11.1; 13.1
	מוש	9		14.4
10	קרא*1	10	7.7, *13* (2×); 8.3	11.7 (2×); *13.9*
	גפן	*10*	*8.12*	

Words omitted from the table, in addition to common words already mentioned: איש, ישב*¹, כה אמר יהוה*¹, ירושלם*¹, יום, הלך, דרך*¹, בית, בין, בחר*¹, בוא, ארץ, אם, מלאך*¹, עוד, ענה, תחת. לפני.

In the majority of cases no real connection can be intended. The context and/or usage is too dissimilar, for example, in the case of לבש, שמר and פתח. Other words are not distinctive enough for an isolated occurrence to establish a link: נצל, אש, נתן, הביא, מוש, קרא. The word ימין is used differently in chs. 4 and 6; in 11.17 the similarity is not very strong. In 13.9 an opportunity is missed, for we do not find איש־ימין (as in Ps. 80.18). We do not find conscious links made by means of common words or phrases, which would be surprising if an editor of the whole book intended his readers to relate the 'messianic' figures of Zechariah 1–8 with the king and/or shepherd and/or pierced one of Zechariah 9–14.[1]

In Zechariah 6–8 the word שמע is used of obeying Yahweh; the exhortation to Joshua to hear (3.8) introduces a promise, but has some affinity with these references.

גפן may be distinctive enough for an association to be intended.

The obvious parallels occur where we should expect: *Joshua* the *high priest* on whose *head* is *set* צניף טהור/עטרות (3.1-5; 6.11). Also there is the mention of צמח in 3.8 and 6.12. We must investigate these connections separately.

The remaining words which might be significant are:

1.   עמד, which forms an inclusio around the two central visions, confirming the rather obvious point that these *occupy a central position together*. We noted the apparently super-fluous use of this in considering Zechariah 3 on its own, and it appears to be an important idea in the series of visions.

2.   עין may have some special use here, but it is difficult to be sure what it might be. With this we should consider the numbers 'seven' and 'one'. There is a strange emphasis on the

1.   Despite the fact that conservative scholars have always held that both parts of Zechariah foretell the coming of the messiah, there is, as far as I know, no attempt to demonstrate concrete links between the figures used. For a summary of views and brief discussion (which, however, concentrates almost entirely on Zech. 9–14), see R.L. Smith, *Nahum–Malachi*, pp. 175-80; also F.F. Bruce, *This Is That* (Exeter: Paternoster Press, 1968), pp. 100-14.

latter: 'one stone', 'one woman', 'one day' (?), 'Yahweh one
and his name one' (3.9; 5.7; 14.7, 9). The other references
do not seem to be significant: 'one on the right. . . left', 'one
to one. . .' and so on.

Checking back to the previous sections we note that there are few
parallels apart from the phrase 'choose Jerusalem' noted in the section
above. With ch. 1 we find: קרא (used differently), דרך and שמע (all
1.4); 'my servant(s)' (1.6; 3.8); עמד is only used in the expression
'standing among the myrtle trees'. It is appropriate that as the fathers
previously followed their own 'evil ways', the command to 'walk in
my ways' is now laid upon Joshua the people's representative.
Parallels with ch. 2 are limited to עין, אש.

Our conclusions must necessarily be somewhat negative here. There
is little evidence that the writer who was responsible for ch. 3 sought
to do more than to link it with ch. 4 as the central part of the series of
visions, and to link it with the final appendage to the visions.

This conclusion is consonant with the view that 3.1-7 + 8-10 has more
affinity with the work of the redactor than the visionary, especially
when we add to the observations above the different introductory
formula and the use of the expression מלאך יהוה. However, the latter
expression does occur in 1.11-12, and the last verse of the final vision
suggests that it is מלאך יהוה who is in mind. The question is: under what
circumstances does a different expression indicate a different hand?[1]

The Connection between Zechariah 3–4 and 6.9-15
We have noted that there are many words common to Zech. 3 and
6.11-15. This connection has been obvious to commentators because
both passages have to do with Joshua the high priest. Nevertheless it is
rare to find a commentary with a concern to show the purpose of the
positioning of the two passages, or the more than usual number of
repeated words.[2] We may say immediately that both units occur in key

---

1.   This question is peripheral to this study. It seems that there is much work to
do before an agreed answer can be given. Statistical studies, such as those of Radday
and Wickmann (see bibliography), have not yet produced precise answers that have
gained widespread agreement.

2.   E.g. Petersen, who regards the author/editor of Zechariah as 'an accomplished literary architect', only treats 6.9-15 on its own, pointing out the general
similarity with ch. 4 in the method of composition (*Haggai and Zechariah*, p. 273).

positions in the section 1.7–6.15. One is in the centre of the overall chiasmus and one is at the very end of the series: usually both are significant places. This emphasizes the importance of Joshua, at least, in the thinking of the prophet and/or the editor of this stage in the tradition.

If we ask what part Zerubbabel plays in this pattern we run into difficulties in giving a detailed and precise answer, and we meet with conflicting theories.[1] However, from the point of view of the finished text, certain statements may confidently be made.

1. Two figures are in focus in both 3.8 and 6.11-14: Joshua and 'Branch'.
2. The identification, in some sense, of Zerubbabel with 'Branch', for he is the one who is to build the Temple (4.9; 6.12-13).
3. Both have some responsibility for ruling God's people, for: Joshua is promised that he will 'rule my house...courts...' in 3.7; the stone set before him seems to be connected specifically with cleansing, but it implies some sort of special authority in any case; ch. 4 features two important individuals who act with Yahweh's authority; the use of olive trees and branches (שׁבלי הזתים) makes a further link with 'Branch' (צמח); at least one crown is placed on Joshua's head (6.11) but 'Branch' will 'bear royal honour, and sit and rule on his throne', either with a priest by his throne or with a priest on another throne (והיה כהן על כסא) (6.13); there will be שׁלום עצת between them (6.13).
4. The expected differentiation between priest and civic ruler is maintained (3.8; 6.13).

The main objections to this would come from the difficulty of knowing how to interpret the plural עטרות in vv. 11 and 14. Rudolph interprets it as a singular form,[2] which most easily makes sense of the singular verbs in v. 14, and many commentators emend the text to agree with some LXX manuscripts and Syr. (LXX and Syr. in v. 14). Some go on to suggest that the crown was originally put on the head of Zerubbabel,[3] but for political reasons this was changed. For details

1. See, e.g., Rignell, *Die Nachtgesichte,* pp. 223-33.
2. *Haggai,* pp. 127-28; cf. Job 31.36.
3. E.g. Amsler *et al., Agée, Zacharie, Malachi,* pp. 105-109.

see Petitjean and Meyers.[1] It remains true that, in the text that we have, both figures 'rule' in some sense. Mason[2] suggests that it is possible that Joshua was crowned symbolically before Zerubbabel had come from Babylon. He makes some useful points:

1. As in the 'messianic' reference of 3.8, the 'Branch' is not identified with Zerubbabel.
2. As in 3.8 the priestly line is seen as the guarantee of the coming of the messianic ruler of the future.
3. The priests do meanwhile exercise the rule.
4. Even when the messianic ruler has come a joint rule with the priestly line is envisaged.
5. Verse 14 suggests that the continuing rule of the priests in the temple is a 'reminder' of God's promises for the community's future.
6. The call to put the crown in the temple suggests a time later than Zerubbabel's coming from Babylon. By the time the temple was there in which to put the crown, he had done his work.

He concludes that this suggests a moulding of the traditions after the event to reflect the actual prominence of the priestly line.

In 6.15 the refrain, 'you shall know that Yahweh of hosts has sent me to you' occurs. This has the effect of tying together this final climax of the series of visions with the completion of the temple by Zerubbabel (4.9) and the climax of the first three visions, the oracle of 2.10-16. They all had to do with Jerusalem, and this fact is emphasized by the refrain 'again choose Jerusalem' (1.17; 2.16, two final phrases). In 3.2 this motif is picked up before the action proceeds to a new subject: the cleansing of Judah and Jerusalem.

Thus, even without being sure of the meaning of every detail, we can observe the logic of the whole construction.[3]

---

1. Petitjean, *Les oracles*, pp. 279-82, 296-97; Meyers, *Haggai, Zechariah*, pp. 336, 349-54.
2. *Haggai, Zechariah and Malachi*, pp. 62-63.
3. This gives some support to Schöttler's labelling of V2 ('Die Entmachtung der äusseren Feinde des Gottesvolkes' and V7 ('Die Beseitigung der inneren Feinde des Gottesvolkes') (*Gott inmitten seines Volkes*, p. 327).

Connections between Zechariah 4 and the Rest of Zechariah

Verse	Word	Occurrences in ch. 4	Occurrences in the rest of 1.1–8.23	Occurrences in chs. 9–14
1	עור*²	1.##5,8		9.13; 12.4; 13.7
2	זהב	2, 12 (2×)	6.11	13.9; 14.14
	גלל	2, 3	5.1, 2 (מגלה)	(גלים 10.11)
	ראש*³	2.##14,24, 7	*6.11*	
3	שנים	3, 11, 12, 14	6.1, 13	11.7; 13.8
	זית	3, 11, 12		14.4 (2×)
	שמאל	3, 11		12.6
5	ידע*²	5, *9*, 13	*6.15*; 7.14	11.11; *14.7*
6	חיל	6		9.4; 14.14
	רוח*²	*6*	5.9; 6.5, *8*; *7.12*	12.1, 10; 13.2
7	הר	7	6.1.##11-13; 8.3.##14,17	14.4.##6,14,24, 5.##3,7
	אבן*³	*7*, 10	*5.4, 8*	9.15, 16; 12.3
	חנן	7.##*13*, *14*	*6.14*	*12.10* (חנונים +)
9	יסד	9	8.9	12.1
	שלח*¹	*9*	*6.15*; 7.2, 12; 8.10	9.11
10	שמח*²	10	8.19(n)	10.7 (2×)
12	שני	12	6.2	11.14
14	אדון כל הארץ	*14*	*6.5*	(אדון 9.4 only)

Words omitted: שוב*¹, אדוני (= angel), אחד/ת*³, איש, ארץ, בית, גדל, יד, יום, ימין*³, שבעה*³, עין, ענה*²עמד, מלאך*¹, לפני, כל, יצא*².

It is plain from this that there are few possibilities of establishing connections with later chapters by means of common vocabulary. The phrase 'know that Yahweh of hosts has sent me to you' has been dealt with above.[1] Other repeated words are used differently, and the connections, if there are any, are too subtle for us to prove an intended link. Although יסד, referring to the founding of the temple in 4.9 and 8.9, confirms the importance of the founding of the temple in the mind of the prophet, it does not seem to be used as a marker for structure. The only supporting link is שלח, 4.9 and 8.10, but the first of these is part of the phrase noted above, and thereby links with 6.15.

Bearing in mind that the phrase 'know...sent me to you' links the

1.　See p. 106 n. 1.

central editorial section of ch. 4 with ch. 6, there may be some
significance in the use of חן. It is repeated in 4.7, the cry that accom-
panies the setting up of האבן הראשה, and is also the name substituted
for Josiah in 6.14 (cf. v. 10).[1] There may even be a connection with
12.10. Other than these note the following.

רוח, 'by my/his Spirit' in 4.6; 7.12. The latter refers to 'the *torah*
and the words that Yahweh. . . sent by his Spirit by the hand of the
former prophets' (the latter phrase also occurs in 7.7). This suggests
that the writer is conscious of the fact that Zechariah stands in the line
of the earlier prophets, and that Yahweh's methods remain the same.

The expression 'Lord of all the earth' forms a very strong link
between the climax of this central section of the visions, and the last
vision of the series.

There are some contacts between 4.6-10 and 12.1 and 10, viz.
'Yahweh who founded the earth and forms the spirit of man' (12.1)
and 'spirit of grace (and supplication)' (12.10), which probably
indicates at least that the writer of ch. 12 knew the earlier section.[2]

We may conclude that there is no other evidence of an attempt to
link this vision plus its oracle with any other section in Zechariah 1–
14. Again the words and phrases most likely to be significant occur in
the editorial section.

Connections between Zechariah 5 and the Rest of Zechariah

Verse	Word	Occurrences in ch. 5	Occurrences in the rest of 1.1–8.23	Occurrences in chs. 9–14
		Vision 6: The Flying Scroll (5.1-4)		
3	שבע	3, 4	8.17 (n)	
4	בית	*4.##7,10,16* (11)	6.10; *7.3*; *8.9*, 13 (2×), 15, 19	9.8; 10.3, 6 (2×); 11.13; 12 (7×); 13.1, 6; 14.2, 20, 21

1. An alternative explanation that has found some favour is that of A. Demsky,
'The Temple Steward Josiah ben Zephaniah', *IEJ* 31 (1981), pp. 100-102. He
refers to the Akkadian *laḫḫinu* (and its Aramaic cognate לחן) which is used of an
official responsible for handling gold and silver in the temple or court. Quoted with
approval in Petersen, *Haggai and Zechariah*, p. 278 n. 8.

2. Cf. Mason, *Zechariah 9–14*, pp. 202-206.

שקר	**4**	**8.17**	10.2; 13.3
עץ	**4**		12.6
אבן*3	4, (8)		9.15, 16; 12.3

Words omitted: אני, ארך*2, ארץ, בוא, יצא*2, כל, מלאך*1, נשא + עין*2, פני, רחב*2,
שוב*1, תוך*2.

Vision 7: The Woman in the Ephah (5.5-11)

6	עין*2	6	8.6.##7,14	9.1, 8; 11.12, 17 (2×); 12.4; 14.12
7	נשא*2	7, 9	6.13	
	אשה	7, 9		11.9; 12 (5×); 14.2
	ישב*1	7	6.13; 7.7 (2×); 8.4, 20-21	9.5-6; 10.6; 11.6; 12 (5×); 13.1; 14.10, 11 (2×)
	אבן*3	8, (4)		9.15, 16; 12.3
8	השלך	8.##4,9		11.13.##4,15
9	רוח*2	**9**	6.5, 8; 7.12	12.1, 10; 13.2
	כנף	9.##9,11,12	8.23	
	שמים*2	**9**	**6.5**; 8.12	12.1
11	בנה	11	6.12, 13, 15; 8.9	9.3
	בית	11 see above		
	חניה	**11**	**6.8**	

Words omitted: אחת*3, איה*2, ארץ, בין, הלך, יצא*2, מלאך*1, כל, נשא + עין*2, פה,
תוך*2.

On examinination, most of these repeated words prove to be incapable of establishing any link between different sections of the book. The only possible ones seem to me to be the following.

נשבע לשקר is applied to one of two types of person who will be cut off by the curse, the other one being 'he who steals'. In 8.17 שבעת שקר occurs in a group of four exhortations, delivered to the people who are restored to favour after the punishment of the exile. Obviously, this is an important part of the necessary purification that is to take place, but there does not seem to be a very strong attempt to link these sections of the book together. The actual form of the combination is different, and the associations are different (e.g. stealing is not mentioned in 8.16-17).

בית occurs at the end of each of these two visions; in v. 4 it is given great emphasis. Perhaps there is a deliberate contrast made between the houses of the sinner and of 'wickedness' itself, and the house of Yahweh.

The former will be destroyed/far away; Yahweh's house will be rebuilt as a sign of his dwelling in the midst of this people again. The use of בנה in 5.11, 6.12-13 and 8.9, would add some support to this. However, only in the first of these is 'house' used: the others have היכל.

Finally the *hiphil* of נוח near the end of the seventh and eighth visions looks like a deliberate play on words. To cause evil to rest in its own place far away in the land of Shinar, causes God's Spirit to rest in the north. This transfer of evil from Jerusalem to Babylon/the north prepares the way for the exiles in Babylon to return to Jerusalem (6.9-15). With these references we should probably note מנחתו in 9.1. It represents a distinctive idea in a prominent place. The root occurs nowhere else in Zechariah.

Other words are used so differently that we must consider this part of the investigation at an end. The only clear links with other sections of Zechariah are those established between VV2-3 and 6-8 above.[1]

Connections between Zechariah 6 and the Rest of Zechariah

Verse	Word	Occurrences in ch. 6	Occurrences in the rest of 1.1–8.23	Occurrences in chs. 9–14
		Vision 8: The Four Chariots (6.1-8)		
3	אמץ	3, 6		12.5
5	רוח*2*4	5, 8	*7.12*	13.2
6	צפון*2	**6, 8** (2×)		14.4
	תימן	6		9.14
7	בקש	7	8.21, 22	11.16; 12.9
		Prophetic Action and Oracle (6.9-15)		
10	לקח	10-11		11.7, 10, 13, 15
	גולה	10		14.2
11	כסף	11		9.3; 11.12, 13; 13.9; 14.14
12	היכל	12-15	8.9	
13	הוד	13		10.3
	משל	13		9.10
	שלום	13	8.10, 12, 16, 19	9.10

1. See pp. 247-51, 252-53.

14	חלם	14		10.2
	זכר	14		10.9; 13.2
15	רחק	15		10.9
	שלח*1	15	7.2, 12; 8.10	9.11
	שמע*1*3	15.##14,15	7.11, 12, 13.##5,9 8.9, *23*	
	קול	15		11.3 (2×)
	אלהים	**15**	8.8, 23	*9.7, 16;* 10.6; *11.4;* *12.5,* 8; *13.9;* *14.5*

Words omitted which occurred in the first vision*1: רכב, סוס, לבן, התהלך, אדום.
Other words: *4הר, גדול, *5בנה, *5בית, *2ארץ, *2ארבע, איש, *2אחר, אדם, אדון, ענה, *2עין, *2עין + נשא + מלאך, כל, *3כהן, כה אמר יהוה, *1ישב, *2יצא, *2יום, *2ידע, חנן, תחת. *4שני, *4שנים, *2שמים, שלש, שלש*1, שוב, *3שים, רביעי, *1ראשון, *1עשה.

אלהים is an important word in its context, and the references in 8.8 and 13.9 provide the strongest link between the major sections of Zechariah. With them must also be considered 2.15, והיו לי לעם. But the other references also appear to have some significance, except for 12.8 (house of David...like God). All the others have a pronominal form, which expresses a significant relationship: Philistia will become a remnant for our God (9.7); Yahweh their God will save them (9.16); the inhabitants of Jerusalem have strength through Yahweh their God (12.5). The shepherd is the agent of 'Yahweh my God' (11.4). In 14.5 the reading is disputed[1] but the context is of salvation by a decisive intervention of Yahweh. The strongest statement, which has most in common with 8.8 and 13.9 is in 10.6, 'for I am Yahweh their God and I will answer them'.

Zech. 6.15b is a conditional promise, which has been taken to be a later addition[2] (cf. the exhortation at the end of 8.19). It fits in well with the thought of Zechariah 1–8 as a whole: judgment came because the fathers did not 'hearken to (the voice of) Yahweh'. It is, therefore,

---

1.   MT reads 'Yahweh my God'. Most commentators explain this as a mistake for אלהיך by haplography with the following כל, and this would explain the absence of the conjunction. It is plain that the verse has suffered in transmission, and this seems to be the best solution, except that there is no manuscript support for it. Three Hebrew manuscripts read 'God', two 'his God' and one 'God of Israel'. See Sæbø, 'Die deuterosacharjanische Frage', p. 114. It is difficult to see any reason why the prophet should say 'my God' (cf. Rudolph, *Haggai,* p. 232).

2.   See p. 148 n. 1.

completely natural to find an exhortation to hearken as the climax of
the promise.

There are few additional connections to be noted. בקשׁ and שׁלום are
used differently in chs. 6 and 8.

Apart from these it is no exaggeration to say that there is not a
single word that is used in the same way in ch. 6 and the remainder of
Zechariah.

Connections between Zechariah 7–8 and Zechariah 9–14

Verse	Word	Occurrences in ch. 7–8	Occurrences in chs. 9–14
Ch. 7			
1	מלך	1	9.5, 9; 11.6; 14.5, 9, 10, 16, 7
2	שׁלח[*1]	2, 12; 8.10	9.11
3	נזר	3	9.16
	עשׂה[*1]	3, 9; 8.16	10.1
5	ספד	5	12.10-12 (5×)
6	אכל	6.##2,7	9.4, 15; 11.1, 9, 16; 12.6
	שׁתה	6.##4,9	9.15
7	ראשׁון[*1]	7, 12; 8.11	12.7; 14.10
9	רחם[*1]	9	10.6
10	עני	10	9.9; 11.7, 11
	לב(ב)	10, 12; 8.17	10.7 (2×); 12.5
11	נתן[*3]	11; 8.12 (3×)	10.1; 12.12
	סור[*3]	11	9.7; 10.11
12	שׂים[*3]	12, 14	9.13; 10.3; 12.2, 3, 6
14	סער	14	9.14
	גוי[*1]	14; 8.13, 22, 23	9.10; 12.3, 9; 14.2, 3, 14, 16, 18, 19
	עבר[*3]	14	9.8.##4,7; 10.11
Ch. 8			
3	קדשׁ[*2]	3	14.5, 20, 21
5	מלא	5	9.13, 15
	ילד	5.##4-5	13.3.##10,21
6	שׁאריח[*]	<u>6</u>, <u>11</u>, <u>12</u>	9.7; 11.9; 12.14
7	ישׁע[*9]	**7, 13**	**9.9, 16; 10.6;** *12.7*
	מזרח	7	14.4
8	הביא[*3]	8	10.10; 13.9

	אלהים*6*9	**8, 23**	*9.7, 16; 10.6; 11.4; 12.5, 8; 13.9; 14.5*
	צדק*9	*8*	*9.9*
9	חזק	9, 13, 23.##8,14	14.13
	יסר*4	9	12.1
	בנה*5	9	9.3
10	שכר	10.##5,9	11.12.##7,13
	בהמה*2	10	14.15
	יצא*2	10	9.14; 10.4; 14.2, 3, 8
	שלום	10, 12, 16, 19	9.10
	צר(ה)	10	10.11
12	זרע	12	10.9; 11.17 (2×)
	שמים	12	12.1
13	ברך	13	11.5
	ירא	13, 15	9.5
14	נחם*1	14	10.2
16	שער	16	14.10.##12,16,19
17	שקר*5	17	10.2; 13.3
	אהב	17, 19	13.6
19	שמח*2	19n	10.7.##4,10
	טוב	19	9.17; 11.12
21	הלך	21.##1,7,8,17,	9.14; 10.12 (*hithpael*)
	cf.*1	23.#19	
	בקש*6	21, 22	11.16; 12.9
23	החזיק	23.##8,14	14.13
	לשון	23	14.12

Words, omitted: אב*1, גם, גוי*1, גוי*5, בית, בוא, ארץ, אני, איש*2, אחר(י)*2, אחר/ת, אדם, *3, כה, ישב*1, ישראל*2, ירושלם*1, יסד*4, יום, יהודה*1, ידע*2, יד, הר, חנן*4, טוב*1, גדול, רב*2, קרא*1, קדש*2, עשה*1, עם*2, עיר*1, עין*2, סבב*2, כל, יהוה אמר, ציון, פה, תחת, שני, שמר*3, שמע, שלש*3*1, שלח*1, שוב*4*2, רוח*1, רביעי.

Despite the large number of repeated words, few show any sign of having been used as markers of structure. From that point of view the labour involved in producing and examining such a table proves disappointing. On the other hand, it demonstrates how many possibilities there are for imaginative theories of structure. For example, 7.1–7 contains a number of words that are also found in 9.1–10.1. So we might surmise that: Bethel sends Regem-melek[1] to enquire of Yahweh

---

1. Note that on the computer tape that was used for the analysis בת־אל שר־אצר was considered to be one word, as was רגם־מלך. This is why מלך does not show in

whether he should fast (נור *niphal*) as he has done for many years, and receives the answer 'When you fasted, did you not fast for your own benefit; and do you not eat and drink for your own benefit . . . ' In the future Gaza's king will perish and Jerusalem's king will come; Yahweh, the one who makes (עשה) the storm clouds, will set Jerusalem's prisoners free; his people will be (not fasting: הנזר, but) a crown (נזר).

In fact this does not stand up to critical scrutiny. We have to discount most of the words in the list because their use is different: any connection between them would be too subtle for anyone we might imagine to be a normal hearer or reader. This excludes: נזר, שלח, מלך, שארית, ילד, מלא, קדש, סער, שים, סור, לבב, עני, ראשון, שחה, אכל, עשה, ירא, ברך, שמים, צרה, שמים, זרע, יצא, בהמה, שכר, בנה, יסד, חזק (probably), מזרח, לשון, בקש, הלך, מוב, אהב, שער, נחם.

Some words might possibly be intentionally connected: ספר (but the passages are very different and there is not much else to link them), רחם (but the reference is different: human and divine compassion), נתן (8.12 and 10.1 only. Both refer to blessing but, in the first reference, the vine, ground and heavens give their increase; in the latter it is God who gives), גוי (but it can only serve to indicate the main focus of the contexts in which it occurs).

שלום refers to relationships between people in 8.16 and 19, to safety for the people of Judah in 8.10 and 12, but to peace to the nations in 9.10.

Some words are used in similar ways but not distinctively enough to be effective in structuring: שקר, שמח.

We have noted the distinctive phrase מעבר ומשב previously. It occurs in a fairly prominent place in both 7.14 and 9.8, almost at the end of a sub-section of the text. In the first passage[1] its absence indicates the devastation of the pleasant land, in the second Yahweh himself stands as a guard so that no one (presumably no unauthorized person) can come and go as they please. The precise meaning, there-

the table: it has been considered separately. I do not think that the individual parts of these names can be used for structuring purposes.

1. Many commentators decline to explain the significance of this phrase. Rudolph translates 'ohne Verkehr' (*Haggai*, pp. 141-42); Perowne suggests 'as we say, *went backward and forward*'; presumably it signifies the everyday business of settled life, cf. Ps. 121.8, יהוה ישמר צאתך ובאך.

fore, is somewhat different, but one can well imagine the author of 9.8 making use of this phrase to express a reversal of fortune for the people of Israel, and I should not delete this as a gloss, as does *BHS* for example. It is difficult to argue for more than this.

This leaves a small group of words which might serve this function: ישע, which is used of Yahweh's action for his people, with the *niphal* participle in 9.9; הביא, used of Yahweh's bringing his people to Jerusalem/from the land of Egypt; אלהים (see above); and צדק, which is remarkably rare in Zechariah (only 8.8, attached to the important climax of chs. 7–8, and 9.9, where the adjective צדיק refers to the coming king). It is noticeable that these all occur in 8.7-8, with their counterparts mostly in a comparatively small compass, 9.7–10.6. It is also interesting that Mason identified some of these verses as having affinities with proto-Zechariah.[1] We shall deal with these in connection with the sections of Zechariah 9–14 since it seems more likely that its author(s)/editor(s) has/have been influenced by proto-Zechariah than vice versa.

I conclude that we have found evidence of a connection between Zechariah 1–8 and 9–14, but not of an overall editing of the whole book.

Arguments for the Unity of Zechariah

Having looked at the verbal links between each section of Zechariah 1–8 and the rest of the book, we should be in a position to offer an opinion on the likelihood that the whole of Zechariah 1–14 is a unity. We have not found evidence in favour of this view, so let us ask if there actually is evidence that this method does not take account of.

One of the most succinct presentations of arguments for the unity of Zechariah is given by Joyce Baldwin.[2] She mentions Barnes who notes the following features:

> centrality of Jerusalem
> sympathetic attitude to Ephraim
> prominent place given to David.

---

1. See, e.g., *Zechariah 9–14*, pp. 11, 26-27, 29, 30-31, 36-38, 85-88, 93, 98-100, 123-24, 124, 127-28; 'The Purpose of the Editorial Framework of the Book of Haggai,' *VT* 27 (1976), pp. 227-31, 233-36.

2. Baldwin, *Haggai, Zechariah, Malachi,* p. 68.

Also Mitchell, who 'was prepared to state that the metre of 13.7-9...resembled that of 3.7', the use of which was 'favourable rather than unfavourable to the authorship of Zechariah'.[1] She also lists various criteria:

1. Characteristic words and phrases:
   2.10–9.9
   7.14–9.8: 'none shall march to and fro' identical phrase, found nowhere else in the OT.[2]
2. Idiosyncrasy of dwelling on an idea:
   6.10, 11, 13 (take...take, crown, throne, throne);
   8.4-5 (streets...streets)
   11.17 (his arm, right eye, both repeated)
   14.5 (you shall flee...you shall flee as you fled...)
   14.9 (Yahweh one and his name one)

Even if some repetitions are excised as glosses, 'enough examples remain to prove the point'. I find this very doubtful, since the examples are uncertain in any case.

3. Mention of the whole then the part:
   5.4 (the house...his house...both timber and stones)
   12.11-13 (every family; specified in 12, 13)
4. Metaphors are followed by their meaning 'as in 10.4'
5. Unusual fivefold development of an idea:
   6.13 and 9.5-7
6. Similarities of thought:
   Cleansing: 1.4; 3.4-9; 5.1-11; 13.1, 9
   Promise that the nations will return: 2.10-11; 8.7; 10.6-12
   Overthrow and conversion of Israel's enemies: 2.4, 12-13; 8.20-23; 9.1-8; 12.4; 14.16
   Hope of messianic ruler: 6.12-13; 9.9-10.[3]

She notes scholars who have given support to these arguments to a greater or lesser extent:

> The force of these similarities is admitted by those who postulate that the second part was the work of a disciple of Zechariah, as well as those scholars, such as C.H.H. Wright, E.B. Pusey, W.H. Lowe, A. van Hoonacker, who have attributed the whole book to Zechariah. In

---

1. Baldwin, *Haggai, Zechariah, Malachi,* p. 68; Mitchell, *Haggai, Zechariah, Malachi and Jonah,* p. 235.
2. Baldwin, *Haggai, Zechariah, Malachi,* pp. 68-69.
3. Baldwin, *Haggai, Zechariah, Malachi,* p. 69.

recent years the cogency of the arguments in favour of the unity of the book has been acknowledged by W.F. Albright[1] (and conservative scholars [E.J. Young, N.H. Ridderbos, R.K. Harrison]).

Again, as P.R. Ackroyd comments, 'The very fact that this linking of 9–14 with 1–8 took place argues for some recognition of common ideas or interests'.[2]

It seems to me that it is important to affirm the affinities between Zechariah 1–8 and 9–14, and that Mason has shown beyond reasonable doubt that there is a strong continuity of thought. Still, the evidence adduced here does not point to unity of authorship, nor even editorial unity.

In his more recent commentary,[3] K.L. Barker summarizes arguments against unity of authorship as based on: (1) differences in style and other compositional features, and (2) historical and chronological references that allegedly require a later date. He quotes with approval (even relish) G.L. Robinson's comment that there is 'no mode of reasoning so treacherous as that from language and style'.[4] In order to demonstrate that one could draw a list to counteract Mitchell's list of differences in vocabulary[5] he offers a 'partial but suggestive list of expression common to both parts of the book':[6]

1. 'No one should come or go', 7.14, and '*against marauding forces*' (his italics), 9.8. (This seems to suggest a difference in usage.)
2. 'Declares the Lord', fourteen times in 1–8 and also in 10.12; 12.1, 4; 13.2, 7-8. (This surely cannot be taken seriously.)
3. 'The LORD Almighty' 1.6, 12; 2.13; 9.15; 10.3; 12.5. (It is interesting that at least two of the three references in Zechariah 1–8 are in sections that I have thought to be redactional.)

---

1. Review of *Introduction to the Old Testament*, by R.H. Pfeiffer, *JBL* 61, (1942), p. 121. He actually says: 'Whether any or all of these oracles [of Zech. 9–14] are to be attributed to Zechariah we cannot say; the reviewer sees no reason why most of them cannot be credited to Zechariah himself'.
2. *PCB*, p. 651.
3. *Haggai, Zechariah and Malachi*, pp. 596-97.
4. *ISBE*, V, p. 3139. This reference is from the original edition.
5. *Haggai, Zechariah, Malachi and Jonah*, p. 236.
6. *Haggai, Zechariah, Malachi and Jonah*, pp. 596-97.

4. 'Will be' (2.4), 'were at rest' and 'were settled' (7.7), 'will
   remain intact' (12.6), and 'remain' (14.10). He notes that 'the
   Hebrew verb. . . is the same for all of these'. (It is clear that
   the use is different, and the verb is a common one [יָשַׁב].)

All in all we must say that Barker has provided evidence against the
unity of Zechariah 1–14 rather than for it.

The detailed tables that I have produced, and our examination of
repeated words, show:

1. That there are many words which are repeated in Zechariah
   1–8 and 9–14.
2. That there are very few words that are used in the same sense
   in both parts of the book.
3. That very often, the distinctive repeated words belong to sections of the book attributed to the same author on other
   (usually form-critical) grounds.

It is true that I have not proved the existence of two or more authors/
editors who were responsible for the composition of Zechariah 1–14,
but the evidence suggests at least two separate individuals who worked
on chs. 1–8 and 9–14.[1] Further, it seems more likely than not that a
different editor moulded the primary material of Zechariah 1–8 in
order to give us our present text. However, there is also strong
evidence that these individuals or groups shared a common background and theological understanding.

Gott inmitten seines Volkes *by H.-G. Schöttler*

I have said that we do not find confirmation of conservative theories
concerning the unity of Zechariah 1–14. At the other end of the scale
we do not find confirmation of the radical theory of Schöttler, who
finds evidence of five stages of redaction in Zechariah 1–6 alone. He
presents his conclusions on p. 448 and they may be summarized as

---

1. Since this book was completed M.G. Kline has written an article, 'The
Structure of the Book of Zechariah' (*JETS* 34 [1991], pp. 179-93), which argues
for a unified editing of the whole book. He finds a 'three-hinge framework' in 3.1-
10, 6.9-15 and 11.1-17. I cannot attempt a detailed criticism at this point, but it
seems that, if my findings concerning the work of Lundbom, Holladay, Lamarche *et
al.* are justified, then Klines's hypothesis must be rejected as highly subjective.

follows ('V1' etc are my labels; titles are Schöttler's; verse numbers are approximate, for not all verses are accepted as given).

Basic text:	V1	'Pferde'	(1.7-9, 10b, 11b)	(pp. 223-39)
519 BC		Yahweh word attached	1.14	(p. 268)
	V3	'Messschnur'	(2.5-8)	(pp. 231-34)
		Yahweh word attached	2.14	(pp. 268-69)
	V5	'Leuchter'	(4.1-3a, 4-5, 6a, 14)	(pp. 235-57)
	V7	'Efa'	(5.5, 6a, 8a, 9-11)	(pp. 257-60)
	V8	'Wagen'	(6.1a, 2-5, 7)	(pp. 261-67)

These five visions form a cycle which shows concentric symmetry:

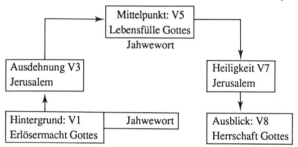

It is unusual to find such an interest in structure in this milieu. In general this agrees with the view of scholars who consider the relationship of the visions to each other, that V1 and V8 balance each other, V5 (with or without V4) is the centrepoint and VV2-3 are in some way parallel to VV6-7. Nevertheless, the way that this is presented without detailed justification is unsatisfactory (see below). Schöttler also compares this five-membered structure to that of Isa. 54.1-3, 4-6, 7-10, 11-13, 14-17.[1]

First Editing:	V2	'Werkleute' (2.3-4)[2]
c. 515 BC		Word of Yahweh: 1.15
	V4	'Jeschua'
		Expansion: 4.10-11, 12b-14
		Word of Yahweh: 4.6b

This produced a seven vision cycle with a different centre:

---

1. *Gott inmitten seines Volkes*, pp. 273-75.
2. *Gott inmitten seines Volkes*, pp. 287-90.

V1	Hintergrund: Erlösermacht Gottes [+ Jahwewort]
V2	Niederwerfung der äusseren Feinde
V3	äussere Daseinfülle [+ Jahwewort]
V4	Vergebung der Schuld des Volkes und des Landes
V5	innere Daseinfülle [+ Jahwewort]
V7	Beseitigung der inneren Feinde
V8	Ausblick: Herrschaft Gottes

The structure presented here is based on rather subjective labelling, and it is impossible to take it seriously as an intended structure, even though we note the accurate observations it contains. For example, it is true that VV2-3 are concerned with the punishment of external enemies, while VV5, 7 look for the removal of 'inner enemies'. It is not clear that the author thought in these terms.

The second editing, according to Schöttler, added V6, together with various motifs (horn, high priest as mediator of salvation, woman in the ephah, and four winds) and Yahweh-words (2.10a, 12-13; 4.6a, 7, 10, [8-9]; 6.8). He dates this in the middle of the fifth century BC, around the time of Nehemiah.

It is very strange that Schöttler should have omitted V6 from the procedure so far. His discussion of 5.1-4[1] is characteristically detailed but yields almost nothing of substance. He notes that it is unclear who the prophet's 'Gesprächspartner' is (unlike 4.1-14; 5.5-11); he notes that, although the prophet sees and understands the vision, the one who speaks with him asks again about the picture (which does not seem strange to me) and the measurements given by the prophet play no further part in the explanation of the vision; and finally, he notes the difficulties involved in translating vv. 3b-4. Uncertainty should not lead to a speculative conjecture with far-reaching consequences.

The next stage is placed at the end of the fifth century or in the fourth century BC. Two 'Zeichenhandlungen' are added (stone on the headband of the high priest 3.8a, 9a, b; crown on the head of the high priest, 6.9, 10b, 11, 13a).

Finally, in the third century BC, the 'Mahnrede' (1.1-6) and the 'Mahnwort' (6.15b) are added, and the introduction (1.7) is revised.

I have little confidence in this radical traditio-historical approach to the text, which seems to build so much on so little. However, this is not the place for a detailed critique of this aspect of Schöttler's work.

---

1. *Gott inmitten seines Volkes*, pp. 126-33.

A few comments concerning my particular interests must suffice.

1. I have not found evidence of more than one or two redactors at most, and the editorial activity that I can detect seems to be self-consistent and skilfully artistic.

2. Even if Schöttler's form-critical and traditio-historical work could be shown to be soundly based, his suggestions concerning the successive structures of the different recensions of the text would have to be rejected. As far as I can see, there is no attempt to determine or be governed by any objective criteria; there is no attempt to demonstrate that the author-editor would have characterized the various sections as Schöttler does.

3. To undertake such a detailed study of Zechariah 1–6 rather than 1–8 must be regarded as rash. (He presents a plan of chs. 7–8[1] with three major divisions: 7.1-14 [1-3, 4-7, 8-14], 8.1-17 [1-2, 3, 4-5, 6, 7-8, 9-17] and 8.18-23 [18-19, 20-22, 23], but the discussion leading to this contains little more reference to chs. 7–8 than a discussion of the introductory formulae). We have found strong evidence of links at least between the editorial sections of Zechariah 1–6 and 7–8, as well as the same kind of structuring method in both blocks of material.

Connections between Zechariah 9.1–11.3 and the Rest of Zechariah

Verse	Word	Occurrences in 9.1–11.3	Occurrences in 1.1–8.23	Occurrences in the rest of 9–14
Ch. 9				
1	עין*2	*9.1, 8*	2.1, 5, 12; 3.9 4.10; 5.1, 5,6, 9; 8.6.##7,14	11.12, *17.##10,15; 12.4; 14.12*
	ישראל*1	9.1	2.2.#17?; 8.13	11.14.#13?; 12.1
3	בנה*5	9.3	1.16; 5.11; 6.12, 13, 15; 8.9	
	כסף*6	9.3	6.11	
4	נכה	9.4; 10.11		12.4 (2×); 13.6 (2×), 7
	חיל*4	9.4	4.6	14.14
	אש*2	*9.4; 11.1*	2.9; 3.2	12.6 (2×); 13.9

---

1. Schöttler, *Gott inmitten seines Volkes*, p. 40.

	אכל[*7]	9.4, 15; 11.1	7.6 (2×)	11.9, 16; 12.6
5	ירא[*7]	9.5	8.13, 15	
	יבש	9.5; 10.5, 11		11.17, 14
	נבם	9.5		12.10
	מלך[*7]	9.5, 9	7.1, (2)	14.5, 9, 10, 16, 17
	ישב[*2]	9.5, 6; 10.6	11×, esp. *2.8, 11;* *7.7.##12,18*	11.6; 12.5, *6,* 7, 8, 10; 13.1; 14.10, 11.##1,7
6	כרת	9.6, 10.##1,6		11.10; 13.2, 8; 14.2
7	סור[*3]	9.7; 10.11	3.4; 7.11	
	נשאר[*7]	9.7	(n. 8.6, 11, 12)	11.9; 12.14
	אלהים[*6*7]	*9.7, 16;* *10.6*	*6.15; 8.8,* 23	**11.4; 12.5,** 8; *13.9; 14.5*
	אלף	9.7		12.5, 6
8	עבר[*3*7]	9.8.##4,7; 10.11	3.4 (*hiphil*); 7.14	
	שוב[*1] cf.[*11]	9.8, 12.##1,9 9; 10.#6?, 9, 10	1.3 (2×), 4, 6, 16; 7.14; 8.3, 15	13.7
9	צדק[*7]	*9.9*	*8.8*	
	ישע[*7]	**9.9, 16;** 10.6	**8.7,** 13	12.7
	עני[*7]	9.9	7.10	11.7, 11
	רכב[*1]	9.9, 10; 10.5	1.8; 6 (5×)	12.4
10	סוס[*1]	9.10; 10.3, 5	1.8.##7,16; 6 (5×)	12.4 (2×); 14.15, 20
	שלום[*6]	9.10	6.13; 8.10, 12, 15, 19	
	משל[*6]	9.10	6.13	
	בריח	9.11		11.10
11	שלח[*1]	9.11	1.10; 2.12, 13, 15; 4.9; 6.15; 7.2, 12; 8.10	
12	יום	9.12, 16	14×	24×
13	מלא[*7]	9.13, 15	8.5	
	שים[*3]	9.13; 10.3	3.5 (2×); 6.11; 7.12, 14	12.2, 3, 6
	חרב	9.13		11.17; 13.7
	גבר (n)	<u>9.13;</u> <u>10.5</u>, 6, <u>7,</u> 12		<u>13.7</u>
14	יצא[*2]	*9.14;* *10.4*	4.7; *5 (6×);* *6 (7×);* 8.10	14.2,3, 8
	הלך[*7]	9.14; 10.12	1.10, 11; 6 (3×); 8.21 (4×); 23.#19	

	סער*7	9.14	7.14	
	תימן*6	9.14	6.6	
	יגן	9.15		12.8
15	אבן*3	9.15, 16	3.9 (2×); 4.7, 10, 5.4, 8	12.3
	שתה*7	9.15	7.6 (2×)	
16	צאן	9.16; 10.2		11.4, 7 (3×), 11, 17; 13.7
	מר*7	9.16	7.3	
	נוס*2	9.16 (נסס?)	2.10	
	אדמה*2	9.16	2.16	13.5
17	טוב*1	9.17	1.13, 17; 8.19	11.12

Ch. 10

1	עשה*1	10.1	1.6 (2×); 2.4; 6.11; 7.3, 9; 8.16	
2	חזה	10.2		13.4 n.
	שקר*5	10.2	5.4; 8.17	13.3
	חלם*6	10.2	6.14	
3	פקד	10.3.##4,9		11.16
	הוד*6	10.3	6.13	
4	יחד	10.4		12.10
6	רחם*1	10.6	1.12, 16; 7.9	
7	שמח*2	10.7.##4,10	2.14; 4.10; 8.19	
9	רחק*6	10.9	6.14	
	זכר*6	10.9	6.15	
	חיה*1	10.9	1.5	13.3; 14.8
	מצא	10.10		11.6
11	צרה*7	10.11	8.10	
	מצ(ו)לה	10.11	1.8	

Ch. 11

1	פתח*3	11.1	3.9.##14,15	13.1
2	אדרת	11.2, 3		11.13; 13.4
3	קול*6	11.3.##1,7	6.15	

Words omitted: ‏זרע*7, התהלך*1, הביא*3, דרך*1, גוי*1, בת*2, בית*5, בחר*1, אדון*4,
יהודה*1, ירושלם*1), לב(ב)*7, נחם*1, נתן*3, עם*2*11, עור*2, ציון*1, רב*2.

In this section, I shall primarily be looking forward to Zech. 11.3–13.9 and Zechariah 14. As we worked through chs. 1–8 there were few signs of any attempt by the editor to give literary unity to the

whole of chs. 1–14, although we did note links between 8.7-8 and
9.9–10.6. I shall attempt to gather these together at the end of this
chapter. Before doing this I shall consider the work done by Mason on
inner-biblical exegesis in Deutero-Zechariah. His work has focused on
the use of earlier biblical material with a view to explaining the
relationship (theological and otherwise) between the persons
responsible for Zechariah 9–14 and the earlier part of the book. He
also looks at the use of earlier material outside Zechariah 1–8. This is
relevant to my own study in at least two ways:

1. I shall have a valuable check on how well my method iden-
    tifies similarities: does it miss important points of contact;
    does it add anything to what scholars have already discovered
    by other methods?
2. I shall have to face the question whether the similarities I
    pick out are due to a concern for structure, or whether they
    are due simply to quoting or alluding to earlier material.
    This may include material originating outside the book of
    Zechariah but used by the writers/editors of both parts.

In my judgment we must ignore the following words (given in the
order in which they occur above): סור, נבט, יבש, ירא, כסף, בנה, ישׂראל,
רחם, חד, הוד, חלם, עשׂה, טוב, אדמה, נוס, נזר, סתה, הלך, מלא, יום, שלח, שוב,
שׂמח, רחק, זכר, מצא, צרה, מצולה, קול. Some dubious examples have been
kept even now, but we are left with a manageable number. I shall
collect together those words which occur in the major sections that I
have isolated.

Contacts with 8.7-8
In this category there are three important words, אלהים, צדק and ישׁע,
which I have already noted in the relevant sections of Chapter 3
above. They certainly provide evidence that the writer/editor of
Zechariah 9–10 shared the same central concerns as the one(s)
responsible for Zechariah 7–8. I have also noted the similarity
between 9.9 and 2.14. However, I do not think that we can demonstrate an intention to integrate these elements into a unified structure
extending across Zechariah 1–8 and 9–14. The most we can say is that
the writer/editor alludes to and re-emphasizes the theme of 'Yahweh
as the God of his people' (found in both 2.10-17 [v. 15] and 8.8, the

centre of chs. 7–8). However, the strongest contact with 8.7-8 is found in 9.16, 10.6, and (above all) 13.9, rather than in 9.9.[1]

Contacts with 11.4-17 + 13.7-9

עין. We must ignore the common expression 'if it is good in your eyes'; this leaves 11.17, the curse upon the worthless shepherd. Even though 'eye' is an important word this cannot plausibly be linked with the obscure references in 9.1, 8. However, 12.4 'on the house of Judah I will open my eyes' looks as if it might be comparable to 9.8.

נכה and אש both occur in 13.7-9. Both are connected with chastening, whereas 9.4 and 10.11 refer to punishment of Israel's traditional enemies, Tyre and Egypt.

אכל refers to 'eating flesh' of the sheep by other members of the flock (11.9) and by the worthless shepherd (11.16). This is not the same as judgment by fire (9.4; 11.1) nor victory in battle (9.15).[2]

יבש is used of the worthless shepherd's arm. In chs. 9-10 it is also used of judgment: of Ekron's hopes, of riders of horses and of the depths of the Nile. This is an average range of meanings for this versatile verb, but it means that we cannot rely on it.

ישב, meaning 'inhabitant' in 11.6, must be disregarded.

כרת is only found in Zechariah 9-14. Usually it signifies judgment, but in 11.10 it is used in the common idiom 'made a covenant'.

נשאר is an important word, and the 'sheep that are left' signify people. Nevertheless, nothing is done to emphasize the word in this context. Zech. 9.7 and 12.14 (Philistia as a clan; families that are left) are different. Moreover, in 13.8 the verb יותר is used.

אלהי is the most significant word in this section, and forms an inclusio. At the start it is used to imply that Yahweh is the prophet's God but the people could not speak in this way. At the end they have been brought into this relationship. There is some continuity established, therefore, throughout 9.1–13.9.

I have already noted that 13.9 is similar to the promise of 2.15 and 8.8. These are linked, by means of the refrain '. . . you will know that

---

1. Cf. pp. 253, 267.
2. This verse is usually emended. See, e.g., Rudolph, *Haggai,* p. 184. Baldwin keeps the MT and understands it as: 'They shall eat (sc. the victory banquet)'. She comments: 'The slingstones that have come their way as missiles will be as useless then as all other weapons of war'. Either way, it cannot be connected with ch. 11.

Yahweh of hosts has sent me to you', with the other most important themes of Zechariah 1–8, viz. the restoration of Jerusalem and the building of the Temple through Zerubbabel, and the purified restored leadership seen in Joshua and 'Branch'. If we take seriously the material included between 11.4 and 13.9, it has to do with cleansing the people through their compassion and supplication (12.10a), and this has some connection with the piercing referred to in 12.10b. This connection is strengthened by the paradoxical command of Yahweh in 13.7, 'Awake O sword against *my* shepherd, against *"my neighbour"* (עמיתי)'. The word עמית means 'associate, fellow' and is only found elsewhere in Leviticus: viz. 5.21; 18.20; 19.11, 15, 17; 24.19; 25.14-15, 17. It always signifies someone who should be treated rightly! Mason[1] notes that

> the reference to the sword of God falling, the word for 'striking', the references to the scattering of the sheep, and the phrase *I will turn my hand against* are all used in the prophetic literature exclusively in a hostile sense and in a context of judgment.

This, I believe, confirms that we have something intentionally puzzling.

עני describes the king who comes on the ass, and also the 'poor of the flock', *if* this reading is correct. We cannot build anything on it, but see צאן below.

I cannot see any convincing connection between the 'blood of the covenant' in 9.11, and the 'covenant with all the peoples'.

חרב גבור, 9.13, describes Israel as a fighting force in the hand of Yahweh. There is at least some resonance with חרב and גבר in 11.17 and 13.7. In all three places חרב is viewed as an implement that carries out Yahweh's will in some sense.

צאן provides a strong connection between the two sections, especially when we consider that the people 'are afflicted (יענו) for there is no shepherd (רעה)'.

פקד did not look promising on its own, but the context in which it occurs has a certain amount in common with 11.16. Yahweh's anger is 'hot against *the shepherds* and he will *visit upon* (i.e. punish)[2] them; for he will *visit* (for good) *his flock*. . .' This forms a strong contrast with the shepherd that Yahweh is raising up in 11.16, who 'will not *visit* (care for) the perishing. . .'

1. *Haggai, Zechariah and Malachi*, p. 111.
2. BDB, p. 823, 3c.

It does not seem possible to link the glory of the trees of Lebanon (11.2-3) with the 'lordly price' of 11.13. We may also disregard the 'hairy mantle' of 13.4.

To sum up so far: I have not found any obvious linking of sections, as in the case of the visions in Zechariah 1–6. Nor have I been able to confirm the structural theories of Lamarche, Lacocque or Otzen. On the other hand there does seem to be a coherence to the whole section 9.1–13.9, brought out by the presence of significant ideas expressed in similar terms. It begins to look as if a connection between the humble king, the shepherd(s) and the pierced one was really intended by the person(s) responsible for the final form of Zechariah. This does not mean that the editor of chs. 1–8 was the same as that of chs. 9–14, or that the latter worked over the former. The impression is given of two separate entities with a considerable amount in common having been put together.

Contacts with 12.1–13.6

If I have been right in regarding 11.4–13.9 as a whole unit, and in seeing an intended unity with 9.1–11.3, then we should look for ways in which this is confirmed or undermined in 12.1–13.6. It appears that there *are* further links: נכה is used twice of Yahweh's judgment in 12.4 ('strike with panic/blindness'); the fire devours Judah's enemies (12.6, as in 9.4, although the figure is different in detail);[1] there is considerable stress upon the idea of 'inhabiting' in the descriptions of blessing and judgment; כרת is used of judgment of idols; 12.5 has 'God' with the personal suffix (12.8 does not fit obviously, but perhaps it recalls Exod. 4.16 and Yahweh's great deliverance through Moses); ישע is an important word used in the context of battle; the רכב and סוס make a clear connection with 9.9-10; שׂים is used each time with Yahweh as the subject in the context of making his people a particular type of instrument for punishing their enemies (warrior's sword, proud battle horse, cup of reeling, heavy stone, blazing pot/flaming torch); Yahweh will shield (יגן) them. I think we must ignore אבן and אדמה.

Looking at the later section, we find חזה and שקר in close proximity in 10.2 and 13.2-3, referring to 'diviners' (קסמים) and the (presumably false) prophet.[2]

---

1. I resist the temptation to reinstate נבב, 9.5; 12.10.
2. Lamarche connected these two sections, 10.2-3a and 13.2-6 (*Zacharie 9–14*,

In 10.9 חיה is used to express blessing for those who have been scattered: they will live, with their children. In 13.3 it is the false prophet's own 'father and mother who bore him' that say, 'You shall *not* live...'

Contacts with Zechariah 14
Here we find a number of words relating to the defeat of Yahweh's enemies and the establishing of his supremacy: חיל is used of the wealth taken away from Tyre/the nations; מלך is used to deny a king to Gaza, then to describe Jerusalem's lowly king. Chapter 14 contains references to Yahweh as king over all the earth, and (twice) the king whom the nations come to worship (vv. 9, 16-17), as well as the apparently incidental references to King Uzziah and the 'king's wine presses'. At least 14.11 mentions being inhabited as a sign of God's blessing. Horses are mentioned as suffering a plague like the one suffered by the nations who came against Jerusalem and then as having bells inscribed 'holy to Yahweh'.

יצא is used of half the city going forth into exile, of Yahweh going forth to battle on Jerusalem's behalf, and of living waters going forth from Jerusalem. These are comparable to 9.14 'his arrow will go forth' and 10.4 'every oppressor will go forth (i.e. depart)' or 'every ruler will go forth'.[1]

There are no distinctive contacts between 9.15–11.3 and ch. 14, except for חיה, which represents a different usage.

Conclusions
Taking together our results from Chapter 3 and the present chapter we seem to have the following situation.

Zech. 9.1–11.3 begins and ends with judgment for Judah's enemies. It contains a hint of salvation for them also in 9.7. As far as Judah is concerned, there will be salvation and peace. Bad leaders will be removed and their king will come נושע and צדיק.

---

pp. 54-55, 88-90, 108-109), but without noting this correspondence, and by working on different principles. In 12.1–14.21, 13.2-6 was left without a counter-part. This unit, 'Suppression of idols', then seemed to match 10.2-3a, 'Presence of idols'. I do not argue here for 10.2-3a as a separate unit.

1. See p. 183 n. 1.

Zech. 11.4–13.9 begins and ends with the questions of leaders, described as shepherds. There are some paradoxical elements, in 11.4-14 as well as in 11.15-17 and 13.7-9. It is difficult to see how the good and bad features of Yahweh's shepherd can fit together. In the middle of this there is a passage dealing with a siege of Jerusalem by the nations, ending in victory for Judah, David and Jerusalem. This leads unexpectedly into a passage about a figure who has been pierced, possibly representing Yahweh,[1] and then mourning over him, cleansing from sin and uncleanness, and the removal of false prophets.

It is as if the first unit has been turned inside out. The inner sections of 9.1–11.3, dealing with leadership, correspond to the outer sections in 11.4–13.9. The outer sections of 9.1–11.3, dealing with war and victory for Israel, correspond to the inner section of 11.4–13.9, namely 12.1–13.6.

Contacts between 9.1–11.3 and ch. 14 are found only in the early verses.

Connections between Zechariah 11.4–13.9 and the Rest of Zechariah

Verse	Word(s)	Occurrences in 11.4–13.9	Occurrences in 1.1–8.23	Occurrences in ch. 14 (verses)
Ch. 11				
4	כה אמר יהוה (צבאה)	11.4.1	chs: 1 (5×); 8 (10×) 2; 3; 6; 7 (1×)	
	אלהים*6*9	*11.4;* 12.*5,* 8; **13.9**	**6.15; 8.8, 23**	5
5	ברך*7	11.5	8.13	
6	מלך*7*9	11.6	7.1	(5×)
	נצל*3	11.6	3.2	
7	לקח*6	11.7, 10, 13, 15	6.10, 11	21
	שנים*4	11.7; 13.8	4.3, 11, 12, 14; 6.1, 13	
	אחד*3 (אחה)	11.7.##12,15, (11.8)	3.9; 4.3##.4,7; (3.9; 5.7; 8.21 [2×])	7, 9 (2×)
	קרא*1	11.7.##13,16 **13.9**	**1.4, 14, 17;** 3.10; **7.7, 13** (2×); 8.3	

9	אשה*⁵	11.9 ch. 12 (5×) (pl.)	5.7, 9	2 (pl.)
	בשר*²	11.9, 16	2.17	12
10	כרת*⁹	11.10		2
11	ידע*²	*11.11*	**2.13, 15;** 4.5, **9,**7 13; **6.15;** 7.14	
	שמר*³	11.11	3.7 (3×); 7.12	
12	עין*²	11.12, 17.##10,15; 12.4	1.1, 5, 12; 2.9; 3.10; 5 (4×); 6.1; 8.1, 8	12
	שכר*⁷	11.12.##7,13	8.10.##5,9	
	כסף*⁶	11.12, 13; 13.9	6.11	14
13	השליך*⁵	11.13.##4,15	5.8.##4,9	
	יקר	11.13.##8,10		6
14	שני*⁴	11.14	4.12; 6.2	
16	נער*²	11.16; 13.5	2.8	
	בקש*⁶	11.16; 12.9	6.7; 8.21, 22	
17	הוי*²	11.17	2.10 (2×), 11	
	ימין*³	11.17.##11,16	3.1; 4.3, 11; 6.6	

Ch. 12

1	נטה*¹	12.1	1.16	
	שמים*²	12.1	2.10; 5.9; 6.5; 8.12	
	יסד*⁴	12.1	4.9; 8.9	
	רוח*²	12.1, 10; 13.2	2.10; 4.6; 5.9; 6.5, 8; 7.12	
	קרב	12.1		1, 3
2	סבב*²	12.2, 6	2.9; 7.7	10, 14
3	אסף	12.3		2, 14
4	סוס*¹	12.4.##7,18	1.8 (2×); 6 (5×)	15, 20
5	אמץ*⁶	12.5	6.3, 7	
6	עץ*⁵	12.6	5.4	
	שמאל*⁴	12.6	4.3, 11	
	רשאון*¹	12.7	1.4; 6.2; 7.7, 12; 8.11	10
	מלאך*¹	12.8.17	chs. 1 (5×); 2 (3×); 3 (4×); 4 (3×); 5 (3×); 6 (2×)	
10	ספד*⁷	12.10 (2×), 11 (2×), 12	7.51	
11	בקע	12.11		4
12	משפחה	12 (9×)		17, 18

Ch. 13

1	חטאת	13.1		19 (2×)
3	חיה*1	13.3	1.5	8
	ילד*7	13.3.##10,21	8.5 (2×)	
4	חזה*9	13.4	10.2	
	לבש*3	13.4	3.3-5	
5	עבד*1	13.5	1.6; 2.13; 3.8	
6	אהב*7	13.6	8.17, 19	
7	פוץ*1	13.7	1.17	
8	יתר	13.8		2, 16
9	זהב*4	13.9	4.2, 12 (2×); 6.11	14
	עם*2	**13.9**	*2.15; 8.7, 8*	

Words omitted: *1ירושלם, *1יהודה, *1*9טוב, *2חבל, *1גוי, *2אש, *7אהב, *2אדמה, *1אב,
*6שלש, *2סבב, *3נתן, *1יהוה + מלאך, *1ישב.

The repetitions here are, as expected, mostly to do with the nations'
onslaught against Jerusalem. Thus we find: כרת, כסף, זהב (as spoil; as
being refined 13.9; cf. the table for 9.11–11.3 for silver), אסף (of all
nations/peoples of the earth), battle horses smitten with plague, יתר
(noun and two different *niphal* verb forms). These serve to draw
attention to the similarity between chs. 12.1 and 14.1. The link
between 13.8-9 and 14.2, 14 (זהב + כסף, יתר) is more tenuous, since
the words are used differently.

As previously, many of the words must be discounted: נשים, לקח,
ידע, יקר,[1] קרב, ראשון, חטאת, חיה. This leaves a miscellaneous collection
of words:

עין, מלך, אלהים, see above.[2]

אחד seems to be important, but its significance is hard to specify. Is
there, for example, an intended connection between the 'one day' of
14.7 and 3.9, and the 'one month' of 11.8, and/or the 'one stone' of
3.9, and even the 'one woman' of 5.7?

משפחה, is used of various families within Israel in ch. 12, and of the
earth/Egypt in 14.17-18. Egypt seems to be a representative enemy
here and in v. 19, where it is also parallel to 'all nations'.

בקע is used of the Valley of Megiddo, and the Valley of the Mount

---

1.   Despite the rarity of the words יָקַר and יְקָר the forms and meanings in 11.13
(noun and verb) and 14.6 are so different that it is impossible to connect them. In
addition the latter text is uncertain.

2.   See Otzen, *Studien*, pp. 169-72. He refers to G. Grützmacher, *Ursprung der
in Zach. 9–14 vorliegenden Profetien* (Heidelberg, 1892).

of Olives. The former is most obviously linked with the death of Josiah, killed in the plain of Megiddo, and for whom laments were uttered at the time of the Chronicler. This might then be linked with the 'martyr' of 12.10.[1]

The 'Mount of Olives', east of Mount Zion,[2] does not occur elsewhere in the OT. Perhaps we should make some connection with the olive trees of ch. 4. There are suggestive allusions here, but nothing that we can say with any certainty. I shall defer further discussion until after consideration of Zechariah 14.

Connections between Zechariah 14 and the Rest of Zechariah

Verse	Word	References in ch. 14	References in chs. 1–8
1	חלק	1	2.16
	שלל	1	2.12, 13
2	גולה	2	6.10
4	אמר	4, 12	1.8, 10, 11; 3 (6×); 4.14
	מזרח	4	8.7
	מוש	4	3.9
	צפון	4	2.10; 6.6, 8 (2×)
	נגב	4, 10	7.7
5	נוס	5.##1,10,12	2.10
	נגע	5	2.12 (2×)
	מפני	5	2.17
	אלהים	5	6.15; 8.8, 23
	קדש	5	2.16, 17; 8.3
7	ידע	7	2.13, 15; 4.5, 9, 13; 6.15; 7.14
9	ארץ + כל	9, 10	1.11, 4.10, 14 (+ אדון); 5.3, 6; 6.5 (+ אדון)
10	שער	10.##12,16,19	8.16
12	בשר	12	2.17
	לשון	12	8.23
13	החזיק	13	8.23 (2×)
14	זהב	14	6.11
	כסף	14	6.11

---

1. Cf. Ezek. 11.23 (BDB has 11.33 wrongly).

2. 2 Sam. 15.30 mentions the מעלה הזיתים, which David ascended weeping as he fled from Absalom; Ezek. 11.23 mentions the 'mountain that is on the east of the city'.

Words omitted: איש, כל הארץ אדון*4, אחד*3, אחר*2, אם, אשה*5, בגד*3, בהמה*2,
ירושלם*2, יצא*2, יום, יד, יד*2, חלק*, חיה*1, חיה*7, חזק*7, זיח*4, זיח*4, הר*4, גם*1, גוי*1, גדל*1, בית*1, בוא*1,
פה*2, עם*1, עיר*1, עוד, עד, סוס*1, סוס*2, סבב*7, מלך*2, לקח*6, לפני, יהודה*1, ישב*1 +
תחת*2, שלל*1, ראשון*1, ראש*2, רב*1, קרא*2, קדש.

In addition I have found contacts with the previous major sections in that:

1. Zech. 12.1-9 and 14.1-15 both present a situation where Israel is under attack by the nations, but is victorious through the intervention of Yahweh.
2. The climax of ch. 14 is that there will no longer be a כנעני in the Temple. If this is read in ch. 11, then a firm link is established, and 14.21 implies also a purified leadership.

I will try to set out the overall pattern of chs. 9–14, as it has emerged.

9

	1-8	Judgment for Judah's enemies (with a hint of salvation)
	9-10	Judah's righteous, saved, humble king comes; peace is established
	11-17	Judgment for enemies and salvation for Judah/Ephraim
10		
	1-5	Further concern about leadership: judgment of corrupt leaders; provision of true leadership (?)
	6-12	Strengthening for Judah/Joseph/Ephraim (with mention of judgment for enemies)
11		
	1-3	Judgment on ? (pride, shepherds, nations?)
	4-14	Judgment against bad leaders and stubborn people
	15-17	Judgment of a leader
12		
	1-9	Judgment for Judah's/Jerusalem's enemies: victory in battle
	10-14	The pierced one. Yahweh's spirit of compassion brings mourning
13 1		Cleansing 'on that day'
	2-6	Idols and false prophets are removed
	7-9	Judgment of 'my shepherd' brings refining and fulfilment of the promise: Yahweh their God etc.
14		
	1-15	Judgment for Judah's/Jerusalem's enemies: destroyed in battle by God's intervention
		Eschatological phenomena; plagues for Yahweh's enemies
	16-21	Blessing for the nations: they come to Jerusalem for the feast of booths (or else they suffer plagues)
		Jerusalem is purified ('holy to Yahweh')

I do not think it is possible to reduce this to a neat diagram without distorting the picture (which, hopefully, at present is not prejudiced by preconceived ideas about structure). It is clear that there is a unity about the whole, despite the wide variety of materials from which this is composed. It seems likely that this is the case because the writers/editors had certain interlocking concerns: those that are listed in the *Summary of Results* below (a' to g') which can probably be traced back to those of Zechariah himself and his contemporaries.

The structure that does appear may be described in simplified terms as a sort of multi-layer sandwich, where the 'bread' consists of passages concerning the enemies of Judah and Jerusalem: it contains varying amounts of judgment and/or salvation for the enemies and for Judah/Jerusalem. The climax is that the nations are given the same opportunity to worship Yahweh as Judah's. The 'filling' concerns the question of leadership. Here there are also variations in content: the right leader is to be installed and bad leaders purged; cleansing is to be achieved somehow in connection with God's representative.[1]

Contacts between Zechariah 1–8 and 9–14 according to Mason

There are at least 34 places where Mason, in his thesis of 1973, comments upon similarities between different parts of the book of Zechariah. They are as follows.[2]

On 9.1–8

1. Zech. 9.1 and 6.8; מנוחתו and הניחו (9.1; 6.8), noting the ambiguity in both passages (pp. 4-6).

2. Zech. 9.1-8 and 6.1-8.

---

1. There is no generally agreed interpretation of 12.10. Traditionally Christian exegetes have taken it to refer to the messiah, but many argue (like Mitchell, *Haggai, Zechariah, Malachi and Jonah,* p. 330) that the pierced figure belongs to past history, and that this rules out a messianic interpretation. It is difficult to be sure of the chronology intended in this section of Zechariah, where so much is mysterious and obscure. In view of the way that the book holds together, and the similarities with the 'smitten shepherd', it seems to me that the pierced one must be, in *some* sense, Yahweh's representative, whether past, present or future. See Mason, *Zechariah 9–14*, pp. 233-40, for a discussion of the various views.

2. The fullest presentation of Mason's views is in the thesis. Since this is still unpublished, it seems worthwhile to present what he says in some detail.

The first (6.1-8) is followed immediately by a promise of the completion of the Temple and the institution of a divinely-ordained leadership. Zech. 9.1-8 also culminates in a promise that Yahweh will again encamp at his house and offer the protection of the divine presence and leadership of his people. Both thus have been *editorially arranged* [emphasis mine] so that they lead towards a Zion-centred tradition. It is possible, then, that in this opening oracle, themes of proto-Zechariah's teaching are being taken up and made the basis for the expression of eschatological hope (p. 11).

3. Zech. 9.3 and 10.5, כטים חוצות, used as a term of contempt in the latter, as in Mic. 7.10 (and also Ps. 18.42 = 2 Sam. 22.43) (p. 19).

4. 'Spiritual renewal' for foreigner and home-born alike; cf. Philistia in 9.6-7, Zech. 3, 5. '...breadth of vision and universalist thought somewhat akin to the circles in which the final form of the oracles of Zech. 1–8 took shape' (pp. 26-27).

5. Zech. 9.8 mentions 'the house' of Yahweh. The Targum renders חניתי as it does 2.14, where 'in my holy house' is also added. The Targum also adds 'like a wall of fire' based on 2.9 (p. 29).

6. Zech. 9.8, מצבה. He notes Jansma (who thinks that the pointing of MT preserves two readings: ה/מצבא, and may 'continuate' a third variant in the 'apparently redundant' מעבר ומשב),[1] and Sæbø,[2] who relates מצבה and מעבר ומשב, seen respectively as two variants, to:

    a.   Zech. 1.16-17, in which the 'house' is also central, and which also contains the word עוד.

    b.   Zech. 7.14 which has been noted above (p. 30).

7. Zech. 9.8 rounds off vv. 1-7

> with the promise that God will protect his people, cleansed and forgiven, stripped of all false self-reliance and cultic apostasy... from the Temple... This echoes the themes of the divine return to Jerusalem and protection of it, the cleansing and renewing of the people, and the making of the Temple a centre for all, Israelite and foreign alike, to come and worship, themes, all of which, are prominent in proto-Zechariah (pp. 30-31).

8. בעיני. Sæbø noted how much emphasis there is on the 'eye' of Yahweh in Zechariah 1–8.[3]

---

1.   *Zechariah 9–14*, pp. 69-70.
2.   'Die deuterosacharjanische Frage', pp. 159-61.
3.   'Die deuterosacharjanische Frage', p. 161; also see above, pp. 254-57.

On 9.9-10

9. An independent oracle but

> its editorial placing here can hardly have been accidental. . . a general resemblance to the pattern and emphases of proto-Zechariah may be recalled.
>
> In both, the promise of the new age, with the role of the Temple central to the fulfilment, leads on to the thought of the agent of the rule of God, and, in both, certain features of royalty are emphasised. Have these emphases of proto-Zechariah influenced the arrangement of oracles here, and, if so, does it mean that the promises of Zechariah concerning the Temple and the leadership are being reinterpreted in a new situation and their fulfilment announced as being at hand? (pp. 36-38).

10. Zech. 9.9; 2.14. Points of contact: the context of judgment against the 'nations' which have plundered and oppressed his people; the contrast of rejoicing to former servitude; many nations will join themselves to Yahweh (cf. also Zeph. 3.14) (pp. 39-45; cf. also pp. 59-60, 77).

On 9.11-17

11. Zech. 9.12; 2.10-13. Refers to Sæbø's espousal of R. Bach's suggestion that 9.12 belongs to a literary type 'invitation to flight'[1] (p. 67).

12. Zech. 9.16; cf. references to stones and crowns in Zechariah 1–8. The crowns may speak of the joint rule of high priest and 'civil' governor in the restored community. 'Is it possible that in this verse there is the thought that the promise of the stone and the crowns, particularly in proto-Zechariah, is to be fulfilled in the life of the community?' This would mean that 'the community are to become what Joshua and Zerubbabel had been' (pp. 85-88).

On 10.1-2

13. Rain as a symbol of God's life-giving activity and presence, as in many earlier prophecies, including Zech. 8.9-13 (p. 93).

14. Points to the moral to be drawn from history as Zech. 1.4 (p. 97).

---

1. Sæbø, 'Die deuterosacharjanische Frage', p. 191; R. Bach, *Die Aufforderungen zur Flucht und zum Kampf in alttestamentlichen Prophetenspruch* (WMANT, 9; Neukirchen–Vluyn: Neukirchener Verlag, 1962), p. 19.

15. Position and pastoral purpose afford another strong link with Zechariah. 1–8, cf. 1.2-6, 16; 2.9, 14-16; 3.7; 6.15b; 7.8-13; 8.16-17, 21-22 (pp. 98-100).

On 10.3-12 + 11.1-3

16. Zech. 10.6 'affords a remarkable reversal of the judgment of Zech. 7.13' (pp. 123-24).

17. Zech. 10.7 cf. 8.5 (children[/sons] rejoicing/playing) (p. 124).

18. Zech. 10.9 זרע either means 'scatter' here only, or should be emended to זרה. The latter might be supported by 2.4 ('horns scattered Israel') and 7.9-14 (סער) (pp. 127-28).

19. 'A continued link with the thought of proto-Zechariah is apparent in the promise of divinely appointed leadership, the destruction by the power of Yahweh of those who opposed his people, perhaps the avenging horsemen who execute Yahweh's will, the joy of the returning exiles extending even to their children, the fertility of the land with its vineyards, the reversal of the "scattering" and the picture of the restored community "walking" in the name of Yahweh (v. 12, cf. 8.21)' (p. 131).

On 11.4-17

20. There is general similarity between this and the 'Night Visions', including first person form, most marked with 6.9-14 (which is not actually a 'night vision'). There is no need to accept Sæbo's suggestion that Zechariah was the one who carried out the action recorded in 11.4-17 (pp. 138-39).

21. The prophet's view of the official cultus is in line with earlier prophecy, and in particular, proto-Zechariah, for example 7.8-10 'on which 11.4-5 might almost be a comment' (pp. 148-49).

22. Was some symbolic act behind throwing the thirty pieces of silver into the smelting furnace (so LXX, χωνευτήριον)? This suggestion, though tentative, is supported by 13.7-9 and Ezek. 22.17-22, and would be in line with Zechariah 3 and 5.1-4; cf. 6.9-14 (pp. 163-64).

On 13.7-9

23. עמיתי, 13.7, 'by its rarity, is meant to carry special emphasis. For elsewhere in the Old Testament it occurs only in the legal sections of Leviticus'. It is used especially of the way Israelites should treat each other and recalls chs. 7–8 (pp. 174-75).

24. Hos. 2.25, Ezek. 37.23, Zech. 8.8, 13.8 represents a line of tradition in which a remnant is purified and enters into a new relationship with God (pp. 185-86).[1]

On 12.1–13.6

25. Prediction of victory against the nations is found (especially in Ezek. 38–39 etc. and in proto-Zechariah in 1.14, 2.4, 8, 10-13, 16 (pp. 198-99).

26. Promises of Zechariah 1–8 were seen to be only partially fulfilled and reinterpreted in the new situation. Many features of VV1-4 are seen in Zechariah 12ff. For example, Jerusalem is the centre of the action; the divine fire has a part to play (2.9; 12.6); Yahweh is a shield (2.9; 12.8); there is a close connection between outward victory and inward cleansing (3; 5; 12.10; 13.6); restored leadership plays a vital part (3; 4.6ff; 12.8 [house of David 'like God']). (He also mentions the penitence of the whole community, apparently in connection with restored leadership, 12.10ff.) (pp. 202-206).

27. סַף can mean 'threshold' or 'sill' as well as 'goblet' or 'basin' and is used especially of the Temple. The use of this term in 12.2, 'cup of reeling', may evoke the Temple and the idea of Yahweh being in the midst of his people, and thus connect again with proto-Zechariah (p. 209).

28. Isa. 28.16 'receives some re-interpretation' in Zech. 3.9 and 4.7-10. The figures in 12.2-3 are not arbitrarily chosen, and do not refer primarily to Greek sports, but are the conscious reinterpretation and reapplication of earlier prophetic motifs' (pp. 211-12).

29. רוּחַ חֵן וְתַחֲנוּנִים, 12.10, recalls 4.7, חֵן חֵן לָהּ. Both signify the favour of God. It is best to take רוּחַ to mean *the* Spirit of God, rather than a human disposition (pp. 231-34).

30. דקר in both 12.10 and 13.3 cannot be co-incidental (pp. 251-52).

On 14

31. Jerusalem is to be judged and spoil taken, a dramatic reversal of the promise of 2.12 (שָׁלָל to become שְׁלָלִים) (pp. 257-58).

---

1.   Note that he treats the shepherd of 13.7-9 as bad, and as belonging with 11.15-17 (Mason, *Zechariah 9–14*, pp. 187-88), but 'this does not detract in general from its connection with 12.1–13.6'.

32. 'The picture of the idyllic prosperity of the land consorts well with Zech. 3.10 and ch. 8, but nothing akin to the eagerness associated with the building of he Temple of those chapters is found here.' There is also no mention of the messianic hopes that were attached to Zerubbabel, nor the 'enthusiasm that attached to Joshua as the second in a dyarchy' (pp. 277-78).

33. The security of Jerusalem expressed in 14.11 echoes 12.6, but also takes up another theme of proto-Zechariah: 2.9; 8.3ff. (which itself repeats the theme of Ezek. 28.26) (p. 282).

34. Ritual emphasis of the final verses is still within the influence of proto-Zechariah (3; 5; 6.13ff.; 8.1ff., 18-19) (pp. 289-90).

Conclusion

There is strong continuity between Zechariah 1–8 and 9–14 as is seen in: the centrality of Zion; God's deliverance and protection and his presence within; divine provision of leadership as a sign of the new age; cleansing of the community to enable it to fulfil its mediatorial role; the note of universalism. The greatest difference is in the nature of the leadership that Yahweh will provide: a tendency towards a greater 'collectivization' or 'democratization' of the hope (pp. 306-307).

Relevance to my own Study

Mason's task was very different from my own: he set out to investigate signs of continuity between proto- and Deutero-Zechariah; I have sought signs of a writer's intention to indicate connections between different parts of the book. The criteria required, have therefore been more stringent than those of Mason. For example, he has noted similarity of themes or ideas (cf. nos. 2, 4, 7, 9-10, 13-15, 19, 21, 23-25, much of 26, 27-28, 31-34), whereas I have not regarded this as a sufficiently strong marker. Examination of the instances noted by Mason reveals that the ideas and themes are almost always expressed differently. This confirms my conclusion that there has been no overall editorial reshaping of Zechariah.

There are, in my opinion, a few places where Mason has identified quite a strong connection between Zechariah 1–8 and 9–14, for example no. 16. How did I miss this, and was it a serious mistake? It is easy to answer the first question: the words used in 7.13 and 10.6 are different: '...they called and I would not *hear*', 'I will *answer* them'. I do not think this was a serious omission, for if the later writer had intended his readers to see a connection, he would probably have used a stronger indicator. This would have been spotted by my method if: (1) I had extended the search to include recognized word pairs; and (2) the words שמע and ענה happened to be such a pair.[1] A similar situation exists for no. 11: I did not connect 'flee' in 2.10 (// נמלט) with 9.12 (although I examined and rejected a possible link with 14.5).

Several of Mason's suggestions are tentative (e.g. nos. 1, 5, 12, 18, 22), and are not, therefore, suitable for the purpose of this study.

The fact that כסית חוצות (no. 3) occurs as a phrase elsewhere in the Hebrew Bible reduces (but does not remove) its significance as a marker of structure. This reminds us that, not only words, but phrases must be evaluated in terms of their distinctiveness.

On the other hand, it is probable that some of the repeated words which we have examined might be of interest to Mason if he ever publishes a revised form of the thesis. The clearest example is probably 2.15, 8.8, 13.9.[2]

Summary of Results

There have been no great surprises in this chapter. The indications noticed in Chapter 3 are confirmed: there is clear evidence of a unified editing of the whole of chs. 1–8, with a concern to emphasize certain important themes. I might mention:

a.   Yahweh's anger with 'the fathers' and the judgment that followed.

b.   Yahweh's anger now transferred to the nations (although they started out in accordance with his intentions), and his compassion for Judah and Jerusalem.

c.   Yahweh's intention, therefore, to dwell in the midst of *his people* in Jerusalem again, and to be their God.

d.   The concern that people should know that Yahweh has sent a messenger to them.

e.   The provision of harmonious civil and religious leadership authorized by Yahweh.

---

1.   In fact these words do not seem to form a recognized word pair. The characteristic pairing with 'answer' is 'call' or 'cry' (most frequently קרע). But קרע is also frequently found with שמע. There is room for further investigation here.

2.   *Zechariah 9–14*, pp. 99-100, 199, 201, 259.

f. The purifying of the Yahweh's people, and their future obedience.

g. The eventual blessing of peoples outside Judah, who will join themselves to Yahweh/come to entreat his favour (2.15; 8.20-23).

In chs. 9–14 we have seen similar concerns, although they are expressed differently:

a'. Yahweh's 'impatience' with 'the flock' and his judgment (partly expressed in the attack by the nations, and partly somehow related to his provision of bad leaders).

b'. Yahweh's giving victory to Judah and Jerusalem (and David), over the nations (although they succeed at first).

c'. Yahweh's promise to be their God (13.9; cf. 10.6; 12.5), worshipped in Jerusalem.

d'. The implicit concern that the people should recognize God's word (11.11, cf. the staffs and the pieces of silver?; 12.5; cf. 10.1-2).

e'. The provision of a 'humble and righteous' king/shepherd (9.9-10; 10.2-4; 11?).

f'. The purifying of the people from all uncleanness, somehow related to the cursing/piercing of an individual, who belongs to but is treated with hostility by Yahweh, yet he achieves Yahweh's purposes by being judged; also the purifying of the temple (14.21).

g'. The eventual (only ch. 14) blessing of nations (including Egypt) outside Judah, who will come to worship Yahweh in Jerusalem (14.16-21).

Put like this, it is easy to see why scholars have argued for both continuity and discontinuity between Zechariah 1–8 and 9–14. The connections are not strong enough to establish overall (and therefore long-range) structuring.[1]

---

1. It is interesting to compare the five headings that Mason gives in order to compare and contrast the main concerns of Zech. 1–8 and 9–14 ('Some Echoes of the Preaching in the Second Temple? Tradition Elements in Zechariah 1–8', *ZAW* 88 [1976], pp. 227-38): prominence of the Zion tradition; cleansing of the community; universalism; appeal to earlier prophets; provision of leadership as a sign of the new

The overall structure of Zechariah 1–8 may be expressed in simplified, but not distorted fashion as follows:

1.1-6   Introduction. Historical reasons for the present disaster; assurance that the situation has changed; appeal to return to Yahweh.
          Report that the people did turn.

1.7–6.15 Series of night visions with attached oracles.
          V1   Horses patrol the earth: nations at ease
          V2   Horns that scattered Jerusalem to be punished
          V3   Jerusalem inhabited without walls
          V4   Joshua the high priest reclothed
          V5   Two anointed: (Joshua) and Zerubbabel
          V6   Scroll/curse going forth against thief etc.
          V7   Ephah and woman: wickedness removed far away
          V8   Horses and chariots patrol the earth: God's Spirit at rest

Visions 1 and 8 are obviously similar, but the situation changes from Yahweh's being angry with the nations, to his being at rest. It may be assumed from the contrast and from the content of the intervening material that the nations have been dealt with, and Judah and Jerusalem are cleansed and protected.

The two pairs of visions 2-3 and 6-7 match each other. Visions 2 and 3 are linked together in a number of ways: their form is similar and both focus on Jerusalem. The oracle 2.10-17 further emphasizes their unity and ties them to V1 with the phrase 'again choose Jerusalem'. It also introduces new elements which become important over the whole of chs. 1–8:

1. 'You will know that Yahweh of hosts has sent me...' (+ 4.9; 6.15)

2. Many nations will join themselves to Yahweh (8.20-23; cf. 6.15a).

3. Yahweh will dwell in the midst of his people and be their God (8.3, 8).

Visions 4 and 5 occupy the central position and, in their present form at least, present a divinely authorized dyarchy of Joshua the high priest, and Zerubbabel/'Branch' who rebuilds the Temple and,

age. For examples of possible connections between sections, see above, pp. 222, 246, 253, 256, 259, 269.

according to 6.13, bears royal honour. They stand before the Lord of the whole earth.

Visions 6-7 belong together: both speak of 'going forth' and deal with the removal of evil from the land. They have contacts with the other pair of visions, 2-3, both together and separately (V2 // V7; V3 // V6); they also have formal links with the last vision.[1]

The last vision rounds off the whole, forming its own climax to the series as it describes the accomplishment of God's purposes: the Lord of the whole earth.[2]

Zech. 6.9-15 is an account of a prophetic word and action, which picks up some of the most important themes mentioned previously: the two leaders; the Temple and regathering of people to rebuild it; and 'you shall know that Yahweh of hosts has sent me to you'. Verse 15b refers back to 1.2-6 (esp. v. 4).[3]

Zech. 7–8 is constructed as a large chiasmus, with the promise mentioned above at the centre (8.8). It refers to themes introduced in 1.1-6, giving an exhortation to obey, a promise for Jerusalem and Judah, and a wider promise (based on the visit of people from Bethel to 'entreat the favour of Yahweh') to many peoples.[4]

This coherent whole is marked out for the reader or hearer by the use of key words and phrases that connect corresponding sections together. Despite the fact that there are passages where it is impossible to be sure what the intended meaning is in detail, the result is a very pleasing and powerful unity.

Within Zechariah. 9–14 we have seen evidence of continuity in that the same basic themes are found throughout, in an alternating pattern. There is no possibility, as far as I can see, of presenting an exact pattern, such as those offered by Lamarche, Lacocque and others. Nevertheless, there do seem to be deliberate attempts to connect different sections with each other. For example, we noted links between the units making up 9.1–11.3, so as to emphasize the main themes of judgment/salvation for Judah/the nations, and in particular the battle

---

1. Pp. 251-53.
2. Pp. 142-43, 245-46, 264.
3. Pp. 147-48, 245-46, 261-63, 268.
4. P. 163; cf. p. 160.

scenes of Zechariah 12 and 14; God's dwelling in the midst of his people; and the suffering of Yahweh's representative[1] (see pp. 289-90 above).

It remains for me to try to draw together my conclusions for the complete study.

---

1.   Pp. 176-77, 193-94, 289-90.

Chapter 5

CONCLUSIONS

The two parts of this study hang together. In the first part I showed that many of the structural studies undertaken in current scholarship are carried out with insufficient regard for academic rigour. The strict criteria advocated by a number of scholars are almost universally ignored. I suggested that one significant way of minimizing the subjective element in structural studies would be to examine all occurrences of repeated words. I showed beyond reasonable doubt that, if I had taken notice of these criteria, I should not have been able to present 'Isaiah 67' as a well-structured whole.

I also suggested that the units to be investigated should be decided without regard to structural considerations, and as far as possible, conform to the results agreed by mainline biblical scholarship.

Words were to be examined for their distinctiveness and potential for acting as markers for the literary structure of a text, and this was done without regard for the particular structure of the unit under consideration. I showed that many studies today make use of very common words.[1]

I noted the tendency for scholars to choose convenient labels for the sub-sections of a unit, so that an apparent regularity of structure was achieved which did not stand up to close scrutiny.[2] I resolved to avoid subjective labelling, and to rely on the content of the unit in question as explicitly stated in its own words.

It was easy to show that the application of these criteria would have removed much of the subjective element in current studies. It seemed likely that scholars studying the same text would no longer be able to produce conflicting results.[3]

1. P. 32 and n. 2; pp. 45, 48.
2. See, e.g., pp. 43-44, 50, 169-71, 180, 181-82, 190-91, 195-97.
3. Pp. 59-61.

However, in order to test the theory it was necessary to apply it rigorously to a self-contained section of the OT. I chose the book of Zechariah, because it gave scope for examining two well-defined and established parts to the book, their internal coherence and their relationship to each other; it has been subjected to a certain amount of structural investigation previously, especially chs. 9–14,[1] and it seemed an interesting project to compare the results already achieved with my own; it seemed likely that there might actually be some 'planned structures' in Zechariah, for example, the arrangement of the visions in chs. 1–6; and possibly a more or less elaborate arrangement of units in 9-14. If nothing could be proved we could at least have the satisfaction of having interacted with Lamarche, Lacocque and Otzen.[2]

In fact we discovered some surprising results. The evidence for editorial structuring in chs. 1–8 was very strong, in individual small units,[3] in the rather large unit of chs. 7–8, and in the arrangement of units in relation to each other.[4] I was not primarily interested in doing redaction criticism, but had noted certain passages as probably due to an editor or editors.[5] The careful structuring of the text seemed to stem from both the original writer *and* the editorial reworking. I noted variations in the way that the structuring was done, but did not theorize about whether this implied more than one hand.[6]

In looking at Zechariah 9–14, we again discovered evidence of a concern for structure. This, however, was noticeably different from the work done in chs. 1–8. The basic material was more varied; the structuring was not so precise; connections were made, not simply between two sections, but between three or more.[7]

For example, connections were found between 10.3-5 and 11, and 9.1-8 and 9–10 (and 13). It would be easy, by selective choice of marker words (some of them quite impressive!), to argue for a chiastic structure:[8]

---

1. Especially by Lamarche; also Lacocque and Otzen.
2. See esp. pp. 167-68, 170-72, 182-83, 191-92, 211-12, 215-16, 220-23, 228-32.
3. E.g. Zech. 1.1-6 + 7-17; 2.5-9 + 10-17.
4. E.g. Zech. 1 with 6 and 7–8; Zech. 2.1-9 with 5.1-11 (and 6.1-8).
5. See the summary at the end of Chapter 2.
6. Cf. e.g. Zech. 1.1-6; 2.1-4; 3.1-7, 8-10; 4.1-14.
7. Pp. 192-95.
8. See the table on p. 193.

9.1-8   10.6-12
    9.9-10   10.3-5
    9.11–10.2

However, we have seen that this does not represent the connections that actually exist in the text, nor does it adequately describe the movement of this overall section. Consequently, I was unable to present a neat diagram of the structure.

In considering the relation between Zechariah 1–8 and 9–14, we have found almost nothing that would argue for a unified editing of the book, let alone common authorship. There *are* similarities of theme, theology and language, but these seem to be adequately explained on the basis of a continuing tradition which was well versed in the prophet's work and in the older traditions of Israel that he also knew.[1]

In asking whether the results of this study were consonant with those of other scholars working in the same field some unexpected points of contact were found (e.g. both Hanson and Willi-Plein, in very different ways, draw attention to connections between chs. 9 and 10). We did not find anything startlingly out of line with OT scholarship, and it seems probable that this sort of study could be combined with more traditional approaches and methods to produce something new and substantial.

In relation to 'structural studies', my conclusion is that, although most of the work considered is lacking in rigour and has not taken to heart the warnings given by various writers, there is every reason to supppose that the aims of scholars working in this area are valid and promise much in the future. If they are to be accepted by the majority of scholars, they need consciously to build on the results of mainline biblical scholarship. In the words of Muilenburg, they need to be 'form criticism and beyond' (and all that preceded form criticism). They also need to take notice of the observations listed in Chapter 1 above.

In applying my method to the book of Zechariah, I found that certain patterns appeared without any effort on my part.[2] Some passages could be set out in different ways, and it was difficult to state *precisely*

---

1. See the section on Mason's thesis in Chapter 4 above.
2. E.g. 1.1-6; 3.1-7, 8-10; 4.1-6aα + 10aβ-14; 5.5-11; the overall structure of chs. 7–8.

what the author/editor's intention was. Nevertheless, the movement and logic of the passage in question could be seen quite clearly.[1] Some passages did not seem to have any clear structure,[2] and although this was disappointing, it does show that the method adopted will not allow all passages to be pressed into some sort of apparently logical pattern.

It is likely that I have *underestimated* the intentions, and the artistry of the authors/editors of the book of Zechariah; and also that some of the patterns discovered by other scholars, that I have regarded as doubtful, may actually have been intended by the writers of the passages in question. This is to be expected, since I have concentrated on trying to discover patterns that could be *shown* to be 'intended', that is they reflect the conscious or even unconscious purposes of the writer. Occasionally, I made suggestions about possibilities that could not be proved or shown to be probable.[3]

I hope that the change already seen in biblical commentaries will continue, and that eventually all commentators will take seriously the overall purpose and literary methods of the authors/editors in question, and that all will attempt to apply more rigorous tests to the structures that they seem to discern.[4] There is scope for and promise of much greater biblical understanding.

1. E.g. 2.1-4; 2.5-17; 6.1-8; 9.1–11.3.
2. E.g. 4.6aβ-7; 5.1-4; 9.1-8.
3. E.g. on 6.9-15, in Chapter 3.
4. In other words I hope for commentaries that will give the factual evidence and sound, considered comment that Rudolph does, and add more imaginative suggestions, such as those of Watts in his commentary on Isaiah, but with more critical evaluation.

BIBLIOGRAPHY

1. Works on Zechariah

Ackroyd, P.R., *Exile and Restoration* (London: SCM Press, 1968).

—'Haggai/Zechariah', in *Peake's Commentary on the Bible* (ed. M. Black and H.H. Rowley; London: Nelson, 1962).

Amsler, S., 'Zacharie et l'origine de l'apocalyptique', in *Congress Volume, Uppsala* (VTSup, 22; Leiden: Brill, 1971), pp. 227-31.

Amsler, S., A. Lacocque, and R. Vuilleumier, *Commentaire de l'Ancien Testament. XI.c. Aggé, Zacharie 1-8, Zacharie 9-14, Malachie* (Neuchâtel: Delachaux & Niestlé, 1981).

Baldwin, J.G., *Haggai, Zechariah, Malachi* (London: Tyndale Press, 1972).

Barker, K.L., 'Zechariah', in *The Expositor's Bible Commentary* (ed. F.E. Gaebelein; Grand Rapids: Zondervan, 1985), VII, pp. 595-697.

Barnes, W.E., *Haggai, Zechariah, Malachi* (Cambridge: Cambridge University Press, 1934).

Beuken, W.A.M., *Haggai-Sacharja 1-8* (Assen: Van Gorcum, 1967).

Beyse, K.-M., *Serubbabel und die Königserwartungen der Propheten Haggai und Sacharja* (Stuttgart: Calwer Verlag, 1972).

Chary, T., *Les prophètes et le culte à partir de l'exil* (Paris: Desclée, 1954).

Coggins, R.J., *Haggai, Zechariah, Malachi* (Sheffield: JSOT Press, 1987).

Coggins, R., A. Phillips and M. Knibb (eds.), *Israel's Prophetic Tradition: Essays in Honour of Peter Ackroyd* (Cambridge: Cambridge University Press, 1982).

Cashdan, E., 'Zechariah', in *The Twelve Prophets* (ed. A. Cohen; London: Soncino, 1957).

Craigie, P.C., *Twelve Prophets*, II (Edinburgh: St Andrew's Press, 1985).

Dahood, M., 'Zacharia 9.1, *ÊN 'ĀDĀM*', *CBQ* 25 (1963), pp. 123-24.

Delcor, M., 'Les allusions à Alexandre le grand dans Zacharie 9.1-9', *VT* 1 (1951), pp. 110-24.

—'Deux passages difficiles: Zech. 12.11; 11.13', *VT* 3 (1953), pp. 67-77.

—'Le trésor de la maison de Yahweh des origines à l'exil', *VT* 12 (1962), pp. 353-77.

Dentan, R.C., and J.T. Cleland, 'Zechariah 9-14', in *The Interpreter's Bible*, VI (ed. G.A. Buttrick; Nashville: Abingdon Press, 1956), pp. 1089-114.

Driver, G.R., 'Linguistic and Textual Problems: Minor Prophets', *JTS* 39 (1938), pp. 393-405.

Driver, S.R., *The Minor Prophets: Nahum, Habakkuk, Zephaniah, Haggai, Zechariah, Malachi* (The Century Bible; Edinburgh: T.C. & E.C. Jack, 1906).

Emerton, J.A., Review of *Zacharie 9-14: Structure littéraire et messianisme*, by P. Lamarche, *JTS* 14 (1963), pp. 113-16.

Finlay, T.J., 'The Sheep Merchants of Zechariah 11', *GTJ* 3 (1982), pp. 51-65.

Gaide, G., *Jérusalem, voici ton roi: Commentaire de Zacharie 9-14* (Lectio Divina, 49; Paris: Cerf, 1968).

Good, R.M., 'Zechariah's Second Night Vision (Zech. 2.1-4)', *Bib* 63 (1982), pp. 56-59.

Halpern, B., 'The Ritual Background of Zechariah's Temple Song', *CBQ* 40 (1978), pp. 167-90.

Hanson, P.D., *The Dawn of Apocalyptic* (Philadelphia: Fortress Press, 1975).

—'Old Testament Apocalyptic Re-Examined', *Int* 25 (1971), pp. 454-79; reprinted in *Visionaries and their Apocalypses* (ed. P.D. Hanson; Philadelphia: Fortress Press, 1938), pp. 37-60.

Hoftijzer, J., 'A propos d'une interprétation récente de deux passages difficiles: Zech. 12.11; 11.13', *VT* 3 (1953), pp. 407-409.

Honeyman, A.M., 'Hebrew *sp* "basin, goblet"', *JTS* 37 (1936), pp. 56-59.

Hoonacker, A. van, *Les douze petits prophètes* (Paris: Gabalda, 1908).

Jansma, A.T., *An Inquiry into the Hebrew Text and the Ancient Versions of Zechariah 9–14* (Leiden: Brill, 1949).

Jeremias, C., *Die Nachtgesichte des Sacharja: Untersuchungen zu ihrer Stellung im Zusammenhang der Visionsberichte im Alten Testament und zu ihrem Bildmaterial* (Göttingen: Vandenhoeck & Ruprecht, 1977).

Jones, D.R., 'A Fresh Interpretation of Zechariah 9–11', *VT* 12 (1962), pp. 241-59.

—*Haggai, Zechariah and Malachi* (London: SCM Press, 1962).

Keil, C.F., *The Twelve Minor Prophets*, II (Edinburgh: T. & T. Clark, 1871).

Kline, M.G., 'The Structure of the Book of Zechariah', *JETS* 34 (1991), pp. 179-93.

Kraeling, E., 'The Historical Situation in Zechariah 9.1–10', *AJSL* 41 (1924), pp. 24-33.

Lamarche, P., *Zacharie 9–14: Structure littéraire et messianisme* (Paris: Gabalda, 1961).

Leupold, H.C., *An Exposition of the Book of Zechariah* (Grand Rapids: Baker, 1965).

Lipiński, E., 'Recherches sur le livre de Zacharie', *VT* 20 (1970), pp. 25-55.

Lutz, H.-M., *Jahwe, Jerusalem und die Völker* (Neukirchen–Vluyn: Neukirchener Verlag, 1968).

McCaul, A., *Rabbi David Kimchi's Commentary on the Prophecies of Zechariah* (James Duncan, 1837).

Mason, R., *The Books of Haggai, Zechariah and Malachi* (Cambridge: Cambridge University Press, 1977).

—'The Purpose of the Editorial Framework of the Book of Haggai', *VT* 27 (1976), pp. 227-38.

—'Some Echoes of the Preaching in the Second Temple? Tradition Elements in Zechariah 1–8', *ZAW* 96 (1984), pp. 221-35.

—'The Use of Earlier Biblical Material in Zechariah 9–14: A Study of Inner Biblical Exegesis' (dissertation, King's College, London, 1973).

Meyers, C.L., and E.M. Meyers, *Haggai, Zechariah 1–8* (AB; Garden City, NY: Doubleday, 1987).

Mitchell, H.G., J.M.P. Smith and J.A. Bewer, *Haggai, Zechariah, Malachi and Jonah* (ICC; Edinburgh: T. & T. Clark, 1912).

Mittman, S., 'Die Einheit von Sacharja 8.1-8', in W. Claasen (ed.), *Text and Context: Old Testament and Semitic Studies for F.C. Fensham* (JSOTSup, 48; Sheffield: JSOT Press, 1988), pp. 269-82.

Moore, T.V., *Zechariah* (Carlisle, PA: Banner of Truth Trust, 1958).

North, R., 'Prophecy to Apocalyptic via Zechariah', in *Congress Volume, Uppsala* (VTSup, 22; Leiden: Brill, 1972), pp. 47-71.

Otzen, B., *Studien über Deuterosacharja* (Copenhagen: Prostant apud Munksgaard, 1964).

Perowne, T.T., *Haggai and Zechariah* (Cambridge: Cambridge University Press, 1888).

Petersen, D.L., *Haggai and Zechariah 1–8* (London: SCM Press, 1985).

—*Late Israelite Prophecy: Studies in Deutero-Prophetic Literature and in Chronicles* (Missoula, MT: Scholars Press, 1977).

—'Zechariah's Visions: A Theological Perspective', *VT* 34 (1984), pp. 195-206.

—'Zerubbabel and the Jerusalem Temple Reconstruction', *CBQ* 36 (1974), pp. 366-72.

Petitjean, A., *Les oracles du Proto-Zacharie* (Paris: Gabalda, 1969).

Pierce, R.W., 'Literary Connectors and a Haggai/Zechariah/Malachi Corpus', *JETS* 27 (1984), pp. 277-89.

Portnoy, S.L., and D.L. Petersen, 'Biblical Texts and Statistical Analysis: Zechariah and Beyond', *JBL* 103 (1984), pp. 11-21.

Pusey, E.B., *The Minor Prophets with a Commentary*. VIII. *Zechariah* (London: Nisbet, 1907).

Radday, Y.T., *An Analytic Linguistic Key-Word in Context to the Books of Haggai, Zechariah and Malachi* (Computer Bible, 4; Biblical Research Associates, 1973).

Radday, Y.T., and M.A. Pollatschek, 'Vocabulary Richness in the Post-Exilic Prophetic Books', *ZAW* 92 (1980), pp. 333-46.

Radday, Y.T., and D. Wickmann, 'The Unity of Zechariah Examined in the Light of Statistical Linguistics', *ZAW* 87 (1975), pp. 30-55.

Richter, H.-F., 'Die Pferde in den Nachtgesichten des Sacharja', *ZAW* 98 (1986), pp. 96-100.

Rignell, L.G., *Die Nachtgesichte des Sacharja* (Lund: Gleerup, 1950).

Robinson, T.H., and F. Horst, *Die zwölf kleinen Propheten* (Tübingen: Mohr, 1964).

Rosenberg, R.A., 'The Slain Messiah in the Old Testament', *ZAW* 99 (1987), pp. 259-61.

Rothstein, J.W., *Die Nachtgesichte des Sacharja* (Leipzig: Hinrichs, 1910).

Rudolph, W., *Haggai—Sacharja 1–8—Sacharja 9–14—Malachi* (Gütersloh: Gerd Mohn, 1976).

Sæbø, M., 'Die deuterosacharjanische Frage: Eine forschungsgeschichtliche Studie', *ST* 23 (1969), pp. 115-40.

—*Sacharja 9–14: Untersuchungen von Text und Form* (Neukirchen–Vluyn: Neukirchener Verlag, 1969).

Schöttler, H.-G., *Gott inmitten seines Volkes: Die Neuordnung des Gottesvolkes nach Sacharja 1–6* (Trier: Paulinus-Verlag, 1987).

Schumpp, P.M., *Die heilige Schrift*. X.2. *Das Buch der zwölf Propheten* (Freiburg: Herder, 1950).

Sellin, E., *Das Zwölfprophetenbuch* (Leipzig: Deichert, 1922).

Seybold, K., *Bilder zum Tempelbau: Die Visionen des Propheten Sacharja* (Stuttgarter Biblestudien; Stuggart: KBW, 1974).

Sinclair, L.A., 'The Redaction of Zechariah 1–8', *BibRes* 20 (1975), pp. 36-47.

Smith, R.L., *Nahum–Malachi* (WBC; Waco, TX: Word Books, 1964).

Stade, B., 'Deuterosacharja: Eine kritische Studie', *ZAW* 1 (1881), pp. 1-96; *ZAW* 2 (1882), pp. 151-72, 275-309.

Strand, K.A., 'The Two Olive Trees of Zech. 4 and Rev. 11', *AUSS* 20 (1982), pp. 257-61.

Stuhlmueller, C., *Rebuilding with Hope: A Commentary on the Books of Haggai and Zechariah* (International Theological Commentary; Grand Rapids: Eerdmans, 1988).

Thomas, D.W., and T.C. Speers, 'Zechariah 1–8', in *The Interpreter's Bible*, VI (ed. G.A. Buttrick: Nashville: Abingdon Press, 1956), pp. 1053-88.

Tidwell, N.L.A., *'wǎ'ōmar* (Zech. 3.5) and the Genre of Zechariah's Fourth Vision', *JBL* 94 (1975), pp. 343-55.

Torrey, C.C., 'The Evolution of a Financier in the Ancient Near East', *JNES* 2 (1943), pp. 295-301.

—'The Foundry of the Second Temple in Jerusalem', *JBL* 55 (1936), pp. 247-60.

Tournay, R., Review of *Zacharie 9–14: Structure littéraire et messianisme*, by P. Lamarche, *RB* 69 (1962), pp. 588-92.

Unger, M.F., *Zechariah* (Grand Rapids: Zondervan, 1963).

Van Dyke Parunak, H., *Linguistic Density Plots in Zechariah* (Computer Bible, 20; Biblical Research Associates, 1979).

Wallis, G., 'Erwägungen zu Sacharja 6.9-15', in *Congress Volume, Uppsala* (VTSup, 22; Leiden: Brill, 1972), pp. 232-37.

Willi-Plein, I., *Prophetie am Ende: Untersuchungen zu Sacharja 9–14* (BBB, 4; Bonn: Peter Hanstein, 1974).

Woude, A.S. van der, 'Zion as Primeval Stone in Zechariah 3 and 4', in Claasen (ed.), *Text and Context*, pp. 237-48.

2. *Other works*

Ackroyd, P.R., 'Teraphim', *ExpTim* 62 (1950–51), pp. 378-80.

—'The Vitality of the Word of God in the Old Testament', *ASTI* 1 (1962), pp. 7-23.

Aitken, K., 'The Oracles against Babylon in Jer 50–51', *TynBul* 35 (1984), pp. 25-63.

Alden, R.L., 'Chiastic Psalms: A Study in the Mechanics of Semitic Poetry in Psalms 1–50', *JETS* 17 (1974), pp. 11-28.

—'Chiastic Psalms: A Study in the Mechanics of Semitic Poetry in Psalms 51–100', *JETS* 19 (1976), pp. 191-200.

—'Chiastic Psalms: A Study in the Mechanics of Semitic Poetry in Psalms 101–150', *JETS* 21 (1978), pp. 199-210.

Alonso-Schökel, L., *Estudios de poética hebrea* (Barcelona: Juan Flors, 1963).

—'Hermeneutical Problems of a Literary Study of the Bible', in *Congress Volume, Edinburgh* (VTSup, 28; Leiden: Brill, 1975), pp. 1-15.

—'Hermeneutics in the Light of Language and Literature', *CBQ* 25 (1963), pp. 371-186.

—'The Poetic Structure of Psalm 42–43', *JSOT* 1 (1976), pp. 4-11.

Alter, R., *The Art of Biblical Narrative* (New York: Basic Books, 1981).

—*The Art of Biblical Poetry* (New York: Basic Books, 1985).

—'A Response to Critics', *JSOT* 27 (1983), pp. 113-17.

Andersen, F.I., *The Sentence in Biblical Hebrew* (Janua Linguarum, Series Practica, 231; Mouton: The Hague, 1974).

Ap Thomas, D.R., 'Some Aspects of the Root HNN in the Old Testament', *JSS* 2 (1957), pp. 128-48.

Auffret, P., 'Essai sur la structure littéraire d'Ex 14', *EstBíb* 41 (1983), pp. 53-82.

—'Essai sur la structure littéraire du Psaume 1', *BZ* 22 (1978), pp. 44-45.

—'Essai sur la structure littéraire du Psaume 11', *ZAW* 93 (1981), pp. 401-18.

—'Essai sur la structure littéraire du Psaume 74', *VT* 33 (1983), pp. 129-48.

—'Essai sur la structure littéraire du Psaume 86', *VT* 29 (1979), pp. 385-402.

—'Essai sur la structure littéraire du Psaume 137', *ZAW* 92 (1980), pp. 346-77.

—'Remarks on J. Magonet's Interpretation of Exodus 6.2-8', *JSOT* 27 (1983), pp. 69-71.

—'The Literary Structure of Exodus 6.2-8', *JSOT* 27 (1983), pp. 46-54.

—*The Literary Structure of Psalm 2* (JSOTSup, 2; Sheffield: JSOT Press, 1977).

—'Notes complémentaires sur la structure littéraire des Psaumes 3 et 29', *ZAW* 99 (1987), pp. 90-93.

—'Note sur la structure littéraire du Psaume 3', *ZAW* 91 (1979), pp. 93-106.

—' "Pivot Pattern": Nouveaux exemples (Jon 2.10; Ps 31.13; Isa 23.7)', *VT* 28 (1978), pp. 103-10.

Bailey, K.E., *Poet and Peasant* (Grand Rapids: Eerdmans, 1976).

—*Through Peasant Eyes* (Grand Rapids: Eerdmans, 1980).

Barré, L.M., 'The Poetic Structure of Genesis 9.5', *ZAW* 96 (1984), pp. 101-104.

Barthes, R., *et al.*, *Structural Analysis and Biblical Exegesis: Interpretational Essays* (Pittsburgh: Pickwick Press, 1974).

Bengel, J.A., *Gnomon of the New Testament* (trans. R. Andrew; Edinburgh: T. & T. Clark, 1958–59).

Berlin, A. (with a response by J. Kugel), 'On the Bible as Literature', *Prooftexts* 2 (1982), pp. 323-32.

Bertman, S., 'Symmetrical Design in the Book of Ruth', *JBL* 84 (1965), pp. 165-68.

Black, E., *Rhetorical Criticism* (New York: Macmillan, 1965).

Bligh, J., *Galatians in Greek: A Structural Analysis of Paul's Epistle to the Galatians* (Detroit: University of Detroit Press, 1966).

Boadt, L., 'The A:B:B:A Chiasm of Identical Roots in Ezekiel', *VT* 25 (1975), pp. 693-99.

—'Notes on Poetic Structure and Style', *CBQ* 35 (1973), pp. 20-34.

Boys, T., *Key to the Book of Psalms* (L.B. Seeley, 1825).

Brandt, W.J., *The Rhetoric of Argumentation* (New York: Bobbs-Merrill, 1970).

Brodie, L., 'The Children and the Prince: The Structure, Nature and Date of Isaiah 6–12', *BTB* 9 (1979), pp. 27-31.

Ceresko, A.R., 'The Chiastic Word Pattern in Hebrew', *CBQ* 38 (1976), pp. 303-11.

—'The Function of Chiasmus in Hebrew Poetry', *CBQ* 40 (1978), pp. 1-10.

Clines, D.J.A., 'Hosea 2: Structure and Interpretation', in *Studia Biblica 1978. I. Papers on Old Testament and Related Themes* (ed. E.A. Livingstone; JSOTSup, 11; Sheffield: JSOT Press, 1979), pp. 83-103.

Clines, D.J.A., D.M. Gunn and A.J. Hauser (eds.), *Art and Meaning: Rhetoric in Biblical Literature* (JSOTSup, 19; Sheffield: JSOT Press, 1982).

Cohn, R.L., 'Narrative Structure and Canonical Perspective in Genesis', *JSOT* 25 (1983), pp. 3-16.

Condamin, A., 'Symmetrical Repetitions in Lamentations 1 and 2', *JTS* 7 (1906), pp. 137-140.

Cross, F.M., and D.N. Freedman, *Studies in Ancient Yahwistic Poetry* (Missoula, MT: Scholars Press, 1975).

Culley, R.C., 'Oral Tradition and the Old Testament: Some Recent Discussion', in *Semeia* (Missoula, MT: SBL, 1976), V, pp. 1-33.

—'Some Comments on Structural Analysis and Biblical Studies', in *Congress Volume, Uppsala* (VTSup, 22; Leiden: Brill, 1972), pp. 129-42.

—*Studies in the Structure of Biblical Narrative* (Philadelphia: Fortress Press, 1976).

—'Structural Analysis: Is it Done with Mirrors?', *Int* 28 (1974), pp. 165-81.

Dahood, M.J., 'Chiastic Breakup in Isaiah 58.7', *Bib* 57 (1976), p. 105.

—'A New Metrical Pattern in Biblical Poetry', *CBQ* 29 (1967), pp. 574-82.

De Roche, M., 'Structure, Rhetoric and Meaning in Hosea 4.4-10', *VT* 33 (1983), pp. 185-98.

De Vries, S.J., *Yesterday, Today and Tomorrow* (Grand Rapids: Eerdmans, 1975).

Detweiler, R., *Story, Sign and Self: Phenomenology and Structuralism as Literary Critical Methods* (Philadelphia: Fortress Press, 1978).

Drijvers, P., *The Psalms: Their Structure and Meaning* (New York: Herder & Herder, 1965).

Fokkelman, J.P., *Narrative Art and Poetry in the Books of Samuel. I. King David (2 Sam. 9–20 & 1 Kings 1–2)* (Assen: Van Gorcum, 1981).

—*Narrative Art and Poetry in the Books of Samuel. II. The Crossing Fates (1 Sam. 13-31 & 2 Sam. 1)* (Assen: Van Gorcum, 1986).

—*Narrative Art in Genesis* (Assen: Van Gorcum, 1975).

Forbes, J., *Symmetrical Structure of Scripture* (Edinburgh: T. & T. Clark, 1854).

Fraenkel, J., 'Chiasmus in Talmudic-Aggadic Narrative', in Welch (ed.), *Chiasmus in Antiquity*, pp. 183-97.

Freedman, D.N., 'The Structure of Job 3', *Bib* 49 (1968), pp. 503-508.

—'The Structure of Psalm 137', in *Near Eastern Studies in Honor of William Foxwell Albright* (ed. H. Goedicke; Baltimore: Johns Hopkins University Press, 1971), pp. 187-205.

Freedman, D.N., and C.F. Hyland, 'Psalm 29: A Structural Analysis', *HTR* 66 (1973), pp. 237-56.

Gevirtz, S., *Patterns in the Early Poetry of Israel* (Studies in Ancient Oriental Civilization, 32; Chicago: University of Chicago Press, 1963).

Gibbs, J.M., 'Chiastic Psalms' (Private circulation, 1971).

—'Luke 24.13-33 and Acts 8.26-39: The Emmaus Incident and the Eunuch's Baptism as Parallel Stories', *Bangalore Theological Forum* 7.1 (1975), pp. 17-30.

Gilbert, M., 'La structure de la prière de Salomon Sg 9', *Bib* 51 (1970), pp. 301-31.

Gileadi, A., 'A Holistic Structure of the Book of Isaiah' (thesis, Brigham Young University, 1981).

Gitay, Y., 'A Study of Amos's Art of Speech: A Rhetorical Analysis of Amos 3.1-15', *CBQ* 42 (1980), pp. 293-309.

Glasson, T.F., 'Chiasmus in St Matthew 7.6', *ExpTim* 68 (1956–57), p. 302.

Goldingay, J., 'The Arrangement of Isaiah 41–45', *VT* 29 (1979), pp. 289-99.

Gooding, D.W., 'The Literary Structure of Daniel and its Implications', *TynBul* 32 (1981), pp. 43-79.

Gordis, R., 'A Rhetorical Use of Interrogative Sentences in Biblical Hebrew', *AJSL* 49 (1933), pp. 212-17.

Greenwood, D., 'Rhetorical Criticism and *Formgeschichte*: Some Methodological Considerations', *JBL* 89 (1970), pp. 418-26.

Grol, H.W.M. van, 'Paired Tricola in the Psalms, Isaiah and Jeremiah', *JSOT* 25 (1983), pp. 55-73.

Gros-Louis, K.R.R., J.S. Ackerman and T.S. Warshaw (eds.), *Literary Interpretations of Biblical Narratives* (Nashville: Abingdon Press, 1974).

Habel, N.C., 'The Narrative Art of Job: Applying the Principles of Robert Alter', *JSOT* 27 (1983), pp. 101-11.

Hagstrom, A.D., *The Coherence of the Book of Micah: A Literary Analysis* (thesis, Union Theological Seminary, Richmond, VA, 1982).

Holladay, W.L., *The Architecture of Jeremiah 1–20* (Lewisburg, PA: Bucknell University Press, 1976).

—'Chiasmus, the Key to Hosea 12.3-6', *VT* 16 (1966), pp. 53-64.

—'Form and Word-Play in David's Lament over Saul and Jonathan', *VT* 20 (1970), pp. 153-89.

Holman, J., 'The Structure of Psalm 139', *VT* 21 (1971), pp. 298-310.

Holmgren, F., 'Yahweh the Avenger: Isaiah 63.1-6', in Jackson and Kessler (eds.), *Rhetorical Criticism*, pp. 133-48.

—'Chiastic Structure in Isaiah 51.1-11', *VT* 19 (1969), pp. 196-201.

Isbell, C.D., and M. Jackson, 'Rhetorical Criticism and Jeremiah 7.1–8.3', *VT* 30 (1980), pp. 20-26.

Jackson, J.J., and M. Kessler (eds.), *Rhetorical Criticism: Essays in Honor of James Muilenburg* (Pittsburgh: Pickwick Press, 1974).

Jacobson, R., 'The Structuralists and the Bible', *Int* 28 (1974), pp. 146-64.

Jebb, J., *Sacred Literature* (T. Cadell and W. Davies, 1820).

Jeremias, J., 'Chiasmus in den Paulusbriefen', *ZNW* 49 (1958), pp. 145-56.

Jobling, D., 'Robert Alter's *The Art of Biblical Narrative*', *JSOT* 27 (1983), pp. 87-99.

—*The Sense of Biblical Narrative* (JSOTSup, 7; Sheffield: JSOT Press, 1978).

Jones, D.R., 'Exposition of Isaiah 1.21-end', *SJT* 21 (1968), pp. 320-29.

Junker, H., 'Die literarische Art von Isa 5, 1-7', *Bib* 40 (1959), pp. 259-66.

Kessler, M., 'Response to Alonso-Schökel's "The Structure of Psalm 42–43" ', *JSOT* 1 (1976), pp. 12-15.

Kessler, R., *Some Poetical and Structural Features of the Song of Songs* (Leeds University Oriental Society Monograph, 8; Leeds: Leeds University Press, 1957).

Kikawada, I.M., 'The Shape of Genesis 11.1-9', in Jackson and Kessler (eds.), *Rhetorical Criticism*, pp. 18-32.

König, E., *Stilistik, Rhetorik, Poetik* (Leipzig, 1900).

Kosmala, H., 'Form and Structure in Ancient Hebrew Poetry', *VT* 14 (1964), pp. 152-80.

—'The Term *geber* in the Old Testament and the Scrolls', in *Congress Volume, Rome* (VTSup, 17; Leiden: Brill, 1968).

Krasovec, J., *Antithetic Structure in Biblical Hebrew Poetry* (VTSup, 35; Leiden: Brill, 1984).

Kselman, J., 'The ABCB Pattern: Further Examples', *VT* 32 (1982), pp. 224-29.

—'Psalm 101', *JSOT* 33 (1985), pp. 45-62.

Kugel, J., *The Idea of Biblical Poetry* (New Haven: Yale University Press, 1981).

—'On the Bible and Criticism', *Prooftexts* 1 (1981), pp. 217-36.

Kuntz, J.K., 'The Canonical Wisdom Psalms of Ancient Israel—Their Rhetorical, Thematic and Formal Dimensions', in Jackson and Kessler (eds.), *Rhetorical Criticism*, pp. 186-222.

—'Psalm 18: A Rhetorical-Critical Analysis', *JSOT* 26 (1983), pp. 3-31.

Lack, R., *La symbolique du livre d'Isaïe: Essai sur l'image littéraire comme élément de structuration* (AnBib, 59; Rome: Pontifical Biblical Institute, 1973).

Lewin, E.D., 'Arguing for Authority: A Rhetorical Study of Jeremiah 1.4-19 and 20.7-18', *JSOT* 32 (1985), pp. 105-119.

L'Hour, J., 'Formes littéraires, structure et unité de Deuteronome 5–11', *Bib* 45 (1964), pp. 551-55.

Lichtenstein, M.H., 'Chiasm and Symmetry in Proverbs 31', *CBQ* 44 (1982), pp. 202-11.

Loader, J.A., *Polar Structures in the Book of Qoheleth* (BZAW, 152; Berlin: de Gruyter, 1979).

Lord, A.B., *The Singer of Tales* (Cambridge, MA: Harvard University Press, 1960).

Lowth, R., *Lectures on the Sacred Poetry of the Hebrews* (Boston: Crocker & Brewster; New York: J. Leavitt, 1829).

Lund, N.W., *Chiasmus in the New Testament* (Chapel Hill: University of North Carolina Press, 1942).

—'Chiasmus in the Psalms', *AJSL* 49 (1933), pp. 281-312.

—'The Influence of Chiasmus upon the Structure of the Gospel according to St Matthew', *ATR* 13 (1931), pp. 405-33.

—'The Influence of Chiasmus upon the Structure of the Gospels', *ATR* 13 (1931), pp. 27-48.

—'The Literary Structure of Paul's Hymn to Love', *JBL* 50 (1930), pp. 266-76.

—'The Presence of Chiasmus in the New Testament', *JR* 10 (1930), pp. 74-93.

—'The Presence of Chiasmus in the Old Testament', *AJSL* 46 (1930), pp. 109-26.

Lundbom, J.R., *Jeremiah: A Study in Ancient Hebrew Rhetoric* (Missoula, MT: Scholars Press, 1975).

—'Poetic Structure and Prophetic Rhetoric in Hosea', *VT* 29 (1979), pp. 300-308.

—'Rhetorical Structure in Jeremiah 1', *ZAW* 103 (1991), pp. 193-210.

McKnight, E.V., *Meaning in Texts: The Historical Shaping of a Narrative Hermeneutics* (Philadelphia: Fortress Press, 1978).

Magonet, J., *Form and Meaning: Studies in Literary Techniques in the Book of Jonah* (Sheffield: Almond Press, 1983).

—'Isaiah 2.1–4.6: Some Poetic Structures and Tactics', *Amsterdamse cahiers voor exegese* 3 (1982), pp. 71-85.

—'The Rhetoric of God: Exodus 6.2-8', *JSOT* 27 (1983), pp. 56-67.

—'A Response to P. Auffret's "Literary Structure of Exodus 6.2-8"', *JSOT* 27 (1983), pp. 73-74.

—'Some Concentric Structures in Psalms', *HeyJ* 23 (1982), pp. 365-76.

—'The Structure and Meaning of Leviticus 19', *HAR* 7 (1983), pp. 151-67.

March, W.E., '*Laken*: Its Function and Meaning', in Jackson and Kessler (eds.), *Rhetorical Criticism*, pp. 256-84.

Marshall, R.J., 'The Structure of Isaiah 1–12', *BibRes* 7 (1962), pp. 19-32.

Malatesta, E., 'The Literary Structure of John 17', *Bib* 52 (1971), pp. 190-214.

Meek, T.J., 'The Structure of Hebrew Poetry', *JR* 9 (1929), pp. 523-50.

Melugin, R., *The Formation of Isaiah 40–55* (Berlin: de Gruyter, 1976).

Miller, A.S., *The Literary Style of the Book of Isaiah and the Unity Question* (thesis, Mid-America Baptist Theological Seminary, 1982).

Morgenstern, J., 'The King-God among the Western Semites and the Meaning of Epiphanes', *VT* 10 (1960), pp. 138-97.

Mosca, P.G., 'Psalm 26: Poetic Structure and the Form-Critical Task', *CBQ* 47 (1985), pp. 212-37.

Muilenburg, J., 'Form Criticism and Beyond', *JBL* 88 (1969), pp. 1-18.

—'The Form and Structure of the Covenantal Formulation', *VT* 9 (1959), pp. 347-65.

—'The Linguistic and Rhetorical Uses of the Particle *kî* in the Old Testament', *HUCA* 32 (1961), pp. 135-60.

—'The Literary Character of Isaiah 34', *JBL* 59 (1940), pp. 339-65.

—'A Study in Hebrew Rhetoric: Repetition and Style', in G.W. Anderson *et al.* (eds.), *Congress Volume* (VTSup, 1; Leiden: Brill, 1953), pp. 97-111.

Murray, D.F., 'Narrative Structure and Technique in the Deborah-Barak Story (Judges 4.4-22)', in *Studies in the Historical Books of the Old Testament* (ed. J.A. Emerton; VTSup, 30; Leiden: Brill, 1979), pp. 155-89.

Naidoff, B.D., 'The Twofold Structure of Isa 45.9-13', *VT* 31 (1981), pp. 180-85.

Niditch, S., 'The Composition of Isa 1', *Bib* 61 (1980), pp. 509-29.

O'Callaghan, M., 'The Structure and Meaning of Gn 38', *Proceedings of the Irish Biblical Association* 5 (1981), pp. 72-97.

Patte, D., *What is Structural Exegesis?* (Philadelphia: Fortress Press, 1976).

Patte, D., and A. Patte, *Structural Exegesis: From Theory to Practice* (Philadelphia: Fortress Press, 1978).

Peter-Contesse, R., 'La Structure de 1 Samuel 1–3', *BT* 27 (1976), pp. 312-14.

Polzin, R., 'The Framework of the Book of Job', *Int* 28 (1974), pp. 182-200.

Porten, B., 'Structure and Chiasm in Aramaic Contracts and Letters', in Welch (ed.), *Chiasmus in Antiquity*, pp. 169-82.

—'The Structure and Theme of the Solomon Narrative (1 Kings 3–11)', *HUCA* 38 (1967), pp. 93-128.

Prinsloo, W.S., 'Isaiah 14.12-25—Humiliation, Hubris, Humiliation', *ZAW* 93 (1981), pp. 432-38.

Radday, Y.T., 'Chiasm in Samuel', *LB* 9-10 (1971), pp. 21-31.

—'Chiasm in Tora', *LB* 19 (1972), pp. 12-23.

—'Chiasmus in Hebrew Biblical Narrative', in Welch (ed.), *Chiasmus in Antiquity*, pp. 50-117.

Radday, Y.T., and H. Shore, *Genesis: An Authorship Study in Computer-Assisted Liguistics* (AnBib; Investigationes Scientificae in Res Biblicas, 103; Rome: Biblical Institute Press, 1985).

Ridderbos, N.H., 'Response to Alonso-Schökel's "The Poetic Structure of Psalm 42–43"', *JSOT* 1 (1976), pp. 16-21.

Riding, C.B., 'Psalm 95.1-7c as a Large Chiasm', *ZAW* 88 (1976), p. 418.

Rittersprach, A.D., 'Rhetorical Criticism and the Song of Hannah', in Jackson and Kessler (eds.), *Rhetorical Criticism*, pp. 68-74.

Rogerson, J., 'Recent Literary Structuralist Approaches to Biblical Interpretation', *Churchman* 90 (1976), pp. 165-77.

Sanders, E.P., 'Chiasmus and the Translation of I Q Hodayot 7.26-27', *RevQ* 23 (1968), pp. 427-31.

Sawyer, J.F.A., 'What was a Mošia'?', *VT* 15 (1965), pp. 475-86.

Saydon, P.P., 'Assonance in Hebrew as a Means of Expressing Emphasis', *Bib* 36 (1955), pp. 36-50, 287-304.

Skehan, P., 'Strophic Structure in Ps 72 (71)', *Bib* 40 (1959), pp. 302-308.

Shea, W.H., 'The Chiastic Structure of the Song of Songs', *ZAW* 92 (1980), pp. 378-96.

Smith, R.F., 'Chiasm in Sumero-Akkadian', in Welch (ed.), *Chiasmus in Antiquity*, pp. 17-35.

Spivey, R.A., 'Structuralism and Biblical Studies: The Uninvited Guest', *Int* 28 (1974), pp. 133-45.

Tromp, N.J., 'Amos 5.1-17: Towards a Stylistic and Rhetorical Analysis', *OTS* 2 (1982), pp. 56-84.

Vermes, G., *Scripture and Tradition in Judaism* (Leiden: Brill, 1961).

Via, D.O., 'A Structuralist Approach to Paul's Hermeneutic', *Int* 28 (1974), pp. 201-20.

Waard, J. de, 'The Chiastic Structure of Amos 5.1-17', *VT* 27 (1977), pp. 170-77.

Wal, A. van der, 'The Structure of Amos', *JSOT* 26 (1983), pp. 107-13.

Walker, H.H., and N.W. Lund, 'The Literary Structure of the Book of Habakkuk', *JBL* 53 (1934), pp. 355-70.

Watson, W.G.E., 'Chiastic Patterns in Biblical Hebrew Poetry', in Welch (ed.), *Chiasmus in Antiquity*, pp. 118-68.

—*Classical Hebrew Poetry* (JSOTSup, 26; Sheffield: JSOT Press, 1984).

—'Further Examples of Semantic-Sonant Chiasmus', *CBQ* 46 (1984), pp. 31-33.

—'The Pivotal Pattern in Hebrew, Ugaritic and Akkadian Poetry', *ZAW* 88 (1976), pp. 239-53.

Watters, W.R., *Formula Criticism of the Poetry of the Old Testament* (BZAW, 138; Berlin: de Gruyter, 1976).

Webster, B.C., 'Strophic Patterns in Job 3–28', *JSOT* 26 (1983), pp. 33-60.

Welch, J.W. (ed.), *Chiasmus in Antiquity* (Hildesheim: Gerstenberg, 1981).

Welch, J.W., 'Chiasmus in Ancient Greek and Latin Literature', in Welch (ed.), *Chiasmus*, pp. 250-68.

—'Chiasmus in the Book of Mormon', in Welch (ed.), *Chiasmus*, pp. 198-210.

—'Chiasmus in the New Testament', in Welch (ed.), *Chiasmus*, pp. 211-49.

—'Chiasmus in Ugaritic', in Welch (ed.), *Chiasmus*, pp. 36-49.

—'Chiasmus in the Book of Mormon' (unpublished thesis, Studies X.1, Brigham Young University, 1969), pp. 69-84.

Wenham, G.J., 'The Coherence of the Flood Narrative', *VT* 28 (1978), pp. 336-48.

Whallon, W., *Formula, Character and Context* (Cambridge, MA: Harvard University Press, 1969).

White, H.C., 'French Structuralism and Old Testament Narrative Analysis: Roland Barthes', in R.C. Culley (ed.), *Semeia* (Missoula, MT: SBL, 1975), III, pp. 99-127.

Whybray, R.N., 'On Robert Alter's *The Art of Biblical Narrative*', *JSOT* 27 (1983), pp. 75-86.

Wiklander, B., *Prophecy as Literature* (Lund: Gleerup, 1984).

Willis, J.T., 'The First Pericope in the Book of Isaiah', *VT* 34 (1984), pp. 63-77.

—'A Lament Reversed—Isaiah 1, 21ff', *ZAW* 98 (1986), pp. 236-48.

—'The Structure of Micah 3–5 and the Function of Micah 5.9-14 in the Book', *ZAW* 81 (1969), pp. 191-214.

Wilson, J.L., *A Rhetorical-Critical Analysis of the Balaam Oracles* (PhD thesis, Southern Baptist Theological Seminary, 1981).

Wright, A.G., 'The Structure of the Book of Wisdom', *Bib* 48 (1967), pp. 165-84.

Yee, G.A., 'An Analysis of Prov 8.22-31 According to Style and Structure', *ZAW* 94 (1982), pp. 58-66.

Yoder, P.B., 'A-B Pairs and Oral Composition in Hebrew Poetry', *VT* 21 (1971), pp. 470-89.

INDEXES

INDEX OF BIBLICAL REFERENCES

OLD TESTAMENT

NEW TESTAMENT

INDEX OF AUTHORS